Light verbs

Light verbs

―

Synchronic and diachronic studies

Edited by
Anna Riccio and Jens Fleischhauer

düsseldorf university press

We acknowledge support by the Open Access Publication Fund of the University and State Library Düsseldorf.

ISBN 978-3-11-138844-1
e-ISBN (PDF) 978-3-11-138887-8
e-ISBN (EPUB) 978-3-11-138893-9
DOI https://doi.org/10.1515/9783111388878

This work is licensed under the Creative Commons Attribution 4.0 International License. For details go to https://creativecommons.org/licenses/by/4.0.

Library of Congress Control Number: 2024952111

Bibliographic information published by the Deutsche Nationalbibliothek
The Deutsche Nationalbibliothek lists this publication in the Deutsche Nationalbibliografie; detailed bibliographic data are available on the internet at http://dnb.dnb.de.

© 2025 with the author(s), editing © 2025 Anna Riccio and Jens Fleischhauer, published by Walter de Gruyter GmbH, Berlin/Boston, Genthiner Straße 13, 10785 Berlin. This book is published open access at www.degruyter.com.

d|u|p düsseldorf university press is an imprint of Walter de Gruyter GmbH.

dup.degruyter.com
Questions about General Product Safety Regulation:
productsafety@degruyterbrill.com

Contents

List of abbreviations — VII

Anna Riccio and Jens Fleischhauer
Introduction to the volume — 1

Natasha Stojanovska-Ilievska
A corpus-based study of the English light verb constructions with *give* denoting bodily actions and physical interaction — 15

Pei-Jung Kuo
The GIVE group of the Mandarin light verbs — 43

Georgina Alvarez-Morera, Jordi Ginebra, and Isabel Oltra-Massuet
Modification in *give* light verb constructions — 65

Niklas Wiskandt
Light verb constructions with experiencer objects in Germanic and Romance — 97

Flavio Pisciotta and Francesca Masini
A paradigm of psych-predicates — 123

John Sundquist
Taking a closer look at light verb constructions in the history of American English — 177

David Nicoletti
Constructional semantics of Italian light verb constructions — 199

Hideki Kishimoto
On the light verb construction in Japanese — 233

Index — 277

List of abbreviations

ABS	absolutive
ACC	accusative
ASP	aspect
AUX	auxiliary
CL	classifier
COMP	complementizer
CONJ	conjunctive
CONT	continuative
COP	copula
DAT	dative
DEF	definite
DEM	demonstrative
DET	determiner
DIST	distal
ERG	ergative
EXP	experiencer
F	feminine
FUT	future tense
GEN	genitive
GER	gerundive
IMP	imperative
INDF	indefinite
INF	infinitive
IPFV	imperfective
LVC	light verb construction
M	masculine
N	neuter
NEG	negation
NOM	nominative
NOML	nominalizer
NP	noun phrase
OBJ	object
PART	partitive
PASS	passive
PERF	perfect
PFV	perfective
PL	plural
POSS	possessive
PP	prepositional phrase
PROG	progressive
PROX	proximate
PRS	present tense
PST	past tense

Open Access. © 2025 the author(s), published by De Gruyter. This work is licensed under the Creative Commons Attribution 4.0 International License.
https://doi.org/10.1515/9783111388878-203

VIII — List of abbreviations

PTCP	participle
REL	relative marker
SG	singular
STIM	stimulus
SV	simplex verb
TOP	topic
TR	transitive
V	verb
VN	verbal noun

Anna Riccio and Jens Fleischhauer
Introduction to the volume

The term 'light verb' originates from Jespersen (1942), who used it to refer to the finite verb in a complex predicative construction where the predicative content is primarily contributed by, for example, a nominal element.[1] A characteristic feature of light verbs is that they are always bound to a construction that we can call a 'complex predicate', i.e. a multi-word expression that forms a joint predication. This specific type of complex predicate is called 'light verb construction' (LVC). An English example of an LVC discussed by, for instance, Butt and Lahiri (2002) is *give a kiss*. In addition to the term 'light verb', other terms can also be found in the literature, some of which are only used in specific individual language linguistics (cf. Pompei et al., 2023, 1). The term 'support verb', which various authors equate with 'light verb' (e.g., Danlos, 1992; Langer, 2004; Storrer, 2007; Mel'čuk, 2022), is still relatively widespread. Accordingly, we also find the term 'support verb construction.' In this volume, we use the terms 'light verb' and 'light verb construction', as they are more widely used overall and lack the connotation that the verb only has a supportive function.

There is another use of the term 'light verb' which we do not explore in this volume. In generative syntax, 'light verb' is used for an "affixal verb [...] to which a noun, adjective or verb adjoins" (Radford, 1997, 264). One example given by Radford is the suffix *-en*, which transforms adjectives into verbs (e.g., in *redden*). Light verbs are associated with little *v* (Folli and Harley, 2007). In the context of the theory, they can also have zero instantiations and occur in various syntactic derivations (VP shells). The term 'light verb' is thus used much more broadly than in the present volume, where it is used to refer to the (overtly realized) verbal constituent of a phrasal complex predicate (as sketched above).

In the prototypical cases, light verbs combine with nouns, or noun phrases, as in English *give* with *a kiss*. In addition, we find – especially in various Indo-European languages such as the Germanic languages but also in Persian – LVCs that consist of

---

[1] The aim of this introduction is not to provide an overview of the extensive literature on light verbs and light verb constructions. Rather, we seek to thematically motivate the papers gathered in this volume and to contextualize them within the wider discourse. A recent overview on light verbs and light verb constructions can be found, for instance, in Pompei et al. (2023).

Anna Riccio, University of Foggia, Foggia, Italy
Jens Fleischhauer, Heinrich Heine University, Düsseldorf, Germany

a light verb and a prepositional phrase (e.g. Dutch *aan het rollen brengen* 'get/ cause rolling' lit. on the rolling bring; cf. Hinderdael, 1987). In some Australian languages, they combine with a so-called coverb. An example from the Bardi can be seen in (1), where the uninflecting coverb *wajim* 'wash' forms an LVC with the light verb.

(1) wajim i-n-ma-n=irr
 wash 3-TR-put-CONT=3PL.OBJ
 'He/she washes them.'

(Bowern, 2014, 264)

Light verb constructions vary in terms of the elements they are made up, but there are certain characteristics that these constructions have. First of all, they always contain a verbal element which, as is often assumed, is also used as a full lexical verb in the language. Light verbs do not form a distinct (syntactic) category of their own, unlike full verbs, auxiliary verbs or modal verbs, for example. Rather, a light verb represent just a specific use of a full verb and is thus in opposition to the 'heavy verb' usage of the verb, as is the case when it is used in a regular predicate-argument construction.

It is often assumed that the verbs that exhibit light verb usages inherently carry a rather abstract semantics. Typically, lexemes that denote directional movement (e.g., 'come') or transfer (e.g., 'give,' 'take,' 'bring') are cited as characteristic light verbs (see Bowern, 2014, 2 for a brief discussion of verbs with light usages in Australian languages). In many languages that have light verb constructions, these verbs certainly form the core of the set of light verbs. Verbs that denote a specific type of locomotion, such as 'sneak up' or 'crawl in', are not found among the light verbs. However, there are also verbs with meanings such as 'hit' or 'stand' that are used as light verbs in some languages. LVCs with a verb meaning 'hit' can be found, for example, in Persian (2a) and the Bantu language Swahili (cf. Olejarnik, 2011; Martin, 2019). Light verbs with the meaning of 'stand' are commonly found in Dutch (2b) and German (Fleischhauer, 2022, 2024; among others).

(2) a. mesâl zadan
 example hit
 'to give an example'
 b. onder observatie staan
 under observation stand
 'to be under observation'

An important question in this context is: how can we distinguish between a light verb use and a heavy verb use of a verb? Everyone would probably agree with the statement that *give* is used as a heavy verb in (3a), but not in (3b). In (3a), *give* denotes a transfer event in which an object (*a ball*) changes ownership. This is different in (3b), the referent of *kiss* does not change its possessor. Instead of a change of possession, *give a kiss* denotes a kissing event. The difference between the two verb usages – the heavy verb usage in (3a) and the light verb usage in (3b) – can also be recognized by the fact that *give* in (3a) can be replaced by verbs of the same semantic class, such as *hand over* (e.g., *The girl handed over a ball to the boy*). This is not possible in (3b), as the light verb has lost its synonymy relationships with the full verb usage (#*The girl handed over a kiss to the boy*).

(3)   a.   *The girl gave the boy a ball.*
       b.   *The girl gave the boy a kiss.*

In (3b), *give* is part of an LVC, which is evidenced by the fact that the predicative meaning is primarily contributed by the nominal element rather than the verb. This can be clearly illustrated by comparing the two examples in (3b). In its heavy verb usage, *give* denotes a transfer event, where the object argument *a ball* specifies only the entity being given (cf. Newman 1996; Butt and Geuder 2001). If we replace *a ball* with *a book* (4a), the entity that the boy receives changes – perhaps even the manner of giving – but what remains constant is that a giving event is denoted. In contrast, (3b) does not denote a giving event; instead, it denotes a kissing event. This is evident because *give a kiss* can be paraphrased with the verb *kiss*.[2] The predicative meaning – specifically, the denoted event – is contributed by the noun *kiss*. If we replace the noun with *answer* (4b), we obtain a different LVC that denotes a different type of event. *Give an answer* refers to an event in which someone responds to someone else (cf. Butt and Geuder, 2001, 339–343). A rough paraphrase for this LVC is 'to answer' Since kissing and answering are clearly distinct event types and also have different event participles, it becomes clear that the denoted event does not depend on the verb but only on the noun. Otherwise, it would be expected that the two LVCs would denote events that can be assigned to a common event type.

(4)   a.   *The girl gave the boy a book.*
       b.   *The girl gave the boy an answer.*

That the denoted eventuality[3] is determined by the nominal element and not by the verb is proposed by Fleischhauer (2020) as an identification criterion for

---

[2] The fact that a light verb construction can be paraphrased by a simplex verb does not mean that the LVC and the corresponding simplex verb are total synonyms (cf. Pisciotta and Masini, this volume). This is explicitly addressed with the LVC *give a kiss* in Wittenberg and Snedeker (2013); Wittenberg and Levy (2017).
[3] This is, following Bach (1986), a cover term for states and events.

LVCs, which allows for a distinction between light verb constructions and regular predicate-argument constructions (such as *give someone a ball*), on the one hand, and idiomatic expressions (in the sense of Nunberg et al. 1994) like *give the shirt off (one's) back*, on the other. The idea behind this is that in regular predicate-argument constructions the denoted eventuality is determined by the verb and the replacement of one argument expression by another – e.g. *ball* by *book* – does not result in a different type of eventuality being denoted. The giving a book is a transfer event in the same way as the giving of a ball; the possession of the referent of the theme argument changes from the agent to the recipient. However, the two events do not have to be identical in all respects, but can differ in the way in which the change of ownership is carried out. However, there is no such difference encoded in the verbal meaning.

If we look at idioms next, we find that neither the verb nor the noun determines the denoted eventuality. The Cambridge English Dictionary paraphrases the idiom *give the shirt off (one's) back* as 'to be be willing to do anything to help another person'.[4] The idiom thus describes a person's state, more specifically: the state of doing everything to help someone else. This meaning is not derived from the meaning of the verb *give*, in particular this state is not a subtype of a giving event, nor is it derived from the meaning of the non-eventive noun *shirt*. Instead, it is the idiom as a whole that determines the meaning and thus the denoted event.

That we can distinguish LVCs from other predicative constructions by which part of the complex predicate denotes the denoted eventuality is at least implicitly assumed in various analyses, but usually as one among a variety of other criteria (see Fleischhauer, 2023 for a brief overview of the debate on German LVCs). In fact, we find this in principle even in Jespersen, who assigns only a supporting role to the light verb, but shifts the semantic content of the predication to the noun.

The discussion has shown that the predicative content of an LVC is primarily contributed by the nominal element. This raises the question of whether the light verb also contributes to the meaning of the complex predicate? Starting with Jespersen's introduction of the term light verb, we can see that the answer to this question has changed over the years. Jespersen assumed that light verbs are semantically empty and that they merely serve to specify functional features of the verb (e.g., tense, subject agreement) and thus license an eventive noun for predication. This observation is correct insofar as the collocation partners with which light verbs form a complex predicate are not verbs themselves and therefore cannot be inflected for tense or subject agreement. The fact that light verbs primarily have such a support-

---

4 https://dictionary.cambridge.org/de/worterbuch/englisch/would-give-the-shirt-off-back; last access: 15/01/2025.

ing function in the sentence was still assumed by authors after Jespersen (Cattell, 1984; Grimshaw and Mester, 1988) and is also reflected, for example, in the use of the term 'support verb' (Mel'čuk, 2022).

The view is now widespread that light verbs are indeed semantically defective verbs, meaning they do not denote an event themselves (Butt and Lahiri, 2002; Butt and Geuder, 2001), but they contribute to the meaning of the LVC (Bonial and Pollard, 2020; Bowern, 2008, 2014; Brugman, 2001; Butt, 2003, 2010; Butt and Lahiri, 2013; Fleischhauer and Neisani, 2020; Isoda, 1991; Ježek, 2023; Pompei and Piunno, 2023; Sanromán Vilas, 2011, Stojanovska-Ilievska, this volume, 17–18 among others). This contribution can be quite subtle and may manifest, for instance, in contrasts of aktionsart (e.g., stativity and inchoation) or volitionality.

This can be illustrated using the Persian examples in (5). In Persian, the noun *sedâ* 'sound' can be combined with different light verbs (*kardan* 'do' and *dâdan* 'give'), which then form LVCs that denotes the emission of a sound. The LVC *sedâ kardan* 'produce a sound' (lit. sound make) is compatible with the adverb *amdan* 'intentionally' (5a), while the LVC *sedâ dâdan* 'produce a sound' (lit. sound give) is not (5b). Both sentences differ only in the choice of light verb, demonstrating that it is the light verbs that create this semantic contrast. As a conclusion, it follows that light verbs must contribute something to the overall meaning of the LVC.

(5) a. *Bačče amdan   sedâ   kard.*
       child intentionally sound do.PST.3SG
       'The child produced a sound intentionally.'
    b. #*Bačče amdan   sedâ   dad.*
       child intentionally sound give.PST.3SG
       intended: 'The child produced a sound intentionally.'
                                            (Fleischhauer and Neisani, 2020, 71–72)

Even though the perspective that light verbs contribute to the overall meaning of LVCs is now shared by – as it seems – most authors, there are still few studies that explicitly examine the semantic contribution of the light verb. The assumption that the light verb makes an identifiable contribution to the overall meaning of the LVC only makes sense if it is also based on the premise that the meaning of the LVC arises from the meanings of its components, and thus that LVCs are formed compositionally (at least to some degree).

The idea that light verb constructions are formed compositionally is not often explicitly stated in the literature (exceptions are Karimi, 1997; Müller, 2010; Samvelian and Faghiri, 2014; Fleischhauer and Gamerschlag, 2019; Fleischhauer et al., 2019; Ježek, 2023). Bonial and Pollard (2020, 578–579) characterize LVCs are 'semi-compositional' as they are partially idiomatic but, at the same time, differ from fixed, non-compositional idioms as the meaning of the nominal element (at least) is transparent. Nunberg et al. (1994) have shown that there need not be a contradiction between compositionality and idiomaticity (here understood as, for instance, non-literalness). Based on this work, LVCs can be understood, as various authors have suggested, as 'idiomatically combining expressions' (e.g., Samvelian and Faghiri, 2013a,b, 2014; Fleischhauer, 2020; Fleischhauer and Neisani, 2020; Fleischhauer and Gamerschlag, 2019 and Nicoletti, this volume).

A central characteristic of LVCs is thus that they distribute their predicative meaning over several elements, with the primary contribution to the predication being made by the nominal element. By distributing the overall meaning over several words of different parts of speech (such as V + NP or V + PP), LVCs differ significantly from simplex verbs, in which the meaning is encoded in a (single) verb lexeme.

LVCs can be paraphrased by simplex verbs in some cases, for example *to kiss* is a suitable paraphrase for *give a kiss* and *to bath* for *take a bath*. However, LVCs differ from simplex verbs in terms of their concrete meaning – LVCs show Aktionsart distinctions that corresponding simplex verbs cannot realize in this way – or in terms of their modification potential. The light verb as a meaning-bearing element of the construction thus also have a meaning-differentiating function with regard to corresponding simplex verbs . This aspect shows that light verbs have a functional motivation that goes beyond the mere licensing of the nominal element in a predicative function, as Jespersen assumed.

Although there is no established definition of the terms 'light verb' and 'light verb construction' on the basis of which light verbs and LVCs can be (comparatively) identified, we nevertheless believe that these terms are useful for identifying and analyzing certain types of complex predicates. Based on these assumptions, we have identified several research questions, which have guided the creation of this volume:

- What meaning do light verbs contribute to LVCs? Can we identify the same meaning features (e.g. Aktionsart, volitionality) in all languages or do languages differ in terms of which meaning features can be realized by a light verb?
- Do light verbs contribute the same meaning in all LVCs or do we have to assume different light verb meanings – for different collocation partners?
- On which levels do light verbs contribute to the constitution of meaning? At the level of argument structure? In the constitution of the complex predicate's Aktionsart properties? In the specification of lexical meaning independently of argument structure and action type?
- What contribution do light verbs make to functionally differentiating the LVCs in which they occur from simplex verbs?

- Is lightness a gradual phenomenon, so that some light verbs can be 'lighter' than others? If so, what gradual gradations are there? At what point does an expression count as 'light' and no longer as 'heavy'?
- Is lightness the result of a desemanticization process? If so, is there a connection between light verbs and auxiliaries, as for example Hopper and Traugott (1993, 112) and Allerton (2002, 7) assume? In other words, do light verbs represent an intermediate step in the auxiliarization process?
- What collocational restrictions do light verbs have? This question can be addressed from two perspectives. Firstly, from the perspective of the light verbs: With which nouns can a light verb combine? Do the nouns with which a light verb can be combined form natural (semantic) classes or are there no regularities with regard to the collocation partners? If there are recognizable regularities, are they language-specific or can they be found across languages for the same light verb types (e.g. 'give' light verbs)? From the perspective of nouns, we can ask with which light verbs a noun – or a certain semantic class of nouns such as psych nouns – is combined? Can nouns of the same class combine with the same light verbs across languages or are there language-specific differences?
- How do diachronic processes, such as grammaticalization and lexicalization, shape the meaning of light verbs over time?
- How do patterns emerge in light verb usages and how do they gain productivity?

These and other questions play a central role in the papers collected in this volume. The individual chapters address these questions, sometimes explicitly and sometimes implicitly, differing not only in the specific research questions but also in the methodological and theoretical approach chosen by the authors. As a result, the volume represents a diverse approach to the phenomenon of light verbs, reflecting its broad thematic range.

Structure of the volume

The papers collected in this volume explore the intricate nature of light verb constructions, highlighting their semantic flexibility, syntactic variation, and cross-linguistic diversity. Through corpus-based analyses of authentic linguistic data from large text corpora, these studies offer valuable insights into how light verbs – such as 'give', 'make' or 'take' – function across various language families (e.g., Germanic vs. Romance languages, English vs. Mandarin, etc.).

Various papers present a detailed analysis of the use of specific light verbs: the chapters by **Stojanovska-Ilievska**, **Kuo**, **Alvarez-Morera, Ginebra and Oltra-Massuet**, as well as **Wiskandt** focus on light verbs with the meaning 'give', while **Sundquist** and **Nicoletti** highlight light verbs with the meaning 'take'. The discussions address issues related to the demarcation of light verbs and their heavy verb uses (e.g., **Stojanovska-Ilievska**), the specific semantic function of light verbs (e.g., **Kuo**), the competition between LVCs and corresponding simplex verbs (e.g., **Pisciotta and Masini**), as well as questions regarding argument realization in light verb constructions (**Kishimoto**). The contributions either take a language-specific perspective or, as in the case of **Alvarez-Morera, Ginebra and Oltra-Massuet** and **Wiskandt**, a comparative linguistic approach that examines properties of LVCs – modification and combination of light verbs with specific nouns—in a Romance-Germanic comparison. Thereby, the volume sheds light on both typological differences and universal patterns in LVC usage, examining the mechanisms that shape their syntactic structures and their role in conveying meaning in different contexts from both synchronic and diachronic perspectives.

Stojanovska-Ilievska investigates the semantic and syntactic features of English LVCs involving the verb *give*, with a particular focus on bodily actions and physical interactions. The results suggest that LVCs exhibit distinct syntactic patterns, including monotransitive constructions for bodily actions and ditransitive constructions for physical interaction. The analysis highlights the role of light verbs in the construction of meaning, demonstrating that their construction extends beyond simple semantic bleaching, influencing the interpretation and functional structure of these constructions.

Kuo's paper explores the syntactic behavior of six light verbs within the 'give'-group in Mandarin, advancing the understanding of these constructions in Chinese, where light verbs undergo a process of semantic reduction or bleaching. The corpus-based analysis reveals varying degrees of lightness, with some light verbs displaying characteristics typical of full verbs, while others show a greater degree of cohesion with their complements. This suggests a progression toward grammaticalization, with light verbs becoming more integrated into the syntactic structure.

The study by **Alvarez-Morera**, **Ginebra**, and **Oltra-Massuet** presents a typology of LVCs based on the presence of determination and modification within 'give'-LVCs across four languages: English (Germanic), German (Germanic), Catalan (Romance), and Spanish (Romance). The analysis distinguishes two primary types of LVCs: (1) those with a determined noun that allows flexible modification, and (2) those with bare nominals, which do not permit modification. The findings provide us empirical support for a neo-constructionist approach to argument structure, proposing that the degree of syntactic cohesion between the light verb and the noun is determined by the syntactic properties of the nominal element, rather than by the light verb itself.

Wiskandt examines LVCs with experiencer objects in both Germanic and Romance languages, analyzing their syntactic and semantic contrastive patterns. The study focuses on a comparative analysis of two LVC patterns involving the light verbs 'make' and 'give', with an emphasis on both cross-linguistic variations and systematic parallels. Special attention is given to the role of transfer verbs and prepositional constructions. A corpus-based analysis of emotion nouns in six languages reveal that the selection of light verbs is not arbitrary; rather, specific emotion nouns tend to co-occur with particular light verbs, indicating a structured relationship between the noun and verb.

This study by **Pisciotta** and **Masini** investigates the competition between denominal psych subject-verb constructions and psych LVCs in Italian, using a corpus-based methodology. The analysis, grounded in Construction Grammar, considers verb derivation schemas and LVC schemas as constructions that can form complex predicates with psychological state nouns. Causatives exhibit the most competition, influenced by such as the semantics of the nominal base, genre, and speech context. A constructional network model is proposed to offer a more refined understanding of the competition between synthetic and analytic predicates.

Sundquist explores the historical development of LVCs in American English, focusing on the expression *take a look* and analogous constructions. The study examines these developments within Goldberg's (2019) notion of 'coverage', analyzing them diachronically. The analysis consider how the coverage of construction reflects its ability to integrate and adapt to established linguistic patterns, influenced by factors such as frequency, variability, and similarity to previously attested constructions.

Nicoletti's paper analyzes Italian LVCs involving the verb *prendere* 'to take' across different contexts, including mental activities, changes of state, and event initiation. The analysis identifies three main subtypes of LVCs, classified according to their semantic functions, with the change-of-state category being the most frequent. The study posits that the meaning of light verbs can be interpreted as extensions of their full counterparts within a cognitivist framework.

Kishimoto, finally, examines the syntactic structure of Japanese LVCs from a generative perspective, focusing on the verb *suru* 'do' in combination with a verbal noun to form a predicative complex. The study concentrates on the realization of arguments within these constructions and investigates whether *suru* possesses its own argument structure, including distinct thematic roles (θ-roles). Additionally, the author explores the argument ascension, where arguments from the verbal noun move and receive case markers based on their thematic roles.

Acknowledgements

We would like to thank the reviewers for their valuable comments on the individual essays. We would also like to thank the team at Düsseldorf University Press/ DE Gruyter, especially Anne Sokoll, Jessica Bartz and Elisabeth Stanciu, for their time and effort in realizing this project and for their competent and very accommodating support throughout the entire process. Additionally, we would like to express our gratitude to the Universitäts- & Landesbibliothek Düsseldorf, which made this Open Access publication possible through financial support via an Open Access grant. Furthermore, the book publication has also been partially funded by Jens Fleischhauer's project 'Funktionsverbgefüge: Familien & Komposition' (HE 8721/1-1) funded by the German Research Foundation (DFG).

Bibliography

Allerton, David. 2002. *Streched verb constructions in English*. London: Routledge. https://doi.org/10.4324/9780203167649.
Bach, Emmon. 1986. The algebra of events. *Linguistics and Philosophy* 9. 5–16.
Bonial, Claire and Kimberly A. Pollard. 2020. Choosing an event description: What a PropBank study reveals about the contrast between light verb constructions and counterpart synthetic verbs. *Journal of Linguistics* 56(3). 577–600. https://doi.org/10.1017/S0022226720000109.
Bowern, Claire. 2008. The Diachrony of Complex Predicates. *Diachronica* 25. 161–185. https://doi.org/10.1075/dia.25.2.03bow.
Bowern, Claire. 2014. Complex predicates in Australian languages. In Harold Koch and Rachel Nordlinger (eds.), *The languages and linguistics of Australia: A comprehensive guide*, 263–294. Berlin: De Gruyter Mouton. https://doi.org/10.1515/9783110279771.
Brugman, Claudia. 2001. Light verbs and polysemy. *Language Sciences* 23. 551–578.
Butt, Miriam. 2003. The Light Verb Jungle. *Harvard Working Papers in Linguistics, Papers from the GSAS/Dudley House Workshop on Light Verbs* 9. 1–49.
Butt, Miriam. 2010. The light verb jungle: Still hacking away. In Mengistu Amberber, Bret Baker and Mark Harvey (eds.), *Complex Predicates in Cross-Linguistic Perspective*, 48–78. Cambridge: Cambridge University Press.
Butt, Miriam and Wilhelm Geuder. 2001. On the (semi)lexical status of Light Verbs. In Norbert Corver and Henk van Riemsdijk (eds.), *Semilexical Categories: On the Content of Function Words and the Function of Content Words*, 323–370. Berlin: Mouton de Gruyter.
Butt, Miriam and Aditi Lahiri. 2002. Historical stability vs. historical change. https://ling.sprachwiss.uni-konstanz.de/pages/home/butt/main/papers/stability.pdf, last access: 13/01/2025.
Butt, Miriam and Aditi Lahiri. 2013. Diachronic pertinacity of light verbs. *Lingua* 135. 7–29.
Cattell, Ray. 1984. *Composite Predicates in English*. Sydney: Academic Press.
Danlos, Laurence. 1992. Support verb constructions: linguistic properties, representation, translation. *Journal of French Language Studies* 2(1). 1–32.

Fleischhauer, Jens. 2020. Predicative multi-word expressions in Persian. In *Proceedings of the 34th Pacific Asia Conference on Language, Information and Computation*, 552–561. Hanoi: Association for Computational Linguistics. https://aclanthology.org/2020.paclic-1.63, last access: 13/01/2025.

Fleischhauer, Jens. 2022. *stehen unter*-Funktionsverbgefüge und ihre Familien. *Zeitschrift für germanistische Linguistik* 50(2). 247–288. https://doi.org/10.1515/zgl-2022-2055.

Fleischhauer, Jens. 2023. The 'principle of no synonymy' and light verb constructions – A case study on German stative light verbs. Presented at the 16th International Cognitive Linguistics Conference, 7–11 August 2023, Düsseldorf, Germany.

Fleischhauer, Jens. 2024. Eine datengesteuerte Untersuchung deutscher Funktionsverbgefüge. Artikelvarianz in *stehen*-Funktionsverbgefügen. *Lingue e Linguaggi* 65. 233–265. http://siba-ese.unisalento.it/index.php/linguelinguaggi/article/view/30024/24502, last access: 13/01/2025.

Fleischhauer, Jens and Thomas Gamerschlag. 2019. Deriving the meaning of light verb constructions – a frame account of German *stehen* 'stand'. In Constanze Juchem-Grundmann, Michael Pleyer and Monika Pleyer (eds.), *Yearbook of the German Cognitive Linguistics Association, vol. 7*, 137–156. Berlin: Mouton de Gruyter. https://doi.org/10.1515/gcla-2019-0009.

Fleischhauer, Jens, Thomas Gamerschlag, Laura Kallmeyer and Simon Petitjean. 2019. Towards a compositional analysis of German light verb constructions (LVCs) combining lexicalized tree adjoining grammar (LTAG) with frame semantics. In *Proceedings of the 13th international conference on computational semantics - long papers*, 79–90. Gothenburg: Association for Computational Linguistics. https://www.aclweb.org/anthology/W19-0407, last access: 13/01/2025.

Fleischhauer, Jens and Mozhgan Neisani. 2020. Adverbial and attributive modification of Persian separable light verb constructions. *Journal of Linguistics* 56(1). 45–85. https://doi.org/10.1017/S0022226718000646.

Folli, Raffaella and Heidi Harley. 2007. Causation, obligation, and argument structure: On the nature of little v. *Linguistic Inquiry* 38(2). 197–238. https://doi.org/10.1162/ling.2007.38.2.197.

Goldberg, Adele. 2019. *Explain Me This*. Princeton: Princeton University Press. https://doi.org/10.1515/9780691183954.

Grimshaw, Jane and Armin Mester. 1988. Light verbs and θ-marking. *Linguistic Inquiry* 19. 205–232.

Hinderdael, Michael. 1987. Zum Artikelgebrauch in deutschen und niederländischen präpositionalen FVG. In Michael Hinderdael and Lieven Van Baelen (eds.), *Deutsch-Niederländisch kontrastiv zwei Aspekte aus dem syntaktischen und lexikalischen Bereich*, 7–48. Ghent: Seminarie voor Duitse Taalkunde.

Hopper, Paul and Elizabeth Traugott. 1993. *Grammaticalization*. Cambridge: Cambridge University Press.

Isoda, Michio. 1991. The light verb construction in Japanese. In *CLS 27: Papers from the 27th Regional Meeting of the Chicago Linguistic Society 1991 Part One, The General Session*, vol. 27 1, 261–275.

Jespersen, Otto. 1942. *A Modern English Grammar on Historical Principles, Part VI, Morphology*. Copenhagen: Ejnar Munksgaard.

Ježek, Elisabetta. 2023. Semantic Co-composition in Light Verb Constructions. In Anna Pompei, Lunella Mereu and Valentina Piunno (eds.), *Light Verb Constructions as Complex Verbs: Features, Typology and Function*, 221–238. Berlin: De Gruyter.

Karimi, Simin. 1997. Persian Complex Verbs: Idiomatic or Compositional? *Lexicology* 3(1). 273–318.

Langer, Stefan. 2004. A linguistic test battery for support verb constructions. *Lingvisticae Investigationes* 27(2). 171–184. https://doi.org/10.1075/li.27.2.03lan.

Martin, Joshua. 2019. Analyzing Complex Predicates in Swahili. In *Proceedings of the Florida Linguistics Yearly Meeting (FLYM) 5*, vol. 6, 25–36.

Mel'čuk, Igor. 2022. Support (= Light) Verbs. *Neophilologica* 34. 1–30. https://doi.org/10.31261/NEO.2022.34.03.

Müller, Stefan. 2010. Persian complex predicates and the limits of inheritance-based analyses. *Journal of Linguistics* 46(2). 601–665. https://doi.org/10.1017/S0022226709990284.

Newman, John. 1996. *Give: A cognitive linguistic study*. Berlin: Mouton de Gruyter. https://doi.org/10.1515/9783110823714.

Nicoletti, David. this volume. Constructional semantics of Italian light verb constructions: The case of *prendere*. In Anna Riccio and Jens Fleischhauer (eds.), *Light verbs: Synchronic and diachronic studies*, 199–231. Düsseldorf: Düsseldorf University Press.

Nunberg, Geoffrey, Ivan A. Sag and Thomas Wasow. 1994. Idioms. *Language* 70(3). https://doi.org/10.1353/lan.1994.0007.

Olejarnik, Magdalena. 2011. An LFG Approach to Complex Predicates in Swahili. In Piotr Banski, Beata Lukaszewicz, Monika Opalinska and Joanna Zaleska (eds.), *Generative Investigations: Syntax, Morphology, and Phonology*, 139–165. Newcastle upon Tyne: Cambridge Scholars Publishing.

Pisciotta, Flavio and Francesca Masini. this volume. A paradigm of psych-predicates: Unraveling the constructional competition between light verb constructions and derived verbs in Italian. In Anna Riccio and Jens Fleischhauer (eds.), *Light verbs: Synchronic and diachronic studies*, 123–175. Düsseldorf: Düsseldorf University Press.

Pompei, Anna, Lunella Mereu and Valentina Piunno. 2023. Introduction. In Anna Pompei, L. Mereu and V. Piunno (eds.), *Light Verb Constructions as Complex Verbs*, 1–18. Berlin: Mouton de Gruyter. https://doi.org/10.1515/9783110747997-001.

Pompei, Anna and Valentina Piunno. 2023. Light Verb Constructions in Romance languages. An attempt to explain systematic irregularity. In Anna Pompei, Lunella Mereu and Valentina Piunno (eds.), *Light Verb Constructions as Complex Verbs*, 99–147. Berlin: Mouton de Gruyter.

Radford, Andrew. 1997. *Syntax: A minimalist introduction*. Cambridge: Cambridge University Press.

Samvelian, Pollet and Pegah Faghiri. 2013a. Introducing PersPred, a Syntactic and Semantic Database for Persian Complex Predicates. In Valia Kordoni, Carlos Ramisch and Aline Villavicencio (eds.), *Proceedings of the 9th Workshop on Multiword Expressions (MWE 2013)*, 11–20. Atlanta: The Association for Computational Linguistics.

Samvelian, Pollet and Pegah Faghiri. 2013b. Re-thinking Compositionality in Persian Complex Predicates. *Berkeley Linguistics Society* 39. 212–226. https://shs.hal.science/halshs-01439564v1, last access: 13/01/2025.

Samvelian, Pollet and Pegah Faghiri. 2014. Persian Complex Predicates: How Compositional Are They? *Semantics-Syntax interface* 1(1). 43–74.

Sanromán Vilas, Begoña. 2011. The unbearable lightness of light verbs. Are they semantically empty verbs? In Igor Boguslavsky and Leo Wanner (eds.), *Proceedings of the 5th International Conference on Meaning-Text Theory*, 253–262.

Stojanovska-Ilievska, Natasha. this volume. A corpus-based study of the English light verb constructions with *give* denoting bodily actions and physical interaction. In Anna Riccio and Jens Fleischhauer (eds.), *Light verbs: Synchronic and diachronic studies*, 15–42. Düsseldorf: Düsseldorf University Press.

Storrer, Angelika. 2007. Corpus-based investigations on German support verb constructions. In Christiane Fellbaum (ed.), *Collocations and Idioms: Linguistic, lexicographic, and computational aspects*, 164–187. London: Continuum Press.

Wittenberg, Eva and Roger Levy. 2017. If you want a quick kiss, make it count: How choice of syntactic construction affects event construal. *Journal of Memory and Language* 94. 254–271. https://doi.org/10.1016/j.jml.2016.12.001.

Wittenberg, Eva and Jesse Snedeker. 2013. It takes two to kiss, but does it take three to give a kiss? Categorization based on thematic roles. *Language, Cognition and Neuroscience* 29(5). 635–641. https://doi.org/10.1080/01690965.2013.831918.

Natasha Stojanovska-Ilievska

A corpus-based study of the English light verb constructions with *give* denoting bodily actions and physical interaction

1 Introduction

This paper reports the findings of a corpus-based investigation into the light verb constructions (LVCs) with *give*. Drawing on examples from the British National Corpus (BNC), it analyses the semantic and syntactic characteristics of these LVCs and explores their similarities and differences to determine whether any meaningful patterns and associations can be discerned. It also discusses the intricate relations between the LVCs with *give* and their full verb (FV) counterparts (e.g. *to give a gasp* vs. *to gasp, to give someone a hug* vs *to hug someone*).

LVCs are bipartite constructions consisting of a verbal and a nominal component. The main semantic contribution of the construction is brought about by the eventive noun within the LVC, which is considered the semantic core of the LVC. On the other hand, light verbs (LVs) have long been considered to be devoid of meaning (hence: light) to a greater or a lesser degree, having derived from their 'heavy' counterparts through semantic bleaching. This paper touches upon the motivation behind the choice of *give*, rather than some other light verb, in these LVCs. In so doing, it lends support to those approaches to LVCs that acknowledge some level of semantic contribution from the light verb to the overall meaning of the LVC.

The heavy use of *give* is demonstrated in example (1a), which is excerpted from the BNC, as are all other examples, unless specified otherwise. It literally indicates the transfer of a concrete material object from one person to another. This idea of a transfer serves as a common thread running through all LVCs with *give*, with the caveat that, in LVCs with *give*, what is transferred is never a concrete, tangible material object. The idea of a transfer of possession of a concrete material object from (1a) has evolved in different directions in the LVCs with *give*, as is shown in examples (1b) through (1d). What elements of the concept of transfer are preserved and which ones are lost in these LVCs is discussed in greater detail in Sections 2 and 4. The use of these LVCs for the expression of a wide range of events, such as: emis-

---

Natasha Stojanovska-Ilievska, Ss. Cyril and Methodius University in Skopje, North Macedonia

∂ Open Access. © 2025 the author(s), published by De Gruyter. (cc) BY This work is licensed under the Creative Commons Attribution 4.0 International License.
https://doi.org/10.1515/9783111388878-002

sion of sounds (1b), physical interaction (1c) and verbal interaction (1d), suggests that LVCs with *give* are semantically quite varied.

(1)   a.   *He gave her a delicate necklace of amethysts and pearls set in Scottish gold.* (APW, 549)
        b.   *She gave a cry* [...] (GW8, 2669)
        c.   *He gave her a brief hug* [...] (HA7, 2634)
        d.   *I gave him a simple answer* [...] (ADY, 3337)

Not only are LVCs with *give* semantically versatile, but they also exhibit some syntactic versatility, which is reflected in the variation of the syntactic patterns that these LVCs occur in, as well as in the different degrees of complexity in the structure of the noun phrase (NP) within the scope of the LVCs.

In this context, the main aims of this paper are: to offer a semantic classification of LVCs with *give* into families, to scrutinize their morphosyntactic features by delving into their structural complexities on a sentential level, as well as to investigate the semantic and discourse-pragmatic differences between the LVCs and their full verb counterparts. Therefore, this paper seeks to address the following research questions:

i.   Are distinct families of LVCs with *give* associated with a specific tense, aspect and voice?
ii.   Are there any semantic and discourse-pragmatic differences between the LVCs with *give* and their FV counterparts that factor into the choice of one structure over the other?

Based on these research questions, the following hypotheses were examined:
1. Each family of LVCs with *give* is associated with a specific tense, aspect and voice. The rationale behind this is that families of LVCs with *give* render prominent different aspects of the transfer of possession typical of the act of giving. These differences are formally reflected in distinct morphosyntactic patterns, which should enable the expression of a range of meanings aligned with the unique semantic background of each family. And it is recognized that meanings are conveyed through various means, including the grammatical categories.
2. There are semantic and discourse-pragmatic differences between the LVCs with *give* and their FV counterparts that motivate the selection of one structure over the other. Based on the principles of language economy, it is very unlikely that two structures would co-exist in a language with no semantic or discourse-pragmatic differences between them whatsoever.

To the best of my knowledge, a corpus-based study of families of LVCs with *give* seeking to uncover their shared and family-specific semantic and syntactic features and tendencies has hitherto not been performed. By filling this research gap, this study aims to provide new insights into LVCs with *give* and would, hopefully, encourage further research in this area.

This chapter is structured in five sections. Having introduced the research topic in the Introduction, I discuss the positions of authors who have made valuable contribution to our understanding of LVCs over the years in the section entitled Background on LVCs (2). The Methodological approach section (3) outlines the procedures that were followed in the research process. The Results and discussion section (4) presents the findings of the study and places them in the context of previous studies done in this field, while the final section (5) summarises the main points from the study and gives directions for further research.

2 Background on LVCs

2.1 Definitions

What is considered a LVC in this paper is a combination of a light verb and a noun phrase with an eventive noun as its head, which is either derivationally or phonetically related to a simple verb that corresponds in meaning to the entire construction (*to give a sigh* vs *to sigh*). An eventive noun may display the basic meaning of a process "whether generalized or a single instance" (Allerton, 2002, 121) or various other 'facet' meanings, including: an effected speech act, a mental or physical effect, a service, etc. (Allerton, 2002, 122–123). While some authors only allow for nouns derived through conversion (zero-derivation) in LVCs (Jespersen, 1942; Dixon, 2005; Wierzbicka, 1982), the approach taken in this paper aligns closely with Allerton (2002); Nesselhauf (2005) and Algeo (2006), whose understanding of eventive nouns within LVCs is broader and allows for nouns derived though various word-formation processes.

In this study of LVCs with *give*, the majority of the LVCs surveyed include nouns that were diachronically derived from the associated verb either through conversion or suffixation (which was verified online through the Oxford English Dictionary[1] and the Merriam-Webster Dictionary[2]). Yet in some cases it was not as straightforward to determine whether the noun predated the verb or vice versa (as was

---

[1] http://www.oed.com, last access: 20.10.2024.
[2] http://www.merriam-webster.com, last access: 20.10.2024.

the case with *kiss*, both the noun and the verb dating back to Old English). Sometimes, what synchronically looks like an instance of conversion, is actually a documented case of two separate borrowings from another language (*to cry* and *a cry* from French). Because of these difficulties, the diachronic approach was abandoned, as well as the traditional qualification of the noun within the LVCs as 'deverbal'.

The terms 'prototypical,' 'literal' and 'heavy' *give* are used interchangeably to refer to the central meaning of *give* to denote an act of transfer of ownership of a concrete material thing from one person to another. They are contrasted with the terms 'light' or 'figurative' *give*, which are reserved for uses of *give* that illustrate more abstract notions reminiscent of an act of giving. The term 'light' underscores the loss of some semantic traits inherent in the heavy verb through the process of semantic bleaching (desemanticization), while the term 'figurative' highlights the extensions of the meaning of the literal verb in different directions. The semantic bleaching evident in light *give* can be understood as a reduction in "the contribution of one or more domains to the matrix domain" of prototypical *give*, thus giving rise to figurative extensions (Pompei, 2023, 165). The uses of *give* in the LVCs analysed in this paper are thus considered to be simultaneously both light and figurative.

For the purposes of this paper, the concept of a LVC family (Fleischhauer and Gamerschlag, 2019; Fleischhauer, 2021) was employed for the first time to LVCs with *give*. A LVC family basically includes LVCs that meet two criteria: (a) they contain the same light verb and (b) they lend themselves to the same interpretation pattern. LVC families demonstrate that the interpretation of LVCs stems from the consistent semantic contribution of the light verb in the first place. This paper is concerned solely with LVCs with *give*. Three general families are distinguished, of which only two will be analysed in this paper due to space limitations.

2.2 On the status of LVCs in phraseology

Based on their degree of fixedness and semantic transparency, phraseological units can be placed at different positions on the phraseological continuum (Granger and Paquot, 2008, 36; Cowie, 1981, 227–229). Idioms are often placed at one end of the spectrum as fixed expressions whose meanings are opaque, i.e. do not derive from the meanings of their constituent parts (e.g. *to kick the bucket*). On the opposite end are free combinations, which are not typically included in phraseology because their meanings are simply the sum of their parts (e.g. *write a letter*). Between pure idioms and free combinations lie two other categories: figurative idioms and restricted collocations (Cowie, 1998, 7; Cowie, 1981, 227–229). On this phraseological continuum, LVCs are often categorized as restricted collocations (Allerton, 2002, 221; Nesselhauf, 2005, 21), in which the light verb is used figuratively, while the noun is used in its literal sense. While typically being semantically transparent (e.g. *to give someone a push* meaning 'to push someone'), LVCs can shift toward idiomatic usage (e.g. *to give someone a push* meaning 'to encourage someone'), further blurring the lines between restricted collocations and idioms. That said, LVCs share some similarities with idioms, as they are stored in memory and recalled as whole units (Allerton, 2002, 221).

2.3 The semantic contribution of the light verbs in LVCs

In the first half of the 20th century light verbs were perceived as verbs "with a vague meaning" primarily functioning as connectives (Poutsma, 1926, 394) or as "insignificant" verbs, operating merely as exponents of the grammatical categories of person and tense (Jespersen, 1942, 117). In the last decades of the 20th century, however, perspectives emerged suggesting that the light verbs within LVCs actually make major semantic contribution to these constructions (Stein, 1991; Wierzbicka, 1982). This perspective is consistent with the dominant views in the late 20th and early 21st centuries (Newman, 1996; Brugman, 2001; Gradečak-Erdeljić, 2004, 2009), which, despite some variations in terminology, propose that: a) light verbs have a more abstract meaning than heavy verbs, but are certainly not devoid of meaning, and b) essential semantic traits of the heavy verb can be recognized in the light verb as well. Applying the cognitive linguistics theory of force dynamics, it has been shown that the force dynamics inherent in the heavy verb is retained in the light verb to varying degrees (Brugman, 2001, 558–561; Gradečak-Erdeljić, 2009, 101–106), thereby indicating that the selection of a light verb in specific LVCs is not arbitrary, but rather highly motivated.

Going back to the examples in the Introduction, it is not by chance that light *give* was used in the LVCs in (1b), (1c) and (1d), rather than some other light verb, such as: *take, have, make* or *do*. *Take* is inappropriate as a substitute for *give* because *give* and *take* are considered relational opposites or converses, albeit "not exact converses" (Hurford and Heasley, 2007, 123, 137). Thus, *take* makes possible the conceptualization of the giving act from the perspective of the recipient, rather than the giver. For example, *take a punch from someone* would be the relational opposite of *give someone a punch*. When it comes to light *have*, it indicates a self-oriented activity that is either "aimless or aimed at some experience of the agent", without any external goal (Wierzbicka, 1982, 758). Hence light *have* is incompatible with LVCs indicating some interaction between two participants. Light *make* specifically points to the active process of creation of a new entity, as in *make a choice* or *make a claim*, while light *do* is more neutral in portraying the performance of an action, as in *do a dance* or *do a jump* (Gradečak-Erdeljić, 2009, 126–127). This is not to say that each eventive noun can be combined with only one specific light verb. For example, multiple light verbs can be used with *a shriek*, but the interpretation is different each time. Specifically, *give* in *give a shriek* would lend the action an involuntary overtone, *do a shriek* would be used to indicate a deliberate act of performing before spectators, while *have a shriek* would be used for an action done willingly and for personal pleasure (Quirk et al., 1985, 752).

On the other hand, verbs that share similar sub-categorization frames with *give* (such as: *donate, grant, bestow, present, confer, hand*, etc.) are also unacceptable as substitutes for light *give* in these LVCs because none of them is as experientially basic and as stylistically neutral as *give*. For example, the verb *grant* is applied in cases of formal giving of rights, permission or privileges from the position of authority, *donate* indicates giving something specifically with the purpose of helping someone, *present* implies giving something at an official or formal occasion, etc. Since all these verbs have highly nuanced meanings, they are not as amenable to a diversity of semantic and pragmatic contexts as is the case with *give*.

2.4 On the figurative extensions of *give* in LVCs

Give is a three-place predicate involving the transfer of ownership (of a material object) from one person to another. The subject argument denotes the first, generally human participant, i.e. the protagonist who has the material object. The indirect object (IO) argument denotes the second animate (usually human) participant in this relation. It is the protagonist to whom the material object is given, i.e. the recipient. The referent of the direct object (DO) argument is usually a concrete material object whose selectional restriction is 'non-human', despite there being examples of human referents of this argument, too. As a result of the process of semantic extension, this relation of transfer of a material object can be understood as a transfer of an immaterial (abstract) object (Topolińjska, 2000, 83). This conceptualization of more abstract concepts by means of more concrete ones is attributable to the experiential basicness of the act of giving and the semantic complexity of the prototypical *give*, both of which make it a rich cross-linguistic source of figurative (or metaphorical) extensions (Newman, 1996, 2, 15, 258).

In languages worldwide, eight major figurative extensions of *give* have been identified: interpersonal communication, emergence/ manifestation, causation/ purpose, permission/ enablement, schematic interaction, recipient/ benefactive marking, movement and completedness, though this list is not exhaustive (Newman, 1996, 134). Based on a survey of *give* + eventive noun combinations listed in specialized dictionaries of English collocations, three of these eight figurative extensions were identified as pertinent to the English LVCs with *give*: emergence (closely related to that of causation), schematic interaction and interpersonal communication. How these figurative extensions are related to the semantics of the prototypical *give* is explained in the next paragraph.

The prototypical *give* typically indicates a transfer of a concrete material object from one person to another, as in (1a), where after the act of giving the referent of the subject argument loses possession of the necklace. In the LVCs (1b) through (1d) the meaning of *give* is semantically somewhat bleached since not all of the elements of the heavy *give* are present in the light *give*. In some LVCs, light *give* is quite distant from the prototypical *give*. For example, in the LVC *give a cry* in (1b), there are not even two participants between whom some kind of transfer occurs. However, what is similar between light *give* in this LVC and the prototypical *give* is that something emerges from a source. While in the prototypical *give*, the giver can be construed as the source from which something (i.e. the material object to be transferred) originates, in the LVC in (1b), the one who voices the cry can be perceived as the source of the sound, which is then emitted in the air. Despite the fact that a recipient is not specified, the concept of a sound emanating from a source is vaguely reminiscent of an act of giving. In such LVCs, we observe the extension of *give* to describe emergence, i.e. to convey the idea of something emerging from somewhere (Newman, 1996, 144–149). On the other hand, in the LVC *give a hug* in example (1c) there are two participants just like in the prototypical *give* and some interaction occurs between them at the initiative of the first participant, only this time it is not a concrete material object that is being transferred, but some form of physical contact is applied by the first participant to the second one. Hence, we can say that in this and other similar examples the meaning of *give* has evolved towards the notion of physical interaction, or what Newman refers to as schematic interaction (Newman, 1996, 201–206). In the LVC in (1d), the referent of the subject argument did not hand anything to anyone, nor did they lose possession of anything. Yet, there are some similarities between the heavy *give* in (1a) and the light *give* in (1d). Namely, there are two human participants, and there is interaction between them in both examples. It is just that the conveyed verbal message in (1d) is construed as the thing being given by the first to the second participant in the prototypical (or heavy) use of *give* in (1a). This is why in such cases it is said that *give* has developed a figurative extension to verbal interaction, or interpersonal communication in Newman's terminology (Newman, 1996, 136–144). These figurative extensions (emergence/ causation, schematic interaction and interpersonal communication) lay the core semantic foundations for the three major families of LVCs with *give*.

3 Methodological approach

Taking into consideration that some LVCs are typical of colloquial speech, while others are more frequently found in more formal discourse (Shahrokny-Prehn and Höche, 2011, 243–245; Allerton, 2002, 29), this study was based on the British National Corpus (BNC), which comprises various genres of written language: fiction (ca. 17%), magazines (ca. 8%), newspapers (ca. 11%), academic texts (ca. 16%), non-academic texts (ca. 17%) and miscellaneous (ca. 21%), as well as transcripts of spoken language (ca. 10%). The BNC is a closed corpus of approximately 100 million words, including materials dating between 1980-1993. All examples excerpted from the BNC include their text code and sentence number within brackets.

The BBI Combinatory Dictionary of English (Benson et al., 2010), the Oxford Collocations Dictionary for Students of English (Crowther et al., 2002), the LTP Dictionary of Selected Collocations (Hill and Lewis, 1997), were all used to compile a list of collocations of the type '*give* + eventive noun'. In cases of discrepancies, the online versions of the Oxford Advanced Learner's Dictionary, the Longman Dictionary of Contemporary English and the Collins English Dictionary were used to verify that specific combinations have actually been attested in the English language as collocations.[3] This manually generated list of LVCs with *give* was surveyed for some underlying semantic patterns. It appeared that my grouping of these LVCs into semantic fields closely (but not completely) mirrored some of Newman's (1996) figurative extensions of *give*. The LVCs were thus classified into three major families: LVCs indicating bodily actions, physical interaction and verbal interaction, of which the first two are analysed in this paper. LVCs that did not clearly fit into any of these categories (such as: *give someone assistance*, etc.), were not analysed any further. Hence, the classification is not exhaustive both in terms of the number of analysed families and in terms of the LVCs included in each separate family.

The search for LVCs was conducted online on the BNC website.[4] Since LVCs consist of two segments (a verbal and a nominal one), and both the verb phrase (VP) and the NP can be of varying length and complexity, of all the search options available on the website, searching for collocates seemed to be the most sensible approach. The rationale for this choice is that the Collocates search menu makes possible the simultaneous search for two words (a node word and its collocate), while capturing all their word-forms, and offering the possibility for specification of the distance

---

[3] The dictionaries have been accessed online. The urls are: *Collins COBUILD Advanced Learner's Dictionary* https://www.collinsdictionary.com/dictionary/english, *Oxford Advanced Learner's Dictionary* https://www.oxfordlearnersdictionaries.com/, last access: 7/10/2024.
[4] https://www.english-corpora.org/bnc/, last access: 7/10/2024.

within which the node and its collocate should occur. The collocation window approach (Gablasova et al., 2017) was applied to search for word co-occurrences within a defined short span, in this case four words to the left and four to the right of the node, as is typical (Sinclair, 1991; Nesselhauf, 2005). This method reveals broader word associations and not just words adjacent to the node. It allows for the occurrence of determiners and/or adjectival modifiers before the noun within a LVC, and it also generates both active and passive voice constructions, as in: *H.H. Barrows gave a presidential address* (GVW, 759) and *The keynote address was given by Sir Desmond Lorimer* (AMH, 438), respectively.

Thus, the lemma GIVE was entered as a node in the first search box in the Collocates menu, while the second box was filled with a lemmatized eventive noun, such as: SMILE_n, GRUNT_n, etc., where the capital letters indicate a lemma and retrieve all word-forms in consequence, while the attached _n restricts the search to nouns in cases when there is also a verb with the same form. Such searches generated exampl sentences with the nouns *smile(s)*, *grunt(s)*, etc. within four positions to the left and to the right of the verb *give* in any of its inflected forms. Such searches were performed for 40 distinct LVCs with *give*.

The search generated 2,261 hits, which were manually individually filtered to discard examples that met the search criteria but were not examples of LVCs. First, examples were discarded if a word-form of *give* and its collocate occurred across sentence boundaries, as is the case with *cry* and *give* in the following stretch of text: *They probably need a good cry. It certainly gives me, an innocent bystander, instant indigestion* [...] (HH0, 117-118). Structures that superficially resemble LVCs, but fail to meet the criteria for LVCs were also discarded. Such was the case with [...] *why worry about them? Erm you've given them a good start in life* [...] (FMS, 607-608), where *start* refers to a beginning, rather than a sudden involuntary movement, as in *Suddenly he gave a frightened start* (CAB, 812). Hence, in this example, a near-paraphrase of 'you've given them a good start' with the lexical verb *start* is impossible, which would be a prerequisite for a structure to be considered a LVC. Constructions with idiomatic meaning, such as: *to give someone the kiss of life* meaning 'resuscitate' in *When they found her she was given the kiss of life* (CH2, 494) were beyond the scope of this study, as well. In addition, phrasal verbs with *give* were excluded from the analysis even if the collocate under investigation occurred in direct object position, as is case with the phrasal verb *give up* and the collocate *laughs* in: *I wouldn't give up those laughs for anything* [...] (HRF, 899). Examples were also discarded where *given* was used as a preposition meaning 'considering,' as in: *Given a good performance today, he will clearly be in line for a place at Wembley* (A8C, 23). Finally, since this study aims to establish some association between particular families of LVCs with *give* and the verbal categories of tense, aspect and voice, non-finite verb forms (infinitives and participles) were also excluded from this study.

The remaining 1,664 examples were manually annotated: the light verb for the verbal categories of tense, aspect and voice, while the nouns within the LVCs for the nominal categories of definiteness and number. A noun was considered to have definite reference if it was preceded by a definite article, a determinative possessive, or a demonstrative determiner (Quirk et al., 1985, 253, 327, 362, 372). A noun was considered indefinite if it was not preceded by any article (zero article), if it was preceded by the indefinite article, or other indefinite determiners, such as: *some, any, either, neither, every, each, all, few, many, one, another*, etc. (Quirk et al., 1985, 253, 261, 376–392). The overall results per family are displayed in tables 1-4 in Section 4.

In each of the two subsections in Section 4, by referring to examples from the BNC and the data from the tables 1–4, the extent to which families of LVCs display syntactic flexibility is assessed, by verifying whether they allow passivization or an overt realization of an IO. In addition, the flexibility within the noun phrase (NP) itself is examined as well, by checking if the pluralization of the noun, and the substitution of the indefinite article with a marker of definiteness are allowed.

4 Results and discussion

4.1 Family 1: LVCs denoting bodily actions

From a semantic point of view, what LVCs from Family 1 have in common is the fact that they all denote an action that involves movement of a part of the body (2a), while many of them additionally indicate the emission of vocal sounds (2b). Thus, we distinguish between two subfamilies within Family 1. They both demonstrate the same general morphosyntactic pattern but exhibit two distinct interpretational patterns.

(2)   a.   *Louise gave a little smile.* (C8S, 1529)
       b.   *I gave a scream of horror.* (H9U, 1745)

A convenient paraphrase for Subfamily 1A would be: 'the subject referent makes a facial or bodily movement denoted by the NP-internal noun', as in (2a), and it is exemplified with the following LVCs: *give a chuckle, give a cough, give a gasp, give a gulp, give a jerk, give a jump, give a laugh, give a shrug, give a shudder, give a sigh, give a smile, give a snort, give a sob, give a start, give a wave* and *give a wink*. These LVCs are generally based on the class of verbs involving the body (Levin, 1993), particularly the subclasses of verbs of gestures/signs involving body parts, verbs of body-internal states of existence and verbs of non-verbal expression. Subfamily 1B includes LVCs that can be paraphrased with 'the subject referent emits the sound denoted by the NP-internal noun', as in (2b), and includes the following LVCs: *give a bellow, give a cry, give a groan, give a grunt, give a moan, give a scream, give a shriek,* and *give a squeak.* These LVCs are based on verbs of sound emission from Levin's (1993) classification, which are oftentimes cross-listed in other (sub)classes too, such as the subclasses of verbs of non-verbal expression, and verbs of manner of speaking, or the class of verbs of sounds made by animals. Thus, it was sometimes a bit problematic whether to include certain LVCs in the first or in the second LVC subfamily, especially if they could rightfully occur in both. For example, *giving a cry* essentially refers to the production of sound, but it is also related to non-verbal expression. Since it foremost denotes the emission of a vocal sound, which can secondarily be interpreted as an emotional expression through involvement of parts of the body, the LVC *give a cry* was included in Subfamily 1B.

The causative figurative extension of *give* is present in all of the LVCs in Family 1, where causativity is generally understood as "causing an event or thing, without any interpersonal manipulation" (Newman, 1996, 176). Closely related to this, the LVCs that denote production of sounds and egress of air instantiate the figurative extension of emergence, or appearance of something from somewhere (Newman, 1996, 145). Thus, the emission of sound in the LVCs resembles the movement of an object outside of the personal sphere of control of the giver in a giving act, while the source of the sound in the LVCs corresponds to the giver (Newman, 1996, 144–148).

Many of these LVCs indicate unintentional, instinctive or physiological reactions (Gradečak-Erdeljić, 2009, 115) or involuntary reactions (Jespersen, 1942, 118), as in (3). Such unintentionality in the performance of the action is not in line with the literal *give*, which indicates a conscious and intentional act.

(3)   *There was no foothold and Maggie gave a cry of fear as she too felt the ground give way beneath them as they slid over the edge towards the lake.* (HGK, 2134)

Since the LVCs from Family 1 are related to intransitive verbs (*to sigh* vs *to give a sigh*), in these LVCs light *give* only requires a subject (S) and a direct object (DO), while an indirect object (IO) is generally not added (Huddleston and Pullum, 2002, 293). This means that LVCs from this family are most distant from the literal *give* understood as a transfer of an object from one person to another, because they usually do not imply directing the movement or sound to anyone in particular. Thus, the majority of LVCs from this family (78.14%) are realized as monotransitive constructions. Likewise, the LVC *give a shrug* occurs within a monotransitive pattern in 93 of the 95 BNC examples, amounting to 97.89%. In example (4), however, the LVC is structurally different from all the hitherto mentioned examples because of its overt expression of the recipient in indirect object position. Thus, in (4) light *give* is syntactically closer to the literal ditransitive *give* because both protagonists necessary for the realization of the transfer (the agent and the recipient) are realized in the LVC in their respective syntactic positions of a subject and an indirect object. The gesture *a shrug of apology* is directed to Mariana (the recipient in IO position), so what is actually communicated with her is the apology, which finds its expression through the shrug. Of the 24 LVCs from this family searched in the BNC, only three other LVCs sometimes occur in the ditransitive pattern: *give a smile, give a wink* and *give a wave*. They all denote gestures and facial expressions used in non-verbal interaction.

(4) *He brushed a few drops of sea water off the top of the carburetor, dabbed the float chamber full and gave Mariana a shrug of apology before kicking the starter.* (AMU, 1750)

In the LVCs from this family the eventive noun is profiled as a discrete unit of an action. This contributes to the understanding of the action denoted by the LVC as time-bounded. In example (5a) we see how the indefinite article in these LVCs is used as an indicator of the singularity of the action. Being quantized through the indefinite article, the NP in DO position adds the end-point required for a telic interpretation of the entire VP. This could be seen as an instance of 'object marking', which is applied in English as a telicity-encoding strategy (Filip, 2008, 234), because giving is an act that becomes telic through the involvement of a theme (van Gelderen, 2017, 58). Example (5b) with the FV *scream* has an atelic interpretation, which is proved by the felicitous use of the adverbial of duration *for hours*. On the other hand, in (5c) we are clearly dealing with a telic eventuality description regarding the same FV, because the presence of the adverbial *once* points to a single atomic screaming event, or a singular eventuality (Landman, 2008, 112) and it is precisely telic predicates that denote events which can be counted and can thus be modified by iterative adverbials (Filip, 1993, 91–92). In other words, "bounded predicates treat their arguments as logical individuals, i.e., as entities which can be counted" (Herweg, 2014, 191) and can thus combine well with temporal count adverbials, such as *once, twice, three times*, etc. Thus, while the FV *scream* can be interpreted as either telic or atelic depending on the context, LVCs with singular nouns within their structure conceptualize the event as an action with an inherent end-point, which licences their telic interpretation. By contrasting (5a) and (5b), we observe that LVCs can actually express Aktionsart (also called inner aspect in van Gelderen, 2017, 57) opposition with the corresponding FVs.

(5) a. *[…] she gave a scream thinking that it was the spider running there.* (KCP, 73)

   b. *In the end she left it to cry. It screamed for hours, probably waking the entire house.* (GUM, 2132-2133)

c. *Sam Somerville screamed once, buried her face in Quinn's back and began to cry.* (CAM, 1764)

Regarding the categories of definiteness and number, as much as 95.13% of all surveyed examples included an indefinite singular noun within the LVC, as in (5a), which is evident from Table 1. This confirms that LVCs from this family are basically used to express singular bounded actions. LVCs with indefinite plural nouns (6a), LVCs with definite singular nouns (6b) and LVCs with a plural noun with definite reference, such as (6c) were marginally represented among the surveyed examples of LVCs with *give* from this family, with 0.89%, 3.91% and 0.07% respectively.

(6) a. *She gave little moans of pleasure* [...]. (FS1, 397)
 b. *Again, he gave that expressive shrug.* (JY7, 5563)
 c. *She gave them her best smiles.* (GUK, 130)

As for tense, as much as 97.02% of the LVCs in active voice have been used in the simple past tense, while only rare examples in the simple present have been recorded, along with sporadic examples in the simple future and the past perfect, as apparent from Table 2. The findings about the predominance of the simple past, coupled with the fact that the NPs within the structure of these LVCs are quantized (by being singular) in 1341 cases (99.04%) speaks of a strong tendency for the LVCs from the 'bodily actions' family to denote telic eventuality descriptions in which the endpoint has been reached, because following Borik (2006, 39), "if a given proposition has the property of defining the event being described as telic, then whenever the past tense is used, we infer that the event has terminated (or reached an end-point)". Thus, in the absence of the perfective/ imperfective aspectual distinction in English, which is typical of many Slavic languages, LVCs could be perceived and employed as markers of telicity (Brinton, 2011), unlike the full verbs that alternate between telic and atelic readings.

LVCs from this family resist passivization, which can be seen from the contrast between (7a) and (7b). In the LVCs from this family the noun in DO position cannot be promoted to the subject position of a passive sentence because passivization operates on arguments (Kearns, 1988, 15). Rare examples of passive constructions (more specifically 2 out of 1354 examples, or 0.15%) were observed in the BNC in which the participant with the role of a non-prototypical recipient in the ditransitive LVCs was advanced to subject position, as is the case with the noun *onlookers* in example (7c).

(7) a. *She gave a cry, and fell to the floor.* (FSL, 443)
 b. **A cry was given by her* [...].
 c. *Onlookers at a charity sponsored walk were given a smile.* (ACM, 136)

Tab. 1: Distribution of NPs within the LVCs from Family 1 across the nominal categories of definiteness and number.

	indefinite singular NP	definite singular NP	indefinite plural NP	definite plural NP	Total
chuckle	21	1			22
cough	19	1			20
gasp	38		1		39
gulp	4				4
jerk	8				8
jump	11				11
laugh	240	8	2		250
shrug	90	5			95
shudder	23	3			26
sigh	148		1		149
smile	406	30	3	1	440
snort	31				31
sob	6				6
start	24	1			25
wave	28	1	1		30
wink	17				17
Total Subfamily 1A	1114	50	8	1	1173
bellow	7				7
cry	64	1	1		66
groan	22	1			23
grunt	29		2		31
moan	14		1		15
scream	24	1			25
shriek	10				10
squeak	4				4
Total Subfamily 1B	174	3	4	0	181
Total Family 1	1288	53	12	1	1354

The use of the LVCs with *give* from the 'bodily actions' family is also motivated by information structure considerations. The simple SV realization of the intransitive pattern oftentimes sounds "oddly incomplete" since the verb is typically not intended to bear the "maximum communicative dynamism in a sentence", resulting in the frequent addition of optional adverbials (Quirk et al., 1985, 1401). LVCs with *give* corresponding to intransitive full verbs actually stretch the predication over two segments (a verbal and a nominal one), thus fitting within the canonical English SVO word order and allowing for the placement of sentence focus on verbal content, profiled as an eventive noun in DO position (Brinton, 1996; Quirk et al., 1985;

Tab. 2: Distribution of the LVCs from Family 1 across the verbal categories of tense, aspect and voice. The numbers for Prog(ressive) and Perfect are summarized for the three tenses: Past, Present, and Future in the active voice.

	Active					Imp.	Passive	Total
	Present	Past	Future	Prog.	Perfect			
chuckle		22						22
cough		20						20
gasp		38			1			39
gulp		4						4
jerk	1	7						8
jump	1	10						11
laugh	8	241				1		250
shrug		95						95
shudder		26						26
sigh	3	146						149
smile	8	420	2		3	5	2	440
snort		31						31
sob		6						6
start		23		1	1			25
wave	1	24	1	1		3		30
wink	2	14			1			17
Total 1A	**24**	**1127**	**3**	**2**	**6**	**9**	**2**	**1173**
bellow		7						7
cry	2	63			1			66
groan	1	21				1		23
grunt	1	30						31
moan		15						15
scream		25						25
shriek		10						10
squeak		4						4
Total 1B	**4**	**175**	**0**	**0**	**1**	**1**	**0**	**181**
Total	**28**	**1302**	**3**	**2**	**7**	**10**	**2**	**1354**

Stojanovska-Ilievska, 2022). This contrast is illustrated in examples (8a) and (8b). In the example illustrating the intransitive pattern (8a) the sentence focus is on non-verbal content (*anxiously*), while in (8b) the sentence focus is on verbal content, profiled in the zero-derived noun *gasp*.

(8) a. 'It won't!' Maggie gasped anxiously.' (HGK, 3229-3230)
b. Suddenly Angela, who was gazing at the red mack her mummy was holding out to her, gave a gasp. (B0B, 2555)

To sum up, the LVCs from this family are clearly associated with the simple past tense and the active voice. The marked predominance of singular (and hence quantized) nouns within these LVCs contributes to their telic interpretation and the establishment of a telic-atelic opposition with their corresponding full verb, as a major motivation for their use. The occurrence of these LVCs in the past tense indicates that the end-point in these telic eventuality descriptions has been reached. The focus on verbal content in these LVCs provides another motivation for their use, since it is not always readily available in the intransitive sentence pattern.

4.2 Family 2: LVCs denoting physical interaction

Family 2 basically deals with LVCs that involve someone performing a physical action upon another person/ object. In these constructions Newman (1996) perceives a figurative extension in which the meaning of *give* is reduced to schematic interaction between participants and the character of that interaction is defined by the noun within the structure of the LVCs. Within the 'physical interaction' family, three subfamilies were differentiated, adopting and partly modifying Levin's (1993) verb classes, understood as semantically relatively unified sets of verbs that exhibit similar patterns in diathesis alternations and other characteristics. These are illustrated in examples (9a) through (9c).

(9) a. *Myles Burke gave a final wipe to the brass knocker, the letter-box and doorknob* [...] (B1X, 1012)
b. *Elizabeth gave him a push, which almost toppled him to the ground!* (C98, 1342)
c. [...] *he gave her a big cuddle.* (CGT, 923)

In Subfamily 2A the physical action concerns maintaining the hygiene of something/someone, as in (9a). It is based on verbs from the subclass of 'wipe verbs' within the 'verbs of removing' class, so relevant LVCs include: *give sb/ sth a rub/ scrub/ squeeze/ sweep/ wash/ wipe*, while a convenient paraphrase is: 'the subject referent removes something from something/someone in a manner specified by the NP-internal noun'. In Subfamily 2B the physical action involves applying force (of variable degrees) upon someone/something, as in (9b). It is based on the (sub)classes of verbs of contact by impact, verbs of surface contact, verbs of exerting force and verbs of throwing, among which there is certain overlap and cross-listing. This subfamily is exemplified by the LVCs *give sb/ sth a kick/ nudge/ push/ scratch/ shake/ shove/ slap* and it can be paraphrased by 'the subject referent applies force to someone/something in a manner specified by the NP-internal noun'. Finally, in Subfamily 2C the physical action involves the expression of tenderness or love for someone, as in (9c). It centers around the 'marry verbs' subclass from the class of verbs of social interaction, so pertinent LVCs include *give sb a hug/ kiss/ cuddle*. A common paraphrase for these LVCs would be: 'the subject referent expresses affection through physical contact with someone/something in a manner specified by the NP-internal noun'. The LVCs from Subfamily 2C typically indicate a unidirectional transfer, unlike their full verb counterparts (*to hug, to kiss, to cuddle*), which are also legitimately used to express a bidirectional (reciprocal) transfer.

In terms of the intentionality of the action, the external argument of these LVCs is almost exclusively limited to people acting intentionally, of their own free will. Regarding the transfer of energy from the first to the second participant, which is typical for almost all LVCs in this family, it developed based on the concept of transfer of a material object in the literal *give*, only in these LVCs it is not a specific object that is transferred, but energy. The recipients of that energy are non-prototypical recipients because, to a greater or lesser extent, they are affected by the action denoted by the LVC. In fact, both in examples (10a) and (10b) we are dealing with the same action (hugging), which is conceptualized in different ways in the constructions with the FV and the LV. In such situations, it is considered that the second human participant has the semantic role of a patient in both constructions, regardless of whether it is realized in DO position, as in (10a) or in IO position, as in (10b) (Quirk et al., 1985, 753). Newman (1996) uses the term RECIPIENT for the second participant in the LVCs when he contrasts it with the GIVER, i.e. the first participant involved in the act of figurative energy transfer. However, when it comes to defining the semantic roles of these two participants, he considers the first protagonist to be an agent and the second one to be a patient.

This highlights the importance of information structure in the selection of either a LVC or a construction with a full verb as a vehicle for conveying one's ideas. LVCs tend to place the focus on the verbal content contained in the eventive noun by placing it in clause-final position, as is the case with *a brief hug* in (10b), assuming the familiarity and givenness of the recipient of the hug. In contrast, in the corresponding structures with full verbs the focus is on the patient in DO position, presuming it constitutes new information, as is the case with *Elaine* in (10a). In a LVC this same participant would be syntactically realized in the IO position, typical for a recipient, but would still be affected by the action of the verb, as in: *Francis gave Elaine a hug*.

(10) a. *Francis hugged Elaine* [...]. (F9X, 3599)
     b. *[...] He gave her a brief hug, then turned towards the jeep.* (JXU, 919)

These LVCs are based on transitive verbs indicating some form of physical contact applied by the first participant onto the second one, such as *to kick, to kiss,* or *to wash*. The patient NP in DO position of these transitive verbs is almost invariably placed in IO position (which is typically reserved for the recipient) in the LVCs, before the nominalization in DO position (as in: *to kick someone* vs. *to give someone a kick*). This double object construction occurs in 296 instances (or 98.67%) out of 300 example sentences where the IO argument was overtly expressed (including statements in the active voice and imperatives). The double object construction is sometimes said to contribute to the perception of the recipient of the physical contact as affected (Newman, 1996, 206), the stronger effect on the IO argument being attributed to the greater proximity to the verb. Other authors do not acknowledge any differences in this regard between the double object construction and the *to* variant and assume that there are other factors that motivate the predominance of the double object construction. Namely, it is the tendency of the recipients (as animate participants) to be more familiar in the discourse than themes and hence to be often pronominalized (Rappaport Hovav and Levin, 2008, 157). In compliance with the principles of information structure, such participants are hardly ever placed in clause-final position, as it is reserved for new information (rheme), as in (11a). Although the recipient in an act of giving, in general, is animate (mostly human), in these LVCs the recipients of the physical contact can be either animate (as in: *to give the baby a wash*) or inanimate (as in: *to give the floor a sweep*). By virtue of their being at the receiving end in a giving act (albeit a figurative one), these inanimate entities are practically construed as animate. This might explain the prevalence of the double object construction not only for animate, but also for inanimate recipients. Apparently, they also often have the status of givenness and are hence pronominalized in these LVCs, just like animate recipients.

LVCs where the NP denoting the recipient of the physical contact is placed within a prepositional phrase (PP) with *to* (aka *to* variant or *to* template) are very rare with LVCs from the 'physical interaction' family: 4 instances (or 1.33%) out of 300 example sentences where the participant was overtly expressed (including statements in the active voice and imperatives). When they do occur, they are usually prompted by an IO that is realized by a longer NP, which therefore tends to be moved towards the end of the sentence based on the end-weight principle (Collins, 1995, 44), as is the case with *the niece who killed her* in (11b). Thus, it is information structure and NP heaviness that determine the selection of the preferred variant (double object or *to* variant), as semantically there are no differences between the two variants and they both entail successful transfer (Rappaport Hovav and Levin, 2008, 146, 156).

(11) a. Her husband gave her a hug and hurried inside [...] (ARK, 761)
b. A grieving mother wept over the body of her daughter, then gave a loving hug to the niece who killed her. (CEN, 1091)

Having said that, one has to bear in mind that the patient (or the affected) semantic role is understood in a scalar fashion depending on the level of affectedness by the action of the verb, where degrees of affectedness are understood as "a hierarchy of monotonically weakening truth conditions about the result state of the theme on the scale" (Beavers, 2011b, 335). On the Affectedness hierarchy, which is based on several diagnostic tests (Change entailed of x, x takes result XP, *Happened/did to* x, φ is dynamic, and Result XP variation), the patients of verbs of surface contact/impact are considered less affected than those of verbs indicating degree achievements (or non-quantized change) since they do not imply change, but only involve potential for change (Beavers, 2011b, 358–359). Thus, the participant in IO position is more affected in *give someone a push/shove*, than the one in *give someone a wash/kick/punch/rub*, etc. Applying the same reasoning to LVCs where the argument in IO position is an object rather than a human being, the patient in *give the car a push* would be considered more affected than the one in *give the table a wipe*.

As is shown in Table 3, the LVCs from this family occur in the passive voice very rarely. This means that, just like the LVCs from Family 1, the LVCs from this family also resist passivization by advancing the NP in DO position in the active sentence to the subject position in the passive sentence. This is shown in examples (12a) and (12b), indicating that the eventive nouns within these LVCs do not have the status of arguments. This points to a close connection between the LV and the eventive noun, and is indicative of its integration within the LVCs.

(12) a. When I got home with it, I gave it a wash, and tried it out almost immediately. (EFH, 187)
b. *[...] a wash was given to it, [...]

In contrast, there are scarce examples of passivization in which the argument from IO position is advanced to S position, as is the case with *one distressed victim* in (13). This was observed in 2.58% of all examples. The possibility for passivization only by advancing the argument in IO position (also called 'outer passive' in Brinton, 2011, 566) testifies to the greater syntactic and semantic unity of the LV with the eventive noun, because in that way the constituent elements of the LVC are not separated (Brinton, 2011, 565–566).

(13) [...] one distressed victim is given a reassuring hug from a concerned friend. (CBF, 6088)

Tab. 3: Distribution of the LVCs from Family 2 across the verbal categories of tense, aspect and voice. The numbers for Progressive and Perfect are summarized for the three tenses: Past, Present, and Future in the active voice.

	Active					Imp.	Passive	Total
	Present	Past	Future	Prog.	Perfect			
rub	1	1			1	3		6
scrub						2		2
squeeze	1	6						7
sweep	1						1	2
wash		1	3	1	1	1	1	8
wipe		1				1		2
Total 2A	3	9	3	1	2	7	2	27
kick	4	14	2	1	2	1		24
nudge	1	4						5
push	2	26	4	2	2	4	3	43
scratch		2						2
shake	1	21	1		1	7		31
shove	4	12			1			17
slap		9	2					11
Total 2B	12	88	9	3	6	12	3	133
cuddle	2	4			2	10	1	19
hug	2	30		1	1	8	2	44
kiss	8	35	5		1	38		87
Total 2C	12	69	5	1	4	56	3	150
Total	27	166	17	5	12	75	8	310

Among all the LVCs in the active voice, the simple past is the prevalent tense (73.13%), but other tenses have also been documented (see Table 3). Another study of LVCs with *give* has also demonstrated that they are primarily used in the past tense, suggesting that the syntactic and semantic characteristics of particular LVCs may be related to a specific inflected form of the verb (which in this case is *gave* to indicate past tense), rather than being spread across the lemma GIVE as a whole (Martínez Caro and Arús-Hita, 2020). The fact that LVCs occur preferentially with the simple past tense suggests a connection with the concept of an inflectional island, meaning that certain syntactic and semantic properties of the verb could be said to reside in a specific inflected form (Newman and Rice, 2006).

Contrary to the typical, actualized use of these LVCs in the simple past tense to denote actions that took place in the past, as in (9a), (9b) and (9c), LVCs from this family can also be used in the simple present tense to express habituality. For example, in (14), the act of people from Somalia hugging those who bring them food is depicted as a regular occurrence. This LVC illustrates a telic eventuality description owing to the quantized NP in DO position, but unlike the LVCs in the simple past, this LVC does not indicate that the end-point has been reached.

(14) *Some of them who can speak English come up to you and give you a hug and say, Thank-you, you give us life.* (K1C, 2417)

LVCs from this family generally do not express longer, continuous actions, but rather actions that are performed momentarily, or last a short time. Consequently, these LVCs occur in the progressive aspect in just 5 out of 227 examples in the active voice, amounting to 2.20%. Example (15) is one such case, where the present progressive is used for an action that is performed at the moment of speaking. The prevalence of the perfect aspect is 5.29%

(15) *I am not hurting you. I am giving you a wash.* (KDE, 2330-2331)

Table 4 demonstrates that, regarding the categories of definiteness and number, in the vast majority of examples (94.19%) the nominal part is realized with an indefinite noun in the singular, as is the case with examples (9a)–(9c). In the BNC there were hardly any examples where the NP within the LVCs was realized as a definite noun in singular (1.94%), as in (16a) or an indefinite plural noun (3.87%), as in (16b). There were no examples of definite plural nouns within these LVCs.

(16) a. *And he gave her the kiss she was waiting for* [...]. (JY0, 6419)
      b. *She made me coffee, gave me hugs* [...]. (G0A, 1605)

The change of possession indicated by literal *give* is non-incremental, as it does not progress in successive stages, but operates on a binary scale, shifting from the recipient's not possessing something to their actual coming into in possession of it, both in the double object construction and in the *to* variant (Beavers, 2011a, 26). Being a non-incremental verb in which a complete change of possession is lexicalized, *give* falls within the achievement aspectual subclass of verbs and always has a telic interpretation with quantized themes and overt recipients (Rappaport Hovav and Levin, 2008, 149; Beavers, 2011a, 20). The actual overt realization of the recipient contributes to the demarcation of the result state. This is demonstrated in (17a) as after the completion of the giving act, it is not Carrie, but Mike who has possession of the watch. The inference of a successful transfer is indefeasible with literal *give* (Beavers and Koontz-Garboden, 2020, 115), as shown in (17b). Such is the inference of a successful transfer with light *give* as well. Although in the LVCs from this family light *give* does not instantiate a change of possession as such, the IO referent receives some form of physical contact from the subject referent nonetheless, as in

Tab. 4: Distribution of NPs within the LVCs from Family 2 across the nominal categories of definiteness and number.

	indefinite singular NP	definite singular NP	indefinite plural NP	definite plural NP	Total
rub	5		1		6
scrub	2				2
squeeze	7				7
sweep	2				2
wash	8				8
wipe	2				2
Total Subfamily 2A	26	0	1	0	27
kick	22	2			24
nudge	5				5
push	41	2			43
scratch	1		1		2
shake	31				31
shove	17				17
slap	11				11
Total Subfamily 2B	128	4	1	0	133
cuddle	17		2		19
hug	42		2		44
kiss	79	2	6		87
Total Subfamily 2C	138	2	10	0	150
Total Family 2	292	6	12	0	310

(17c). Even if Dot was reluctant to receive the hug from Gloria, yet from (17c) it is indisputable that Gloria wrapped her arms around Dot, thereby establishing unilateral physical contact with Dot. This can be interpreted as a successful (figurative) transfer of energy from Gloria, as an energy source, to Dot, as an energy sink (Langacker, 1991, 292–293; Newman, 1996, 49, 204). The successfully completed transfer is irrefutable, as shown in (17d).

(17)   a.   *Carrie gave Mike a watch as a Christmas present.* (EF1, 1803)
           b.   *#Carrie gave Mike a watch as a Christmas present, but he didn't receive it.*
           c.   *Gloria gave Dot a hug* [...]. (AC5, 6)
           d.   *#Gloria gave Dot a hug, but Dot didn't receive it.*

The use of the literal *give* with frame adverbials like *in five minutes* is felicitous, but since *give* indicates a simple transition which is completed instantaneously, its combination with such adverbials does not indicate that an event was completed within the given time frame, but that it took place after the specified interval elapsed (Dowty, 1979; Jackendoff, 1996; Rappaport Hovav and Levin, 2008; Rappaport Hovav, 2008). On the other hand, combinations of *give* with durative adverbials like *for five minutes* are infelicitous by virtue of the fact that the act of giving is momentary by default, as is shown in (18a). Example (18b) demonstrates that the same reasoning obtains with LVCs with *give*. Namely, (18b) means that it took Gloria five minutes to decide to give Dot a hug. Should we substitute the LVC *give a hug* with the corresponding full verb *hug* in the same sentence, as in (18c), we would see that the event of hugging could be understood as taking full five minutes (with the adverbial *for five minutes*), or it could be interpreted as occurring after the five-minute interval has passed (with the adverbial *in five minutes*), the latter being exactly the same interpretation as the one of the LVC in (18b).

(18) a. *Carrie gave Mike a watch as a Christmas present in five minutes/ *for five minutes.*
      b. *Gloria gave Dot a hug in five minutes/ *for five minutes.*
      c. *Gloria hugged Dot in five minutes/ for five minutes.*

Verbs in which a non-incremental change is lexicalized, such as *give*, are inherently telic and their use in the simple past tense entails that the end-point of the predicate has been reached (Rappaport Hovav and Levin, 2008, 151; Rappaport Hovav, 2008, 28). For example, *Carrie gave Mike a watch* entails that Mike received a watch. The same applies to LVCs with *give* too, as *Gloria gave Dot a hug* entails that Dot was hugged. In addition, the uses both of literal and of light *give* in the progressive aspect would give rise to the imperfective paradox (Rothstein, 2008, 48): *Carrie was giving Mike a watch* does not entail that Carrie gave Mike a watch and *Gloria was giving Dot a hug* does not entail that Gloria gave Dot a hug. This again is indicative of telicity.

However, the FV *hug* being a semelfactive (which is considered a subclass of activity verbs), has two distinct valid interpretations depending on the context. Namely, *Gloria hugged Dot in five minutes* or *Gloria hugged Dot once* would entail that Dot was hugged by Gloria, the telic interpretation stemming from the use of *hug* as a semelfactive verb, indicating the completion of a single, atomic, minimal event of hugging. However, the addition of the duration adverbial *for five minutes* in *Gloria hugged Dot for five minutes* would induce an activity reading (involving multiple iterations of the single event), thus lending the predicate an atelic interpretation (Rothstein, 2008, 49), because activities do not have an end-point and are by their nature unbounded without the inclusion of some indicators of measure or direction. The telic-atelic dichotomy in the interpretation can also be verified by the application of the progressive test: on a semelfactive, 'single occurrence' reading,

Gloria was hugging Dot does not entail that Gloria hugged Dot because she might have been interrupted midway. In contrast, on the activity (or iterative) reading, *Gloria was hugging Dot* does entail that Gloria hugged Dot, provided that the event of hugging included at least one minimal interval.

Unlike full verbs, such as *hug* above, which are ambiguous between a telic or an atelic interpretation without linguistic or extra-linguistic cues, the LVCs with *give* from Family 2 generally license telic interpretations, except when non-quantized nouns (bare plural nouns) occur in DO position. The fact that such examples are scarce in family 2 (3.22%) renders their significance negligible. Thus, just like in Family 1, we observe an aspectual opposition between the LVCs with *give* (18b) and their corresponding full verbs (18c), the former yielding almost exclusively telic readings, while the latter licencing atelic interpretations as well.

In summary, observations relating to the aspectual profile of literal *give* were found to translate to light *give* as well, although in the LVCs from the 'physical interaction' family we are not dealing with an actual transfer of possession, but rather with an application of physical contact by the subject referent onto another entity, as a form of figurative transfer of energy. The strong preference for the NPs in DO position within these LVCs to be quantized as one (evident in their occurrence as singular nouns in 96.13% of all cases) coupled with the overt expression of the recipient of the physical contact, either in a double object construction or a *to*-template, in 99.34% of the sentences (statements in the active voice and imperatives) licenses the telic interpretation of these constructions. These findings, together with the fact that (73.13%) of the LVCs in the active voice were used in the simple past tense, suggest that speakers may be inclined to use LVCs with *give* as opposed to their corresponding full verbs when they wish to clearly communicate that the end-point of an event was reached at some point prior to the moment of speaking. Passivization was uncommon, and was exclusively realized though the promotion of the IO argument to S position. Information structure and the heaviness of the NP denoting the recipient of the physical contact were found to be relevant factors determining the order of constituents within the sentence. Information structure considerations prove also relevant when choosing either a LVC or a construction with a full verb as a vehicle for conveying one's ideas.

5 Conclusion

This corpus-based study provides a semantic classification of LVCs with *give* into families and examines their morphosyntactic characteristics by exploring their structural complexities at sentence and phrase level. It also analyzes the semantic and discourse-related differences between these LVCs and their full verb equivalents. More specifically, this paper sought to address two research questions and consequently tested two hypotheses. The findings corroborated these hypotheses. By examining examples from the BNC, it was revealed that each family of LVCs with *give* was indeed associated with a specific tense, aspect and voice. The study demonstrated that there exist considerable similarities between the two analysed families of LVCs in terms of their resistance to passivization and their preference for the past simple tense. In addition, the findings suggest that an aspectual opposition can be established between the full verbs and the corresponding LVCs, such that the LVCs with a quantized, singular noun within their structure are perceived to indicate telicity, while the corresponding full verbs allow atelic interpretations. All these findings collectively indicate that LVCs, unlike their full verb counterparts, provide speakers with the means to unambiguously express that the end-point of a past event has been reached, with the understanding that it will be interpreted as completed. Seeking additional evidence for factors that could potentially motivate the choice of either LVCs of full verbs, it was shown that information structure considerations could also determine the selection of one structure over the other. It was also made clear that the choice of the light verb *give* in these LVCs is not arbitrary, but strongly motivated.

In this study three LVC families were identified (bodily actions, physical interaction and verbal interaction) based on Newman's (1996) research into the most common figurative extensions of *give*. This paper focuses only on the first two families due to space limitations. The LVCs from Family 1 indicate movement of parts of the body and production of sounds. The LVCs from Family 2 make possible a different conceptualization of the actions portrayed by their corresponding FVs. These two families demonstrate some obvious parallels to the prototypical *give*, even though there are some discernible differences as well. The LVCs from Family 1 tend to lack an obvious correspondent for the recipient in the giving act, while the LVCs from Family 2 are vaguely reminiscent of the transfer between the participants evident in the prototypical *give*. Hence the LVCs from the 'bodily actions' family are primarily realized in a monotransitive pattern, while the LVCs from the 'physical interaction' family are almost exclusively realized in a ditransitive pattern. Within these two families denoting bodily actions and physical interaction, several subfamilies were differentiated based on their semantic properties. In practice, the boundaries between the individual (sub)families were not always so clear-cut, as was the case when some LVCs from Family 1 (typically denoting involuntary emission of sounds or performance of bodily actions) were used to denote deliberate acts of non-verbal communication and it is Family 3 that revolves around interpersonal communication.

Looking ahead, a similar analysis of the third family of LVCs with *give* would make a valuable contribution to our overall understanding of these constructions, by allowing us to view the findings from this study from a new, broader perspective. Another area worth exploring is the distribution of LVCs with *give* across different text types in online corpora, which could reveal patterns in usage frequency and stylistic preferences associated with specific genres. By complementing this one, such studies would offer new insights into this issue and would deepen our understanding of the diversity and complexity of LVCs in general.

Bibliography

Algeo, John. 2006. *British or American English: A Handbook of Word and Grammar Patterns*. Cambridge: Cambridge University Press.

Allerton, David. 2002. *Streched verb constructions in English*. London: Routledge. https://doi.org/10.4324/9780203167649.

Beavers, John. 2011a. An aspectual analysis of ditransitive verbs of caused possession in English. *Journal of Semantics* 28. 1–54.

Beavers, John. 2011b. On affectedness. *Natural Language and Linguistic Theory* 29. 335–370. 10.1093/jos/ffq014.

Beavers, John and Andrew Koontz-Garboden. 2020. *The Roots of Verbal Meaning*. Oxford: Oxford University Press. https://doi.org/10.1093/oso/9780198855781.001.0001.

Benson, Morton, Evelyn Benson and Robert Ilson. 2010. *The BBI Combinatory Dictionary of English: Your Guide to Collocations and Grammar*. Amsterdam: John Benjamins 3rd edn.

Borik, Olga. 2006. *Aspect and Reference Time*. Oxford: Oxford University Press. https://doi.org/10.1093/acprof:oso/9780199291298.001.0001.

Brinton, Laurel J. 1996. Attitudes toward Increasing Segmentalization: Complex and Phrasal Verbs in English. *Journal of English Linguistics* 24. 186–205. https://doi.org/10.1177/007542429602400304.

Brinton, Laurel J. 2011. The grammaticalization of complex predicates. In Bernd Heine and Heiko Narrog (eds.), *The Oxford Handbook of Grammaticalization*, 559–569. Oxford: Oxford University Press. 10.1093/oxfordhb/9780199586783.013.0045.

Brugman, Claudia. 2001. Light verbs and polysemy. *Language Sciences* 23. 551–578.

Collins, Peter. 1995. The indirect object construction in English: an informational approach. *Linguistics* 33(1). 35–50. https://doi.org/10.1515/ling.1995.33.1.35.

Cowie, Anthony P. 1981. The treatment of collocations and idioms in learners' dictionaries. *Applied Linguistics* 2(3). 223–235.

Cowie, Anthony P. 1998. *Phraseology: Theory, Analysis, and Applications*. Oxford: Oxford University Press.

Crowther, Jonathan, Sheila Dignen and Lea Diana. 2002. *Oxford Collocations Dictionary for Students of English*. Oxford: Oxford University Press.

Dixon, Robert M. W. 2005. *A Semantic Approach to English Grammar*. Oxford: Oxford University Press.

Dowty, David. 1979. *Word Meaning and Montague Grammar*. Dordrecht: Reidel.

Filip, Hana. 1993. *Aspect, Situation types and Noun Phrase Semantics*. New York: Garland.

Filip, Hana. 2008. Events and maximalization: The case of telicity and perfectivity. In Susan Rothstein (ed.), *Theoretical and Crosslinguistic Approaches to the Semantics of Aspect*, 217–256. Amsterdam: John Benjamins.

Fleischhauer, Jens. 2021. Light Verb Constructions and Their Families – A Corpus Study on German '*stehen unter*'-LVCs. In *"Proceedings of the 17th Workshop on Multiword Expressions (MWE 2021)*, 63–69. Online: Association for Computational Linguistics. 10.18653/v1/2021.mwe-1.8. https://aclanthology.org/2021.mwe-1.8, last access: 13/01/2025.

Fleischhauer, Jens and Thomas Gamerschlag. 2019. Deriving the meaning of light verb constructions – a frame account of German *stehen* 'stand'. In Constanze Juchem-Grundmann, Michael Pleyer and Monika Pleyer (eds.), *Yearbook of the German Cognitive Linguistics Association, vol. 7*, 137–156. Berlin: Mouton de Gruyter. https://doi.org/10.1515/gcla-2019-0009.

Gablasova, Dana, Vaclav Brezina and Tony McEnery. 2017. Collocations in Corpus-Based Language Learning Research: Identifying, Comparing, and Interpreting the Evidence. *Language Learning* 67(S1). 155–179. https://doi.org/10.1111/lang.12225.

Gradečak-Erdeljić, Tanja. 2004. Periphrasis in the coding of events. In Barbara Lewandowska-Tomaszczyk and Alina Kwiatkowska (eds.), *Imagery in Language. Festschrift in Honour of Professor Ronald W. Langacker*, 431–443. Frankfurt am Main: Peter Lang.

Gradečak-Erdeljić, Tanja. 2009. Proces shematizacije engleskih laganih glagola. *Jezikoslovlje* 10(2). 95–131.

Granger, Sylviane and Magali Paquot. 2008. Disentangling the phraseological web. In Sylviane Granger and Fanny Meunier (eds.), *Phraseology. An interdisciplinary perspective*, 27–49. Amsterdam: John Benjamins.

Herweg, Michael. 2014. Spatio-temporal modification and the determination of aspect: a phase-theoretical account. In Doris Gerland, Christian Horn, Anja Latrouite and Albert Ortmann (eds.), *Meaning and Grammar of Nouns and Verbs*, 185–222. Düsseldorf: Düsseldorf University Press.

Hill, Jimmie and Michael Lewis. 1997. *LTP Dictionary of Selected Collocations*. Hove: Language Teaching Publications.

Huddleston, Rodney and Geoffrey K. Pullum. 2002. *The Cambridge grammar of the English language*. Cambridge: Cambridge University Press.

Hurford, James R. and Brendan Heasley. 2007. *Semantics: a coursebook*. Cambridge: Cambridge University Press.

Jackendoff, Ray. 1996. The proper treatment of measuring out, telicity, and perhaps even quantification in English. *Natural Language and Linguistic Theory* 14. 305–354.

Jespersen, Otto. 1942. *A Modern English Grammar on Historical Principles, Part VI, Morphology*. Copenhagen: Ejnar Munksgaard.

Kearns, Kate. 1988. *Light Verbs in English*. Doctoral dissertation: Massachusetts Institute of Technology, Cambridge, MA.

Landman, Fred. 2008. 1066: On the differences between the tense-perspective-aspect systems of English and Dutch. In Susan Rothstein (ed.), *Theoretical and Crosslinguistic Approaches to the Semantics of Aspect*, 217–256. Amsterdam: John Benjamins.

Langacker, Ronald. 1991. *Foundations of cognitive grammar. Vol. 2*. Stanford: Stanford University Press.

Levin, Beth. 1993. *English Verb Classes and Alternations: A Preliminary Investigation*. Chicago: University of Chicago Press.

Martínez Caro, Elena and Jorge Arús-Hita. 2020. *Give* as light verb. *Functions of Language* 27(3). 280–306. https://doi.org/10.1075/fol.16036.mar.

Nesselhauf, Nadja. 2005. *Collocations in a Learner Corpus*. Amsterdam: John Benjamins.

Newman, John. 1996. *Give: A cognitive linguistic study*. Berlin: Mouton de Gruyter. https://doi.org/10.1515/9783110823714.

Newman, John and Sally Rice. 2006. Transitivity schemas of English EAT and DRINK in the BNC. In Stefan Th. Gries and Anatol Stefanowitsch (eds.), *Corpora in cognitive linguistics: Corpus-based approaches to syntax and lexis*, 225–260. Berlin: Mouton de Gruyter. https://doi.org/10.1515/9783110197709.225.

Pompei, Anna. 2023. How light is 'give' as a Light Verb? A case study on the actionality of Latin Light Verb Constructions (with some references to Romance languages). In Anna Pompei, Lunella Mereu and Valentina Piunno (eds.), *Light Verb Constructions as Complex Verbs*, 149–200. Berlin: Mouton de Gruyter. https://doi.org/10.1515/9783110747997-006.

Poutsma, Hendrik. 1926. *A Grammar of Late Modern English, Part 2: The Parts of Speech*. Groningen: P. Noordhoff.

Quirk, Randolph, Sidney Greenbaum, Geoffrey Leech and Jan Svartvik. 1985. *A Comprehensive Grammar of the English Language*. London: Longman.

Rappaport Hovav, Malka. 2008. Lexicalized meaning and the internal structure of events. In Susan Rothstein (ed.), *Theoretical and Crosslinguistic Approaches to the Semantics of Aspect*, 13–42. Amsterdam: John Benjamins.

Rappaport Hovav, Malka and Beth Levin. 2008. The English dative alternation: A case for verb sensitivity. *Journal of Linguistics* 44. 129–167. https://doi.org/10.1017/S0022226707004975.

Rothstein, Susan. 2008. Telicity and atomicity. In Susan Rothstein (ed.), *Theoretical and Crosslinguistic Approaches to the Semantics of Aspect*, 43–78. Amsterdam: John Benjamins.

Shahrokny-Prehn, Arian and Silke Höche. 2011. Rising through the registers – A corpus-based account of the stylistic constraints on Light Verb Constructions. *Corpus* 10. 239–257. https://doi.org/10.4000/corpus.2110.

Sinclair, John. 1991. *Corpus, Concordance, Collocation*. Oxford: Oxford University Press.

Stein, Gabriele. 1991. The Phrasal Verb Type 'to have a look' in Modern English. *IRAL* 29. 1–29. https://doi.org/10.1515/iral.1991.29.1.1.

Stojanovska-Ilievska, Natasha. 2022. Information packaging strategies serving the communicative needs of speakers. *Crossroads. A Journal of English Studies* 38. 5–17.

Topolińjska, Zuzanna. 2000. *Polish-Macedonian: Grammatical Confrontation 3. Studies in Morphosyntax*. Skopje: Macedonian Academy of Sciences and Arts.

van Gelderen, Elly. 2017. *Syntax: An Introduction to Minimalism*. Amsterdam: John Benjamins. https://doi.org/10.1075/z.214.

Wierzbicka, Anna. 1982. Why can you have a drink when you can't *have an eat? *Language* 58(4). 753–799. https://doi.org/10.2307/413956.

Pei-Jung Kuo
The GIVE group of the Mandarin light verbs

A corpus-based investigation

1 Introduction

In this paper, I discuss the GIVE group of light verbs in Mandarin Chinese and aspects of their syntactic behavior based on my examination of the Academia Sinica Balanced Corpus of Modern Chinese.[1] A typical light verb construction is composed of a verb and a complement. Typically, the complement is a verbal noun, as shown in (1) in English and (2) in Japanese. In some languages, such as German, the verbal noun is realized as a PP, as in (3).

(1) *He took a drink of the soda.* (Bonial, 2021, 6)

(2) *Taroo-ga eigo-no benkyoo-o sita.*
     Taro-NOM English-GEN study-ACC did
     'Taro studied English.' (Shimada and Kordoni, 2003, 1)

(3) *Der Mann steht* [PP *unter* [NP *Schock*]].
     the man stands under shock
     'The man is shocked.' (Fleischhauer, 2021a, 63)

The examples above show that the complement, rather than the main verb, denotes the main event content. Since the verbs in the examples do not function as typical main verbs, they are referred to as 'light verb' constructions (LVC). A 'light verb' can be contrasted with a 'heavy verb,' which takes a genuine noun as its complement. Interestingly, although light verbs were assumed to be semantically empty in the early literature (e.g. Jespersen, 1942), an increasing number of cross-linguistic studies suggest that they are semantically reduced or bleached (e.g. Grimshaw and Mester, 1988; Di Sciullo and Sara Thomas Rosen, 1990; Gross and de Pontonx, 2004; Fleischhauer and Neisani, 2020, among others).

In addition to syntactic and semantic studies of light verb constructions, the literature has benefited in recent years from cross-linguistic corpus studies, including

---

1 Online source: https://asbc.iis.sinica.edu.tw/, last access 30/9/2024.

Pei-Jung Kuo, National Chiayi University, Taiwan

Open Access. © 2025 the author(s), published by De Gruyter. This work is licensed under the Creative Commons Attribution 4.0 International License.
https://doi.org/10.1515/9783111388878-003

those of Hanks et al. (2006), Rácz et al. (2014), and Fleischhauer (2021a). In Chinese, light verbs can be divided into DO and GIVE groups semantically (i.e. Lu and Huang, 2023). In corpus studies of Chinese light verbs, the DO group has received the most attention (e.g. Wang, 2004; Jiang and Huang, 2018). Therefore, thoroughly investigating the GIVE group can also benefit our understanding of light verbs in Mandarin Chinese.

The paper is organized as follows: In Section 2, I first identify possible light verbs that can be categorized as part of the GIVE group. In Section 3, I present my corpus study that draws on the Academia Sinica Balanced Corpus of Modern Chinese and focuses primarily on the syntactic patterns following light verbs in the GIVE group. Section 4 includes a discussion of the results and possible implications. I conclude the paper in the last section.

2 Two Groups of light verbs in Chinese

In this section, I first identify possible light verbs in Mandarin Chinese. To the best of my knowledge, Zhu (1982, 1985) is probably the earliest discussion of Chinese light verbs. Zhu has proposed that there are five light verbs in Chinese and that they share similar syntactic features. Specifically, he suggests that the primary meanings of the five verbs have been bleached, and that they all take a verbal noun that denotes the primary meaning of the predicate. These five light verbs and the possible verbal nouns that can follow them, as discussed by Zhu (1985, 1-2), are shown from (4) to (8).

(4) Light verb: 進行 *jìnxíng* 'proceed'
Verbal nouns: 調查 *diàochá* 'investigation', 研究 *yánjiù* 'research', 登記 *dēngjì* 'registration', 鬥爭 *dòuzhēng* 'fighting', 教育 *jiàoyù* 'education', 指導 *zhǐdǎo* 'guidance', 觀察 *guānchá* 'observation', 合作 *hézuò* 'incorporation', 交涉 *jiāoshè* 'negotiation'

(5) Light verb: 加以 *jiāyǐ* 'give'
Verbal nouns: 說明 *shuōmíng* 'explanation', 解釋 *jiěshì* 'explanation', 干涉 *gānshè* 'interference', 改造 *gǎizào* 'change', 指導 *zhǐdǎo* 'guidance', 解決 *jiějué* 'solution', 限制 *xiànzhì* 'limitation', 控制 *kòngzhì* 'control', 訓練 *xùnliàn* 'training'

(6) Light verb: 給予 *jǐyǔ* 'give'
Verbal nouns: 支持 *zhīchí* 'support', 幫助 *bāngzhù* 'help', 獎勵 *jiǎnglì* 'praise', 鼓勵 *gǔlì* 'encouragement', 補助 *bǔzhù* 'subsidy', 同情 *tóngqíng* 'sympathy'

(7) Light verb: 予以 *yǔyǐ* 'give'
Verbal nouns: 考慮 *kǎolǜ* 'consideration', 解釋 *jiěshì* 'explanation', 挽救 *wǎnjiù* 'rescuing', 表揚 *biǎoyáng* 'praising', 安排 *ānpái* 'arrangement', 發表 *fābiǎo* 'publication', 保障 *bǎozhàng* 'protection', 答覆 *dáfù* 'reply', 照顧 *zhàogù* 'taking care of'

(8) Light verb: 作 *zuò* 'do'
Verbal nouns: 準備 *zhǔnbèi* 'preparation', 紀錄 *jìlù* 'record', 檢討 *jiǎntǎo* 'review', 指示 *zhǐshì* 'indication', 交代 *jiāodài* 'explanation', 補充 *bǔchōng* 'replenishment', 決定 *juédìng* 'decision', 貢獻 *gòngxiàn* 'contribution', 研究 *yánjiù* 'research', 統計 *tǒngjì* '(doing) statistics'

Examples of the five light verbs and verbal noun combinations listed in Zhu that I observed in the Sinica Corpus are shown in (9) to (13).

(9) 教師 研習中心 遂 針對 此一問題 **進行** 研究。
Jiàoshī yánxízhōngxīn suì zhēnduì cǐyīwèntí jinxing yánjiù
teacher learning_center then against this_question proceed research
'The Teacher Learning Center then researched this issue.'

(10) 進行 工程 時 亦 未 將 生態因素 **予以** 考慮 在內。
Jinxing gōngchéng shí yì wèi jiāng shēngtàiyīnsù yǔyǐ kǎolǜ zàinèi
proceed project when also not will ecological_factor give consider inside
'Ecological factors were not taken into account when carrying out the project.'

(11) 機車 佔用 公有巷道 非法 停車 問題, 交通部 應 提出 具體辦法 **加以** 解決。
Jīchē zhànyòng gōngyǒuxiàngdào fēifǎ tíngchē wèntí
motorcycle occupy public_lane illegal park problem
jiāotōngbù yīng tíchū jùtǐbànfǎ jiāyǐ jiějué
Ministry_of_Transport should propose specific_measures give solve
'The Ministry of Transport should propose specific measures to solve the problem of illegal parking of motorcycles occupying public lanes.'

(12) 用 多年的 時間 來 **作** 準備。
Yòng duōnián-de shíjiān lái zuò zhǔnbèi
use many_year time come do preparation
'It takes many years to do the preparation.'

(13) 公營事業 民營化 為 政府 政策, 希望 公營事業 員工 能 **給予** 支持。
Gōngyíngshìyè mínyínghuà wéi zhèngfǔ zhèngcè xīwàng
public_enterprise privatization be government policy hope
gōngyíngshìyè yuángōng néng jǐyǔ zhīchí
public_enterprise employee can give support
'The privatization of public sector enterprises has become a government policy, and we hope that public sector employees can support it.'

In the later literature, somehow 作 *zuò* 'do' is replaced by its synonym 做 *zuò* 'do' in the relevant discussions. An example from the Sinica Corpus is shown in (14).

(14) 她 是 為了替 即將 演出的 角色 **做** 準備。
Tā shì wéiliǎotì jíjiāng yǎnchū-de juésè zuò zhǔnbèi
she be for upcoming perform-DE role do prepare
'She is preparing for her upcoming role.'

Subsequent to Zhu (1985), Zhou (1987a), Zhou (1987b) and Qiu (1994) proposed that 給以 *gěiyǐ* 'give', as shown in example (15) taken from the Sinica Corpus, should be considered a light verb as well.

(15) 芮妮齊薇格 因 此片 獲 獎 連連, 美國國家評論獎 還 頒發 最佳 突破表現 獎 **給以** 肯定。
Ruìníqíwéigé yīn cǐpiàn huò jiǎng liánlián
Renée Zellweger because this_film receive award repeatedly
měiguóguójiāpínglùnjiǎng hái bānfā zuìjiā
American National Critics Award even award best
túpòbiǎoxiànjiǎng gěiyǐ kěndìng
breakthrough_performance give affirmation
'Renée Zellweger won numerous awards for this film, including the National Critics Award for Best Breakthrough Performance.'

Later, in Huang et al. (2014) and Lin et al. (2014), 從事 *cóngshì* 'engage' and 搞 *gǎo* 'do' are examined and compared with 加以 *jiāyǐ* 'give', 進行 *jìnxíng* 'proceed' and 做 *zuò* 'do', as illustrated in (17) and (16).

(16) 這個 老糊塗, 自己 什麼 都 沒有, 還要 去 **搞** 統一。
Zhège lǎohútú zìjǐ shénme dū méiyǒu háiyào qù gǎo tǒngyī
this old_fool self what all not-have still go do unity
'This old fool himself has nothing and still wants to unify.'

(17) 學術單位 像 中研院 民族所 就 鼓勵 研究人員 往國外 從事 研究。
Xuéshùdānwèi   xiàng zhōngyányuàn mínzúsuǒ   jiù
Academic_institution like Academia Sinica Institute_of_Ethnology JIU
gǔlìyán   jiùrényuán wǎngguówài cóngshì yánjiù
encourage researcher go.abroad   engage research
'Academic institutions like the Institute of Ethnology, Academia Sinica encourage researchers to engage in research abroad.'

In addition to the light verbs discussed in the literature, I would like to add two more possible candidates here. In Lu and Huang (2023), the light verb *jiyu* 'give' is mentioned and compared to the other two light verbs 予以 *yǔyǐ* 'give' and 加以 *jiāyǐ* 'give'. However, the authors do not indicate the Chinese characters nor tonal information for *jiyu*. For *jiyu*, the first character can have two possible tones (third tone or fourth tone), and the two pronunciations are associated with different phrasal combinations. According to the online Chinese Dictionary published by the National Academy for Educational Research in Taiwan[2], if the first character is pronounced as the third tone, the corresponding Chinese characters could be 給予 *jǐyǔ* or 給與 *jǐyǔ*. An example from the Sinica Corpus of 給予 *jǐyǔ* is shown in (13) and an example of 給與 *jǐyǔ* is shown in (18). In addition, based on my own anecdotal observations from daily life and internet searches, it is also quite common in Taiwan to pronounce these two light verbs as *gěiyǔ* 'give',

(18) 而 某 肇事者 家屬 在 媒體 上 對 其 行為 給與 支持。
Ér mǒu zhàoshìzhě jiāshǔ zài méitǐ shàng duì qí xíngwéi jǐyǔ
and certain perpetrator family on media up   to his behavior give
zhīchí
support
'The family of a perpetrator supported his behavior in the media'

If the first character of *jiyu* is pronounced as the fourth tone, the light verb combination 寄予 *jìyǔ* is also possible. An example of this variant from the Sinica Corpus is shown in (19). According to the online Chinese Dictionary of the National Academy for Educational Research in Taiwan, 寄予 *jìyǔ* can also be defined as 給予 *jǐyǔ*.

(19) 選擇 離開的, 大家 也 寄予 祝福。
Xuǎnzé líkāi-de dàjiā   yě jìyǔ zhùfú
choose leave-DE everyone also give bless
'For those who choose to leave, everyone also sends their blessings to them.'

---

[2] https://dict.revised.moe.edu.tw/index.jsp; last access: 7/10/2024.

Overall, the light verbs presented so far can be divided into two groups: The DO group and the GIVE group. I summarize what we have found in (20).

(20) a. The DO group: 進行 *jìnxíng* 'proceed', 作/做 *zuò* 'do', 從事 *cóngshì* 'engage', 搞 *gǎo* 'do'
b. The GIVE group: 加以 *jiāyǐ* 'give', 給予/給與 *jǐyǔ* 'give/gěiyǔ* 'give', 予以 *yǔyǐ* 'give', 給以 *gěiyǐ* 'give', 寄予 *jìyǔ* 'give'[3]

By considering the tonal profile of light verbs and their Chinese characters, there appear to be six possible light verbs in the GIVE group. In the following section, I will use these six light verbs as keywords when searching the Sinica Corpus.

3 The corpus data

In this section, I present an empirical corpus study of Chinese light verb constructions. As mentioned, the DO group has received most attention in previous corpus studies in the literature, so here I focus on the six GIVE group members. In addition, among the GIVE group, 加以 *jiāyǐ* 'give' is the light verb which is usually compared to the other members of the DO group (i.e. Huang et al., 2014; Lin et al., 2014; Jiang et al., 2016; Jiang and Huang, 2018; Jiang et al., 2018; Xu et al., 2020, among others). However, since we have identified six members in the GIVE group, it will be interesting to see whether there are any similarities or differences within the GIVE group itself.

In my investigation, I examined the syntactic elements following the six GIVE light verbs, with a significant focus on the appearance of genuine NPs and verbal nouns. As noted in the Introduction, in the literature, it has been proposed that the so-called light verbs take verbal nouns (i.e. Jespersen, 1942), while typical verbs take genuine NPs. Typical verbs are thus considered 'heavy' rather than 'light'. It seems reasonable to hypothesize, therefore, that the 'weight' of verbs in the corpus will relate to the kind of noun that appears after them. In the following, I examine the verbal nouns and the genuine NPs (if any) taken by these six GIVE light verbs. A noun is considered to be a 'verbal noun' here if it has a verbal use that is noted in the online Chinese Dictionary published by the National Academy for Educational Research in Taiwan. In addition, I also examine the incidence and role of modifiers that follow the verbs and propose that a light verb's position on a 'scale of lightness'

---

[3] For ease of annotation, in the following discussion, I will follow the pronunciation of the on-line Chinese Dictionary published by the National Academy for Educational Research in Taiwan and mark 給予/給與 as *jǐyǔ* 'give'.

relates not only to the kind of noun that follows it, but also to the degree of morphosyntactic cohesion between the light verb and its verbal noun.

The corpus examined is the Academia Sinica Balanced Corpus of Modern Chinese, completed in 1997. The current version used is the 4.0 version. This corpus contains 19,247 articles, 1,396,133 sentences, and 11,245,330 word tokens collected from different subject domains, such as literature, life, society, science, philosophy, and art.

The search procedure was conducted as follows. The six light verbs of the GIVE group were searched as keywords in the corpus. No specific subject domain was targeted; hence, the default setting of the search engine was used. Note that although some light verbs in this group may have different pronunciations since the search uses Chinese characters, the different pronunciations should not affect the search results. The data examined was retrieved on January 22, 2024. The number of lines of text which contain the keywords found in the corpus are listed in Table 1.

Tab. 1: The available lines of the six members of the GIVE group.

	給以 *gěiyǐ*	寄予 *jìyǔ*	給與 *jǐyǔ*	予以 *yǔyǐ*	給予 *jǐyǔ*	加以 *jiāyǐ*
line numbers	10	39	45	584	978	1253

Next, the search results were listed line by line using Microsoft Excel. Then, they were examined line by line again, and syntactic annotations of what followed these light verbs were marked manually. After all the annotations were completed, the possible syntactic patterns were sorted according to what followed the light verbs. The following possible patterns shown in Table 2 were observed.[4]

Since this study focuses on the heaviness and lightness of the six light GIVE verbs, I focused on the contrastive patterns of the NPs and VNs that follow them. However, while making annotations, I also took note of the modifiers preceding the NPs or VNs, as well as other syntactic categories that follow them. In (21), I collapse the syntactic patterns into the two possibilities in (21).

(21)   a.   (Mod) + NP + (...)
        b.   (Mod) + VN + (...)

The breakdown of the data is illustrated in Table 3. Note that the other patterns that do not belong to (21a) or (21b) will be categorized as 'others' in this table.

---

[4] I have tried to collapse similar syntactic patterns together to make the table as concise as possible. Hence, there are in fact more possible syntactic patterns than those shown in Table 2.

Tab. 2: The syntactic Patterns.

Syntactic Patterns		給以 gěiyǐ	寄予 jìyǔ	給與 jǐyǔ	予以 yǔyǐ	給予 jǐyǔ	加以 jiāyǐ
NP (+…)		1	2	18	9	186	10
Mod NP (+…)		—	18	6	4	345	3
VN (+…)		2	9	9	463	139	1092
Mod VN (+…)		6	9	3	78	220	79
Others	Verb + object	—	—	—	16	3	20
	VO compound (+ …)	—	—	—	11	5	1
	(Mod) AP	—	—	—	2	—	2
	的 de …	—	1	3	—	46	—
	了 le …	—	—	—	—	4	—
	者 zhě …	—	—	—	—	2	—
	LV VN	—	—	—	1	1	—
	Sentence	—	—	—	—	—	46
	X	—	—	6	—	23	—
	?	1	—	—	—	4	—
Total		10	39	45	584	978	1253

Usage-wise, we can see that 加以 *jiāyǐ* is the most frequent light verb in the GIVE group, followed by 給予 *jǐyǔ*, 予以 *yǔyǐ*, 給與 *jǐyǔ*, 寄予 *jìyǔ*, and 給以 *gěiyǐ*. The numbers in Table 3 are translated into percentages in Table 4. For the light verbs 給以 *gěiyǐ*, 寄予 *jìyǔ* and 給與 *jǐyǔ*, because the examples are few, it is hard to say whether the categorization has any significance here. Hence, it is better that we put them aside and focus on the comparisons of the other three light verbs 予以 *yǔyǐ*, 給予 *jǐyǔ* and 加以 *jiāyǐ*. This also gives us an excellent opportunity to compare our results with those of Lu and Huang (2023), who studied these light verbs in the ToRCH 2009 Corpus.[5]

At first glance, in Table 3, the light verb 給予 *jǐyǔ* is much heavier than expected, although it is considered one of the light verbs in Zhu's (1985) list. On the other hand,

Tab. 3: The categorization results (Version 1).

	給以 *gěiyǐ*	寄予 *jìyǔ*	給與 *jǐyǔ*	予以 *yǔyǐ*	給予 *jǐyǔ*	加以 *jiāyǐ*
(Mod) + NP + (…)	1	20	24	13	531	13
(Mod) + VN + (…)	8	18	12	541	359	1171
others	1	1	9	30	88	69
Total	10	39	45	584	978	1253

---

5 https://corpus.bfsu.edu.cn/info/1070/1558.html; last access 11/10/2024.

Tab. 4: The data in percentage (Version 1).

	給以 *gěiyǐ*	寄予 *jìyǔ*	給與 *jǐyǔ*	予以 *yǔyǐ*	給予 *jǐyǔ*	加以 *jiāyǐ*
(Mod) + NP + (...)	10%	51%	53%	2%	54%	1%
(Mod) + VN + (...)	80%	46%	27%	93%	37%	93%
others	10%	3%	20%	5%	9%	6%
Total	100%	100%	100%	100%	100%	100%

if we focus on the (Mod) + VN + (...) pattern, we can see that 予以 *yǔyǐ* and 加以 *jiāyǐ* are very 'light' in that their complements are mostly verbal nouns. Although the percentage of tokens of 加以 *jiāyǐ* that follow this pattern (93 %) is the same as that of 予以 *yǔyǐ*, 加以 *jiāyǐ* is probably the lightest light verb among the six members. This is because 加以 *jiāyǐ* itself is ambiguous. In addition to being a light verb, 加以 *jiāyǐ* can also mean 再加上 *zàijiāshàng* 'plus/in addition' and take a sentence or an NP according to the online Chinese Dictionary published by the National Academy for Educational Research in Taiwan. Fortunately, it is not hard to distinguish between these two uses. Since the light verb 加以 *jiāyǐ* does not contribute any meaning to the sentence, if it is removed, the sentence remains intact. However, if 加以 *jiāyǐ* means 'plus/in addition,' the omission of 加以 *jiāyǐ* will make the preceding and following context challenging to understand. This contrast is shown in (22) and (23).

(22) Light verb 加以 *jiāyǐ*
 這些 都是 可以 分別（加以）深入 研討的。
 zhèxiē dūshì kěyǐ fēnbié jiāyǐ shēnrù yántǎo-de
 these all can separately give deep discuss-DE
 'these all be studied in depth separately.'

(23) 'Plus/in addition' 加以 *jiāyǐ*
 其 生產量 遠 超過 本國 需求量，*（加以）油價 飄漲
 qí shēngchǎnliàng yuan chāoguò běnguó xūqiúliáng jiāyǐ
 its production far exceed domestic demand plus
 yóujià piāozhàng
 oil_price_soar
 'its production far exceeds domestic demand, and oil prices soar'

If we remove the cases where 加以 *jiāyǐ* means 再加上 *zàijiāshàng* 'plus/in addition', we are left with the following two revised Table 5 and Table 6.

For 予以 *yǔyǐ*, 給予 *jǐyǔ* and 加以 *jiāyǐ*, the results in the revised Table 6 echo the corpus results by Lu and Huang (2023), where 加以 *jiāyǐ* is the most grammaticalized light verb, followed by 予以 *yǔyǐ* and 給予 *jǐyǔ*. Note that their grammaticalization ranking of 予以 *yǔyǐ*, 給予 *jǐyǔ* and 加以 *jiāyǐ* is determined by the appearance of

Tab. 5: The categorization results (Version 2).

	給以 *gěiyǐ*	寄予 *jìyǔ*	給與 *jǐyǔ*	予以 *yǔyǐ*	給予 *jǐyǔ*	加以 *jiāyǐ*
(Mod) + NP + (...)	1	20	24	13	531	0
(Mod) + VN + (...)	8	18	12	541	359	1159
others	1	1	9	30	88	19
Total	10	39	45	584	978	1178

Tab. 6: The data in percentages (Version 2).

	給以 *gěiyǐ*	寄予 *jìyǔ*	給與 *jǐyǔ*	予以 *yǔyǐ*	給予 *jǐyǔ*	加以 *jiāyǐ*
(Mod) + NP + (...)	10%	51%	53%	2%	54%	0%
(Mod) + VN + (...)	80%	46%	27%	93%	37%	98%
others	10%	3%	20%	5%	9%	2%
Total	100%	100%	100%	100%	100%	100%

the aspect marker following the light verb. However, this distinguishing feature is not available in the current study since 給予 *jǐyǔ* is the only light verb that can take an aspect marker in the corpus investigated. However, we have seen that we can get the same ranking as Lu and Huang under the current hypothesis in which verbs followed by VNs are lighter than those followed by genuine NPs. Thus, in addition to using the appearance of an aspect marker as a diagnostic, it also appears possible to assess verb lightness and heaviness by examining the kind of noun that follows it.

Finally, despite the low number of 給以 *gěiyǐ*, it is among the three light verbs, including 予以 *yǔyǐ* and 加以 *jiāyǐ*, that are most likely to exhibit the (Mod) + VN + (...) pattern. A commonality among these three light verbs is that their second character is 以 *yǐ*. This character is used as a particle that is placed after a verb and denotes no meaning, such as in 得以 *déyǐ* and 能以 *néngyǐ*.[6] A quick search in the Sinica Corpus shows that there is no aspect marker following 得以 *déyǐ*, either.[7] This is consistent with what we have found for 給以 *gěiyǐ*, 予以 *yǔyǐ*, and 加以 *jiāyǐ* in the Sinica Corpus.

---

[6] The definition is taken from the online Chinese Dictionary published by the National Academy for Educational Research in Taiwan.

[7] There are 644 lines for 得以 *déyǐ*, while there are no lines available for 能以 *néngyǐ*. On the other hand, there are two cases where the aspect markers 了 *le* and 著 *zhe* follow the combination of 得以 *déyǐ* plus a verbal noun in the corpus.

4 Further discussion

In this section, I discuss some exciting phenomena exhibited by 給以 *gěiyǐ*, 予以 *yǔyǐ*, and 加以 *jiāyǐ*, giving us enough data for further examination in the corpus search. Note that these three light verbs are the GIVE light verbs shown in Zhu's (1985) list.

4.1 The aspect marker

As shown in Table 2, only 給予 *jǐyǔ* can be followed by the aspect marker 了 *le*, and there are four examples of this in the corpus.[8] The syntactic patterns of the four examples with 了 *le* are shown in (24).

(24) a. 對 *duì* NP + 給予 *jǐyǔ* + 了 *le* + Mod NP
 b. 對 *duì* NP + 給予 *jǐyǔ* + 了 *le* + Mod VN
 c. 給予 *jǐyǔ* + 了 *le* + NP + NP
 d. 給予 *jǐyǔ* + 了 *le* + NP + Mod NP and Mod NP

From these four patterns, it can be inferred that 給予 *jǐyǔ* functions as a ditransitive verb, in which the indirect object (IO) can be introduced by a preposition *duì* 'to' or preceding the direct object (DO) directly.

The possibility for 給予 *jǐyǔ* to take an aspect marker echoes the previous observation that it is not as light as the other light verbs 予以 *yǔyǐ* and 加以 *jiāyǐ*, and, therefore, can take genuine NPs. In the corpus research, we found a lot of examples in which 給予 *jǐyǔ* takes a genuine NP or a coordinated NP, as shown in (25). In some sentences, 給予 *jǐyǔ* is used as a ditransitive verb, as in (26). Also note that in example (26a), the DO is a verbal noun, while the DO in (26b) is a genuine NP.

(25) a. 給予 一個 時代
 jǐyǔ yīgè shídài
 give one-CL era
 'to give an era'
 b. 給予 時間 與 機會
 jǐyǔ shíjiān yǔ jīhuì
 give time and opportunity
 'to give time and opportunity'

---

[8] The results here partially echo Lu and Huang's (2023) generalization for the aspectual properties of 予以 *yǔyǐ*, 給予 *jǐyǔ* and 加以 *jiāyǐ*. In their corpus study, they have concluded that the perfective -*le* can occur with 予以 *yǔyǐ* and 給予 *jǐyǔ*. However, I did not find any examples of 予以 *yǔyǐ* in the Sinica Corpus.

(26) a. 給予 岳飛 平反
   jǐyǔ YuèFēi píngfǎn
   give Yue Fei redress_a_grievance
   'to give Yue Fei to redress a grievance'
b. 給予 我們 意見
   jǐyǔ wǒmen yìjiàn
   give we   opinion
   'to give us opinions'

In other words, it is evident that 給予 *jǐyǔ* 'give' is indeed heavier in taking genuine NPs and is used frequently as the common verb 給 *gěi* 'give' in Chinese. The verb 給 *gěi* 'give' is a common and typical ditransitive verb that denotes the meaning of giving, as shown in (27). It is also possible for this verb 給 *gěi* to take 了 *le* as its aspect marker.

(27) 張三 給 (-了) 李四 錢。
   Zhāngsān gěi(-le)   Lǐsì qián
   Zhangsan give(-ASP) Lisi money
   'Zhangsan gave Lisi some money.'

Diachronically, it is not surprising to see that the light verb 給予 *jǐyǔ* 'give' is used as the verb 給 *gěi* 'give'. If we examine the light verb 給予 *jǐyǔ* 'give', it is composed of two characters: 給 *gěi* 'give' and 予 *yǔ* 'give'. The first character is the same as the verb 給 *gěi* 'give', as shown in (27). As for the second character 予 *yǔ* 'give', although it cannot be used independently in modern Chinese, it can be used separately in archaic Chinese and means 'give' exactly. An example is cited in (28).

(28) 牛 羊 倉廩, 予 父母
   niú yang cānglǐn yú   fùmǔ
   cow goat granary give parents
   '...(as for) cows, goats, and granary, give to (my) parents.'

(Shi Ji: Ben Ji, 91 B.C.)

Since the meaning of both characters is 'to give,' it seems pretty natural to see that the light verb 給予 *jǐyǔ* 'give' can be used as a heavy verb as 給 *gěi* 'give' (see also Lu and Huang, 2023, 320).

As a final note, recall that 寄予 *jìyǔ* can be defined as 給予 *jǐyǔ*. Although there are just a few instances of 寄予 *jìyǔ* in the corpus, as noted in Table 6, the percentage that takes a VN is low, and this is also the case for the light verb 給與 *jǐyǔ*. Hence, we may conclude that these three 'light' verbs are not so light and are in a stage between being heavy verbs and light verbs.

4.2 Modifiers

During the investigation, it was observed that sometimes modifiers precede the VN, while sometimes they do not, which seemed to warrant further consideration. Here, I focus on the two relatively light verbs 予以 *yǔyǐ* and 加以 *jiāyǐ* and examine their VN syntactic patterns.

Below, I note the two possible VN syntactic patterns under consideration, as shown in (29). The Pattern in (29a) indicates that the light verb takes VNs directly, while the pattern in (29b) indicates that there are modifiers preceding the verbal nouns.

(29) a. VN (+ …)
 b. Mod + VN (+ …)

Based on (29), the tokens and the corresponding percentages of the VNs with or without the modifiers are shown in Table 7.

Tab. 7: Line numbers and percentage of VNs.

	予以 *yǔyǐ*	加以 *jiāyǐ*
VN (+ …)	463 / 86%	1092 / 93%
Mod VN (+ …)	78 / 14%	67 / 7%
Total	541 / 100%	1159 / 100%

As shown in Table 7, 加以 *jiāyǐ* has a greater tendency to take the VN directly. But it is not totally impossible for 加以 *jiāyǐ* and 予以 *yǔyǐ* to have modifiers before the verbal noun. This then argues against Kuo's (2012, 141) claim that 加以 *jiāyǐ* and 予以 *yǔyǐ* cannot be separated by any modifier between them and their verbal nouns (see also Lu and Huang, 2023, 309).

Next, we examine the length of the modifiers for the verbal noun as measured by whether the modifier is made up of a single or multiple characters. Below, if the number of characters is greater than four, the modifier is categorized as a longer modifier. The results are shown in Table 8. Number-wise, 予以 *yǔyǐ* has more modifiers preceding the VN than does 加以 *jiāyǐ*. For both 予以 *yǔyǐ* and 加以 *jiāyǐ*, two-character modifiers have the highest percentage and account for more than half. However, when it comes to longer modifiers, 予以 *yǔyǐ* has more tokens in this case.

The modifier length results echo the patterns of the light verb and the verbal noun in Table 7. Overall, the light verb 加以 *jiāyǐ* takes more VNs directly when compared to 予以 *yǔyǐ*. In addition, even if 加以 *jiāyǐ* takes modified VNs, the mod-

Tab. 8: Length and percentages of the modifiers.

	予以 *yǔyǐ*	加以 *jiāyǐ*
One-character Modifier + VN	1 / 1%	1 / 1.5%
Two-character Modifier + VN	49 / 63%	41 / 61%
Three-character Modifier + VN	12 / 15%	22 / 33%
Four-character Modifier + VN	8 / 10.5%	3 / 4.5%
Longer Modifier + VN	8 / 10.5%	0 / 0%
Total	78 / 100%	67 / 100%

ifiers tend to be short. Hence, the percentage of the short modifiers of 加以 *jiāyǐ* is also higher than the ones of 予以 *yǔyǐ*. This gives us the following generalization: When a light verb is lighter, it takes more VNs directly. Even if there are modifiers of the VNs, the modifiers tend to be short. This generalization then provides us with another perspective on the further lightness of 加以 *jiāyǐ* when compared to 予以 *yǔyǐ*. Since 加以 *jiāyǐ* is a very light verb, its combination with the following VN has to be very close to form a complex predicate.

Cross-linguistically, the strong bond between the light verb and the verbal noun might first remind us of the VN-*o suru* and the VN-*suru* constructions in Japanese. The latter has been proposed to involve incorporation, as discussed in Kageyama (1976–1977); Kishimoto (2019), among others. However, I am not equating the bond between the light verb and verbal noun with the solid bond of incorporation here, since incorporation will involve head movement, and there should not be any modifier between the VN and the light verb.[9] Following Simone (2007), it would be better to say that there is a high degree of morpho-syntactic cohesion between the light verb and the verbal noun.[10] The high degree of morpho-syntactic cohesion between the light verb and its verbal noun can be verified from the following topicalization cases. In Chinese, the object of a lexical verb in (30) can be topicalized, as in (31).

(30) 我 很 喜歡 吃 蘋果。
  wǒ hěn xǐhuān chī píngguǒ
  I very like eat apple
  'I like eating apples very much.'

---

9 See also Fleischhauer (2020, 2021b) and Fleischhauer and Neisani (2020) for arguing against incorporation for Persian light verb constructions.
10 For example, in a complex predicate such as *to have a cold*, the object cannot undergo passivization or be focalized, which is due to a high degree of morpho-syntactic cohesion between *have* and *a cold*.

(31) 蘋果 我 很 喜歡 吃。
píngguǒ wǒ hěn xǐhuān chī
apple I very like eat

However, topicalization is only available for the light verb 進行 jìnxíng, but not for 加以 jiāyǐ. This contrast is shown in (32) and (33).

(32) 調查 已經 進行 很久 卻 還 沒有 結果。
diàochá yǐjīng jìnxíng hěnjiǔ què hái méiyǒu jiéguǒ
investigation already proceed long but yet not result
'The investigation has been ongoing for a long time but no results have yet been obtained.'

(33) *調查 已經 加以 很久 卻 還 沒有 結果。
diàochá yǐjīng jiāyǐ hěnjiǔ què hái méiyǒu jiéguǒ
investigation already give long but yet not result
'The investigation has been ongoing for a long time but no results have yet been obtained.'

As shown in Jiang et al. (2016), 進行 jìnxíng has its heavy verb counterpart and can take an aspect marker 了 le or event nouns, such as 進行 (了) 會議 jìnxíng (le) huìyì 'proceed a meeting'. In this respect, 進行 jìnxíng is not so light and does not maintain a high degree of morpho-syntactic cohesion with its verbal noun. Therefore, topicalizing its verbal noun is allowed, as in (32). On the other hand, the verbal noun following 加以 jiāyǐ cannot be topicalized. Hence, this shows that 加以 jiāyǐ and its following verbal nouns have to be very close to each other so that a certain high degree of morpho-syntactic cohesion can be maintained.

4.3 From LV to auxiliary

Lastly, I discuss some more interesting cases of 予以 yǔyǐ, 給予 jǐyǔ, and 加以 jiāyǐ observed in the corpus search. These cases lead us to rethink the syntactic status of light verbs in the relevant examples.

Firstly, it is observed that for the light verbs 予以 yǔyǐ and 給予 jǐyǔ, there are two exceptional cases. That is, 予以 yǔyǐ can take another light verb 進行 jìnxíng and a coordinated VN, as cited in (34).

(34) 予以 進行 調處 及 仲裁
yǔyǐ jìnxing tiáochǔ jí zhòngcái
give proceed mediation and arbitration
'to conduct mediation and arbitration'

The light verb 給予 *jǐyǔ* can also take another light verb 做 *zuò* with a modified VN, as in (35).

(35) 因 小芬的 水腦症 一直 沒有 改善 故 給予 做 腦室腹膜 引流
yīn   Xiǎofēn-de shuǐnǎozhèng yīzhí   méiyǒu gǎishàn gù   jǐyǔ
because Xiaofen-DE hydrocephalus always not   improve therefore give
zuò nǎoshìfùmò   yǐnliú
do   ventriculoperitoneal drainage
'Because Xiaofen's hydrocephalus has not improved, she was given ventriculoperitoneal drainage.'

In addition, there are also cases where 予以 *yǔyǐ*, 給予 *jǐyǔ*, and 加以 *jiāyǐ* are followed by a VO compound, as shown from (36) to (38).

(36) 乃 表示 稻子 結實 方 予以 課稅
nǎi biǎoshì dàozi jiēshí   fang yǔyǐ   kèshuì
so express rice fructify just give tax
'so to express that after the rice ripen, we then tax it'

(37) 再 給予 去蕪存菁
zài   jǐyǔ qùwúcúnjīng
then give remove_bad_keep_good
'then give away the bad and keep the good.'

(38) 再 由 謝德錫 加以 把文引薦
zài   yóu Xièdéxí jiāyǐ bǎwényǐnjiàn
then by Xiedexi give article_introduction
'Xie Dexi then introduced the article'

Finally, there are examples where these three light verbs can take VPs, where the VP is composed of a verb and an object, as shown from (39) to (41).

(39) 縣府 應 予以 吊銷 執照
Xiànfǔ   yīng   yǔyǐ diàoxiāo zhízhào
County_Government should give revoke   license
'the county government should revoke the license.'

(40) 由 內政部 給予 補貼 保費
yóu nèizhèngbù   jǐyǔ bǔtiē   bǎofèi
by Ministry_of_the_Interior give subsidy premium
'premiums subsidized by the Ministry of the Interior'

(41) 為 行政院的 有所保留， 加以 說明 原因
      wéi xíngzhèngyuàn-de   yǒusuǒbǎoliú jiāyǐ shuōmíng yuányīn
      for Ministry_of_Executive-DE reservation give explain   reason
      'explain the reasons for the Ministry of Executive's reservations'

The above syntactic patterns are summarized in (42).

(42) a. LV + LV + VN and VN / Modified VN
      b. LV + VO compound
      c. LV + Verb + Object

One might wonder how these examples can be explained if the LVs are light 'verbs.' In (42a), why can there be two light verbs in a row? In addition, it seems that what follows the light verbs are complete VPs since the verbs all have their objects as in (42b) and (42c). Traditionally, in a light verb construction, the LV is the main verb while the VN is the object. If a VP follows the light verb, how can the light verb be maintained as a verb? Note that semantically, the LV in (42b) and (42c) does not function as a ditransitive verb here, even if one considers the following verb as a verbal noun. Hence, this possibility can be excluded first.

For these cases, I suggest in light of the following proposals that the light verbs in the relevant examples have been further grammaticalized and have become auxiliaries. Hopper and Traugott (1993) proposed that a lexical verb may eventually undergo the following cline in (43) to become an affix:

(43) Full verb > (vector verb) > auxiliary > clitic > affix

(Hopper and Traugott, 1993, 108)

Later, Lu and Huang (2023) considered adding a light verb to the above verb-to-affix cline and have light verbs parallel to the vector verb. Although there are controversies, Lu and Huang assume that light verbs are considered to be part of the grammaticalization cline in (44) and will become an auxiliary through further grammaticalization.[11]

(44) IV > (vector verb/LV) > auxiliary > clitic > affix

(Lu and Huang, 2023, 307)

In (44), we can see that the light verb can be further grammaticalized into an auxiliary. If the LV in (42) functions as an auxiliary, we have the following syntactic patterns in (45).

---

[11] The IV in (44) is equivalent to the full verb in (43).

(45) a. Auxiliary LV + [vp LV + VN and VN / Modified VN]
     b. Auxiliary LV + [vp VO compound]
     c. Auxiliary LV + [vp Verb + Object]

Since these VPs already have a verb and an object, the additional preceding LV as an auxiliary would be a possible syntactic explanation. The auxiliary LV then provides a way to accommodate the co-existence of the light verbs and their further grammaticalized counterparts.

Other than the auxiliary account, another possible explanation is that the light verbs in (45) are adverbs. Since there is already a main verb in the examples in (45), what precedes the main verbs could be adverbs. More generally, this adverb account might be extended to all light verbs under examination.[12] That is, the so-called light verb constructions are adverbs preceding regular verbs. This explains several pieces of the phenomenon observed in the light verb constructions. As shown above, a very light verb like 加以 *jiāyǐ* does not take aspect markers, nor can its verbal noun be topicalized. Under the adverb account, an adverb, of course, does not take aspect markers. In addition, if the light verb is an adverb, what follows is a genuine verb, and a verb independently cannot be topicalized. Under this perspective, the adverb account seems to work as well.

However, I would argue that, based on the current corpus investigation, the auxiliary account outranks the adverb account. First, we have seen that the so-called light verb has different degrees of lightness. If light verbs are adverbs, we have to say that adverbs also have different degrees. Moreover, some not-so-light verbs can take genuine NPs or even form a double object construction, as in (25) and (26), and the indirect objects apparently can be genuine NPs or pronouns. An adverb, being an adverb, is not compatible with NPs or pronouns.

Secondly, adverbs are considered adjuncts syntactically. Being adjuncts, they are stackable, and their positions are changeable, as illustrated in (46).

(46) a. *The children did not unthinkingly, deliberately break the vase.*
     b. *The children did not deliberately, unthinkingly break the vase.*

However, if we reverse the order of the two light verbs in (34), the sentence becomes ungrammatical, as in (47).

(47) *進行 予以 調處 及 仲裁
     jinxing yǔyǐ tiáochǔ jí zhòngcái
     proceed give mediation and arbitration
     'to conduct mediation and arbitration'

---

[12] The author would like to thank one of the reviewers who brought up this point.

The same restriction can be observed in the following example (48), taken from the corpus. If we reverse the order between the light verb and the AdvP/AdjP before the verbal noun, the result is unnatural and even ungrammatical, as in (49).

(48) 應 由 政府 立法 加以 必要的 保護
yīng yóu zhèngfǔ lìfǎ jiāyǐ bìyàode bǎohù
should by government legislate give necessary projection
'necessary protection should be provided by government legislation.'

(49) *?應 由 政府 立法 必要的 加以 保護
yīng yóu zhèngfǔ lìfǎ bìyàode jiāyǐ bǎohù
should by government legislate necessary give projection
'necessary protection should be provided by government legislation.'

Thirdly, we have seen that light verbs like 給予 *jǐyǔ*, can have the following kind of sentence shown in (50).

(50) 給予 氧氣 及 呼吸 支持
jǐyǔ yǎngqì jí hūxī zhīchí
give oxygen and breath support
'provide oxygen and respiratory support'

In this example, 氧氣 *yǎngqì* is a genuine NP, and it coordinates with the following phrase by a coordinator. Coordination requires coordinated components to be of the same syntactic category and to form a larger constituent of the same syntactic type. Hence, in example (50), the right conjoint has to be an NP, and the bigger syntactic unit coordinated is an NP. Again, this shows that 給予 *jǐyǔ* cannot be an adverb here since an adverb does not modify NPs.

Fourthly, although the adverb account can explain the aspect marker taking and *no*-topicalization cases discussed above, it does not necessarily describe all the facts observed in the corpus. Empirically, we have seen that it is not the case that all light verbs cannot take aspect markers. In addition, while the verbal noun cannot be topicalized, it does not necessarily mean it must be a verb. From examples (32) and (33), we have seen cases where the verbal noun can be topicalized. The instances where the verbal noun cannot be topicalized may be due to the close relationship between the light verb and the verbal noun.

Finally, even if we adopt the adverb account just to explain the patterns in (45), we have to explain why it is the case that while most of the light verbs remain light verbs, some have become adverbs. Theoretically, being an adverb does not conform to the cline of grammaticalization shown in (44).

To summarize, currently, in our corpus study, we have seen only a few examples showing the pattern in (45), and I have proposed that they are auxiliaries. While most light verbs remain light verbs, these few examples indicate and support a grammaticalization process of the light verbs into auxiliaries.[13]

5 Conclusion

In the paper, I discuss my corpus study of the GIVE group of Mandarin light verbs and examine its six members. The results show that in addition to number differences, light verbs also have different degrees of lightness. It is evident that the various degrees of lightness can be observed by the appearance of the verbal nouns that follow the light verbs. Some light verbs are fairly close to typical verbs in their behaviors. Moreover, it is also observed that lighter light verbs show a higher degree of morpho-syntactic cohesion between the light verb and its verbal noun. Finally, there are also some instances in the corpus data where the light verbs have undergone grammaticalization and have become auxiliaries. Overall, the results of the corpus search support certain previous theoretical studies and highlight some new patterns that would be difficult to discern without running a corpus study.

Bibliography

Bonial, Claire. 2021. Précis of Take a Look at This! Form, Function, and Productivity of English Light Verb Constructions. *Colorado Research in Linguistics* 25. 1–20. https://doi.org/10.33011/cril.v25i.1341.

Bruening, Benjamin. 2015. Light verbs are just regular verbs. *U. Penn Working Papers in Linguistics* 21(1). 1–10.

Di Sciullo, Anna Maria and Sara Thomas Rosen. 1990. Light and Semi-light Verb Constructions. In Katarzyna Dziwirek, Patrick Farrell and Errapel Mejías-Bikandi (eds.), *Grammatical Relations: A Cross Theoretical Perspecive*, 109–125. Stanford: Center for the Study of Language and Information.

Fleischhauer, Jens. 2020. Predicative multi-word expressions in Persian. In *Proceedings of the 34th Pacific Asia Conference on Language, Information and Computation*, 552–561. Hanoi: Association for Computational Linguistics. https://aclanthology.org/2020.paclic-1.63, last access: 13/01/2025.

Fleischhauer, Jens. 2021a. Light Verb Constructions and Their Families – A Corpus Study on German 'stehen unter'-LVCs. In "*Proceedings of the 17th Workshop on Multiword Expressions (MWE 2021)*,

---

13 There also exists the proposal that light verbs are just regular verbs, as in Bruening (2015). Due to the space limit, I will not go into this issue deeply. However, if light verbs are regular verbs, it would be hard for this verb proposal to explain why there are different degrees of lightness in the light verbs under the current examination.

63–69. Online: Association for Computational Linguistics. 10.18653/v1/2021.mwe-1.8. https://aclanthology.org/2021.mwe-1.8, last access: 13/01/2025.

Fleischhauer, Jens. 2021b. Simplex and Complex Predicates in Persian: An RRG Analysis. In Robert Van Valin (ed.), *Challenges at the Syntax-Semantics-Pragmatics Interface*, 31–62. Newcastle upon Tyne: Cambridge Scholars Publishing.

Fleischhauer, Jens and Mozhgan Neisani. 2020. Adverbial and attributive modification of Persian separable light verb constructions. *Journal of Linguistics* 56(1). 45–85. https://doi.org/10.1017/S0022226718000646.

Grimshaw, Jane and Armin Mester. 1988. Light verbs and θ-marking. *Linguistic Inquiry* 19. 205–232.

Gross, Gaston and Sophie de Pontonx. 2004. Les verbes supports: nouvel état des lieux. *Lingvisticae Investigationes* 27(2).

Hanks, Patrick, Anne Urbschat and Elke Gehweiler. 2006. German Light Constructions in Corpora and Dictionaries. *International Journal of Lexicography* 19(4). 439–457. https://doi.org/10.1093/ijl/ecl027.

Hopper, Paul and Elizabeth Traugott. 1993. *Grammaticalization*. Cambridge: Cambridge University Press.

Huang, Chu-Ren, Jingxia Lin, Menghan Jiang and Hongzhi Xu. 2014. Corpus-based study and identification of Mandarin Chinese light verb variations. In *Proceedings of the First Workshop on Applying NLP Tools to Similar Languages, Varieties and Dialects*, 1–10. Dublin: Association for Computational Linguistics and Dublin City University.

Jespersen, Otto. 1942. *A Modern English Grammar on Historical Principles, Part VI, Morphology*. Copenhagen: Ejnar Munksgaard.

Jiang, Menghan and Chu-Ren Huang. 2018. A Comparable Corpus-Based Study of Three DO Verbs in Varieties of Mandarin: gao. In Jia-Fei Hong, Qi Su and Jiun-Shiung Wu (eds.), *Chinese Lexical Semantics*, 147–154. Cham: Springer.

Jiang, Menghan, Natalia Klyueva, Hongzhi Xu and Chu-Ren Huang. 2018. Annotating Chinese Light Verb Constructions according to PARSEME guidelines. In Nicoletta Calzolari, Khalid Choukri, Christopher Cieri, Thierry Declerck, Sara Goggi, Koiti Hasida and Hitoshi Isahara (eds.), *Proceedings of the Eleventh International Conference on Language Resources and Evaluation (LREC 2018)*, Miyazaki: European Language Resources Association (ELRA).

Jiang, Menghan, Dingxu Shi and Chu-Ren Huang. 2016. Transitivity in light verb variations in Mandarin Chinese–a comparable corpus-based statistical approach. In *Proceedings of the 30th pacific asia conference on language, information and computation: Posters*, 459–468. Seoul. https://aclanthology.org/Y16-3000, last access: 13/01/2025.

Kageyama, Taro. 1976–1977. Incorporation and Sino-Japanese verbs. *Papers in Japanese Linguistics* 5. 117–156.

Kishimoto, Hideki. 2019. Keidooshi-koobun-no idoo-genshoo: Koo-jooshoo-to meishi hennyuu [Movement phenomena in verb consturctions: Argument ascension and noun incorporation]. In Testuo Nishihara, Haruko Miyakoda, Koichiro Nakamura, Yoko Yonekura and Shinichi Tanaka (eds.), *Gengo-niokeru Intaafeisu [Interfaces in Language]*, 11–24. Tokyo: Kaitakusha.

Kuo, Pei-Jung. 2012. A Case Study of Obligatory Object Fronting in Mandarin Chinese. In *On-line Proceedings of GLOW in Asia: Workshop for Young Scholars*, 138–150. Tsu: Mie University. https://www.yumpu.com/en/document/view/36202265/a-case-study-of-obligatory-object-fronting-in-mandarin-chinese, last access: 13/01/2025.

Lin, Jingxia, Hongzhi Xu, Menghan Jiang and Chu-Ren Huang. 2014. Annotation and classification of light verbs and light verb variations in Mandarin Chinese. In *Proceedings of the Workshop on*

Lexical and Grammatical Resources for Language Processing, 75–82. Dublin: Association for Computational Linguistics and Dublin City University.

Lu, Lu and Chu-Ren Huang. 2023. A diachronic insight into the aspectual meaning in Light Verb Constructions. A case study in Mandarin Chinese. In Pompei Anna, Mereu Lunella and Piunno Valentina (eds.), *Light Verb Constructions as Complex Verbs*, 305–336. Berlin: De Gruyter. https://doi.org/10.1515/9783110747997-012.

Qiu, Rongshang. 1994. ingdongci zhiyi – ping Zhu, Dexi guagyu mingdongci de shoufa. *Language Construction Communication* 44. 67–71.

Rácz, Anita, István Nagy and Veronika Vincze. 2014. 4FX: Light verb constructions in a multilingual parallel corpus. In *Proceedings of the Ninth International Conference on Language Resources and Evaluation (LREC'14)*, 710–715. Reykjavik: European Language Association (ELRA).

Shimada, Atsuko and Vlia Kordoni. 2003. Japanese "Verbal Noun and suru" Constructions. In Dorothtee Beermann and Lars Hellan (eds.), *Proceedings of the workshop on multi-Verb constructions*, 1–21. Trondheim: Norwegian University of Science and Technology.

Simone, Raffaele. 2007. Categories and Constructions in Verbal and Signed Languages. In Elena Pizzuto, Paola Pietrandrea and Raffaele Simone (eds.), *Verbal and signed languages. Comparing Structures, Constructs and Methodologies*, 197–252. Berlin: Mouton De Gruyter.

Wang, Leslie Fu-mei. 2004. A corpus-based study of Mandarin verbs of doing. *Concentric: Studies in Linguistics* 30(1). 65–85.

Xu, Hongzhi, Menghan Jiang, Jingxia Lin and Chu-Ren Huang. 2020. Light verb variations and varieties of Mandarin Chinese: Comparable corpus driven approaches to grammatical variations. *Corpus Linguistics and Linguistic Theory* 18(1). 145–173. https://doi.org/10.1515/cllt-2019-0049.

Zhou, Gang. 1987a. Xingshi dongchi de cifenglei. [The subcategorization of form verbs.]. *Chinese learning* 37. 11–115.

Zhou, Xiaobing. 1987b. "jinxing" "jiayi" juxing bijiao. [A syntactic pattern comparison between "jinxing" and "jiayi".]. *Chinese Learning* 42. 1–5.

Zhu, Dexi. 1982. *Yufa jiangyi [Lecture notes on grammar]*. Beijing: Commercial Press.

Zhu, Dexi. 1985. *Xiandai shumain hanyu li de xuhua dongci han mingdongchi, Zhu Dexi wenji disijuan. [Light verbs and nominalized verbs in modern written Chinese, Selected Papers of Zhu, Dexi: the fourth volume.]*. Beijung: ShangWu publishers.

Georgina Alvarez-Morera, Jordi Ginebra, and Isabel Oltra-Massuet
Modification in *give* light verb constructions

A corpus-based study in Germanic and Romance languages

1 Introduction

Since Wierzbicka (1982), light verb constructions (LVCs) have been regarded as the telic counterpart (1a) of atelic verbs (1b), thus accounting for the existence of such similar constructions. However, that cannot be the whole story, since the number of the nominal element affects the telicity of the construction, as illustrated in the contrasts (1a–(1c)).

(1)   a.   *Melinda had a thought*   [+telic]
       b.   *I thought that the advice I was giving my clients was special.*   [–telic]
       c.   *She also had thoughts of suicide.*   [–telic]

(Bonial and Pollard, 2020, 15)

In more recent approaches, the higher frequency of LVCs tends to be attributed to their more flexible modification properties, at least in English (Leech et al., 2009, 179; Huddleston and Pullum, 2002, 293; Bonial and Pollard, 2020, 18). Yet, corpus-based studies, such as Storrer (2007) or Levin and Ström Herold (2015), have shown that modification is not common in LVCs in Germanic languages (e.g. English, German and Swedish). The fact that previous corpus findings are all based on the same language family hinders the possibility of finding the underlying generalization across languages.

Thus, there is a need for corpus-based studies that conduct a cross-linguistic analysis that includes additional language families with a focus on the nominal component of the LVC (as pointed out in Alvarez-Morera, 2023). With this aim, the present study investigates *give*-LVCs across Germanic (English, *give*, and German, *geben*) and Romance languages (Catalan, *donar*, and Spanish, *dar*). Taking a random sample of 6,794 tokens of *give*-LVCs from online annotated corpora for the four languages within the time frame of the 21st Century as a basis, we review the morphosyntactic properties of the nominal element, with a special focus on their modifi-

Georgina Alvarez-Morera, University of Oxford
Jordi Ginebra, Universitat Rovira i Virgili
Isabel Oltra-Massuet, Universitat Rovira i Virgili

cation patterns. After the quantitative analysis of the corpus sample in terms of frequency and modification patterns, we observe that the majority of LVCs in all four languages appear unmodified, although there are significant differences within and across language families: modified nominal elements are most frequent in English, while German patterns with Romance languages in that it shows lower percentages of modification of about a third of the instances. Interestingly, Wiskandt (this volume) also concludes that no significant contrast can be established between Germanic LVCs and their Romance counterparts.

We take these findings as a basis for an analysis of LVCs within a neo-constructionist approach to argument structure (Acedo Matellán, 2010, 2016, based on Hale and Keyser, 53–109, 2002), which focuses on the determination and modification properties of the nominal in LVCs. The results point towards a compositional hierarchy of the nominal domain based on Grimshaw's (2005) notion of extended projection: the more independent the nominal from the light verb (LV), the more structure is projected within the nominal domain. Unlike previous studies which focus on the role of the light verb to explain restrictions on the nominal element (Mendívil, 1999), our claim is that it is the nature of the syntactic nominal phrase that establishes the combinatorial patterns of the LVC as a whole.

The structure of the chapter is as follows. In section 2, we briefly review the analysis of LVCs, focusing on how modification in LVCs has been dealt with in previous studies. In section 3, we describe the methodology employed in our corpus-based study on Germanic and Romance languages. Section 4 presents the quantitative results of the study, as well as the statistical analysis 4.2, and discusses the results 4.3. Taking our corpus-based, empirical results as a basis, section 5 establishes a typology of LVCs based on the presence of determination and modification. It further outlines a syntactic account of the various LVCs that is grounded on the layered approach to the nominal domain within a neo-constructionist approach to argument structure. Section 6 concludes and suggests directions for future research.

2 Properties of LVCs across frameworks

This section provides a brief overview of how LVCs are typically defined, their basic properties and what the consensus is on the presence of nominal modification.

The term *light verb* was first coined by Jespersen (1942, 117) to refer to verbo-nominal constructions in English like *have a sigh* or *take a shower*, where a deverbal noun is combined with a semantically impoverished verb to form a complex predicate. After this initial definition, different proposals within various frameworks have examined these structures. While in the 1970s and 1980s, there was certain consensus in considering the LVs completely devoid of predicational force and the argument structure of LVC as inherited from the nominal element (Cattell, 1984; Grimshaw and Mester, 1988), more recent accounts suggest that the LV also contributes to the argument and event structure of the construction (Ginebra, 2003; Ramchand, 2014; Acedo Matellán and Pineda, 2019).

It is also important to bear in mind that LVCs usually have a synthetic verb which a priori conveys the same meaning (Sanromán Vilas, 2009; Butt, 2010): *walk* for *take a walk* or *pasear* for *dar un paseo* Sp.'take a walk'. However, this equivalence is not always available within a particular language and there are four possibilities (Piera and Varela, 1999): (i) the synthetic counterpart is equivalent in both its morphology and semantics (2), (ii) there is morphological affinity but no semantic equivalence (3), (iii) there is only a semantic equivalence (4), and (iv) there is no synthetic counterpart (5).[1]

(2) a. Eng. *take a shower* – *to shower*
 b. Ger. *Antwort geben* lit. 'give answer' – *antworten* 'answer'
 c. Sp. *dar besos* lit. 'give kisses' – *besar* 'kiss'
 d. Cat. *fer una còpia* lit. 'make a copy' – *copiar* 'copy'

(3) a. Eng. *give voice* – *to voice* 'express'
 b. Sp. *hacer fiesta* lit. 'do holiday' – *festejar* 'celebrate'
 c. Cat. *donar propina* lit. 'give tip' – *propinar* 'give/administer'

(4) a. Eng. *make a mistake* – *to err*
 b. Ger. *Platz nehmen* lit. 'take (a) place' – *setzen* 'put'
 c. Sp. *hacer punto* lit. 'do stitch' – *tricotar* 'knit'
 d. Cat. *donar un mastegot* lit. 'give a slap' – *pegar* 'hit'

(5) a. Eng. *take advantage*
 b. Ger. *Abstand nehmen* 'reject' (lit. take distance)
 c. Sp. *hacer deporte* 'do sport' (lit. do sport)
 d. Cat. *donar conferéncia* 'lecture' (lit. give conference)

Even when there is a synthetic verb, as in (2–4), the semantic equivalence between the pairs is not always complete in every context. As mentioned above, Wierzbicka

---

[1] German LVCs with the nominal introduced by a preposition do not generally have a corresponding paraphrasis available, as pointed out in Fleischhauer (2021, 2022) and, hence, they fall into the (iv) pattern. These PP LVCs have been widely studied in German because they appear to be the most representative type of LVCs in that language; however, they are less present in the rest of the languages included in this study (English, Catalan and Spanish). Therefore, the focus of our work focuses on the pattern of a LV followed by a noun phrase.

(1982, 764) points to aspectual differences between English LVCs and their synthetic counterpart as the key motivation for the use of LVCs.

(6) a. *I had a look at all the files in ten minutes.*
b. ?*I looked at all the files in ten minutes.*

(Wierzbicka, 1982, 764)

English LVCs have been further investigated by Bonial and Pollard (2020) on the basis of corpora and they find telicity differences only when the nominal element is singular (7b). The instance in (7c) shows that a plural noun does not express a telic event.

(7) a. *I thought that the advice I was giving my clients was special.* [–telic]
b. *Melinda had a thought: Maybe there would be some way for her husband to collect Mann's DNA [...]* [+telic]
c. *She also had thoughts of suicide.* [–telic]

(Bonial and Pollard, 2020, 15)

Other LVs in English are combined with nouns that are already inherently telic, as in (8) and (9), so the choice of a LVC over the synthetic verb cannot be said to have an aspectual motivation.

(8) a. *Twelve hours into the siege, darkness was beginning to set in, and police decided to make a move.* [+telic]
b. *The governor made a decision to release his tax records.* [+telic]

(9) a. *She appeared with me on VH1 'Celebrity Rehab.'* [+telic]
b. *Bahrain's King Hamad made a rare appearance on television.* [+telic]

(Bonial and Pollard, 2020, 16)

Therefore, there is systematic relation between the aspect of the event denoted by the noun, and the telicity of the whole construction. Yet, as pointed out in Storrer (2007, 186), the choice between the LVC and the corresponding synthetic verb "is not as arbitrary as it has been assumed in the literature", hence a thorough description of which factors favors one or the other type of construction is necessary.

When analysing the paraphrases of synthetic verbs with LVCs in German, Storrer (2007, 180) finds that less than 50% of the instances occurred in contexts compatible with the LVC. LVCs seem, thus, to be semantically more specific, since they can only paraphrase the synthetic verb in those instances where they share the specific meaning.

These observations have also been made for other languages, such as Italian (Bratánková, 2013), where some LVCs have developed a lexicalized meaning independent from the synthetic verb: *fare festa* 'make party' vs. *festeggiare* 'celebrate' or *dare peso* 'give importance' (lit. give weight) vs. *pesare* 'weigh'. This does not apply to all LVCs, since some LVCs are still used as an analytic variant of the synthetic verb (*fare una telefonata* 'make a call' vs. *telefonare* 'call'). However, the use of the LVC in Italian is prevalent where there is a qualitative denotation of the action through the modification of the nominal. This finding is in line with the results presented by Bonial and Pollard (2020, 19–21) for English LVCs.

Nonetheless, Storrer's (2007, 184) corpus study on German LVCs finds that a considerable number of nouns are modified by adjectives to different degrees:

Tab. 1: Noun modified by adjectives (Storrer, 2007, 184).

LVC	Instances	Modified by an adjective
Hilfe leisten 'provide assistence'	310	85 (27.4%)
Unterricht erteilen 'give lecture'	122	34 (27.9%)
Wirkung ausüben 'exert influence'	275	196 (71.3%)
Absage erteilen 'give rejection'	82	42 (51.2%)

Some cases of adjectival modification in LVCs cannot keep their original meaning when transformed into an adverbial modifier of the synthetic counterpart, as in (10), where the modifier is ambiguous or does not sound natural. Also, there are cases, as in (11), where the adjective does not have an adverbial equivalent.

(10) a. *We had – we had a really good laugh and then things happened.*
 b. *?We laughed really well and then things happened.*

(11) a. *President Bush gave a very big speech in September of that year – transferring those detainees to Guantanamo.*
 b. **President Bush spoke very bigly in September of that year – transferring those detainees to Guantanamo.*

(Bonial and Pollard, 2020, 20)

The ease of modification of the noun in contrast with the adverbial modification of the synthetic verb has been considered one of the reasons for the high productivity of LVCs cross-linguistically (Huddleston and Pullum, 2002, 293, Rácz et al., 2014, 5–6, Bonial and Pollard, 2020, 21).

Therefore, Levin and Ström Herold (2015) examine the modification of LVCs in Germanic languages (English, German and Swedish), and they find that the most frequent modification of the nominals in LVCs is adjectival modification. However, this is not present in the majority of instances (see Table 2): the LV with the highest percentage is *give* (32% in English, 19% in Swedish and 24% in German), while *take*-LVCs are comparatively less modified (22% in English, 13% in German and only 5% in Swedish).

Tab. 2: LVCs with adjectival modification (Levin and Ström Herold, 2015, 20).

	English	German	Swedish
give / geben / ge	32% (58/184)	24% (23/94)	29% (41/140)
take / nehmen / ta	22% (39/174)	13% (9/71)	5% (13/265)

Thus, one of the aims of our study is to contribute new and comparable data from a larger set of languages that examines and contrasts the properties of modification in Germanic (English, German) and Romance (Catalan and Spanish) languages.

3 Data and methodology

The present study is based on data from online available corpora in the four languages under study: *Corpus of Contemporary American English* (COCA), *Das Digitale Wörterbuch der Deutschen Sprache* (DWDS), *Corpus textual informatitzat de la llengua catalana* (CTILC), and *Corpus del Español del Siglo XXI* (CORPES XXI). Although there are certain differences between these corpora, especially based on the number of words and the time span they cover (see Table 3), the time frame set for the extraction was the 21st Century in order to concentrate on the most contemporary data of the four corpora and maximally avoid potential biases.[2]

Among the various LVs available, the verb *give* has exhibited stability in terms of frequency since early modern English, as indicated by Butt (2010, 68) and Elenbaas (2013, 66). In contrast, the German verb *geben* does not hold the status of being the most prevalent LV (Bruker, 2011, 45). However, some researchers (i.e. Levin and Ström Herold, 2015), have opted for *geben* over its formal counterpart *erteilen* when comparing it with the English LV *give*. Turning to Romance languages, the LV *dar* in

---

[2] There are no corpora in these four languages that are the same size and cover the same time span and the same textual typology, so we have considered those that are the most homogeneous despite certain divergences and have constrained the time span. In all cases, there is some institution behind these corpora that is responsible for the text selection, annotation and the open access availability of their data (the scholar Mark Davies for COCA, the Berlin-Brandenburg Academy of Sciences and Humanities for DWDS, the Institute of Catalan Studies for CTILC, and the Royal of the Academy Spanish Language for CORPES XXI).

Tab. 3: Comparison of the corpora.

Lang.	Corpus	Size	Genres	Time
English	COCA	+1 billion words of text (25+ million words each year 1990-2019)	8 genres: spoken, fiction, magazines, newspapers, academic texts, blogs, and TV and movies subtitles	2000–2019
German	DWDS	28 billion words of text (1900-2020)	6 genres: spoken, fiction, newspapers, academic texts, blogs, and TV and movies subtitles	2000–2020
Catalan	CTILC	+100 million words of text (1832-2018)	3 genres: fiction, newspapers and academic texts, but there are no instances of spoken language	2000–2018
Spanish	CORPES XXI	312 million words of texts (21st Century)	6 genres: spoken, fiction, newspapers, academic texts, blogs and others	2000–2020

Spanish and *donar* in Catalan rank among the most frequently used verbs. In Spanish, *dar* holds the distinction of being the most widespread verb in the language, according to Sánchez Rufat (2016, 118), and it also represents the LV with the highest number of potential combinations, as noted by De Miguel (2011, 142). Conversely, in Catalan, *donar* is not the most popular LV, it is *fer* 'make/do', but *donar* still maintains a notable frequency, as highlighted in Ginebra and Navarro (2015, 222).

The sample was obtained by searching for the collocation of the LV *give* (and its corresponding translation in each language: *geben*, *donar* and *dar*) and the specific nominal element with which it builds an LVC. The final selection of *give*-LVCs to be analyzed for each language was set to a maximum of 15 LVCs per language, with a range from highly frequent LVCs to less frequent. The highest number of lemmas (n=15) is found in Spanish *dar* LVCs, whereas the number of Catalan (n=14), English (n=13) and German (n=9) LVCs is slightly lower (Table 4). This is due to the fact that LVCs are more diverse in Spanish than in other languages, while in German LVCs with *geben* followed by a noun phrase is not a common pattern within the language (Rácz et al., 2014, 5).

After manually excluding instances of non-LV structures, for every LVC a sample of up to 200 occurrences was analyzed. The LVCs were organized according to the degree of frequency in the corpora under the label frequency: high, medium,

Tab. 4: LVCs analysed in the four languages under study.

	High frequency	Medium frequency	Low frequency
give (English)	advice, speech, answer, example	try, hug, smile, kiss	notice, nod, push, chase, sigh
geben (German)	*Hinweis* 'hint', *Antwort* 'answer'	*Rat* 'advice', *Unterricht* 'lesson', *Erlaubnis* 'permission'	*Kuss* 'kiss', *Warnung* 'warning', *Beschreibung* 'description', *Versprechen* 'promise'
donar (Catalan)	*suport* 'support', *cop* 'blow', *resposta* 'answer', *volta* 'stroll', *explicació* 'explanation'	*consell* 'advice', *permís* 'permission'	*empenta* 'push', *definició* 'definition', *conferència* 'conference', *ajuda* 'help', *bufetada* 'slap', *pallissa* 'beating', *bes/ada* 'kiss'
dar (Spanish)	*vuelta* 'stroll', *paso* 'step', *respuesta* 'answer', *beso* 'kiss'	*golpe* 'blow', *clase* 'lesson', *salto* 'jump', *cambio* 'change', *consejo* 'advice'	*instrucción* 'instruction', *giro* 'turn', *permiso* 'permission', *ayuda* 'help', *bofetada* 'slap', *autorización* 'authorization'

and low.[3] Also, all examples were classified according to the following grammatical factors:[4]

(i) determination (yes/no),
(ii) modification (different classes: unmodified (UNMOD), adjectival (Adj), prepositional phrase (PP), relative clauses (Rel), noun classifiers (NC), genitive (Gen), or various, that is, a combination of two of the former),
(iii) number of the noun (singular/plural).

The final database of *give*-LVCs instances consists of 6,789 tokens of LVC with some differences in the distribution among the four languages (Table 5); although these divergences are consistent with the differences presented in the size of the corpora. The variables were coded in all examples, and then fed into the Lancaster Stats Tools online.[5] First, chi-square tests were used as an initial means to identify potentially

---

[3] The degree of frequency of the LVC has been decided on the co-occurrence between the LV and the different nouns according to the search tool for collocates in each corpus. The list was divided into quartiles and the LVCs were selected randomly from each quartile (high, medium, and low).
[4] Some methodological limitations must be pointed out. The manual coding for variables is a usual method in corpus linguistics but it might lead to measurement errors (Egbert et al., 2020). The possible errors are compensated with a high number of instances. All remaining errors are the researchers' own responsibility.
[5] Available at: http://corpora.lancs.ac.uk/stats/toolbox.php, last access 05/12/2024.

significant from non-significant variables. Second, a logistic regression analysis was performed to find out which features were the strongest predictors of modification. We report the results in the next section.

Tab. 5: Distribution of the number of LVCs of the database for each language.

	English	German	Catalan	Spanish	TOTAL LV
give / geben / donar / dar	2,030	995	931	2,842	6,798

4 General results

4.1 Overview

The analysis of the data on modification in *give*-LVCs shows that LVCs with modified nominal elements are most frequent in English (53.26%), while German (31.76%) and the Romance languages show slightly lower percentages of modification: 28.57% in Catalan and 27.69% in Spanish (Figure 1). The majority of *give*-LVCs appear unmodified in these three languages. This distribution is statistically significant when all languages are compared ($\chi^2(3)$= 376.95, p<.0001, Cramer's V=0.236, medium effect), but not within both language families: when Germanic languages are contrasted, statistical tests prove a significant difference ($\chi^2(1)$=124.09, p<.0001, Cramer's V=0.203, small effect). However, the difference is not significant in the case of the two Romance languages ($\chi^2(1)$=0.27, p=0.60, Cramer's V=0.008, negligible effect).

The results thus point towards a difference in the tendency to appear modified between English and the other three languages, as shown in Table 6. The modification subclasses tagged are: no modification (Unmod), adjectival (Adj), prepositional phrases (PP), relative clauses (Rel), noun classifiers (NC), genitive (Gen), and various. As seen in Table 6, adjectival modification is the most common in all languages: 41.17% in English (versus 12.09% of the rest of modification subclasses), 27.74% in German (versus 4.02% of the rest of modification subclasses), 19.33% in Catalan (versus 9.24% of the rest of modification subclasses), and 19.56% in Spanish (versus 8.13% of the rest of modification subclasses). In fact, relative clauses (Rel), noun classifiers (NC), genitive (Gen) and a combination of subclasses (Various) are residual in the four languages (below 3% of instances in all languages), where NC and Gen are only found in Germanic languages. However, prepositional phrases (PP)

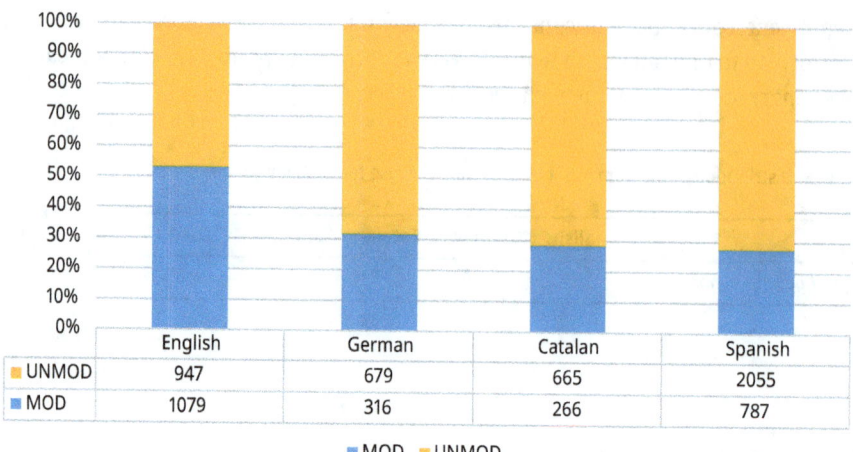

Fig. 1: Distribution of modification in *give*-LVCs.

present similar percentages in the Romance languages, as exemplified in (12): 6.55% in Catalan *donar*-LVCs (12a), and 6.86% in Spanish *dar*-LVCs (12b). These differences in the choice of Germanic languages for NC and Gen and Romance languages for PP reflect the general nominal modification patterns of these language families.

(12) a. i comença a donar-li cops de puny.
       and starts to give-3SG.DAT hits of fist
       'and starts punching him'   (Catalan, CTILC, 2001)
    b. al   dar instrucciones de neutralidad a la Guardia Civil.
       at.the.SG give instructions of neutrality to the Guard Civil
       'when giving neutrality instructions to the Police'
                                                         (Spanish, CORPES XXI, 2001)

Tab. 6: Distribution of modification subclasses in *give*-LVCs (all four languages)

Modification	English	German	Catalan	Spanish
Unmod (No)	947 (46.74%)	679 (68.4%)	665 (71.42%)	2055 (72.31%)
Adj	834 (41.17%)	276 (27.74%)	180 (19.33%)	556 (19.56%)
PP	61 (3.01%)	3 (0.30%)	61 (6.55%)	195 (6.86%)
Rel	36 (1.78%)	13 (1.30%)	12 (1.29%)	24 (0.84%)
NC	59 (2.91%)	1 (0.10%)	-	-
Gen	29 (1.43%)	11 (1.11%)	-	-
Various	60 (2.96%)	12 (1.21%)	13 (1.40%)	12 (0.43%)
TOTAL	2026	995	931	2842

It can be concluded that general differences in the modification of the noun in *give*-LVCs are statistically validated.

Furthermore, a closer look at the correlation between the degree of frequency of LVCs in the corpora and the presence or lack of modification is needed to determine whether frequency has an influence on the overall results.[6]

Figure 3 shows that English *give*-LVCs with high frequency appear modified in most cases (61.42%); those with medium frequency are modified in half of the cases (51.43%); low-frequency LVCs are modified in only 44.10% of the instances. Interestingly, the differences between the degrees of frequency are statistically significant ($\chi^2(2)$=40.23, p<.0001, Cramer's V=0.141, small effect).

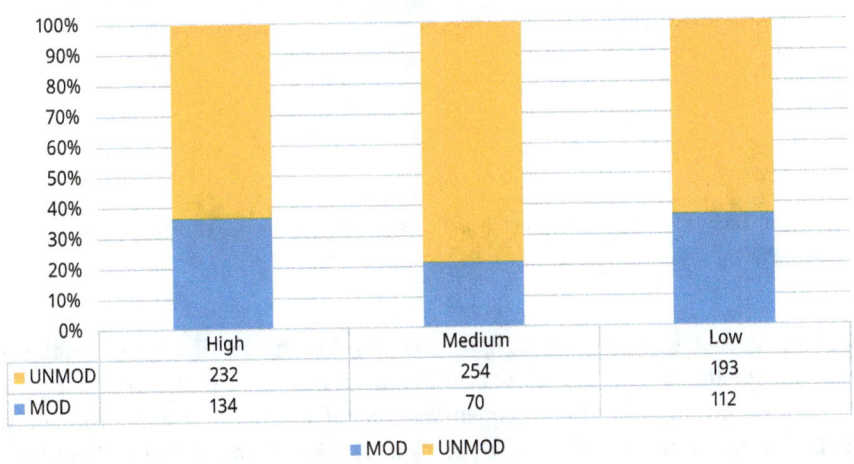

Fig. 2: Distribution of modification in German *geben*-LVCs according to the degree of frequency (high, medium or low).

Hence, the results for English point to a correlation between degree of frequency and levels of modification: the more frequent an LVC, the more likely it will appear modified.

In a similar line, Figure 2 shows that the German high-frequent *geben*-LVCs are modified as often as the low frequency group (36.61% and 36.72% respectively), and to a lesser extent the medium frequent (21.60%). The differences between the de-

---

[6] Frequency is treated here as a categorical variable although it is not a naturally categorial variable for an intention of homogeneity between the four corpora. Moreover, token frequencies are the most widely used corpus statistic, but they are problematic and corpus-dependent (as pointed out in Gries, 2023, 82).

grees of frequency are, again, statistically significant ($\chi^2(2)$=22.86, p<.0001, Cramer's V=0.152, small effect).

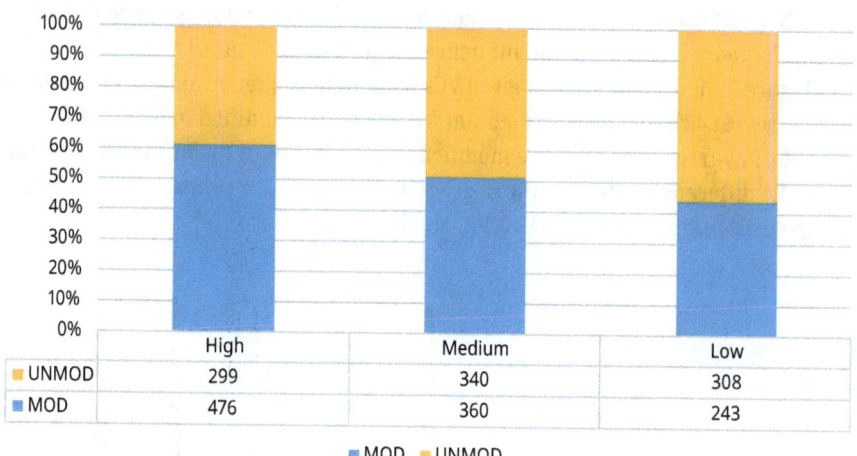

Fig. 3: Distribution of modification in English *give*-LVCs according to the degree of frequency (high, medium or low).

Turning to Romance languages, Figure 4 shows that the distribution of modification in Catalan *donar*-LVCs presents a different trend that radically contrasts with Germanic languages. The high-frequency Catalan *donar*-LVCs are modified in only 28.12% of instances and medium-frequency in 20.15%, which contrast with the low-frequency LVCs that appear modified in 40% of instances.[7] The difference between the groups of frequency is statistically significant ($\chi^2(2)$=12.72, p=0.001, Cramer's V= 0.117, small effect).

A closer analysis of the morphosyntactic properties of Catalan *donar*-LVCs shows that there are certain restrictions to adjectival modification which are related to the bareness of the nominal element (Espinal and McNally, 2011, 113). Bare nominals tend to be modified by relational adjectives (13a), and they only accept qualitative adjectives in restricted contexts (13a).

---

[7] The percentual divergence can be explained by the lower number of examples extracted for the low-frequency LVCs, which is due to the examples available in the CTILC corpus for the 21st Century.

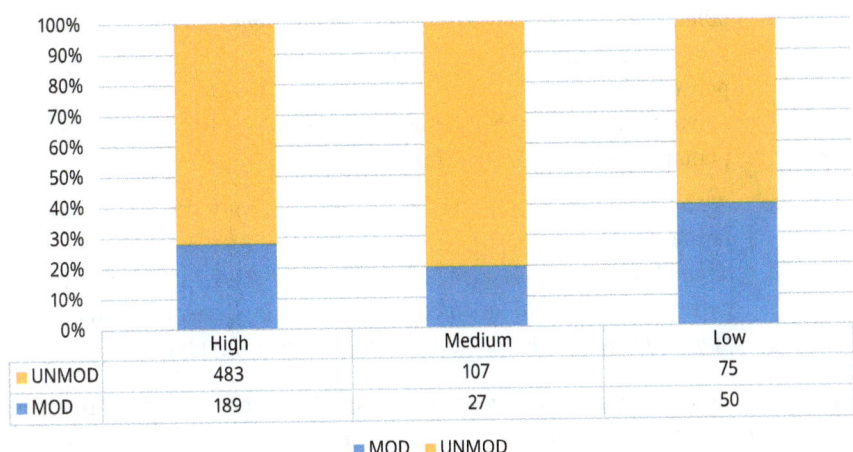

Fig. 4: Distribution of modification in Catalan *donar*-LVCs according to the degree of frequency (high, medium or low).

(13) a. i dóna suport tècnic i personal a la resta d'unitats.
and gives support technical and personal to the rest of-units
'and [it] gives technical and personal support to the rest of the units.'

(Catalan, CTILC, 2010)

b. catalans i balears es donaran suport mutu.
Catalan.PL and Balearic.PL SE give.3PL.FUT support mutual
'Catalan and Balearic [people] will give mutual support'

(Catalan, CTILC, 2005)

These restrictions could have an impact on the results of Catalan *donar*-LVCs which accept the nominal to appear bare. In the sample of Catalan *donar*-LVCs, high and medium-frequency LVCs include constructions which accept both determined and bare nominals (14a), as well as others which only accept the nouns with a determiner in singular (14b); while low-frequency LVCs mainly accept determined nominals (15b) and only two instances can combine with bare nominals (15a).[8]

---

[8] The fact that determined nominals show fewer restrictions in accepting modification might have influenced the results and the differences presented in Figure 4, where the low-frequency *donar*-LVCs show the highest percentages of modification.

(14) a. *donar (un) suport* 'give (a) support', *donar (una) resposta* 'give (an) answer', *donar (un) consell* 'give (an) advice', *donar (un) permís* 'give (a) permission'

b. *donar *(un) cop* 'give *(a) blow', *donar *(una) explicació* 'give *(an) explanation', *donar *(una) volta* 'give *(a) walk'

(15) a. *donar (una) ajuda* 'give (a) help', *donar (una) conferència* 'give (a) conference'

b. *donar *(una) empenta* 'give *(a) push', *donar *(una) definició* 'give *(a) definition', *donar *(una) bufetada* 'give *(a) slap', *donar *(una) pallissa* 'give *(a) beating', *donar *(un) bes/besada* 'give *(a) kiss'

For Spanish *dar*-LVCs, Figure 5 shows that medium-frequency LVCs have the highest percentage of modified instances (36.16%), followed by the high-frequency LVCs (25.12%), and low-frequency are the least modified (23.27%). The difference between the frequency groups is, again, statistically significant ($\chi^2(2)$=45.02, p<.0001, Cramer's V = 0.126, small effect).

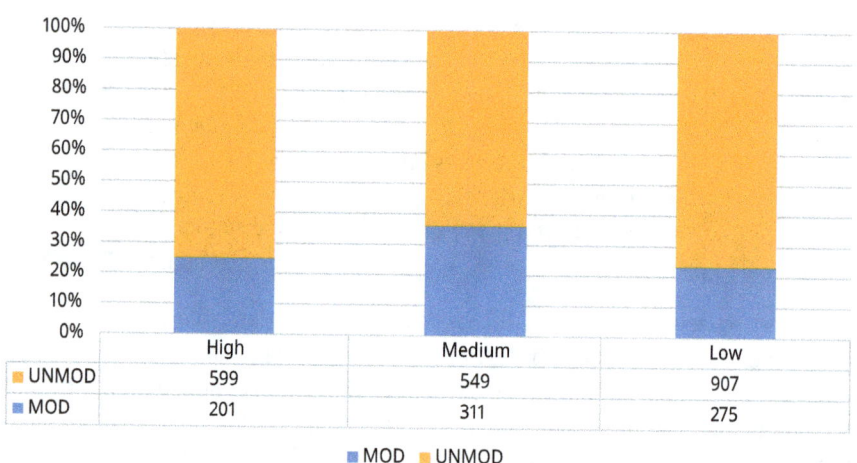

Fig. 5: Distribution of modification in Spanish *dar*-LVCs according to the degree of frequency (high, medium or low).

In sum, the degree of frequency of LVCs in corpora has proven to have contradictory effects on the results. There is a positive correspondence between high-frequency LVCs and a higher presence of modification in the languages with bigger corpora, English and Spanish, although the proportion is lower in Spanish. This tendency is also relevant in German LVCs but to a lesser extent since low-frequency *geben*-LVCs are also equally modified. In contrast, there is a negative correspondence between frequency of LVCs and their possibilities to be modified in Catalan *donar*-LVCs, as it is the low-frequency constructions which are the most frequently modified.

4.2 Statistical analysis

In order to confirm the corpus-based, empirical trends attested in the previous section, we employed a binomial logistic regression as statistical method, which is performed with the most significant variables, to determine which of them are the strongest predictors for modification in LVCs. The implementation of this statistical test aims at examining the extent to which the morphosyntactic variables considered in the previous sections (number and determination), as well as the degree of frequency, can predict the patterns of modification attested.[9]

The result of the logistic regression analysis is given in Table 7, which was overall statistically significant (LL: 442.57; p < 0.0001).

Tab. 7: Output of the logistic regression model for predictor factors in modification with *give* LVCs. Logistic Regression Model: Response variable: Mod (unmodified | modified) (4344 | 2448). Overall model statistics: Likelihood ratio test (LL): 442.57 (p < 0.0001); C-index: 0.65; Nagelkerke R2: 0.09; AIC: 8454.56.

Coefficients	Estimate (log odds)	Standard Error	Z value (Wald)	p-value
(Intercept)	0.299	0.058	5.110	0.000
Langb_de	-0.879	0.082	-10.757	0.000
Langc_ca	-0.978	0.089	-10.960	0.000
Langd_es	-0.998	0.063	-15.850	0.000
Detb_no	-0.461	0.065	-7.058	0.000
Numb_plur	0.086	0.069	1.239	0.215
Freqb_medium	-0.078	0.065	-1.206	0.228
Freqc_low	-0.258	0.066	-3.893	0.000

According to the regression analysis of the corpus material tabulated in Table 7, the variables language and determination are the strongest distinguishing factors. First, three languages, German, Catalan and Spanish, are all less likely than English to be

---

[9] Predictors included in the model are language (Lang), determination (Det), number (Num), and frequency (Freq). No predictor interactions are included. For the calculation, the Lancaster Stats Tools online (Brezina, 2018) is used, which includes the possibility to generate a logistic regression model in the section 'Lexico-grammar'. Available at: http://corpora.lancs.ac.uk/stats/toolbox.php

modified. Second, bare nouns are also less likely than nouns introduced by a determiner to be modified. In contrast, number does not show any significant predicting power.

Regarding the predictor variable frequency, only low frequent LVCs show a negative estimate, which indicates that it is less likely to be modified than the reference variable (highly frequent LVCs). The comparison with medium-frequency LVCs does not show significant results.

Thus, the results of the statistical model are fully in line with the findings reported in the descriptive presentation of the data in section 3.

4.3 Interim discussion

The main purpose of this corpus study was to review the morphosyntactic properties of the nominal element in LVCs, with a special focus on their modification patterns. The results show that modification is clearly more frequent in English, while it is less frequent in German, Catalan, and Spanish to different degrees. Moreover, the corpus data show very little prominence of modification subclasses other than adjectival modification in the four languages. This is in line with previous research by Levin and Ström Herold (2015, 24) who discard the in-depth analysis of clausal modifiers because they represent only 5% of instances with *give*-LVCs and 2% in *geben*-LVCs. The proportions are even lower in our data: in English *give*-LVCs, relative clauses represent 41 out of 2026 instances (2.02%); in German *geben*-LVCs, 14 out of 995 instances (1.41%). In the case of Romance languages, relative clauses also show residual presence: in Catalan *donar*-LVCs, 12 out of 931 (1.21%), and in Spanish *dar*-LVCs, 25 out of 2842 (0.88%).

Regarding PP modification, however, there are no previous studies which can be compared to, because the focus on this kind of modification is not relevant for Germanic languages. In fact, nominal modification through PPs is low to residual in Germanic languages: 5.53% in English *give*-LVCs (112 out of 2026) and only 0.60% in German *geben*-LVCs (6 out of 995). In contrast, PP modification shows a higher presence in the two Romance languages under study: 7.95% in Catalan *donar*-LVCs (74 out of 931) and 10.12% in Spanish *dar*-LVCs (205 out of 2026). Even if PP-modification is more present in the two Romance languages studied, it is still low and only more relevant than adjectival modification with certain nouns: *cop* 'blow', *conferència* 'conference' and *permís* 'permission' in Catalan; *clase* 'lesson' and *permiso* 'permission' in Spanish.

The results on adjectival modification in *give*-LVCs in Germanic languages show that English LVCs are the most frequently modified in 834 out of 2026 instances (41.16%), and German presents lower numbers in 276 out of 995 instances (27.73%).

In Levin and Ström Herold (2015, 20), the results are slightly lower: 32% in *give*-LVCs in English (58/184) and 24% in *geben*-LVCs in German (23/94). However, their sample was smaller and less representative, since it was restricted to the genre of fiction. At the same time, the levels of modification found in our study are slightly lower than the findings by Bonial and Pollard (2020, 16–17) which represented more than 64% on average. However, their results are not comparable to ours either, due to the kind of modifiers included in their analysis, which involved quantifiers, determiners, and relative clauses alongside adjectival modification.

To our knowledge, all previous studies have only included data from Germanic languages, so the results for Catalan *donar*-LVCs and Spanish *dar*-LVCs are novel. In this case, results on adjectival modification are more similar within the Romance language family, but they sharply contrast with the Germanic languages in that they represent a much lower percentage: 180 out of 931 instances in Catalan (19.33%) and 556 out of 2,842 in Spanish (19.56%).

Regarding the degree of frequency of the LVC lemmas, this parameter has contradictory effects on the results, as clearly shown by the logistic regression analysis. Hence, the degree of frequency is a parameter which cannot homogeneously predict the levels of modification in LVCs cross-linguistically without considering the properties of particular LVCs. In fact, previous studies on the use of LVCs versus their synthetic counterparts (i.e. Storrer, 2007; Sanromán Vilas, 2009; Bratánková, 2013) point towards the tendency of frequent LVCs to develop a lexicalized meaning, which would favor their use over that of a synthetic verb. In our data, however, a majority of specific LVCs (regardless of their degree of frequency) combine with a wide range of adjectives, both relational and qualitative, and the tendencies of co-occurring adjectives and nouns are residual.

5 A typology of LVCs across Germanic (English/ German) and Romance (Catalan/ Spanish)

Based on the restrictions and interactions found between modification – relational or qualitative – and determination detected in our corpus-based study, we propose a corpus-based typology of LVCs across Germanic (English/German) and Romance (Catalan/Spanish) languages based on the morphosyntactic structure of these constructions taking into account the deverbal nature of the nominal component, as well as additional restrictions on adjacency and the presence of quantifiers, as summarized in Table 8.

In this section, we discuss the properties of each type and subtype of LVC and suggest a syntactic analysis that focuses on the compositional hierarchy within the

Tab. 8: Typology of LVCs.

	Type 1	Type 2 Deverbal	Type 2 Non-deverbal	Type 3
Deverbal	Yes	Yes	No	—
Determination	Yes	No	No	No
Quantification	Yes	Yes	Yes	No
Adjectival modification	Yes	Yes	Yes (relational)	No
Adjacency	No	No	No	Yes
Examples	*dar un abrazo efusivo* (Sp., give a warm hug)	*dar respuesta afirmativa* (Sp., give positive answer)	*donar consell econòmic* (Cat., give economic advice)	*dar vuelta el partido* (Sp., turn the match around)

DP, where the structure above N determines the degree of integration between the nominal and the verb. The basic idea underlying our syntactic analysis builds on Grimshaw's (1990; 2005), notion of extended projection. Specifically, we suggest that the more independent the nominal from the light verb, the more structure is projected within the nominal domain.

Unlike previous studies which focus on the role of the light verb to explain restrictions on the nominal element (Mendívil, 1999), our claim is, thus, that it is the nature of the syntactic nominal phrase that establishes the combinatorial patterns of the LVC as a whole. The proposal is further framed within the Hale & Keyser's model of argument structure as developed in Acedo Matellán (2016) and Myler (2016).

5.1 Type 1: LVCs with a determiner and flexible modification

The first type of LVCs that we propose are LVCs with a determiner or a quantifier introducing the noun, in which case modification is flexible; if the noun is deverbal, and modification is adjectival, it may be multiple (16).

(16) a. *I will do my best to give brief and unbiased advice.*

(English, COCA, 2011)

b. Le dio un largo beso en la boca a su marido
him gave a long kiss in the mouth to her husband
'She kissed her husband in the mouth for a long time'

(Spanish, CORPES XXI, 2001)

c. *En català, el diccionari Fabra dóna una definició senzilla, però de*
   in Catalan the dictionary Fabra gives a definition simple but of
   caràcter més enciclopèdic que no pas lingüístic
   character more encyclopedic than not not linguistic
   'In Catalan, the Fabra dictionary gives a simple definition, but with a more encyclopedic approach than linguistic'
   (Catalan, CTILC, 2005)

d. *Nur einmal wollte ihr ein Mann einen sogenannten guten Rat*
   only once wanted her a man a so-called good advice
   geben
   give
   'Only once a man wanted to give her a so-called good piece of advice'
   (German, DWDS, 2011)

In the case of non-deverbal nouns, adjectival modification is facilitated by the presence of the determiner in the two Romance languages,[10] as exemplified in (17). That is, modification requires the presence of a determiner, in which case there are no restrictions (as noticed by Alonso Ramos, 2004, 198); otherwise, when the nominal is bare, modification is not possible (18).

(17) a. *los senadores dieron el permiso correspondiente para que el*
   the senators gave the permission corresponding for that the
   gobernante mexicano se ausente del territorio nacional
   governor Mexican SE leaves of.the territory national
   'the senators gave the corresponding permission for the Mexican ruler to leave the country'
   (Spanish, CORPES XXI, 2001)

b. *o bé donava un consell deliberadament ingenu.*
   or well gave a advice deliberately naïve
   'or he gave a deliberately naïve advice'
   (Catalan, CTILC, 2012)

(18) a. *los senadores dieron *(el) permiso correspondiente*
   the senators gave the permission corresponding
   'the senators gave (the) corresponding permission'   [Spanish]

b. *o bé donava *(un) consell ingenu*
   or well gave a advice naïve
   'or he gave (a) naïve advice'   [Catalan]

---

[10] This restriction on bareness is, however, only found in the corpus data of the two Romance languages under study, as will be further developed in the upcoming section 5.2.

Besides the ease in modification, the nouns introduced by a determiner show argumental properties and pass tests, such as the possibility to passivize and pronominalize, exemplified in (19) and ((20) respectively, which have been taken as proof for the referential properties of arguments (Van Valin, 2001, 90, Carnie, 2002, 35–36).

(19)   a.   *Otros pasos han sido dados con la destitución, averiguación y*
                other steps have been given with the dismissal   inquiry   and
                hasta detención de varios funcionarios
                until arrest   of several civil servants
                'Other steps have been taken with the dismissal, inquiry and even arrest of several officials'

                                                        (Spanish, CORPES XXI, 2013)

       b.   *La bufetada havia estat donada i   assumida.*
                the slap   had   been given   and assumed
                'The slap was given and accepted'

                                                          (Catalan, CTILC, 2003)

       c.   *A few examples were given*

                                                            (English, COCA, 2012)

       d.   *Es ist zu vermuten, dass damit   die Erlaubnis   gegeben ist*
                it is to assume   that this.with the permission given   is
                'It is to assume that with this the permission is given'

                                                         (German, DWDS, 2012)

(20)   a.   *Había dado una respuesta y   la defendió hasta el final.*
                had   given a   answer   and it defended until the end
                'He had given an answer and defend it to the end'   [Spanish]

       b.   *El   comte va   donar el permís   a l'abat,   però el*
                the count goes.AUX.PST give   the permission to the_abbot but it
                va   donar a contracor.
                goes.AUX.PST give   at reluctantly
                'The Count gave permission to the abbot, but he gave it reluctantly.'
                                                                       [Catalan]

       c.   *She gave a speech and they remembered it.*   [English]

       d.   *Hat Van der Vaart die Antwort gegeben? Er hat sie endlich gegeben.*
                has Van der Vaart the answer given   he has it finally given
                'Has Van der Vaart given the answer? He has finally given it.'
                                                                           [German]

Hence, our proposal of analysis for Type 1 LVCs in (21) is that the complement of the LV is a canonical DP within a basic dyadic or transitive construction that would parallel Hale & Keyser's basic V+N structure for unergative verbs,[11] as developed in Acedo Matellán (2016); Myler (2016), *i.a.*

(21)   *dar un largo paseo*
       give a long walk
       'take a long walk'

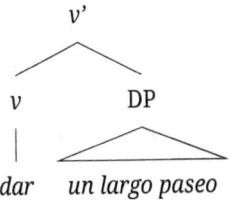

This would also be further in line with Bruening's (2015, 58–59) hypothesis that LVCs behave as traditional verb-noun constructions.

5.2 LVCs with bare nominals

Bare nominals in LVCs cannot behave as canonical arguments due to the lack of the determiner (as predicted in Longobardi, 2005, 36). That is, they cannot be passivized (22b) and pronominalization is restricted to the partitive in languages where this pronoun is in use (i.e. Catalan, 22b). Therefore, they cannot be said to take a DP as a complement, unlike Type 1, but they must rather take some other projection below D, as proposed in e.g. Oggiani (2021, 330), Oggiani (2022, 263) for bare nouns in Spanish.

(22)   a.   *El passaport donava permís   per anar arreu d'Europa i*
            the passport gave   permission to go   over of_Europe and
            Amèrica.
            America
            'The passport gave permission to travel all over Europe and America'
                                                                  (CTILC, 2013)

---

[11] In some of the *give*-LVCs that are ditransitive, the indirect object (IO) would be introduced through an applicative head ApplP, as standardly assumed since Pylkkänen (2008).

b. *Permís   era donat pel   passaport per anar arreu d'Europa i
   permission was given for.the passport to go   over of=Europe and
   Amèrica.
   America
   'Permission was given by the passport to travel all over Europe and America.'

c. El   passaport dona permís   per anar arreu d'Europa i
   The passport gives permission to go   over of_Europe and
   Amèrica, però només en/   #el   donava als   ciutadans majors
   America but only it.PART/ it.ACC gave   to.the citizens old
   d'edat.
   of_age
   'The passport gave permission to travel all over Europe and America, but gave it only to citizens of legal age.'

Some crucial differences are found between bare singular nouns and bare plurals, as the latter do not present restrictions in terms of argument properties nor modification. This difference can also be traced back to Cyrino & Espinal's (2019, 192) proposal that bare plurals have a D layer in their syntax which is introduced by the plural marker. Therefore, bare plurals pattern with Type 1 LVCs in terms of determination and flexible modification, as expected.

In the remainder of the section, we focus on the patterns found regarding bare singulars in *give*-LVCs. First, they present some restrictions related to the type of modification and the verbal base of the noun. That is, when the noun selected by the LV *give* is deverbal and bare, modification is acceptable, though not especially frequent, with both relational adjectives (23) and qualitative adjectives (24).

(23) a. Hay   que darle   respuesta afirmativa a este interrogante.
        have.IMP that give.it.DAT answer   affirmative to this question
        'One must give positive answer to this question'
                                                          (Spanish, CORPES XXI, 2001)

   b. una entitat catòlica que donava suport mèdic i   financer a
      a   entity Catholic that gave   support medical and financial to
      les textiles dones.
      the women
      'a Catholic entity that gave medical and financial support to the women'
                                                          (Catalan, CTILC, 2006)

   c. didn't really ask you here to give me spiritual advice
                                                          (English, COCA, 2019)

(24) a. *no es posible dar respuesta precisa aún a ciertas preguntas*
not is possible give answer precise still to certain questions
'it is still not possible to give precise answer to certain questions'
(Spanish, CORPES XXI, 2002)

b. *A causa de la facilitat de fabricació i d'utilització, la prellosa*
at cause of the facility of fabrication and use the pre-slab
dóna resposta eficient a la demanda de versatilitat funcional i
gives answer efficient to the demand of versatility functional and
arquitectònica del sostre.
architectonical of.the ceiling
'Due to the ease in production and use, the pre-slab gives efficient answer to the demand of functional and architectural versatility in the ceiling.'
(Catalan, CTILC, 2001)

c. *I will do my best to give brief and unbiased advice.*
(English, COCA, 2012)

d. *Er gab später folgende Beschreibung*:
ge gave later following description
'He later gave (the) following description'
(German, DWDS, 2004)

However, non-deverbal bare nominals in *give*-LVCs exhibit certain cross-linguistic differences regarding modification. On the one hand, with non-deverbal nouns, Spanish and Catalan *give*-LVCs allow modification by a relational adjective, but reject qualitative modification, as shown in (25). In contrast, neither Germanic language includes modified bare singular non-deverbal nouns in our sample.

(25) a. *El profesor dio clase {particular/ magistral/ *especial}*
the teacher gave class particular master special
'The teacher gave a {private / master / special} class' (Spanish)

b. *Va donar consell {mèdic/ formal/ *interessant}*
goes.AUX.PST give advice medical formal interesting
'S/he gave a {medical/ formal/ interesting} advice' (Catalan)

Interestingly, the two kinds of adjectives (qualitative and relational) have been claimed to occupy different syntactic positions within the nominal domain, which are based on their restrictions; namely, a more internal position of the relational adjectives and a more external for the qualitative adjective (e.g. Fábregas, 2017, 77; see also Bonet and Solà, 1986, 313, for Catalan; and Bosque and Picallo, 1996, 379, for Spanish).

Partially following Oggiani's (2021; 2022) analysis of bare nouns in Spanish, where the different kinds of adjectives must be inserted at different levels within the noun phrase, depending on their closeness to the nominal, we suggest that bare nouns in *give*-LVCs can thus not project D, as in (26).

(26) dar consejo medico
      give advice medical
      'give (a) medical advice'

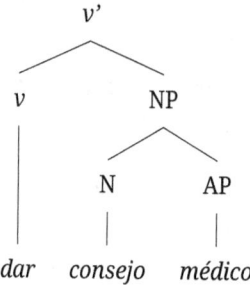

5.3 Type 3: An exceptional case of incorporation

There is an exceptional case of an LVC that does not fit into the previous types. It is the case of *dar vuelta* (lit. 'give turn') in Rioplatense Spanish[12] which can be built with a second direct object,[13] *la cabeza* 'the head', as in (27a), and can also be pronominalised with the accusative pronoun *la* (27b).

---

[12] Spanish spoken in el Río de la Plata (Argentina) has the tendency to select bare nouns in more contexts than other varieties of Spanish (Rinaldi, 2018; Oggiani, 2021, 2022).

[13] It is important to note that this is not a case of accusative doubling (typical from Rioplatense Spanish, as analyzed in Zdrojewski and Sánchez, 2014, 169, Di Tullio et al., 2019, 219) because it can also pronominalise a masculine antecedent with *lo*, as in (i), which refers to *el partido* 'the match'.

(i) Con uno menos, Estudiantes se lo   dio   vuelta a River.
     with one less, Estudiantes SE it.ACC gave.3SG turn to River
     'With one less, Estudiantes turned it over to River.'
     (https://www.ambito.com/deportes/river/con-uno-menos-estudiantes-se-lo-dio-vuelta-n5169973)

(27) a. *Para que un día un macho cualquiera te   diera vuelta la cabeza*
      for that a day a male   any   you.DAT give turn the head
      como una veleta.
      like a   weathercock
      'So that one day any man would turn your head around like a weathercock.' (Spanish, CORPES XXI, 2001)
   b. *te   la   diera vuelta como una veleta.*
      you.DAT it.ACC give turn like a   weathercock
      'would turn it around like a weathercock'

However, the noun *vuelta* cannot be pronominalized (28b) nor extracted in interrogatives (28c). This is proof that it is not a canonical argument of the LV (as pointed out by Galbarini, 2017, 14).

(28) a. *Juan dio vuelta la hoja* = *Juan giró   la hoja*
      Juan gave turn the page   Juan turned the page
      'Juan turned the page'
   b. **Juan la   dio la hoja*
      Juan it.ACC gave the page
      'Juan turned it, the page'
   c. **¿Qué dio Juan la hoja?*
      what gave Juan the page
      'What did Juan do the page?'

A third key aspect is adjacency, as there is no possibility of inserting any element between the LV *dar* and the noun *vuelta*, as in (29).

(29) *Dio {*ya/   *súbitamente} vuelta el partido*
     gave already suddenly   turn the match
     'S/he gave {already/ suddenly} a turn to the match'

According to Acedo Matellán and Pineda (2019, 206), in similar Basque instances which allow a second DO, as in (30), "a lexicalization process has taken place, so that the argument structure of the LVC includes a slot for a DO with a Theme-role". Structurally, there is no trace preventing the merger of a DO and the LVCs can take a DP as a complement which is assigned absolutive case (as pointed out in Martinez, 2015, 376–377).

(30) a. Ume-a-k   eskol-ak   huts   egin ditu.
       kid-DET.ABS-ERG class-ABS.PL failure do AUX.PRS.ERG.3SG.ABS.3PL
       'The kid missed the classes.'
   b. Gizon-a-k   berrion-a   hots   egin
      man-DET.ABS-ERG good_news-DET.ABS noise do
      du.
      AUX.PRS.ERG.3SG.ABS.3SG
      'The man spread the good news.'

These properties are aligned with a case-manipulating type of incorporation (Mithun, 1984, 857): the case left by the incorporated argument (the noun *vuelta*) is available for the other argument, i.e. the oblique argument, which is then promoted. For Mithun (1984, 856), the noun loses the syntactic status as an argument of the clause, when it is incorporated by the verb, which then leaves a case position vacated that can be occupied by the oblique argument.[14] Going back to the specific case of *dar vuelta*, in an early description of this construction, Masullo (1996, 194) suggests that the noun *vuelta* lacks reference due to low transitivity and, hence, allows for the second object to occupy its position. Also, Alonso Ramos (2004, 246–250) defends that there is no need for incorporation in such constructions because it is a ditransitive construction with two objects: one with a defective direct object (*vuelta*) and a full direct object (*hoja*). Although double object constructions are not typical of present-day Spanish, they were attested in Medieval periods of the Romance languages.[15] Their main particularity is that there is no univocal correspondence between the morphological case and the syntactic function.

Interestingly, Pineda (2014, 242) and Pineda (2015, 91–92) defends that some Catalan and Spanish ditransitive constructions should be analyzed as double object constructions. In her analysis, the object with accusative marking is a true IO. Following Pylkkänen (2008), she argues that the possibility that the IO presents accusative marking is explained by the fact that the low Applicative is not the regular Romance low Appl but rather the Anglo-Saxon applicative found in English double object constructions, which does not assign dative case and, hence, assigns the only available case (accusative) by default.

Besides the assignation of accusative case to the oblique object, the analysis of *dar vuelta* should account for the fact that the noun remains in situ (*vuelta*) and does not incorporate as an unergative verbs. At the same time, it should explain the fact

---

[14] As pointed out by an anonymous reviewer, this could potentially be analyzed as a case of pseudo-incorporation (Dayal, 2011; Espinal and McNally, 2011). We leave this for further research.
[15] Matute Martínez (2012, 960) studies these constructions in the history of Spanish and shows how the LVC followed by a direct object is not a productive structure after the 13th Century.

that there is no possibility to introduce an element between the LV and the noun, as previously seen in (29).

Within the extended projection framework (Grimshaw, 2005), the fact that the noun does not receive the accusative marking can be explained through the internal structure of the noun: *vuelta* does not project over n, and thus it cannot be case marked. The other object (oblique IO) has the accusative case available and can take it through the Applicative head proposed by Pineda (2015, 90).

Spanish is a language that a priori does not fall into the group of polysynthetic languages that undergo nominal incorporation (a la Mithun, 1984; Baker, 1988), which is a morphosyntactic process where a noun integrates in a verb or preposition which selects it, and it creates a complex predicate. In this case, the incorporated noun is highly defective and does not have number, case or definiteness marking, thus showing important differences with other more regular cases of incorporation. As Verdecchia (2021, 5) argues, the analysis of Spanish bare nominals cannot be done in terms of incorporation, since there is no strict adjacency between the verb and the noun (as would be the case in LVCs from Type 2). However, this is not the case for *dar vuelta* + DO and, hence, an incorporation analysis should be applied here to explain this unique LVC.

6 Conclusions

The present study reports the findings of a corpus-based study of adjectival modification in *give*-LVCs in two Germanic and two Romance languages. Our results have shown that the frequency of modification in LVCs is only higher than 50% in English, while results of modification in German, Catalan and Spanish LVCs are around a third of all instances. Such a contrastive approach to modification has proven that there are certain differences between language families, and even within the Germanic languages.

Taking the empirical results into account, which show certain restrictions and interactions, we have proposed a typology of LVCs which focuses on the possibilities of determination and modification of the nominal element. The data from Germanic and Romance languages presented in this study confirm that the presence (or absence) of the determiner is crucial for the degree of cohesion between the LV and the noun, which also affects modification.

First, there are LVCs with a determined noun that takes flexible modification (Type 1). The analysis for such constructions within a neo-constructionist approach to argument structure is that of a transitive creation verb, where the verb is followed by a DP that behaves like a canonical argument (Acedo Matellán, 2016; Myler,

2016). Second, there are LVCs with bare nominals (Type 2). The analysis proposed for this type is that they cannot project the DP layer, because they are not argumental. The inability of such noun phrases to behave like canonical arguments in LVCs explains why LVCs have traditionally been analyzed as complex predicates (Butt, 2010) or pseudo-incorporated nominals (Massam, 2001; Espinal and McNally, 2011). However, there is no need for such an analysis of LVCs, because there is no actual adjacency between the LV and the noun. Finally, there is an exceptional case of a LVC (*dar vuelta*) restricted to Rioplatense Spanish where there is an extra direct object and strict adjacency between the LV and the noun *vuelta*.

Therefore, the present proposal defends that all LVCs behave like regular verbnoun constructions (in line with Bruening, 2015), because the differences in the degree of cohesion between the LV and the noun are in fact due to the nature of the nominal rather than the LV itself.

Finally, our findings raise relevant issues in relation to the syntactic analysis of nouns in general and in LVCs in particular. Specifically, the general tendency of English LVCs is to have modified nominals, which was also found in previous studies (i.e. Bonial and Pollard, 2020). This has previously been used to argue that the weight of the nominal is the main reason for the coexistence of LVCs and the corresponding synthetic verb. However, our corpus findings have proven that English LVCs considerably diverge from the behavior of LVCs in the other three languages: German, Catalan, and Spanish, and thus cast doubt on this largely accepted hypothesis. Thus, the coexistence of LVCs and their synthetic counterparts, more specifically their semantic correspondence, should be the focus of future investigation. This further shows that the literature on LVCs would benefit from more contrastive-focused studies which pay attention to the morphosyntactic properties of LVCs across languages.

Bibliography

Acedo Matellán, Víctor. 2010. *Argument structure and the syntax-morphology interface. A case study in Latin and other languages*. Doctoral dissertation: Universitat de Barcelona. http://hdl.handle.net/10803/21788, last access: 13/01/2025.

Acedo Matellán, Víctor. 2016. *The Morphosyntax of Transitions*. Oxford: Oxford University Press. https://doi.org/10.1093/acprof:oso/9780198733287.001.0001.

Acedo Matellán, Víctor and Anna Pineda. 2019. Light verb constructions in Basque and Romance. In Ane Berro, Beatriz Fernández and Jon Ortiz de Urbina (eds.), *Aligning grammars: Basque and Romance*, 176–220. Leiden: Brill. https://doi.org/10.1163/9789004395398_007.

Alonso Ramos, Margarita. 2004. *Las construcciones con verbos de apoyo*. Madrid: Visor Libros.

Alvarez-Morera, Georgina. 2023. *The nominal in light verb constructions: a corpus-based study in present-day English, German, Catalan and Spanish*. Doctoral dissertation: Universitat Rovira i Virgili, Tarragona.

Baker, Mark. 1988. Theta theory and the syntax of applicatives in Chichewa. *Natural Language & Linguistic Theory* 6. 353–389.

Bonet, Sebastià and Joan Solà. 1986. *Sintaxi generativa catalana*. Barcelona: Enciclopèdia Catalana.

Bonial, Claire and Kimberly A. Pollard. 2020. Choosing an event description: What a PropBank study reveals about the contrast between light verb constructions and counterpart synthetic verbs. *Journal of Linguistics* 56(3). 577–600. https://doi.org/10.1017/S0022226720000109.

Bosque, Ignacio and Carme Picallo. 1996. Postnominal adjectives in Spanish DPs. *Journal of linguistics* 32(2). 349–385. https://doi.org/10.1017/S0022226700015929.

Bratánková, Leontýna. 2013. Le costruzioni italiane a verbo supporto. Un'analisi condotta sul corpus parallelo ceco-italiano. *Acta Universitatis Carolinae Philologica* 2. 55–70.

Brezina, Vaclav. 2018. Lancaster Stats Tools online. http://corpora.lancs.ac.uk/stats, last access: 13/01/2025.

Bruening, Benjamin. 2015. Light verbs are just regular verbs. *U. Penn Working Papers in Linguistics* 21(1). 1–10.

Bruker, Astrid. 2011. *Entwurf und Realisierung von Lexikon-Einträgen für Funktionsverbgefüge der deutschen Sprache*. Hamburg: Diplomica.

Butt, Miriam. 2010. The light verb jungle: Still hacking away. In Mengistu Amberber, Bret Baker and Mark Harvey (eds.), *Complex Predicates in Cross-Linguistic Perspective*, 48–78. Cambridge: Cambridge University Press.

Carnie, Andrew. 2002. *Syntax: A Generative Introduction*. Oxford: Blackwell.

Cattell, Ray. 1984. *Composite Predicates in English*. Sydney: Academic Press.

Cyrino, Sonia and M. Teresa Espinal. 2019. On the Syntax of Number in Romance. *Studia Linguistica* 74. 165–203. https://doi.org/10.1111/stul.12123.

Dayal, Veneeta. 2011. Hindi pseudo-incorporation. *Natural Language & Linguistic Theory* 29(1). 123–167. https://doi.org/10.1007/s11049-011-9118-4.

De Miguel, Elena. 2011. En qué consiste ser verbo de apoyo. In M. Victoria Escandell Vidal, Manuel Leonetti and Cristina Sánchez López (eds.), *60 problemas de gramática dedicados a Ignacio Bosque*, 139–147. Madrid: Akal.

Di Tullio, Ángela, Andrés Saab and Pablo Zdrojewski. 2019. Clitic Doubling in a Doubling World: The Case of Argentinean Spanish Reconsidered. In Ángel Gallego (ed.), *The Syntactic Variation of Spanish Dialects*, 215–244. Oxford: Oxford University Press. https://doi.org/10.1093/oso/9780190634797.003.0008.

Egbert, Jesse, Tove Larsson and Douglas Biber. 2020. *Doing linguistics with a corpus: Methodological considerations for the everyday user*. Cambridge: Cambridge University Press. https://doi.org/10.1017/9781108888790.

Elenbaas, Marion. 2013. The synchronic and diachronic status of English light verbs. *Linguistic Variation* 13(1). 48–80. https://doi.org/10.1075/lv.13.1.02ele.

Espinal, M. Teresa and Louise McNally. 2011. Bare nominals and incorporating verbs in Catalan and Spanish. *Journal of Linguistics* 47. 87–128. https://doi.org/10.1017/S0022226710000228.

Fleischhauer, Jens. 2021. Light Verb Constructions and Their Families – A Corpus Study on German 'stehen unter'-LVCs. In "*Proceedings of the 17th Workshop on Multiword Expressions (MWE 2021)*, 63–69. Online: Association for Computational Linguistics. 10.18653/v1/2021.mwe-1.8. https://aclanthology.org/2021.mwe-1.8, last access: 13/01/2025.

Fleischhauer, Jens. 2022. *stehen unter*-Funktionsverbgefüge und ihre Familien. *Zeitschrift für germanistische Linguistik* 50(2). 247–288. https://doi.org/10.1515/zgl-2022-2055.

Fábregas, Antonio. 2017. The syntax and semantics of nominal modifiers in Spanish: interpretations, types and ordering facts. *Borealis. An International Journal of Hispanic Linguistics* 6(2). 1–102. https://doi.org/10.7557/1.6.2.4191.

Galbarini, Paola. 2017. Diferentes usos del verbo dar: análisis desde un modelo (neo)construccionista. *Revista Pilquen* 20(4). 1–17.

Ginebra, Jordi. 2003. Fraseologia, concurrències lèxiques i llengua estàndard. In Miquel Àngel Pradilla (ed.), *Identitat lingüística i estandardització*, 7–55. Valls Tarragona: Cossetània Edicions.

Ginebra, Jordi and Pere Navarro. 2015. Concurrències lèxiques en català i en espanyol: uns quants contrastos. In Àlex Martín Escribà, Adolf Piquer Vidal and Fernando Sánchez Miret (eds.), *Actes del Setzè Col·loqui Internacional de Llengua i Literatura Catalanes. Universitat de Salamanca, 1-6 de juliol de 2012. Vol. II*, 217–228. Montserrat: Publicacions de l'Abadia de Montserrat.

Gries, Stefan. 2023. Statistical methods in corpus linguistics. In Foluke O. Unuabonah, Rotimi O. Oladipupo and Florence Daniel (eds.), *Readings in corpus linguistics: A teaching and research guide for scholars in Nigeria and beyond*, 78–114. Ibadan: Kraft Books Ltd.

Grimshaw, Jane. 1990. *Argument Structure*. Cambridge, MA: The MIT Press.

Grimshaw, Jane. 2005. *Words and Structure*. Stanford: CSLI Publications.

Grimshaw, Jane and Armin Mester. 1988. Light verbs and θ-marking. *Linguistic Inquiry* 19. 205–232.

Hale, Ken and Samuel Keyser. 2002. *Prolegomenon to a theory of argument structure*. Cambridge, MA: The MIT Press.

Hale, Ken and Samuel Keyser. 53–109. On argument structure and the lexical expression of syntactic relations. In Ken Hale and Samuel Keyser (eds.), *The View from Building 20: Essays in Linguistics in Honor of Sylvain Bromberger*, Cambridge, MA: The MIT Press.

Huddleston, Rodney and Geoffrey K. Pullum. 2002. *The Cambridge grammar of the English language*. Cambridge: Cambridge University Press.

Jespersen, Otto. 1942. *A Modern English Grammar on Historical Principles, Part VI, Morphology*. Copenhagen: Ejnar Munksgaard.

Leech, Geoffrey, Marianne Hundt, Christian Mair and Nicholas Smith. 2009. *Change in Contemporary English. A Grammatical Study*. Cambridge: Cambridge University Press. https://doi.org/10.1017/CBO9780511642210.

Levin, Magnus and Jenny Ström Herold. 2015. Give and Take: A contrastive study of light verb constructions in English, German and Swedish. In Signe Oksefjell Ebeling and Hilde Hasselgård (eds.), *Cross-Linguistic Perspectives on Verb Constructions*, 144–168. Newcastle upon Tyne: Cambridge Scholars Publishing.

Longobardi, Giuseppe. 2005. Toward a Unified Grammar of Reference. *Zeitschrift für Sprachwissenschaft* 24. 5–44. https://doi.org/10.1515/zfsw.2005.24.1.5.

Martinez, Arantzazu. 2015. *[Izen + egin]a aditz-lokuzioak: inkorporazio mailak*. Doctoral dissertation: Deustuko Uniberstitatea, Bilbao.

Massam, Diane. 2001. Pseudo noun incorporation in Niuean. *Natural Language & Linguistic Theory* 19. 153–197. https://doi.org/10.1023/A:1006465130442.

Masullo, Pascual José. 1996. Los sintagmas nominales sin determinante: una propuesta incorporacionista. In Ignacio Bosque (ed.), *El sustantivo sin determinación: la ausencia del determinante en la lengua espanola*, 169–200. Madrid: Visor.

Matute Martínez, Cristina. 2012. Aspectos de variación de las locuciones verbales con sustantivos escuetos en la historia del españo. In E. Montero Cartelle and C. Manzano Rovira (eds.), *Actas del*

VIII Congreso Internacional de Historia de la Lengua Española, I, Santiago de Compostela, 959–970. Santiago de Compostela: Meubook.

Mendívil, José-Luis. 1999. *Las palabras disgregadas: sintaxis de las expresiones idiomáticas y los predicados complejos*. Zaragoza: Prensas Universitarias de Zaragoza.

Mithun, Marianne. 1984. The evolution of noun incorporation. *Language* 60(4). 847–894. 10.1353/lan.1984.0038.

Myler, Neil. 2016. *Building and interpreting possession sentences*. Cambridge, MA: The MIT Press. https://doi.org/10.7551/mitpress/9780262034913.001.0001.

Oggiani, Carolina. 2021. "escribir artículo": nombres singulares escuetos en posición de objeto en español rioplatense. *Borealis. An International Journal of Hispanic Linguistics* 10(2). 313–333. https://doi.org/10.7557/1.10.2.5782.

Oggiani, Carolina. 2022. Los escuetos definidos débiles en español rioplatense / Bare weak definites in Rioplatense Spanish. *Revista de Estudos da Linguagem* 30(1). 239–269. https://doi.org/10.17851/2237-2083.30.1.239-268.

Piera, Carlos and Soledad Varela. 1999. Relaciones entre morfología y sintaxis. In Violeta Demonte and Ignacio Bosque (eds.), *Gramática descriptiva de la lengua española, vol. 3*, 4367–4422. Madrid: Espasa Calpe.

Pineda, Anna. 2014. *Les fronteres de la (in) transitivitat. Estudi dels aplicatius en llengües romàniques i basc*. Doctoral dissertation: Universitat Autònoma de Barcelona. http://hdl.handle.net/10803/283926, last access: 13/01/2025.

Pineda, Anna. 2015. Del Datiu a l'acusatiu. Un canvi sintàctic en procés en llengües romàniques i basc. *Llengua i literatura* 25. 73–98. Url=https://raco.cat/index.php/LlenguaLiteratura/article/view/298801, last access: 13/01/2025.

Pylkkänen, Liina. 2008. *Introducing arguments*. Cambridge, MA: The MIT Press.

Rácz, Anita, István Nagy and Veronika Vincze. 2014. 4FX: Light verb constructions in a multilingual parallel corpus. In *Proceedings of the Ninth International Conference on Language Resources and Evaluation (LREC'14)*, 710–715. Reykjavik: European Language Association (ELRA).

Ramchand, Gillian. 2014. On structural meaning vs conceptual meaning in verb semantics. *Linguistic Analysis* 39(1-2). 207–243.

Rinaldi, Melisa Gisele. 2018. *Bare Singulars and So-Called Bare Singulars*. Doctoral dissertation: Queen Mary University, London. https://qmro.qmul.ac.uk/xmlui/handle/123456789/56405, last access: 13/01/2025.

Sanromán Vilas, Begoña. 2009. Diferencias semánticas entre construcciones con verbo de apoyo y sus correlatos verbales simples. *ELUA: Estudios Lingüísticos de la Universidad de Alicante* 23. 289–314.

Storrer, Angelika. 2007. Corpus-based investigations on German support verb constructions. In Christiane Fellbaum (ed.), *Collocations and Idioms: Linguistic, lexicographic, and computational aspects*, 164–187. London: Continuum Press.

Sánchez Rufat, Anna. 2016. El uso transitivo y ditransitivo de dar en un corpus escrito contrastivo. *Revista Fuentes* 18(2). 117–133. https://revistascientificas.us.es/index.php/fuentes/article/view/2917, last access: 13/01/2025.

Van Valin, Robert D. 2001. *An introduction to syntax*. Cambridge: Cambridge University Press.

Verdecchia, Matías. 2021. Nombres escuetos en contextos no verídicos. *Verba: Anuario Galego de Filoloxía* 48. 2–24. https://doi.org/10.15304/verba.48.6109.

Wierzbicka, Anna. 1982. Why can you have a drink when you can't *have an eat? *Language* 58(4). 753–799. https://doi.org/10.2307/413956.

Wiskandt, Niklas. this volume. Light verb constructions with experiencer objects in Germanic and Romance – A corpus-based contrastive perspective on 'make' and 'give' patterns. In Anna Riccio and Jens Fleischhauer (eds.), *Light verbs: Synchronic and diachronic studies*, 97–122. Düsseldorf: Düsseldorf University Press.

Zdrojewski, Pablo and Liliana Sánchez. 2014. Variation in accusative clitic doubling across three Spanish dialects. *Lingua* 151. 162–176. 10.1016/j.lingua.2014.08.003.

Niklas Wiskandt
Light verb constructions with experiencer objects in Germanic and Romance

A corpus-based contrastive perspective on 'make' and 'give' patterns

1 Introduction

This paper investigates light verb constructions (LVCs) with experiencer objects in Germanic and Romance languages from a contrastive perspective. They have been attested in several languages of these families, e.g. German (1) and Portuguese (2).

(1) Die Band **versetzt** das Publikum **in** Begeisterung.
    DEF band transfer.3SG DEF audience into rapture
    'The band puts the audience in raptures.' [German]

(2) A explosão **deu** medo a todas as crianças.
    DEF explosion give.PST.3SG fear to all DEF children
    'The explosion scared all the children.' [Brazilian Portuguese]

Object-experiencer verbs (e.g. 'frighten', 'annoy', 'delight') in Germanic and Romance languages have been a subject of vigorous debates for decades. Complex experiencer predicates, such as the LVCs in (1) and (2), add to the complexity of this domain but have received only little attention. Winhart (2005, 161–166) first describes LVCs with emotion nouns in German, and Wiskandt and Turus (2023, 2025) provide systematic studies for selected patterns; Viñas-de-Puig (2014) studies psych LVCs in Spanish and Catalan; Staudinger (2018) analyzes LVCs of 'make/give fear' patterns in Spanish and French; Pisciotta and Masini (this volume) discuss several psych LVC patterns in Italian. Broader cross-linguistic studies have not been conducted so far. In light of the coexistence and competition between object-experiencer verbs, their different voice constructions, and complex predicate structures, taking the latter into account is imperative in order to thoroughly describe the morphosyntactic variation of experiencer verbs and to understand which construction is used under which conditions. Furthermore, a cross-linguistic investigation of constructions like (1) and (2) can contribute to our knowledge on LVCs in general: The use of different light verbs in constructions that at first glance seem to fulfill the same function, and

---

Niklas Wiskandt, Heinrich-Heine-Universität Düsseldorf, Germany

cross-linguistic lexical restrictions on light verbs in object-experiencer patterns are two aspects that might provide insights into fundamental properties of light verbs.

LVCs with experiencer objects employ several different light verbs. At first sight, however, the different light verbs seem to fulfill the same function. The non-verbal element of the LVC can be a PP (1) or a NP (2). In PPs, different prepositions are attested, e.g. *zu* 'to' vs. *in* 'into' in German. This variation gives rise to several different patterns of LVCs with experiencer objects in the target languages. As becomes apparent from the examples above, Germanic and Romance languages differ in the light verbs and prepositions they use, but systematic parallels, e.g. in the use of transfer verbs, can be identified as well. As a case study within this domain, this paper investigates the contrast between two patterns attested across both language families, involving 'make' and 'give' light verbs, as described, for example, by Staudinger (2018). Example (3a) shows the 'make' pattern in Portuguese, and example (3b) shows the 'give' pattern in Spanish.

(3)   a.   e   poderá **fazer inveja** a todos os seus amigos.
              and can.FUT make envy to all DEF POSS friends
              'and you will be able to make all your friends envious'
                                               [Portuguese; ptTenTen20 32788506]

       b.   Qué **envidia** me   dais
              what envy   1SG.OBJ give.2PL
              'How envious you make me!'   [Spanish; esTenTen18 532736]

The paper is structured as follows: The research background and necessary definitions are exposited in section 2. Section 3 explains the methodology of the study. The results of the corpus study are presented in Section 4, followed by several dimensions of cross-linguistic analysis. A discussion of the results of the present study against the context of previous research is in place in Section 5, before Section 6 concludes the paper.

2 Research background

This section introduces the grammatical domains relevant for this paper, i.e., experiencer predicates and light verb constructions, provides working definitions for the study, and summarizes previous research on the phenomenon under investigation.

2.1 Experiencer verbs and experiencer predicates

Experiencer verbs such as English *frighten*, German *ärgern* 'annoy', Portuguese *preocupar* 'worry' or Catalan *divertir* 'amuse' are transitive verbs that take an experiencer[1] as one of their arguments. They fall into at least two subclasses: Subject-experiencer verbs (short: SE verbs) realize the experiencer argument as their subject, while object-experiencer verbs (OE verbs), such as the exemplary verbs listed above, realize the experiencer argument as their object. For the present study, the latter subclass is of greater importance. The second argument of experiencer verbs has been labeled a stimulus (e.g. Verhoeven, 2010), theme (e.g. Belletti and Rizzi, 1988), causer (e.g. Pesetsky, 1995), or correlate (e.g. Kailuweit, 2005) in previous research, depending on different theoretical assumptions. In this paper, I do not make any claim on the nature of that argument, and thus I use the descriptive, theory-neutral term 'non-experiencer argument'. The category of experiencer verbs has been extensively discussed in recent decades since the seminal work of Belletti and Rizzi (1988), especially with respect to the object-experiencer subtype. Germanic and Romance OE verbs have recently been investigated with respect to aspectual properties (e.g. Hirsch, 2018; Melis, 2019; Fritz-Huechante et al., 2020; Fábregas and Marín, 2020; Cançado et al., 2024), agentivity (e.g. Verhoeven, 2017; Ganeshan, 2019; Fritz-Huechante et al., 2020), word order (e.g. Temme and Verhoeven, 2016; Fábregas et al., 2017), case marking (e.g. Miglio et al., 2013; Ganeshan, 2019; Royo, 2020), and valency alternations (e.g. Pijpops and Speelman, 2017; Rott et al., 2020, 2024; Wiskandt, 2021; Cançado et al., 2024).

In contrast to OE verbs, complex predicates with experiencer objects have received much less attention despite being very productive in several languages. In a corpus study on European languages, Becker and Guzmán Naranjo (2020) show that not only experiencer verbs, but a large variety of simplex and complex predicate structures are used to express emotion meanings. Within the spectrum of complex predicates, numerous languages feature LVCs with experiencer arguments. Similarly to experiencer verbs, LVCs with experiencer objects fall into two subclasses: Subject-experiencer LVCs (SE-LVCs) realize the experiencer as their subject, whereas object-experiencer LVCs (OE-LVCs) realize the experiencer as an

---

[1] The terms 'experiencer' and 'experiencer predicate' are used ambiguously in the literature: 'Experiencer' is used either as a generic label for all argument referents experiencing mental and cognitive states and processes, or as a more specific label only for those argument referents that experience an emotion (a subtype sometimes referred to as 'emoter'). This paper discusses the latter, more specific category: An experiencer argument as understood in this paper refers to a sentient being that feels an emotion denoted by the predicate of which the experiencer is an argument.

object. The latter subclass constitutes the object of research in this paper. The next subsection 2.2 introduces this domain in detail.

A description of the use of OE-LVCs in Germanic and Romance languages is further complicated by the circumstance that many LVCs like in (4a) are in competition with simplex object-experiencer verbs (4b) and with predicates with a 'cause' verb like (4c), for which a classification as either LVCs or a separate type of complex predicates is debatable.

(4) a. *O vizinho (lhe) **deu** horror à menina.*
       DEF neighbor 3SG.DAT give.PST.3SG horror to:DEF girl
       'The neighbor horrified the girl.'
    b. *O vizinho **horrorizou** a menina.*
       DEF neighbor horrify.PST.3SG DEF girl
       'The neighbor horrified the girl.'
    c. *O vizinho (lhe) **causou** horror à menina.*
       DEF neighbor 3SG.DAT cause.PST.3SG horror to:DEF girl
       'The neighbor horrified the girl.'

[Brazilian Portuguese]

2.2 Light verb constructions with experiencer objects

Before we turn to the definition of and previous research on LVCs with experiencer objects, I briefly describe my understanding of LVCs in general.

Light verb constructions (LVCs) are difficult to define, since their structure and properties vary significantly across languages; furthermore, the term has been used to refer to a large range of different constructions even within Germanic and Romance languages. For the purpose of this study, I adopt the definition of LVCs used in Wiskandt and Turus (2025), which is based on those presented in Fleischhauer and Turus (2021, 74) and Fleischhauer and Hartmann (2023, 117):

> A light verb construction (LVC) [...] consists of a semantically light verbal head and a non-verbal phrasal element, for instance, a nominal phrase [...] or a prepositional phrase [...], which together form a single complex predicate. (Wiskandt and Turus, 2025, 3)

Consequentially, I define light verb constructions with experiencer objects (object-experiencer light verb constructions, OE-LVCs) as follows: An OE-LVC is a LVC according to the general definition provided above that has two arguments, of which one, realized as an object, can be attributed the semantic role of an experiencer. The experiencer object can be either a direct object (DO) or an indirect object (IO). In LVCs with a NP as its non-verbal element, the second participant regularly bears the grammatical relation of an indirect object, because the grammatical relation of direct object is already occupied by the NP.

At this point, I do not engage any further in debates about how exactly LVCs should be defined; I adopt these definitions because they are adequate for the object languages of this study (i.e., Germanic and Romance languages). I do not claim any universal applicability, although they can certainly be applied to languages of many other families with similar grammatical prerequisites as well.

Broad cross-linguistic or cross-family studies on LVCs with experiencer objects are not available so far. But, as the following brief literature summary shows, a few patterns of such LVCs in Germanic and Romance languages have already been described in previous research.

Within a comprehensive analysis of the behavior of LVCs in German, Winhart (2005, 161–165) describes several constructions that are OE-LVCs as defined above[2]. She characterizes them as a subtype of her 'Aktiv-Lesart' ('active reading') category of German LVCs. The OE-LVC patterns covered by Winhart's (2005) description are: *zu N bringen* + DO ('bring so. to N'), *in N bringen* + DO ('bring so. into N'), and *in N versetzen* + DO ('transfer so. into N').[3] While Winhart (2005) also treats patterns with the light verb *geben* 'give', none of those constitute OE-LVCs.

Wiskandt and Turus (2023) provide a more detailed and contrastive analysis of the three OE-LVC patterns mentioned in Winhart (2005), showing that they differ in semantic details and with respect to the emotion nouns can take as their non-verbal element. Wiskandt and Turus (2025) conducted a corpus study on the *in N versetzen* + DO pattern and its relation to lexically corresponding object-experiencer verbs. They argue that, when both a simplex verb and the corresponding LVC are available, they form an alternation pair, and choosing the LVC is a means of marking causative semantics.

Turning to Romance languages, Chishman and Abreu (2014) study the syntax and semantics of LVCs in Brazilian Portuguese with the light verbs *dar* 'give' and *fazer* 'make' and bare nouns as non-verbal elements, which they state are very productive. In their data, there are OE-LVCs of the pattern *dar N* + IO, but none with the light verb *fazer*.

Viñas-de-Puig (2014) studies psych predicates in the form of LVCs in Spanish and Catalan from a generative perspective, focusing on event structure. He treats

---

2 Winhart's (2005) understanding of the term 'experiencer' is much broader than than the one assumed in this paper. Thus, Winhart (2005) describes a wide range of LVCs that, in her formulation, involve an experiencer argument; here, I only refer to those included in the definition of this paper.
3 Here and henceforth, *N* is used as a placeholder for a noun denoting an emotion. The complement '+ DO' signals that the patterns take their experiencer arguments as direct objects. Likewise, '+ IO' signals that a pattern takes an indirect object.

patterns with both experiencer subjects and experiencer objects, among them *dar N* + IO 'give N' in Spanish, and *fer N* + IO 'make N' in Catalan.

Staudinger (2018, 240) analyzes 'make/give fear' LVCs in French and Spanish as "complex lexicalized three-place predicates that are syntactically intransitive". Indeed, from a syntactic perspective, the experiencer argument is realized as an indirect object. Following the usual assumption that syntactic transitivity requires a direct object, this fact makes them syntactically intransitive. Semantically, however, these predicates are clearly transitive, since they denote events with two participants in which one participant influences the other.

On the side of semantics, Staudinger (2013, 2018) also highlights that the patterns do not fit any established aktionsart class.

Acedo-Matellán and Pineda (2019) contrast Basque (isolate) LVCs with those in Romance languages, particularly Spanish and French. They include several examples of OE-LVCs, such as Spanish *dar miedo/vergüenza* lit. 'give fear/shame', and French *faire peur/honte* lit. 'make fear/shame'. Interestingly, they report that the patterns 'make N' and 'give N' are also used with emotion nouns and experiencer objects in Basque, a language not genetically related to Germanic and Romance, but in close contact with Spanish and French (Acedo-Matellán and Pineda, 2019, 6–9).

Pompei and Piunno (2023a) provide a comprehensive study of LVCs in Romance languages, particularly treating Italian, French, Spanish, Portuguese, and Romanian. They assume that in Romance languages, "selection of LVs in LVCs, far from being arbitrary, is often sensitive to the semantics of the predicative noun they combine with" (Pompei and Piunno, 2023a, 104), and that "both LVs and predicative nouns may contribute to the selection of the arguments of LVCs" (Pompei and Piunno, 2023a, 106). These assumptions are essential for an analysis of LVCs with experiencer objects. Indeed, in the case of the latter, the selection of an experiencer as the second argument of the predicate is not made by the light verb or by the non-verbal element alone, but by their interaction. In a central part of their article, Pompei and Piunno (2023a, 111–116) analyze Romance LVCs in which the non-verbal element is a noun denoting a psychological state. They divide the class of nouns that denote psychological states into the subclasses 'emotional states or feelings', 'sensations', and 'mental states and aptitudes'. Their categorization of nouns into these subclasses is partly questionable, e.g. the classification of Italian *fastidio* 'annoyance' not as an emotional state or feeling but as a sensation, but generally the 'emotional states or feelings' subclass covers the nouns that occur in LVCs with experiencer objects as understood in this paper. Pompei and Piunno mainly discuss LVCs with experiencer subjects, which encompass 'have' light verbs, but also LVCs with experiencer objects, employing 'give' and 'make' light verbs.

The 'make N' and 'give N' patterns are discussed for Italian, French, Spanish, Portuguese, and Romanian, with reference to a small number of emotion nouns.

They argue that in LVCs of these patterns, the light verb contributes to the semantics of the construction by acting as a causative marker (Pompei and Piunno, 2023a, 113). Furthermore, based on Italian data, they point out an important difference between the two light verbs that possible results in a semantic difference between the resulting LVC patterns (Pompei and Piunno, 2023a, 114–115): They state that 'make' "marks the 'production' of the state in which the Experiencer enters" by the subject of the LVC, and that the resulting emotional state is directly tied to that subject, which is the non-experiencer argument of the predicate. In the absence of that argument, "the state does not exist" (Pompei and Piunno, 2023a, 134). In contrast to that, they argue that the emotion nouns in 'give' LVCs, by contrast, "denote emotional states which may exist regardless of the presence of a Stimulus", that is, emotional states not directly caused (though possibly indirectly triggered) by the actual presence of the referent of the non-experiencer argument in a given situation. However, both patterns are assumed to have a causative meaning and can be employed in "weaker or stronger causative uses" (Pompei and Piunno, 2023a, 137), i.e. they are semantically variable with respect to their degree of causativity. Furthermore, some language-specific mechanisms seem to influence the choice of 'make' vs. 'give' in Romance languages, which have not yet been decoded.

Most recently, Pisciotta and Masini (this volume) include 'make N' and 'give N' as OE-LVC ("causative" in their terms) patterns in their analysis of Italian psych LVCs and corresponding synthetic verbs. Their study also considers another OE-LVC pattern, 'put N', as well as several SE-LVC patterns (cf. e.g. Pisciotta and Masini, this volume, 137). Alvarez-Morera et al. (this volume) investigate the general 'give N' LVC pattern and its modification behavior in a sample covering Romance and Germanic (English, German, Spanish, and Catalan), but their data sample does not include constructions that qualify as OE-LVCs as per the definition assumed in this paper.

The state of research as summarized above provides a solid background, but leaves many open issues: It would be interesting to see whether the general preferences for different light verbs that languages have been attributed in the literature are visible in empirical data, e.g. in corpora.

More empirical data are also needed to support or falsify the assumption (e.g. in Pompei and Piunno, 2023a) that the selection of light verbs and patterns is not arbitrary: Can a distinction in meaning between different light verbs be determined at least on the level of one language, or even cross-linguistically? Are there restrictions with respect to what type of noun can appear in which LVC pattern, and if there are such restrictions, are they language-specific, language family-specific, or language-independent?

For such restrictions, it would be desirable to determine the lexical properties of the nouns and light verbs that are responsible for them. Finally, the role that competition between simplex verbs, LVCs, and other complex predicates plays in the domain of experiencer predicates has occasionally been addressed in the literature, but apart from one study on another OE-LVC pattern in German and its alternation with simplex verbs (Wiskandt and Turus, 2025, see above), and the study of Pisciotta and Masini (this volume) on Italian, there are no detailed accounts available for it.

This paper addresses the research gaps mentioned above by conducting a detailed cross-linguistic corpus study on OE-LVCs of the 'make N' and 'give N' patterns. Its focus is descriptive. Before any kind of causal or theoretical explanation for the behavior of those OE-LVCs is possible, it is necessary to analyze which pattern is used in which language, which emotion nouns can form their non-verbal elements, and whether any regularities can be determined in these dimensions of variation.

3 Methodology

Emanating from the descriptions in the literature and the gaps in the state of research as summarized in the previous section, I conducted a parallel corpus study for a sample of six languages: German, English, Danish (Germanic), Portuguese, Spanish, and Catalan (Romance).

Of the numerous patterns used to build LVCs with experiencer objects in those languages, this study focuses on two patterns that the literature, as referenced in the previous section, has shown to be particularly frequent cross-linguistically: 'make N + IO' and 'give N + IO'. Restricting the scope to one pair of patterns is necessary to make an in-depth cross-linguistic study feasible. Table 1 shows the 'make' and 'give' light verbs of the six sampled languages, as well as the LVC patterns based on them. In each pattern, *N* is a placeholder for the emotion noun that functions as the non-verbal element of the LVC.

Testing the use of these patterns in corpus data requires checking their occurrence with a sample of nouns. I compiled a set of 25 emotion nouns per language. In each language, the noun sample should cover a broad sample of emotion qualities

Tab. 1: Sample of languages and LVC patterns.

Language	MAKE LV	MAKE N + IO	GIVE LV	GIVE N + IO
German	*machen*	*jemandem N machen*	*geben*	*jemandem N geben*
English	*make*	*make someone N*	*give*	*give someone N*
Danish	*gøre*	*gøre nogen N*	*give*	*give nogen N*
Portuguese	*fazer*	*fazer N a alguém*	*dar*	*dar N a alguém*
Spanish	*hacer*	*hacer N a alguien*	*dar*	*dar N a alguien*
Catalan	*fer*	*fer N a algú*	*donar*	*donar N a algú*

and intensities, in order to achieve the highest possible representativeness. Where possible, equivalent nouns were chosen for as many languages of the sample as possible. However, if in a language the noun that is the most equivalent to, or a cognate of, the nouns in the other languages was considered antiquated, very style-specific, or found to be very infrequent in the corpus, another noun, representing a similar emotion nuance, was chosen instead.

All nouns were checked against the requirement that statements of the type 'Person X feels N', where 'N' represents the noun in question, must be felicitous. The noun samples for all languages are listed in Table 2.

Tab. 2: Noun sample for the corpus study.

German	English	Danish	Portuguese	Spanish	Catalan
Angst	fear	angst	medo	miedo	por
Panik	panic	panik	pânico	pánico	pànic
Sorge	worry	bekymring	preocupação	preocupación	preocupació
Verzweiflung	despair	fortvivlelse	desespero	desespero	desesperació
Entsetzen	horror	forfærdelse	horror	horror	horror
Bestürzung	dismay	bestyrtelse	consternação	consternación	consternació
Traurigkeit	sadness	sørgmodighed	tristeza	tristeza	tristesa
Ärger	anger	ærgrelse	irritação	enojo	enuig
Wut	rage	vrede	raiva	rabia	ràbia
Langeweile	boredom	kedsomhed	tédio	aburrimiento	avorriment
Verunsicherung	unsettledness	usikkerhed	insegurança	inseguridad	incertesa
Verwirrung	confusion	forvirring	confusão	confusión	confusió
Scham	embarrassment	skam	vergonha	vergüenza	vergonya
Reue	regret	anger	arrependimento	arrepentimiento	remordiment
Neid	envy	misundelse	inveja	envidia	enveja
Überraschung	surprise	overraskelse	surpresa	sorpresa	sorpresa
Aufregung	excitement	ophidselse	excitação	excitación	emoció
Interesse	interest	interesse	interesse	interés	interès
Erleichterung	relief	lettelse	alívio	alivio	alleujament
Freude	pleasure	glæde	prazer	placer	plaer
Fröhlichkeit	joy	munterhed	alegria	alegría	alegria
Begeisterung	enthusiasm	begejstring	entusiasmo	entusiasmo	entusiasme
Spaß	fun	sjov	diversão	diversión	diversió
Mut	courage	mod	coragem	coraje	coratge
Stolz	pride	stolthed	orgulho	orgullo	orgull

On the level of samples, the noun samples of each language as a whole are comparable, but full comparability on the level of individual nouns is not possible. While there are certainly some similarities in the lexification of emotions in the languages under investigation, there are too many disparities in the meaning of – even cognate – emotion nouns across even closely related languages, and different patterns of colexification of emotion nuances. Limited comparability of individual nouns is an inevitable consequence, but it does not pose a serious problem for this study, since the aim of finding equivalent nouns across languages is essentially a vehicle for ensuring that the noun samples as a whole are equally diverse and comparable.

In the selection of corpora for the study, several criteria were taken into account. For the purpose of the present study, corpora need to feature part-of-speech tagging and lemmatization, but do not need fine-grained grammatical or semantic annotation. The corpora have to be large, and should not only contain formal data, so that LVCs with a low token frequency or predominantly colloquial use can be covered. Since the perspective of the study is synchronic, reasonably recent data are preferred. Furthermore, in order to avoid bias in cross-linguistic comparison, different corpora for the six languages of the sample need to be comparable in age, genre, and composition. To this end, I used corpora from the TenTen corpus family (Jakubíček et al., 2013). TenTen corpora are automatically compiled corpora consisting of web texts from a variety of genres. The compilation follows a consistent set of criteria across languages, which makes the resulting corpora reasonably comparable. For each language, I used the most recent TenTen version available and accessed them through the interface of Sktech Engine (see Kilgarriff et al., 2004, 2014). The corpora used in the study are listed in Table 3.

Tab. 3: Selection of corpora.

Language	Corpus	Year of Compilation	Size (words)
German	deTenTen20	2020	17.5 bn
English	enTenTen21	2021	52 bn
Danish	daTenTen20	2020	3.4 bn
Portuguese	ptTenTen20	2020	12.5 bn
Spanish	esTenTen18	2018	16.9 bn
Catalan	caTenTen14	2014	183.6 mn

The CQL query strings for the corpus study are based on a consistent pattern that searches for the light verb and the noun in question, occurring within the same sentence and with a maximum distance of five words. This maximum distance is essentially arbitrary, but turned out to be the best compromise between covering all tokens of the target LVCs and reducing the number of false hits. Corpus occurrences of the target LVCs with a distance of more than five words between the light verb and the emotion noun are extremely rare. (5) shows an exemplary corpus query string, used to extract data in German *Angst machen* 'make so. fear'.

(5) (meet [lemma="machen"] [lemma="Angst"] -5 5) within <s/>

In the data retrieved by these queries, the occurrences of the target LVCs were identified. Up to 200 hits were checked for each search string, using the random sampling function of Sketch Engine.

A corpus hit was identified as an actual occurrence of the LVC when it matched the intended morphosyntactic structure of the LVC pattern, this structure included both the verb and the noun targeted by the search string, and the meaning of the structure could be roughly covered by the periphrasis 'to cause someone to feel the emotion N'. On the other hand, a false hit was identified when the verb and the noun occurred in a different morphosyntactic structure (6) or in two separate clauses (7). A hit was also classified as false when one of the two elements targeted by the search string fell into the wrong lexical category, for example, due to the homonymy of a noun and a corresponding verb or adjective (8), or the construction deviated semantically from the targeted emotion meaning (9).

(6) A   nova crise política [...] fez   o   mercado entrar em pânico
     DEF new crisis political   make.PST.3SG DEF market enter in panic
     'The new political crisis made the market panic.'
     [Portuguese; ptTenTen20 46506607]

(7) Die Wut entfacht   das Feuer und macht   es   stark.
     DEF rage ignite.3SG DEF fire and make.3SG 3SG.N   strong
     'The rage ignites the fire and makes it strong.'
     [German; deTenTen20 184649401]

(8) They [...] made   him   fear   for his life
     3PL   make.PST 3SG.OBJ   fear(v) for his life
     [English; enTenTen21 6364743]

(9) No utilicen   este medicamento en periodos de mucho cansancio ya que
     not use.SBJV.3PL   this drug   in periods of much fatigue   as
     da   excitación y   un   efecto rebote
     give.3SG   stimulation and INDF effect rebound
     'Do not use this drug during periods of high fatigue as it causes stimulation and a rebound effect.'
     [Spanish; esTenTen18 26450086]

English data presents a special annotation challenge and a good example for the above-described identification process due to the high rate of homonymous pairs of nouns and verbs, e.g. *fear, panic* or *regret*. To distinguish target nouns from homonymous verbs that occur with the verb *make*, one of two criteria was applied, which resolved the doubt: When the word in question takes an argument, it can be classified as a verb, and thus as a false hit, since the nouns in the target LVCs cannot take any arguments of their own. In other cases, coordination of the element provided clarity: The target nouns can be coordinated with another noun inside the non-verbal element of the LVC, but not with a verb. If the word in question allows for coordination with a verb, the corpus token was classified as a false hit.

4 Results

This section presents an overview (4.1) and a contrastive analysis (4.2–4.3) of the results of the corpus study.

4.1 Overview

Two LVC patterns checked for occurrence with 25 nouns in six languages add up to 300 corpus-based statements. This form of results allows for qualitative and limited quantitative conclusions about our object of research. However, no quantitative claims will be made about the frequency of individual LVCs. This study investigates whether a particular pattern is used to form LVCs with experiencer objects in a language, and not how frequent the resulting constructions are. This would be another interesting dimension, but goes beyond the scope of the present paper.

A LVC was counted as attested (+, green color in Table 5) in a language when the following criteria were met:
i. the target construction was found at least twice with the target meaning in tokens from two different sources,
ii. at least one occurrence had an overt indirect object,
iii. and at least one occurrence featured a singular noun without a determiner.

A LVC was counted as dubitable (orange color) when there was only one occurrence that met all these criteria, that is, a hapax (1), or when there was more than one occurrence, but criteria (ii) or (iii) were violated (~). A LVC was counted as not attested (-, red color) when there was no corpus token that met the criteria.

Table 4 summarizes the results of the study. For each pattern in each language, the table specifies how many of the 25 checked LVCs were attested, dubitable, and not attested in the corpus data. Detailed results for all queries are presented in Table 5.

Tab. 4: Summary of corpus study results. + = LVC attested in corpus data; 1 = LVC attested as hapax; ~ = LVC dubitable; – = LVC not attested

Language	MAKE N + DAT	+/1/~/–	GIVE N + DAT	+/1/~/–
German	jemandem N machen	7/1/0/17	jemandem N geben	3/1/0/21
English	make someone N	0/0/0/25	give someone N	10/5/1/9
Danish	gøre nogen N	3/2/1/19	give nogen N	20/1/0/4
Portuguese	fazer N a alguém	3/0/1/21	dar N a alguém	19/0/1/5
Spanish	hacer N a alguien	0/3/0/22	dar N a alguien	21/1/1/2
Catalan	fer N a algú	8/2/1/14	donar N a algú	8/4/1/12

The non-occurrence of a LVC in a corpus does not necessarily mean that this LVC is not understood by speakers of the respective language, since competent speakers are able to reconstruct the intended meaning from the meaning of the noun and the use of the pattern that they know from other LVCs of the same pattern. For example, the hypothetical German LVC ?*Fröhlichkeit machen* lit. 'make joy' cannot be found in corpus data, and native speakers would not use it, but would certainly understand it as expressing a meaning such as 'make someone happy/joyful'. Empirical evidence for this hypothesis would support the assumption that the pattern has a meaning of its own that goes beyond a pure addition of the semantics of 'give' and the respective noun, but this has to be left to future studies.

The overall results can be summarized as follows: The 'give' pattern is attested in all languages, occurring with the most nouns in Spanish and the least nouns in German. The 'make' pattern is clearly attested in four languages, being found with the most nouns in Catalan. It occurs in hapaxes in Spanish, and not at all in English. Generally, the 'give' pattern is much more frequent in the sample. German is the only language of the sample where the 'make' pattern is found with more nouns than the 'give' pattern, and in Catalan both patterns are found to a similar extent. For each pattern found in the data, a corpus example of a LVC is given in (10)–(15) below.

Tab. 5: Detailed results for the corpus study. M – 'make' pattern; G – 'give' pattern; + = LVC attested in corpus data; 1 = LVC attested as hapax; ~ = LVC dubitable; – = LVC not attested

English noun	Ger M	Ger G	Eng M	Eng G	Dan M	Dan G	Por M	Por G	Spa M	Spa G	Cat M	Cat G
fear	+	–	–	–	–	+	–	+	–	+	+	+
panic	+	–	–	+	–	+	–	+	–	+	+	–
worry	+	–	–	1	+	+	–	–	–	+	–	–
despair	–	–	–	–	+	+	–	+	–	+	–	–
horror	–	–	–	1	1	–	–	+	–	+	1	–
dismay	–	–	–	–	–	1	–	–	–	+	–	–
sadness	–	–	–	–	–	–	–	+	–	+	+	1
anger	+	–	–	–	+	+	–	–	1	+	–	–
rage	–	–	–	1	–	–	–	+	1	+	+	+
boredom	1	–	–	–	–	+	+	+	–	+	–	–
unsettledness	–	–	–	–	–	+	–	+	–	+	–	1
confusion	–	–	–	~	–	+	+	+	–	1	–	1
embarrassment	–	–	–	1	–	+	–	+	–	+	+	+
regret	–	–	–	–	–	+	–	+	–	–	–	–
envy	–	–	–	1	–	+	+	+	–	+	+	+
surprise	–	–	–	+	–	+	~	~	–	~	~	~
excitement	–	–	–	+	–	–	–	–	–	+	–	–
interest	–	–	–	–	–	+	–	–	–	–	–	–
relief	–	–	–	+	–	+	–	+	–	+	–	–
pleasure	+	+	–	+	1	+	–	+	–	+	+	+
joy	–	1	–	+	–	+	–	+	–	+	+	+
enthusiasm	–	–	–	+	~	+	–	+	–	+	–	–
fun	+	–	–	+	–	+	–	+	–	+	–	+
courage	+	+	–	+	–	+	–	+	–	+	–	+
pride	–	+	–	+	–	+	–	+	1	+	1	1

(10)   *It **gives** me **panic**.*   [English; enTenTen21 233399416]

(11) a.   *Ihre Sprache **macht** mir **Angst**.*
        her language make.3SG 1SG.DAT fear
        'Her language frightens me.'   [German; deTenTen20 29160]

     b.   *Was aus eigener Kraft* [...] *erworben wurde, **gibt** dem*
        what from own strength acquired AUX.PASS give.3SG DEF.DAT

        *Menschen **Stolz**.*
        human pride
        'What has been acquired through one's own strength gives people pride.'
        [German; deTenTen20 54819051]

(12) a.   *smerte* [...], *der **gjorde** mig **fortvivlelse***
        pain REL make.PST 1SG.OBJ despair
        'pain that made me despair'   [Danish; daTenTen20 923561830]

     b.   *Dette har **givet** mange af os **angst** og **stress**.*
        this AUX.PERF give.PTCP many of 1PL anxiety and stress
        'This has caused many of us anxiety and stress.'
                                       [Danish; daTenTen20 1590288]

(13) a.   *E ver passar a vida **faz**-me **tédio**.*
        and see pass DEF life make.3SG-1SG.OBJ boredom
        'And watching life go by makes me bored.'
                                       [Portuguese; ptTenTen20 903976976]

     b.   *É algo que me **dá medo**.*
        be.3SG something REL 1SG.OBJ give.3SG fear
        'It is something that frightens me.'   [Portuguese; ptTenTen20 107343]

(14) a.   *la verdad me **hace rabia***
        DEF truth 1SG.OBJ make.3SG rage
        'The truth makes me angry.'   [Spanish; esTenTen18 9291254589]

     b.   *y la idea de operarme me **daba pánico***
        and DEF idea of operate.REFL 1SG.OBJ give.PST.3SG panic
        'and the idea of having surgery made me panic'
                                       [Spanish; esTenTen18 6843149]

(15) a.   *el totalitarisme li **fa horror***
        DEF totalitarianism 3SG.DAT make.3SG horror
        'Totalitarianism horrifies him.'   [Catalan; caTenTen14 53268725]

     b.   *Per això ens intenten **donar por**.*
        because of that 1PL.OBJ intend.3PL give fear
        'Because of that they try to scare us.'   [Catalan; caTenTen14 3443479]

A remark on the quantity of data for Catalan shall be in place here: Probably because of the smaller total corpus size, there were only very few hits for some Catalan corpus queries, among which the target LVC was not found. This could be a potential problem for the reliability of the data. However, these cases are not problematic for the specific purpose of this study: If the target construction were productive in Catalan, it would be found among those query hits. In fact, there are also cases of LVCs that were classified as attested because even among very few corpus hits, there were enough occurrences to show that the target LVC exists.

The following subsections present a contrastive analysis based on the data presented in this subsection, taking into account three different dimensions of contrast. I treat contrasts between the two language families, among individual languages, and between the sets of emotion nouns that appear in the LVCs.

4.2 Contrasts between languages and families

First, we focus on a possible contrast between the two language families under investigation. Is there a significant difference between Germanic and Romance families? This would be the case if all Romance languages were more similar to each other than to any Germanic language, and vice versa. Or should the cross-linguistic differences in the data be described on the level of individual languages?

Portuguese and Spanish are, in terms of the use of the two LVC patterns, the languages that are closest to each other: As visible in Table 5, they share the most corresponding LVCs and 'gaps', i.e. non-attested LVC candidates. This is not unexpected, given that they are also the genetically closest languages in the sample. However, the next language closest to them is not the third Romance language Catalan, but Danish, a Germanic language. This manifests in the attestation of a similarly high number of 'give' LVCs and a similarly restricted use of the 'make' pattern. On the other hand, Danish also behaves more like the Romance languages in the sample than like the other two Germanic languages.

German and Danish share the property that they use both patterns, distinguishing them from English. Danish and English share the preference for the 'give' pattern. Overall, Danish is closer to English than to German, but no pair of Germanic languages is nearly as close to each other as Portuguese and Spanish. German is clearly the most different from the rest of the language sample, and there is more heterogeneity within Germanic than within Romance.

In conclusion from these observations, no significant contrast can be established between the Germanic and Romance families. Significant differences can, however, be established between individual languages rather than between entire families. Therefore, we proceed to highlight how the behavior of the patterns in specific languages distinguishes them within the sample.

German data show the lowest frequency of the patterns under investigation in general. A possible explanation for this lies in the productivity of other patterns for LVCs with experiencer objects: Patterns with the light verbs *bringen* 'bring' and *versetzen* 'transfer', as mentioned in section 2, seem to be dominant. Where the patterns were found, they seem to cover different sets of nouns, with the exceptions of *Freude* 'pleasure' and *Mut* 'courage', which occur in both patterns.

English features the only case where not even a hapax was found for one of the two target patterns: The 'make' pattern is clearly not available for English emotion nouns. Though the 'give' pattern is rather restricted in English as well.

In Danish, the corpus data indicate more competition of the target LVC patterns with complex predicates formed by 'make' and an adjective denoting an emotional state, such as 'make angry' or 'make worried'. The 'give' pattern is used very widely in Danish. In contrast, the 'make' pattern is clearly restricted to a few emotion nouns. With three nouns of the sample, it seems to be very productive: *bekymring* 'worry', *fortvivlelse* 'despair' and *ærgrelse* 'anger'. For the nouns where occurrences of the 'make' pattern were found, the 'give' pattern is also productive, with only one exception: For *forfærdelse* 'horror', a hapax was found for 'make', and no occurrence at all for 'give'. This indicates that the 'make' pattern does not fill any gaps.

Portuguese behaves, as indicated above, similar to Danish in that the 'make' pattern is very restricted, but still productive with a small set of nouns, while the 'give' pattern is widely used. For all nouns that occur productively in the 'make' pattern, the 'give' pattern is productive as well; no gaps are filled.

The tendencies in Spanish are again similar to those in Portuguese, but still more explicit: The 'make' pattern was only found in three hapaxes, and the 'give' pattern in Spanish shows the widest use of all patterns and languages in this study.

Catalan is the only language in the sample in which the occurrence of both patterns is balanced. While the Catalan standard prefers *fer* 'make', the data show that *donar* 'give' is actually used to a quite similar extent. Interestingly, there are even corpus tokens in which comments about this relation between the two patterns are made, such as (16).

(16) *No és "donar por", és "fer por". Quin nivell, el*
not be.3SG *donar por* be.3SG *fer por* what.a standard DEF
d'e-noticies, què trist ...
of:online.news what sad
'It is not *donar por*, it is *fer por*. What a standard in these online news, how sad ...'
[Catalan; caTenTen14 65290238]

For the 'give' pattern, there is a significantly higher number of hapaxes, which supports the assumption that LVCs of the pattern exist but are not standard. A possible explanation for this trend lies in the close contact with Spanish, where the 'give' pattern is dominant. As it happens, the result that Catalan is, in contrast to the rest of the sample, balanced with respect to the two LVC patterns actually mirrors its position between the Ibero-Romance and Gallo-Romance subfamilies, although that is not necessarily due to its genetic status, but probably significantly influenced by the close current contact to Spanish. This study shows that Ibero-Romance languages, i.e. Portuguese and Spanish, tend strongly towards the 'give' pattern, while previous literature (e.g. Staudinger, 2018), has described 'make' as the preferred light verb in French, the dominant Gallo-Romance language.

4.3 Contrasts among emotion nouns in LVCs

In the previous subsections, the data was analyzed with a focus on languages and verbs. For this subsection, I shift to a noun-centered perspective in order to provide some qualitative insights into the behavior of different sets of emotion nouns in LVC patterns. As addressed in Section 3, there are limits to the comparability of individual emotion nouns across languages. I only set up cross-linguistic comparisons for any nouns in this subsection if I consider them sufficiently close in meaning.

A basic parameter frequently used to characterize emotions in the literature is their valence, i.e. whether they are associated with positive or negative affect (see King, 2013 and references therein for an elementary description). The dimension is still under debate. For example, there is no consensus on whether positive and negative affect are opposite poles on a scale or whether they are orthogonal parameters. But it is evident that positive and negative affects are important features for the characterization of emotions, and that in many emotions referred to by emotion nouns, either positive or negative affect is clearly dominant. For simplicity, I refer to emotions clearly associated with positive affect, but not with negative affect, as 'positive emotions', and to emotions with opposite association as 'negative emotions'. For most nouns in the sample, the classification of the denoted emotion as positive or negative is intuitive. In some cases, classification is not intuitively possible because the valence of the emotion is underspecified ('excitement', 'confusion', 'surprise'). The observations in the following refer only to those nouns denoting indisputably positive or negative emotions, not to the latter, which are unclear cases.

The valence distinction between positive and negative emotions shows an effect in the corpus data, visible in the results of the study in Table 5. In English, for example, the 'give' pattern appears to be productive with several nouns denoting positive emotions (e.g. *pleasure, joy, courage*), but not with nouns denoting negative emotions (the only exception being *panic*). Interestingly, the only nouns that were found to occur in the 'give' pattern in German also denote positive emotions. Taking a deeper look at the possible correlation between positive emotion meanings and the use of 'give', we can determine (see Table 5) that nouns denoting 'pleasure', 'courage' and 'pride', the latter including one hapax case, are used with 'give' in all six languages, and for 'joy' and 'fun' nouns, only German deviates. In contrast, only German and Catalan data show productive use of the 'make' pattern with any noun in the sample that denotes a clearly positive emotion. For nouns that denote clearly negative emotions, there is no equally clear picture. However, the proximity of Danish to Spanish and Portuguese described in Subsection 4.2 is particularly visible with negative emotion meanings such as 'despair', 'boredom', 'embarrassment' and 'envy'.

After treating the positive-negative contrast, I conclude this section with some separate observations on particular emotion nouns:

- For 'panic' nouns, all six languages use exactly one of the two patterns, although they differ in which of the two they use.
- 'Rage' and 'sadness' nouns occur in the two patterns in Romance languages, but not in Germanic.
- Only Danish corpus data featured any LVC for an 'interest' noun. Data for the other language did not provide a single occurrence of an 'interest' LVC.
- Finally, 'surprise' nouns occur in LVCs with the target meaning in Germanic languages, while the occurrences of the target patterns in Romance languages carry a meaning that includes an event, which would usually cause the emotion of surprise, rather than the actual emotion.

5 Discussion

This section is dedicated to discussing a few particular aspects of the corpus study results against the wider research background.

First, we will look at how the results relate to assumptions from the literature. As explained in Section 2, there are only a few pertinent previous studies, but a set of claims about the 'make' and 'give' patterns can be identified that the results of the corpus study can confirm or, in some cases, contradict.

Staudinger (2018, 238), discussing the 'give' pattern in Spanish, states that its productivity is very limited, if existent at all. Although my study shows restrictions with respect to the productivity of the pattern, it also finds that the pattern occurs regularly with 21 of 25 emotion nouns. This is no concluding proof of productivity, but certainly an indication towards it. In addition to that, my results are compatible with the theoretical assumptions of Staudinger (2018), but since this study produced a significantly different type of results than the former, no further confirmations or contradictions can be pointed out.

The cross-Romance study in Pompei and Piunno (2023a) provides several points of contact for this discussion, and the corpus data for my sample can complement their findings. Pompei and Piunno (2023a, 115, 131) stated that in Spanish, 'give' is always chosen over 'make', and that for LVCs in general, Spanish features the broadest extension of the use of 'give' among Romance languages (Pompei and Piunno, 2023a, 136). The corpus study fully confirms this. For Portuguese, Pompei and Piunno (2023a, 134) did not expect the clear preference for 'give'; my data show, however, that the preference is almost as strong as in Spanish. The 'make' pattern is used for Portuguese OE-LVCs, but only with a few nouns, and nowhere near as broadly as in French.

Regarding the selection of different light verbs, Pompei and Piunno (2023a, 104) argued that it "is often sensitive to the semantics of the predicative noun they combine with". In Subsection 4.3 this paper demonstrates tendencies about which type of emotion noun appears with which light verb. Both the apparent correlation between positive emotions and 'give' light verbs and the impressions on similar behavior of cross-linguistic groups of nouns with near-equivalent meanings support the assumption of Pompei and Piunno (2023a): The selection of light verbs is evidently not entirely arbitrary.

As a common property, Pompei and Piunno (2023a, 137) attribute a causative meaning to both patterns. Assuming this, nouns which denote emotions that cannot usually be externally caused should be incompatible or at least rare with both patterns. As described in the previous section, nouns of 'interest' are incompatible with the patterns in five out of six languages. This finding also matches the argument of Wiskandt and Turus (2023) that German *Interesse* does not occur in any LVC patterns with a causative meaning because the emotion in question cannot be externally caused. However, due to the flexible degree of causativity in OE-LVC patterns (cf. Pompei and Piunno, 2023a, 137), constraints like this are rather probabilistic than categorical in nature.

Through such aspects, the present paper contributes to our understanding of the cross-linguistic behavior of LVCs in general: The light verbs in LVCs are semantically light, but empty enough to be fully interchangeable.

The corpus data analyzed for this paper revealed that a large proportion of the occurrences of the LVCs is modified, displaying either adverbial modification of the predicate or attributive modification of the emotion noun. While the former occurs analogously with OE verbs, the latter option is particular to LVCs. For instance, Alvarez-Morera et al. (this volume) prove the importance of the different types of modification for the behavior of the 'give N' LVC pattern in Germanic and

Romance, analyzing a sample of English, German, Catalan and Spanish corpus data. The extended modification options would be a plausible motive to choose a particular type of psych predicate. Pisciotta and Masini (this volume, 155–156) found a small effect of modification on the form of psych predicates in general, and a particularly large effect in written texts, which they attribute to higher competition in those environments. Although the present paper did not analyze modification patterns, its results combined with those of Alvarez-Morera et al. (this volume) and Pisciotta and Masini (this volume) provide a starting point for a subsequent study on the role of modification in the variation of OE predicates in Germanic and Romance.

A significant gap in previous research as addressed in Section 2 concerned the relationship between different forms of experiencer predicates that seem to be in competition with each other. Although this problem was not in the focus of this study, the data provide some insights of interest for this debate with respect to two dimensions of competition:

First, there are several, although not many cases in the data where both LVC patterns were found for the same noun in one language. Excluding hapax and dubitable occurrences, this is still the case for German *Freude* ('pleasure') and *Mut* ('courage'=, Danish *bekymring* ('worry'), *fortvivlelse* ('despair') and *ærgrelse* ('anger'), Portuguese *tédio* ('boredom'), *confusão* ('confusion') and *inveja* 'envy', and Catalan *por* ('fear'), *ràbia* ('rage'), *vergonya* ('shame'), *enveja* ('envy'), *plaer* ('pleasure') and *alegria* ('joy').

Such pairs of LVCs, which share the same structure and noun, but employ different light verbs, can provide evidence for the contribution of the light verb to the meaning of the LVC if meaning differences between the two LVCs in a pair can be established. As mentioned in Subsection 2.2, Pompei and Piunno (2023a, 114–115) argue for Italian data that there is a difference between the two light verbs with respect to the role that the referent of the non-experiencer argument plays: In the 'make' pattern the emotional state denoted by the noun is directly tied to the non-experiencer argument of the predicate and would not exist in its absence. In the 'give' pattern, by contrast, the emotional state is not directly caused by the presence of the referent of the non-experiencer argument. This explanation seems to be well-suited for several of the above-mentioned pairs, although it should not be assumed as a categorical distinction between the two patterns, but rather as a gradual or probabilistic distinction. For example, Portuguese *fazer confusão* (lit. 'make confusion') and *dar confusão* (lit. 'give confusion') confirm the prediction in so far that *fazer confusão* describes a situation in which a particular event or an animate participant actively or in the latter case even voluntarily causes a state of confusion in an experiencer. The counterpart *dar confusão* rather describes a situation in which a state of affairs or the temporary presence of a participant contributes to a state of confusion that either already exists, or is brought about by that state or participant but continues without the necessary continuous presence of the other participant. A corpus study scrutinizing the difference between 'make' and 'give' light verbs could look into the semantic types of non-experiencer arguments of LVC tokens, and into the wider context, in order to find effects of a semantic distinction like the one assumed by Pompei and Piunno (2023a). For specifically investigating the role of the presence and active involvement of non-experiencer argument referents, an experimental study seems to be better suited.

As a second related aspect, in all languages of the sample, there are lexically corresponding simplex OE verbs for at least some of the LVCs described in this study, which constitute possible alternation pairs. For example, German *Freude machen/geben* (lit. 'make/give pleasure') coexists with *freuen* ('please'), English *give pleasure* coexists with *please*, Danish *gøre/give ærgrelse* (lit. 'make/give anger') coexists with *ærgre* ('anger/annoy'), Portuguese *dar horror* (lit. 'give horror'), as already shown in example (4) in Section 2, coexists with *horrorizar* ('horrify'), Spanish *dar alegría* (lit. 'give joy') coexists with *alegrar* ('gladden'), and Catalan *dar diversió* (lit. 'give fun') coexists with *divertir* ('amuse'). These observations can serve as a starting ground for a subsequent study that focuses on these dimensions of competition and their potential status as alternations, building on the works of Pisciotta and Masini (this volume), and Wiskandt and Turus (2025). Wiskandt and Turus (2025) classify a German OE-LVC pattern with a transfer verb as causative marking, in line with the argument of Pompei and Piunno (2023b, 113), and analyze the LVCs formed by this pattern as causative counterparts in an alternation relation with lexically corresponding simplex OE verbs. Simplex OE verbs are analyzed as less semantically marked compared to the LVCs, a view shared by Pisciotta and Masini (this volume).

The variation in LVC pattern use across Germanic and Romance has, of course, a diachronic dimension, which Pompei and Piunno (2023a) addressed for Romance languages. While a more detailed discussion of diachronic implications would go beyond the scope of this paper, it is worth noting that the present corpus study showed significant differences among the languages of the sample, but not between the two families. Thus I assume that any mechanism for choice of LVC patterns with different emotion nouns was not inherited from any Proto-Germanic or Proto-Romance ancestor, but developed more recently; the parallel development across families can be attributed to language-independent factors. Furthermore, Subsection 4.2 of this study also touched on possible signs of language contact in the availability of LVC patterns, particularly for Catalan, where the productivity of the use of the 'give' pattern is likely a result of intense influence from Spanish. Whether the choice of light verb can indeed be established as an indicator for language contact cannot be determined here; a future cross-linguistic study on historical corpus data could shed light on these dimensions of diachrony and contact.

As a last aspect of the discussion, some limitations of this study need to be addressed: I could not determine which properties, e.g. of aspectual or other semantic nature, decide whether an emotion noun combines with one of the light verbs under investigation or whether this is at all conditioned by any semantic properties of the nouns. This could be the goal of a possible follow-up study from a semantic perspective. A potentially critical point with respect to the representativeness of the study lies in the sample composition: The subsamples for Germanic and Romance do not represent their families equally well. All three Romance languages belong to the Western Romance branch and are more closely related to each other than either of them is to Italian or Romanian. The three Germanic languages in the sample better represent the diversity of their family, since they cover different branches within the family.

6 Conclusion

Light verb constructions with experiencer objects have long been an understudied subcategory in the extensively investigated field of psych predicates. This paper presents the first cross-family corpus study on the use of different patterns for LVCs with experiencer objects. A corpus study on the patterns 'make N + IO' and 'give N + IO' in six languages, testing 25 emotion nouns per language, mapped a significant amount of variation, and some previously undescribed regularities.

We conclude from the results that the situation with respect to the use of the two patterns in Germanic and Romance languages is more complex than previous literature had captured. Cross-linguistic contrasts in the use of the pattern are better established among individual languages than between the two families of Germanic and Romance. Furthermore, there are tendencies about which type of emotion noun appears in which patterns, supporting the assumption that the selection of light verbs is not entirely arbitrary. Coexistence of 'make' and 'give' LVCs and simplex verbs provides a promising testing ground for semantic differences between light verbs and for the semantic contribution of light verbs in general. At the same time, it remains unclear which exact properties of emotion nouns favor particular light verbs, and which role the competition between different forms of predicates, which the data show to be attested, actually plays. For subsequent research, this paper showed that further investigation is necessary with respect to how light verb selection is conditioned, and whether there is a common cross-linguistic mechanism for selection, and that systematic and cross-linguistic empirical studies facilitate results that studies on single languages might miss.

Acknowledgments

I would like to thank the editors of this volume for the initiative and the great selection of articles. The cross-linguistic profile of the volume, as well as exchanges with Dila Turus, fertilized the idea behind this paper. I am grateful to Jens Fleischhauer and Jordi Ginebra for their helpful comments on the manuscript. Furthermore, I really appreciate the constructive discussions on aspects of this work with the audiences of the Workshop on Psych Predicates in Romance Languages, hosted in Düsseldorf in 2023, and of the 54th Linguistic Symposium on Romance Languages, hosted at Brigham Young University in Provo, Utah, in 2024.

Bibliography

Acedo-Matellán, Víctor and Anna Pineda. 2019. Light Verb Constructions in Basque and Romance. In Ane Berro, Fernández Beatriz and Jon Ortiz De Urbina (eds.), *Basque and Romance*, 176–220. Leiden: Brill.

Alvarez-Morera, Georgina, Jordi Ginebra and Isabel Oltra-Massuet. this volume. Modification in *give* light verb constructions: a corpus-based study in Germanic and Romance languages. In Anna Riccio and Jens Fleischhauer (eds.), *Light verbs: Synchronic and diachronic studies*, 65–96. Düsseldorf: Düsseldorf University Press.

Becker, Laura and Matías Guzmán Naranjo. 2020. Psych predicates in European languages: A parallel corpus study. *STUF - Language Typology and Universals* 73(4). 483–523. https://doi.org/10.1515/stuf-2020-1017.

Belletti, Adriana and Luigi Rizzi. 1988. Psych-verbs and θ-theory. *Natural Language and Linguistic Theory* 6(3). 291–352. https://doi.org/10.1007/BF00133902.

Cançado, Márcia, Luana Amaral, Letícia Meirelles and Maria José Foltran. 2024. Psych verbs: the behavior of ObjExp verbs in Brazilian Portuguese. *Linguistics* 62(1). 121–158. https://doi.org/10.1515/ling-2022-0024.

Chishman, Rove Luiza De Oliveira and Debora Tais Batista De Abreu. 2014. Construções com verbo suporte: propriedades gramaticais e discursivas. *Linha D'Água* 27(1). 153. https://doi.org/10.11606/issn.2236-4242.v27i1p153-168.

Fleischhauer, Jens and Stefan Hartmann. 2023. Der Weg von kommen zum Funktionsverb. In Christian Braun and Elisabeth Scherr (eds.), *Methoden zur Erforschung grammatischer Strukturen in historischen Quellen*, 117–138. Berlin: De Gruyter. https://doi.org/10.1515/9783110784282-008.

Fleischhauer, Jens and Dila Turus. 2021. Der Angeklagte steht unter Schutz, wird er aber auch geschützt? –Eine Analyse passivischer Funktionsverbgefüge des Typs 'stehen unter'. *Germanistische Werkstatt* 11. 73–81. DOI:10.25167/pg.4671.

Fritz-Huechante, Paola, Elisabeth Verhoeven and Julian A. Rott. 2020. Agentivity and non-culminating causation in the psych domain: Cross-linguistic evidence from Spanish and Korean. *Glossa: a journal of general linguistics* 5(1). https://doi.org/10.5334/gjgl.896.

Fábregas, Antonio, Ángel L. Jiménez-Fernández and Mercedes Tubino Blanco. 2017. What's up with dative experiencers? In Ruth E.V. Lopes, Juanito Ornelas de Avelar and Sonia M. L.

Cyrino (eds.), *Romance Languages and Linguistic Theory*, 29–48. Amsterdam: John Benjamins. https://doi.org/10.1075/rllt.12.03fab.

Fábregas, Antonio and Rafael Marín. 2020. Datives and stativity in psych predicates. In Anna Pineda and Jaume Mateu (eds.), *Dative constructions in Romance and beyond*, 221–238. Berlin: Language Science Press. 10.5281/ZENODO.3776549.

Ganeshan, Ashwini. 2019. Examining agentivity in Spanish reverse-psych verbs. *Studies in Hispanic and Lusophone Linguistics* 12(1). 1–32. https://doi.org/10.1515/shll-2018-0011.

Hirsch, Nils. 2018. *German psych verbs – insights from a decompositional perspective*. Doctoral dissertation: Humboldt-Universität zu Berlin. https://doi.org/10.18452/19574.

Jakubíček, Miloš, Adam Kilgarriff, Vojtěch Kovář, Pavel Rychlý and Vít Suchomel. 2013. The TenTen Corpus Family. *7th International Corpus Linguistics Conference CL 2013* 125–127.

Kailuweit, Rolf. 2005. *Linking: Syntax und Semantik französischer und italienischer Gefühlsverben:*. Tübingen: De Gruyter. https://doi.org/10.1515/9783110943351.

Kilgarriff, Adam, Vít Baisa, Jan Bušta, Miloš Jakubíček, Vojtěch Kovář, Jan Michelfeit, Pavel Rychlý and Vít Suchomel. 2014. The Sketch Engine: ten years on. *Lexicography* 1. 7–36.

Kilgarriff, Adam, Pavel Rychlý, Pavel Smrž and David Tugwell. 2004. The Sketch Engine. *Proceedings of the 11th EURALEX International Congress* 105–116.

King, Pamela S. 2013. Emotions: Positive and Negative. In Marc D. Gellman and J. Rick Turner (eds.), *Encyclopedia of Behavioral Medicine*, 676–678. New York, NY: Springer.

Melis, Chantal. 2019. Los causativos emocionales del español. Un estudio aspectual. *Anuario de Letras. Lingüística y Filología* 7(1). 105. https://doi.org/10.19130/iifl.adel.7.1.2019.1531.

Miglio, Viola G., Stefan Th. Gries, Michael J. Harris, Eva M. Wheeler and Raquel Santana-Paixão. 2013. Spanish lo(s)-le(s) Clitic Alternations in Psych Verbs: A Multifactorial Corpus-Based Analysis. In Jennifer Cabrelli Amaro, Gillian Lord, Ana de Prada Pérez and Jessi Elana Aaron (eds.), *Selected Proceedings of the 16th Hispanic Linguistics Symposium*, 268–278. Somerville, MA: Cascadilla Proceedings Project.

Pesetsky, David Michael. 1995. *Zero syntax: experiencers and cascades* (Current studies in linguistics 27). Cambridge, MA: The MIT Press.

Pijpops, Dirk and Dirk Speelman. 2017. Alternating argument constructions of Dutch psychological verbs: A theory-driven corpus investigation. *Folia Linguistica* 51(1). https://doi.org/10.1515/flin-2017-0006.

Pisciotta, Flavio and Francesca Masini. this volume. A paradigm of psych-predicates: Unraveling the constructional competition between light verb constructions and derived verbs in Italian. In Anna Riccio and Jens Fleischhauer (eds.), *Light verbs: Synchronic and diachronic studies*, 123–175. Düsseldorf: Düsseldorf University Press.

Pompei, Anna and Valentina Piunno. 2023a. Light Verb Constructions in Romance languages. An attempt to explain systematic irregularity. In Anna Pompei, Lunella Mereu and Valentina Piunno (eds.), *Light Verb Constructions as Complex Verbs*, 99–148. Berlin: De Gruyter.

Pompei, Anna and Valentina Piunno. 2023b. Light Verb Constructions in Romance languages. An attempt to explain systematic irregularity. In Anna Pompei, Lunella Mereu and Valentina Piunno (eds.), *Light Verb Constructions as Complex Verbs*, 99–147. Berlin: Mouton de Gruyter.

Rott, Julian A., Elisabeth Verhoeven and Paola Fritz-Huechante. 2020. Valence orientation and psych properties: Toward a typology of the psych alternation. *Open Linguistics* 6(1). 401–423. https://doi.org/10.1515/opli-2020-0020.

Rott, Julian A., Elisabeth Verhoeven and Paola Fritz-Huechante. 2024. Directionality in the psych alternation: a quantitative cross-linguistic study. *Linguistic Typology* 28(1). 147–191. https://doi.org/10.1515/lingty-2021-0060.

Royo, Carles. 2020. The accusative/dative alternation in Catalan verbs with experiencer object. In Anna Pineda and Jaume Mateu (eds.), *Dative constructions in Romance and beyond*, 371–393. Berlin: Language Science Press. 10.5281/ZENODO.3776563.

Staudinger, Eva. 2013. *Syntax, Subjektivität, Subjektivierung - Schmerzprädikate im Französischen: eine Untersuchung der Konstruktionen französischer Schmerzprädikate in Lesarten unterschiedlicher Subjektivierungsstufen* (Freiburger Romanistische Arbeiten 4). Freiburg: Rombach.

Staudinger, Eva. 2018. French and Spanish 'MAKE/GIVE + FEAR" '-type LVCs – an RRG Constructional Account. In Rolf Kailuweit, Lisann Künkel and Eva Staudinger (eds.), *Applying and Expanding Role and Reference Grammar*, 237–261. Freiburg: Albert-Ludwigs-Universität Freiburg.

Temme, Anne and Elisabeth Verhoeven. 2016. Verb class, case, and order: A crosslinguistic experiment on non-nominative experiencers. *Linguistics* 54(4). https://doi.org/10.1515/ling-2016-0018.

Verhoeven, Elisabeth. 2010. Agentivity and stativity in experiencer verbs: Implications for a typology of verb classes. *Linguistic Typology* 14(2-3). https://doi.org/10.1515/lity.2010.009.

Verhoeven, Elisabeth. 2017. Scales or features in verb meaning?: Verb classes as predictors of syntactic behavior. *Belgian Journal of Linguistics* 31. 165–194. https://doi.org/10.1075/bjl.00007.ver.

Viñas-de-Puig, Ricard. 2014. Predicados psicológicos y estructuras con verbo ligero: del estado al evento. *RLA. Revista de lingüística teórica y aplicada* 52(2). 165–188.

Winhart, Heike. 2005. *Funktionsverbgefüge im Deutschen: Zur Verbindung von Verben und Nominalisierungen*. Doctoral dissertation: Eberhard-Karls-Universität Tübingen.

Wiskandt, Niklas. 2021. Paul ärgert sich, nervt sich aber nicht. Semantische Merkmale deutscher Objekt-Experiencer-Verben und ihr Einfluss auf Antikausativkonstruktionen. *Germanistische Werkstatt* 11. 245–259. https://doi.org/10.25167/pg.4685.

Wiskandt, Niklas and Dila Turus. 2023. Wie man Linguisten in Begeisterung versetzt: Drei Muster von Funktionsverbgefügen mit Objekt-Experiencern. *Germanistische Werkstatt* 12. 149–162. https://doi.org/10.25167/pg.5226.

Wiskandt, Niklas and Dila Turus. 2025. Verb-LVC pairs with experiencer objects in German: Differences in usage and meaning. In Torsten Leuschner, Anaïs Vajnovszki, Gauthier Delaby and Jóhanna Barðdal (eds.), *How to Do Things with Corpora – Methodological Issues and Case Studies on Grammar*, Berlin: J.B. Metzler.

Flavio Pisciotta and Francesca Masini
A paradigm of psych-predicates

Unraveling the constructional competition between light verb constructions and derived verbs in Italian

1 Introduction

The study of Light Verb Constructions (henceforth LVCs) has gained growing attention, especially in recent years (e.g., Pompei and Mereu (eds.), 2019; Pompei et al., 2023). Their peculiar nature has been analyzed from different theoretical perspectives[1], leading to different interpretations of the phenomenon, and in several languages, including Italian (e.g., Elia et al., 1985; Cicalese, 1999; Mastrofini, 2004; Ježek, 2004, 2011; Quochi, 2016; Pompei, 2017; Ganfi and Piunno, 2019). However, the behavior of LVCs still poses many theoretical challenges that are still waiting to be addressed.

For instance, it has been noticed that the existence of LVCs in some languages seems to contradict the Principle of No Synonymy[2] (Bonial and Pollard, 2020), which holds that different forms in a language must have different meanings (Goldberg, 1995, 67). As a matter of fact, at least in Romance and Germanic languages, it is common for LVCs to have a near-synonymic synthetic verb counterpart (henceforth SV) (Alba-Salas, 2002; Sanromán Vilas, 2009; Bonial and Pollard, 2020; Alvarez-Morera, 2022a), often morphologically related. See the following examples from Italian:

(1)   a.   *dare un bacio*   b.   *baciare*
           give a kiss   'kiss'
           'give a kiss'

---

1 Among others: Lexicon-Grammar (Gross, 1976); Lexical-Functional Grammar (Butt, 2003); Relational Grammar (Alba-Salas, 2002); Role and Reference Grammar (Fleischhauer, 2021); Generative Lexicon (Ježek, 2023); Construction Grammar (Jiménez Martínez and Melis, 2023).
2 Variously named in the literature: isomorphism, no synonymy, contrast (e.g., Haiman, 1980; Clark, 1987).

Flavio Pisciotta, University of Salerno
Francesca Masini, Alma Mater Studiorum – University of Bologna

The partial overlap of meanings covered by both LVCs and SVs entails a situation of potential competition between multiword expressions and morphological words for the same semantic niche (Masini, 2019a,b). Since competition between forms is expected to result in functional differentiation (Aronoff, 2016, 42–44), scholars have often looked for the presence of distributional and semantic peculiarities of LVCs with respect to their SV counterparts. It is generally assumed that the main function of LVCs is an aspectual one, i.e., that they denote a telic variant of the SV by expressing a bounded, single instantiation of a larger event (2) (Wierzbicka, 1982; Butt, 2003; Pompei and Piunno, 2023). However, a notable counterexample is represented by LVCs including state nouns, such as nouns denoting psychological states (3) (Bonial and Pollard, 2020).

(2) a. *fare una telefonata* b. *telefonare*
       make a phone_call   'phone'
       'make a (phone) call'

(3) a. *fare paura*   b. *impaurire*
       do fear   'frighten'
       'frighten'

As a matter of fact, not only psych-LVCs such as (3) do not denote a bounded event, but they differ in their semantics and behavior from event-denoting LVCs such as (2). Firstly, they generally involve bare nouns (**fare la paura*, lit. do the fear), that are less referential and less syntactically flexible (e.g., they can't be extracted, nor the construction can be passivized, cf. Marini, 2003, 260-262; Mastrofini 2004, 390-391; Masini, 2009a, 195-196). Secondly, the light verb (henceforth LV) plays a greater role in determining the semantics of the predication, by imposing an argument/ event structure that could differ from the ones expressed by the noun: for instance, in (3) *fare paura* does not simply denote a psychological state (*paura* 'fear'), but the event of causation of such psychological state (Mastrofini, 2004, 388). Thus, LVCs involving state nouns have been considered as distinct constructions from event-denoting LVCs (Alba-Salas, 2004) (although connected in a radial network, cf. the usage-based analysis of *fare*-LVCs in Quochi, 2016).

From this brief overview, psych-LVCs appear to be more fixed, and closer to the semantics expressed by word-formation processes[3], while retaining some degree of transparency and compositionality. Nonetheless, there is a rather complex situation

---

[3] Several studies observed that Verb+Noun LVCs resemble lexical items for their behaviour (Masini, 2009a; Fernández-Domínguez, 2019). This would be compatible with Goldberg's (2003b) analysis of Persian LVCs as stored objects associated with a semantics.

of competition between psych-SVs and psych-LVCs (Masini, 2019a): for instance, the existence of a LVC (4b) sometimes blocks the corresponding denominal verb (4c) – although this is not always the case (5a vs. 5b) – while it may allow the use of another LVC with different light verb and same noun (5b and 5c).

(4) a. ***paura***
         'fear'
     b. *avere* ***paura***
         have fear
         'fear'
     c. °*paurare*

(5) a. *im****paur****ire*
         'frighten'
     b. *fare* ***paura***
         do   fear
         'frighten'
     c. *mettere* ***paura***
         put   fear
         'frighten'

Since, to the best of our knowledge, there is no systematic quantitative study on the matter in Italian, we will tackle the competition between denominal psych-SVs and psych-LVCs following a corpus-based methodology. We will do so from a Construction Grammar perspective, thus considering denominal verb derivation schemas (conversion, suffixation, and parasynthesis) and LVCs schemas as (semi)schematic constructions whose empty slot can be filled by nouns expressing psychological states in order to form complex predicates.

The chapter is structured as follows. In Section 2 we present previous accounts of the competition between LVCs and SVs, focusing on psych verbs and LVCs. In Section 3 we sketchily introduce Construction Grammar tenets and tools that are relevant for the present analysis. Section 4 reports on a two-step analysis, consisting of (i) the collection and description of a dataset of SVs and LVCs based on psych nouns, and (ii) a mixed-effects regression analysis on a sample of synonymous SVs and LVCs found in the dataset. Finally, in Section 5 we discuss our findings and propose a formalization of the relationship between SVs and LVCs in constructional terms. Section 6 draws some conclusions and traces future lines of research.

2 The competition between LVCs and SVs: the case of psych predicates

The coexistence of near-synonymic pairs of LVCs and SVs has been regarded in the literature as an exception to the Principle of No Synonymy (Goldberg, 2003a). So, scholars tried primarily to assess what motivates the very existence of LVCs, i.e., why such constructions should emerge at all. While sometimes the existence of an LVC fills a lexical gap, there are several cases in which a synthetic alternative does exist. First, we will briefly look at general studies on LVCs and SVs (Section 2.1), and then we will focus on psych-verbs (Section 2.2).

2.1 Motivating the existence and use of LVCs

Several studies on different languages have tackled the problem of the semantic overlap between LVCs and SVs. It is important to note, however, that while in our analysis we will focus on the competition between Verb+Noun LVCs and denominal verbs (both containing the same nouns), the treatment of analytic vs. synthetic verbs in the literature often encompasses also morphologically unrelated synonyms, such as Spanish *hacer punto* (lit. do stitch) and *tricotar* 'knit' (Piera and Varela, 1999; Alvarez-Morera, 2022a).[4]

From a semantic point of view, a first difference between corresponding LVCs and SVs is that often the SV tends to be more polysemous than the LVC counterpart, which is instead generally constrained to its most basic meaning (Giry-Schneider, 1978; Sanromán Vilas, 2009).

Furthermore, as mentioned in Section 1, in the case of eventive predicates the use of LVCs delimits a portion (or isolates one instance) of the event described by the SV, thus making it telic (cf. 2; Pompei and Piunno, 2023, 133). However, it has been observed that LVCs are not necessarily telic predicates, and that this aspectual func-

---

4 Furthermore, not always a SV morphologically related to an LVC implies a relationship of synonymy between the two: *dare noia* 'annoy/bother' vs *annoiare* 'bore', both created from *noia* 'boredom/nuisance' (see also Stichauer, 2000). Clearly, we won't focus on these cases, since there is no competition between the two forms.

tion cannot be applied consistently to all noun classes[5] (Bonial and Pollard, 2020, 15).

Although meaning is often called upon, the most cited motivations for the use of LVCs is not strictly semantic and pertains to the possibility to modify the nominal element through the use of adjectives or relative clauses (Huddleston, 2002; Sanromán Vilas, 2009; Bonial and Pollard, 2020; Pompei and Piunno, 2023). Such a possibility is granted by the fact that in LVCs the predication is dispersed over more than one lexical unit (Hopper, 1991). As a matter of fact, even though in some cases there is a semantic equivalence between adjectival modification of the noun in an LVC (6a) and adverbial modification of an SV[6] (6b) (Mirto and Granifero, 2022, 45-47), the first option seems to be chosen significantly more frequently (Bonial and Pollard, 2020):

(6) a. *Anzi tutto questo* mi **dà** **molto**
prior all DEM.PROX.M.SG to_me give.PRS.3SG much.M.SG
fastidio.
annoyance.M.SG
'First of all, this annoys me a lot (lit. gives me much annoyance).'
(CORIS[7], NARRAT)

b. *Anzi tutto questo* mi **infastidisce molto**.
prior all DEM.PROX.M.SG to_me annoy.PRS.3SG much
'First of all, this annoys me a lot.'

However, Alvarez-Morera (2022b) showed that this motivation could be at best language-dependent. Indeed, in languages different from English, the frequency of LVCs showing noun modification is quite low (Alvarez-Morera, 2022b). Thus, modification might be not so available as a cue for determining the choice of LVCs over SVs.[8]

Notwithstanding this, the multiword nature of LVCs can still be considered to be an explanation for the use of LVCs, especially in unplanned communicative situations. Since, as we said, in LVCs the predicate is distributed over more than one lexical unit, this could facilitate information monitoring and processing (Brugman,

---

[5] In some cases, there is indeed an aspectual function, but it is not related to telicization: with nouns indicating an indefinite process the use of the LVC can trigger a habitual, more specific interpretation with respect to some activity, while still creating an atelic predicate, e.g., *nuotare* 'swim' vs *fare nuoto* 'do/go swimming' (Pompei and Piunno, 2023, 133).
[6] Or between an adjectivally modified and an adverbially modified LVC (Fleischhauer and Neisani, 2020).
[7] Corpus available at https://corpora.ficlit.unibo.it/TCORIS/, last access 27/10/2024.
[8] For the concept of 'cue availability' as opposed to 'cue reliability' in the prediction of alternations, see Nesset and Janda (2023, 73).

2001). This, combined with the fact that generally the words that form a LVC are more frequent than the corresponding SVs (Amenta, 2008, 539), could explain the preference for LVCs in spoken discourse observed in the literature (Shahrokny-Prehn and Höche, 2011).

To sum up, even though there is no definitive answer, several functional motivations have been proposed to account for the use of LVCs over (or along with) SVs, ranging from semantic differences to information processing. Although not all of them are extensible to all noun classes, nor to all languages, what emerges clearly is that there is not a unique motivation for selecting analytic predicates over synthetic ones. Therefore, a multifactorial approach is needed to disentangle this complex relationship.

2.2 LVCs and SVs as alternative strategies of predicate formation from psych-nouns

The relationship between LVCs and SVs becomes even more complex by looking at the specific case of psych-predicates. Psych-verbs have been a subject of debate in syntactic research due to the high amount of variation in their argument structure (Croft, 1993; Verhoeven, 2010; Pijpops and Speelman, 2017). The most renown peculiarity pertains to the alignment between semantic roles (Experiencer, i.e., in our case the animate entity affected by the mental state; Stimulus, i.e., the animate or inanimate entity that causes the Experiencer to enter the mental state) and syntactic arguments. Generally, for Italian, Belletti & Rizzi's (1988) classification is assumed, consisting of three different configurations: Subject-Experiencer and Object-Stimulus (7a), Subject-Stimulus and Object-Experiencer (7b), Subject-Stimulus and Indirect Object-Experiencer (7c).

(7) a. $[I\ vampiri]_{Exp}$ temono $[la\ luce]_{Stim}$
 [the vampires]$_{Exp}$ fear [the light]$_{Stim}$
 b. $[Le\ tempeste]_{Stim}$ preoccupano $[i\ marinai]_{Exp}$
 [the storms]$_{Stim}$ worry [the sailors]$_{Exp}$
 c. $[Ai\ topi]_{Exp}$ piace $[il\ formaggio]_{Stim}$
 [to mice]$_{Exp}$ like [cheese]$_{Stim}$

This tripartite distinction is relevant also in terms of event structure, since the configuration in (7b) generally includes verbs with causative meaning (where the Stimulus causes the Experiencer to enter some psychological or emotional state).

While this classification has been largely discussed and revisited by later studies (e.g., Cifuentes Honrubia, 2015; Vietri, 2017), argument realization does not represent the only way to classify psych-verbs. For instance, Jackendoff (1990, 140) cites at least two other criteria, namely: (i) the distinction between positive and negative affect (e.g., *please* vs *hate*); (ii) the distinction between stative and eventive verbs (*bore* vs *annoy*). This last bipartition intertwines with the causative/non-causative nature of the verbs, and this is quite evident in Italian since causative and non-causative eventive verbs are often formally related. As is well known, Italian psych-verbs take part into the anticausative alternation, by adding the reflexive pronoun -*si* to the causative form of the verb to create (usually) an inchoative predicate (8) (Centineo, 1995; Ježek, 2000; Vietri, 2017).[9]

(8)   *appassionare – appassionarsi*
       'excite'   'get passionate'

By intersecting the stative/ eventive and the causative/ non-causative dimensions, we find that psych-verbs cover all three main event types proposed by Croft (1991) (or aspect-causative types, cf. Talmy, 2000): stative, inchoative, agentive (or causative). This is true not only of SVs, but also of psych-LVCs. Therefore, both synthetic and analytic psych-noun-based verbs can express three different kinds of events, as illustrated in (9).

(9)   a.   *simpatizzare* ∼ *avere simpatia*
          sympathize   have sympathy
          'sympathize'   [stative]
    b.   *impaurir-si* ∼ *prendere paura*
          frighten-SI   take   fear
          'get frightened'   [inchoative]
    c.   *angosciare* ∼ *mettere angoscia*
          distress   put   anguish
          'distress'   [causative]

This situation becomes more complex if we take into account the various possible patterns available for creating psych predicates from nouns. As for SVs, denominal psych-verbs can be formed by means of suffixation (9a), parasynthesis (9b), and

---

[9] Nonetheless, even though generally it is assumed that the anticausative *si*- counterpart is an eventive, inchoative predicate expressing a change of state, in some cases it could also be a stative, non-telic predicate (Marín and McNally, 2011). This is due to the fact that not all causatives are actually eventive, even though it is not always easy to draw this distinction at the type-level (Vietri, 2017, 115–116):

(i)   *annoiare* ∼ *annoiarsi*
       'bore'   'be/to get bored'

conversion (or zero-derivation) (9c). All three processes can form both causative verbs and dynamic non-causative verbs, while suffixation and conversion can form also stative verbs (Grossmann, 2004a,b; Iacobini, 2004). If we look at LVCs, we often find more than one pattern to express each of the mentioned event types: statives can be expressed by LVCs with *avere* 'have' and *essere in* 'be in'; inchoatives by LVCs with *prendere* 'take'; causatives by LVCs with *dare* 'give', *fare* 'do', and *mettere* 'put' (Pompei, 2017, 120).

Recently, the competition between the three strategies of denominal verb formation in Italian has been investigated (Iacobini and De Rosa, 2024), and also the rivalry between each of them and LVCs has been acknowledged (Mirto, 2008; Masini, 2009a; Iacobini and Pompei, 2022). In this multifaceted situation, a critical point is that it is generally impossible to predict which LVC will have a corresponding SV (and vice-versa), and which LVC pattern will be selected by a specific noun (Alba-Salas, 2002, 49, 51). However, at least with regard to the selection of the LVC pattern, some tendencies were found by classifying psych-nouns according to various semantic criteria: for instance, as regards Spanish, Sanromán Vilas (2003, 2012) analyzed stative and inchoative psych-LVCs, and proposed that the choice of the LVC depends on the external or internal nature of the cause of the psych noun, i.e., if the noun denotes a state that originates from the experiencer itself or as a reaction to an external source. Instead, a contrastive analysis on MAKE/GIVE causative LVCs in various Romance and Germanic languages by Wiskandt (this volume) shows an effect of the (positive or negative) valence of the psych-noun on the selection of the light verb. However, such effect is configured as a probabilistic rather than categorical constraint.

Hence, there is competition both at the level of predicate-formation schemas (several alternative options being available), and between specific forms, since in some cases both an SV and one (or more) LVC patterns are created from the same noun. Some recent studies on German have addressed the issue of the rivalry both between synthetic vs analytic psych-verbs, and between different analytic patterns, finding an effect of semantic features of the arguments (animacy, eventivity, etc.; Wiskandt and Turus, 2022; Fleischhauer, 2023; Fleischhauer and Turus, 2023).

It is by now clear that, in order to disentangle the relationship between denominal psych-SVs and psych-LVCs in Italian, we need to consider several aspects, both at the level of patterns and at the level of specific expressions. At the level of patterns, we first need to distinguish between stative, inchoative and causative predicates: for each of them we need to identify which nouns enter in which patterns of predicate formation. At the level of specific forms, we need to take into account both 'general' factors (cf. Section 2.1) and psych-verbs' specific argument structure features in order to motivate the coexistence of LVCs and SVs expressing the same meaning.

3 Theoretical background: Construction Grammar

Before delving into the analysis of the competition between psych SVs and LVCs, we briefly outline the theoretical framework adopted in the present case-study, namely Construction Grammar (henceforth CxG), and we explain why it is a fitting choice.

CxG approaches (Goldberg, 1995; Hoffmann and Trousdale (eds.), 2013; Hilpert, 2019; Ungerer and Hartmann, 2023) rely on the notion of 'construction' as a conventionalized form-function pairing, namely a sign. Our linguistic knowledge is modeled on constructions, which vary in both complexity and schematicity, therefore spanning from words to argument structures. All together, constructions form a complex network called 'constructicon' (Fillmore, 1988; Diessel, 2023), which ultimately captures the totality of our knowledge of language (Goldberg, 2003a, 219). Given its non-modular nature (the language architecture is not organized in separate and sequential modules, but in symbolic and holistic entities – constructions – that subsume formal and functional information of various type), phenomena straddling the boundaries of (what we traditionally call) morphology and syntax (like multiword expressions, including LVCs) are expected rather than exceptional.

In the next two subsections we focus on two conceptual tools of constructionist approaches that are relevant for our current purposes: (i) constructional schemas as intended in Construction Morphology (Booij, 2010) (Section 3.1), and (ii) links that connect constructions and are ultimately responsible for the network-like shape of the constructicon.

3.1 Constructional schemas

Although CxG originally began as a syntactic theory with a passion for idiomatic structures (cf. Fillmore et al., 1988), it recently extended to all linguistic structures including morphology. Construction Morphology (henceforth CxM) is the theory developed by Booij (2010) to account for morphological facts in a constructionist fashion and today is a full-fledged part of CxG. As summarized by Masini and Audring (2019), CxM is signed-based, word-based, and usage-based. It is signed-based in that, like CxG, it regards form-function pairings ('constructions') as the basic units of language and assumes a continuum between grammar and lexicon. It is word-based in that the minimal constructions is the word (not the morpheme), therefore adhering to word-based approaches such as Word-and-Paradigm theories of morphology (see, e.g., Blevins et al., 2019; Stump, 2019). It is usage-based (and exemplar-based), since it assumes that morphology is acquired bottom-up from the input (Tomasello, 2003) and that speakers are sensitive to usage and frequency in building and shaping their linguistic representations (Bybee, 2013).

The main consequences of this view of word knowledge are that both words and multiword expressions (like LVCs) may be stored in memory (as constructions), and that there is no principled distinction between words and 'rules', since both concepts are encompassed by the notion of construction: complex words (like *impaurire* 'frighten' or *simpatizzare* 'sympathize') are fully specified constructions in the constructicon, whereas the processes that lead to their creation (namely, parasynthesis and *-izzare* suffixation, respectively) are not represented as 'rules' of some sort but are constructions themselves but with a higher level of abstraction (Booij, 2010 calls them 'schemas').

See for instance (10a) (adapted from Masini and Iacobini, 2018, 97), which represents the schema for Italian denominal parasynthetic verbs with causative meaning. This schema can be unified with a suitable nominal base (e.g., the noun *paura* 'fear', which is independently stored as a fully lexically specified construction) to form a complex verb (e.g., *impaurire* 'frighten', see 10b).[10] Crucially, the schema in (10a) and the complex verb in (10b) are connected via an Instance Inheritance Link (Goldberg, 1995, 79), which connects a more general construction (sometimes called 'mother construction') to one or more specific ('daughter') constructions. The mother construction motivates the daughter(s); the daughter construction is an instance of the mother, from which it inherits many properties while adding new (more specific) ones, that may even override the mother's properties (default inheritance).

(10) a. $< [\text{PREF } [[x]_{N\alpha k}]_{Vi}]_{Vj} \leftrightarrow [\text{CAUSE to have SEM}_k]_j >$

   Instance Inheritance Link

   b. $< [impaurire]_{V\gamma j} \leftrightarrow [\text{CAUSE to have FEAR}]_j >$

Therefore, words and word formations processes are both constructions: they are just represented at different levels of schematicity or abstractness. In this way, schemas (mothers) capture generalizations over stored lexical items and at the same time serve as templates for the formation of new lexical items.

Things work similarly for those multiword lexical items that have the same concept-naming function as lexemes (so-called 'phrasal lexemes'; Booij, 2009; Masini, 2009b) and may be argued to be productive at least to some extent. LVCs fall

---

[10] As Masini and Iacobini (2018, 101) explain, "[s]ince parasynthetic verbs are largely equivalent semantically independently of the prefix used (*ad-/in-/s-*), and the combinations of their properties (prefix, base, inflectional class) show [...] no systematic correlation, new verbs are formed by analogy with actual verbs, thus clustering in 'paradigmatic families' " (cf. Crocco Galèas and Iacobini, 1993). This is the reason why the PREF slot is not specified.

in this category. For instance, for causative LVCs with *fare* 'do/make' (see Section 2.2), we may posit a semi-specified construction like (11a) (where *fare* 'do/make' is specified whereas the N slot remains variable and can be filled by psych nouns), which motivates fully lexically specified constructions like *fare paura* in (11b). Also in this case, an Instance Inheritance Link applies between mother construction and daughter construction.

(11) a. < [[*fare*]$_{V\alpha k}$ [y]$_{N\beta i}$]$_{V\gamma j}$ ↔ [CAUSE to have SEM$_i$]$_j$ >

Instance Inheritance Link

b. < [*fare paura*]$_{V\gamma j}$ ↔ [CAUSE to have FEAR]$_j$ >

To sum up, a constructionist view to complex lexical items allows to keep together, in the same representational space (the constructicon), morphologically complex lexemes and multiword lexemes, creating the conceptual ground for studying the interplay between these two strategies, including competition, when it applies. Let us now turn to links.

3.2 Connecting the dots of the network: vertical and horizontal links

As we saw in (10) and (11), higher-level (mother) constructions are instantiated by lower-level (daughter) constructions. Both entities are available for analysis, the formation pattern and the specific lexical item, thus making it possible to speak of competition at both levels: the (morphological) schema in (10a) can be thought of as competing with the (multiword) schema in (11a) by virtue of the constructions' similar meaning, whereas the parasynthetic verb in (10b) can be thought of as competing with the LVC in (11b), on the same semantic basis. What does this competition entail in terms of representation?

We already saw that the relationship between (10a) and (10b), and between (11a) and (11b) is a vertical or taxonomic one, similarly to the hypernym-hyponym relation in lexical semantics. The Instance Inheritance Link is just one type of vertical link: Goldberg (1995, 75-78, 81) identified three more types of Inheritance Links, namely Metaphorical, Polysemy, and Subpart. Whereas the use of these vertical links is quite established in constructional analyses, the horizontal dimension has been much less explored, until recently, when a discussion about horizontal links emerged.

In fact, Goldberg (1995, 67, 91) already mentioned (albeit cursorily) two types of horizontal relations, namely 'S-synonymous' and 'P-synonymous', to represent the equivalence, either in semantic (S) or in pragmatic (P) terms, between constructions that are not related syntactically. These synonymy relations do not constitute, technically, motivation links and are used by Goldberg (1995, 67) to shape the 'Principle of No Synonymy': "If two constructions are syntactically distinct, they must be semantically or pragmatically distinct".

Later, horizontal relations, intended as "relations that combine two or more constructions at the same level of specificity" (Diessel, 2023, 58), have been explored more in depth and various types of links have been proposed (see Diessel, 2023 for a recent overview).

Cappelle (2006) introduces the notion of 'allostruction' to refer to "(truth)semantically equivalent but formally distinct manifestations of a more abstractly represented construction" (Cappelle, 2009, 187). Cappelle (2006) applies this notion to the continuous and discontinuous orders of transitive particle verbs in English (*pick up the book* vs. *pick the book up*), which would be two allostructions of a more general verb-particle construction underspecified for word order.

Within CxM, Booij and Masini (2015) develop the notion of 'second-order schema' for capturing relations between morphological schemas that display a semantics-morphosyntax mismatch. Second-order schemas are claimed to be exploitable for paradigmatic word formation. Audring (2019) further develops this idea and puts forward the concept of 'sister relation' to account for morphological constructions (like $[N\text{-}ful]_A$ and $[N\text{-}less]_A$, or *helpful* and *helpless*) that are systematically related although they are not motivated or licensed by a shared higher-order schema. Second-order schemas and sister relations are also used in CxM to model inflectional paradigms (Booij, 2010; Masini and Audring, 2019; Jackendoff and Audring, 2020). In a similar fashion, Diewald (2020) proposes to regard inflectional paradigms as complex signs or 'hyper-constructions' where word forms (e.g., singular vs. plural) are related to one another by horizontal links.

Diessel (2023, 62) argues that, like lexemes and word forms, also "phrases and sentences are organized in paradigms of contrastively related constructions", like for instance inflectional periphrasis and clause types (declarative main clauses vs. yes/no questions, etc.). Diessel points out that, like morphological paradigms, also syntactic paradigms exhibit asymmetry, with a member of the paradigm being unmarked with respect to others.

Diessel (2023) also distinguishes horizontal relations within paradigms from horizontal relations modeling so-called 'families' and 'neighborhoods', namely groups of constructions that share some salient properties, in either form or function or both. Diessel (2023, 66) further proposes to distinguish families and neighborhoods along the following terms (although he points out the distinction is rather blurred): the former concept "describes a group (or pair) of similar constructions that are categorized as subtypes of the same schema", whereas the latter "describes a group (or pair) of similar constructions that are licensed by different schemas".

Since families and neighborhoods are reminiscent of 'associative' relations à la de Saussure (1916), for simplicity, here we will use the term 'associative' to refer to horizontal links within families and neighborhoods, whereas we use 'paradigmatic' to refer to horizontal links within paradigms. According to Diessel (2023, 74), associative links are based on similarity, are open-ended, and do not entail differences in marking; instead, paradigmatic links are based on contrast, are (tendentially) closed, and display an opposition between overt and zero marking.

At this point, we may therefore ask what kind of link connects schemas for complex verb formation (like (1a)) and schemas for LVC formation (like (2)) on the one hand, and – at the lower level – SVs like (1b) and LVCs like (3). The main difference between our case and what has been discussed in the literature so far is that the two constructions belong to different levels of complexity (morphologically complex verb vs. multiword verb), thus displaying different internal structure despite similarities in form (the psych noun) and, obviously, in meaning. We come back to this theoretical issue in Section 5.3, after exploring the empirical evidence and discussing the results.

4 Methods, data and analysis

Even though LVCs in Italian have been explored by several works (cf. Section 1), to the best of our knowledge there is no systematic study on the competition between SVs and LVCs, and Italian psych-LVCs, despite being often cited in the literature, have not been thoroughly investigated yet. This situation has two consequences: firstly, an empirically collected list of Italian psych-LVCs is not available, and studies tend to take into account and generalize from a handful of very frequent ones, such as *fare paura* 'frighten'; secondly, the relationship between psych-SVs and LVCs expressing different event types has not been systematized yet.

The aim of this study is to fill these gaps by analyzing the relationship between denominal verb formation and light verb constructions as two competing strategies for the creation of complex predicates from psych-nouns.

First and foremost, we provide a comprehensive list of Italian psych-SVs and psych-LVCs by means of lexicographic and corpus data (Section 4.1), since a clear picture is needed to address this topic. The core of the study will concern the competition between forms, i.e., the coexistence between SVs and LVCs from the same noun.[11] Our hypothesis, coherently with the Principle of No Synonymy, is that the co-existence of the two strategies is regulated by their tendency to occupy different functional and distributional niches. We assess this hypothesis by taking into account several linguistic and extra-linguistic factors (Section 4.2).

4.1 Data collection: the distribution of denominal SVs and LVCs across nouns and event types

Since our aim is to study the behavior of predicate formation from nouns, we started by collecting a list of psych-nouns.

The most complete source for Italian is ItEM (Italian EMotive lexicon; Passaro et al., 2015), which comprises a large list of lemmas with their association score, expressed as cosine similarity, with Plutchik's (1994) basic emotion terms (Passaro et al., 2015). ItEM includes ca. 9300 nominal lemmas. We selected the relevant ones by testing their acceptability in the construction *provare/ sentire* N 'feel N', ending up with a list of 199 nouns. We further enriched the list by comparing it with the one provided in Zammuner (1998), thus reaching the number of 217 nouns. For the sake of simplicity and feasibility, we decided to take into account only underived psych-nouns.[12] Hence, we filtered out deadjectival and deverbal nouns. We did so by relying on the data contained in the Italian dictionary GRADIT (Grande dizionario italiano dell'uso; GRADIT, 2007). The final list contains 86 nouns.

For each of the nouns we annotated the frequency, found in the Italian corpus itWaC (Baroni et al., 2009), and we collected the corresponding SVs and LVCs, dividing them into the three aspect-causative categories (see Section 2.2), based on the meanings in (12):[13]

---

[11] For reasons of space, we cannot adequately discuss competition at the level of patterns. However, we propose some preliminary considerations on trends in the formation of causative predicates through qualitative observations.

[12] We chose to do so to avoid making the picture more complex. For instance, if we had taken into account deadjectival nouns, we would have had to consider also Light Verb + Adjective patterns as a competing strategy. Instead, by taking into account deverbal nouns, we would have had to broaden the pool of actional meanings expressed by nouns, since psych-nouns formed from verbs have been said to denote not only states but also events (Melloni, 2017).

[13] Such a tripartition was elaborated from typological literature on event types and from theoretical literature on Italian psych-LVCs (e.g., Croft, 1991; Pompei and Piunno, 2023). The assessment of the meanings of the actual predicates was carried out by using lexicographic resources in the case of SVs, while for LVCs we employed both classifications from the literature and our own intuition.

(12) stative = X feels/is in a state of N (towards Y)
inchoative = X begins to feel N
causative = Y causes X to feel/begin to feel N

For the SVs, we collected for each noun the corresponding denominal verbs we found in GRADIT, filtering out the ones marked as obsolete or literary-only. Instead, for the LVCs we first restricted our search to 9 patterns selected from the literature:
- *essere in* N 'be in N', *avere* N 'have N', *provare* N 'feel N', and *sentire* N 'feel N' for the stative meaning;[14]
- *prendere/si* N 'take N', *farsi* N 'do oneself N', for the inchoative meaning;
- *fare* N 'do N', *mettere* N 'put N', and *dare* N 'give N' for the causative meaning.

We added to this list another pattern generally overlooked in the literature (though briefly mentioned in Vietri 2017, 112), namely *andare in* N 'go in N', which seems to show an inchoative meaning in opposition with the stative *essere in* N. We then checked for the occurrence of all these patterns filled by the 86 nouns from our list in itWaC small[15], assuming that their presence in a reasonably large corpus speaks in favor of their existence as LVCs. We did this by crossing the pattern and the noun lists and by searching the frequency list of the resulting 860 possible multiword expressions in itWaC small. Multiword expressions with frequency lower than 5 were discarded; moreover, the ones that are attested but do not actually correspond to the meanings in (11) were discarded. The SVs and LVCs were coded for type of word formation process or LVC pattern, and for their frequency in itWaC. Table 1 illustrates the top five nouns by frequency in the dataset with the corresponding synthetic and analytic predicates.

By looking at the dataset, we notice that there is generally only one SV per noun (except for *paura* 'fear', that has both *impaurire* and *spaurire* 'frighten') and the only

---

14 While most light verbs are basic ones, *provare* and *sentire* 'feel' are light verb extensions used instead of (and sometimes more often than) *avere* 'have' in the case of stative psych predicates (Salvi, 1988; Cicalese et al., 2016; Pompei and Piunno, 2023). However, despite being defined as extensions in the literature, they do not seem to point at any relevant semantic (e.g., modal, aspectual, etc.; cf. Ježek, 2004) difference from the basic stative light verbs. Their peculiarity is that they can only be combined with psych-nouns, hence they result to be specific to a particular semantic class. As we mentioned, we used these two constructions as tests to select psych-nouns from ItEM. Thus, we could say that *provare/sentire*-LVCs seem to be less idiomatic and less restricted than generic LVCs with respect to the selection of the nouns filling the construction slot. However, we should remember that the sole acceptability of *provare* and *sentire* with a noun doesn't imply that the pattern is actually used frequently enough to be considered as a LVC.
15 https://bellatrix.sslmit.unibo.it/noske/public/#dashboard?corpname=itwac1, last access 27.10.2024.

Tab. 1: The top five nouns by frequency in the dataset and the corresponding predicates.

noun (freq.)	stative predicate (= feel N)		inchoative predicate (= begin to feel N)		causative predicate (= cause X to feel N)	
	SV	LVC	SV	LVC	SV	LVC
interesse 'interest' (260748)	interessarsi	avere interesse; provare interesse	interessarsi	prendere interesse	interessare	dare interesse
amore 'love' (186567)		avere amore; provare amore; sentire amore	innamorarsi			
dubbio 'doubt' (93128)		essere in dubbio				
paura 'fear' (89449)		avere paura; provare paura; sentire paura	impaurirsi	prendere paura	impaurire; spaurire	fare paura; mettere paura; dare paura
pena 'pain' (71264)	penare	essere in pena; avere pena; provare pena; sentire pena		prendersi pena		fare pena; dare pena

cases in which we find more than one SV per noun is when the anticausative alternation applies (e.g., *interessare* 'interest' and *interessarsi* 'be/ get interested' in Table 1). This could be taken as evidence for blocking preventing to form a potential SV while a synonymous one already exists; however, blocking is not the only phenomenon that can explain this distribution, since it would not make sense for a stative SV to be blocked by the existence of a causative SV. Thus, this situation also shows a relative scarcity of predicates expressed by SVs, since we generally find only one event type per noun expressed through SVs (if we do not take into account anticausative SVs). Instead, we often find more than one LVC per noun, expressing both the same and different event types. In order to understand this distribution better, we can analyze the whole dataset along the two axes also used in Table 1: nouns and event types.

If we look at the nouns ordered by raw frequency per lemma, we notice that higher ranked nouns have generally more corresponding predicates than lower ranked ones (Figure 1). The positive correlation between the $\log_{10}$ of the frequency of nouns and the number of predicative constructions results to be quite high by calculating Kendall's tau coefficient of correlation (tau = 0.55, p < 0.001). This is quite expected since the more frequent a noun is, the more available it is as a base for predicate formation.

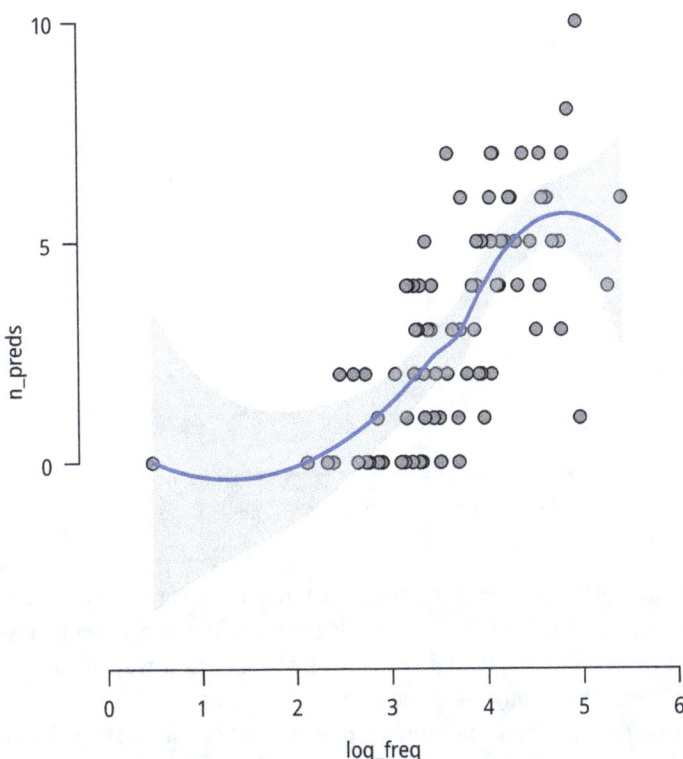

Fig. 1: Log frequency of nouns plotted against the number of predicates per noun.

However, if we separate SVs from LVCs, we see that the correlation is mainly driven by the increase of LVCs (tau = 0.57), while the number of SVs per noun shows a low positive correlation with noun log frequency (tau = 0.26).

The fact that more frequent nouns have a higher possibility of forming predicates has consequences also on the expression of different event types from the same noun. If we divide the nouns in four groups, based on how many event types are lexicalized by both SVs and LVCs (from 0 to 3), we see that the groups expressing more event types comprise more frequent nouns on average[16] (Figure 2, left part). This is probably due to the fact that the more predicates are created from a noun, the more plausible it is that this abundance helps to express all the three possible meanings, as testified by the very high correlation between the number of predicates created from a noun and the number of event types expressed for each noun (tau = 0.8, p < 0.001) (Figure 2, right part).

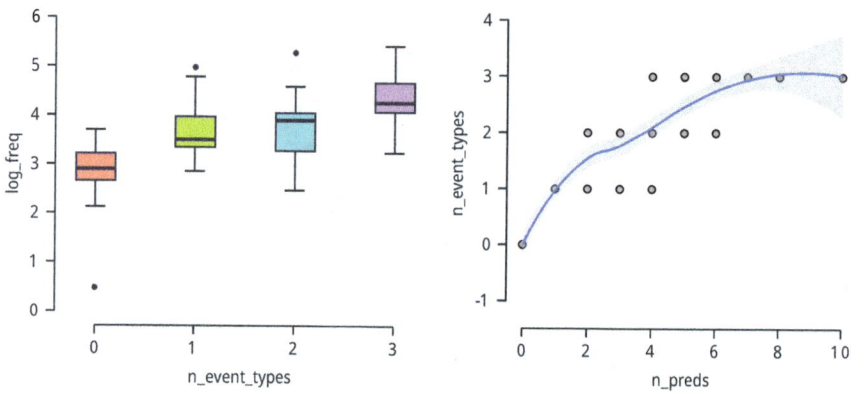

Fig. 2: Log noun frequency grouped by number of event types expressed per noun (left) and number of predicates per noun by number of event types expressed per noun (right).

Since the constructions actually increasing are LVCs and not SVs, we could hypothesize that the expression of different types of events from psych-nouns is made possible by the use of LVCs. However, the situation is quite complex if we look at the distribution of LVCs and SVs among the three event types (Table 2).

While the difference between the number of stative LVCs and stative SVs is quite high[17], and thus we could say that stative psych-predicates are mostly LVCs on the type-level, inchoatives tend to be expressed by means of SVs (see below), while

---

[16] Kruskal-Wallis test yields a p-value < 0.001 for the difference in frequency between the four groups.
[17] If we took into account only basic LVs (*avere* 'have' and *essere in* 'be in'), excluding *provare* and *sentire* 'feel', LVCs would still be more than SVs (53 vs 16).

causatives show a more even distribution between LVCs and SVs.[18] Thus, the contribution of LVCs differs through the different event types.

Finally, a relevant point to highlight is that causatives are the most lexicalized event type: not only they are more numerous than statives and inchoatives, but some of the statives (n = 6) and most of the inchoatives (n = 23) are actually anticausative constructions, formed by adding -*si* to the causative SV (hence, a secondary derivation). Given the apparent 'primacy' of causative events as expressed by SVs and the high number of causative LVCs, we expect to find greater competition between the two strategies within this class.

4.2 The choice between SVs and LVCs

As we mentioned in Section 2.2, there is competition between SVs and LVCs both at the level of patterns and at the level of forms. At the level of patterns, our dataset displays many different constructional schemas used to create predicates from nouns:
- statives: conversion (N-*are*/-*ire*), suffixation (N-*izzare*), *avere* N, *essere in* N, *provare* N, *sentire* N, plus converted or parasynthetic causatives + *si*;
- inchoatives: converted or parasynthetic causatives + *si*, *prendere* N, *farsi* N, *andare in* N;
- causatives: conversion (N-*are*/-*ire*), suffixation (N-*izzare*), parasynthesis (*ad-*/*in-*/*s*-N-*are*/-*ire*), *fare* N, *dare* N, *mettere* N.

As suggested in the literature, the choice between the LVC schemas is at least partially idiosyncratic, and the same goes for the choice between LVC and one of the morphological schemas available (Alba-Salas, 2002, 51). By this, we mean that there

Tab. 2: Number of LVCs and SVs expressing the three event types.

	LVC	SV	total
statives	121	16	137
inchoatives	14	27	41
causatives	63	31	94
total	198	74	272

---

[18] This is confirmed by looking at the standardized residuals from a chi-squared test (p < 0.001) on the contingency table (Table 2): stative events are associated with LVCs (std.res. 5.7), while inchoatives with SVs (std.res. 6.0). As for causatives, we find positive residuals in the LVC cell, but they do not reach the threshold of 2 (std.res. 1.5), and thus we cannot assume causatives to influence the significance of the test.

seems to be no inherent reason why *essere in paura* (lit. be in fear) is not acceptable, while *avere paura* 'have fear' is perfectly acceptable, and the selection seems to depend upon the nominal base. The question seems to be even more complex since there are also less frequent LVCs whose acceptability could be speaker-dependent (e.g., *dare paura* 'give fear').

While it would be impossible to address this topic here with quantitative methods, our data suggest that there may be some trends based on the semantics of the nouns. For instance, by looking at causatives, the *fare*-LVC schema seems to apply quite regularly to nouns associated with disgust and pity (e.g., *fare schifo/ ribrezzo/ pena/ pietà*, lit. do disgust/repugnance/pain/pity), while the *mettere*-LVC seems to be mostly associated with nouns of fear and anxiety[19] (e.g., *mettere paura/ ansia/ angoscia/ inquietudine/ soggezione*, lit. put fear/anxiety/anguish/restlessness/awe).[20] Conversion, instead, seems to be associated more than other schemas with positive sentiment nouns (e.g., *emozionare* and *entusiasmare* 'excite', *interessare* 'interest', *calmare* 'calm down').

However, more in-depth research is needed to disentangle pattern competition in this field. In our analysis, we focus on the competition between different forms, therefore considering cases in which one of the three possible event types is expressed by more than one predicate. More specifically, we concentrate on cases where we find an SV along with one or more LVCs. The analysis aims to unveil which functional and contextual variables motivate the use of the synthetic vs. analytic strategy. We will do so by analyzing a subset of eleven alternations through fitting two mixed-effects regression models.

4.2.1 Sampling, annotation parameters and statistical methods

As we illustrated in Section 4.1, we found a high number of SV and LVC predicates formed from psych-nouns. However, looking at their distribution (cf. Table 2, Section 4.1), we expect the coexistence of synthetic and analytic forms to actually emerge in a relatively limited number of cases.

---

[19] This could suggest an exemplar-based analysis of the phenomenon (cf. Sundquist, 2022), whereby a very frequent LVC such as *fare schifo* or *mettere paura* is used as an exemplar for the creation of LVCs with semantically similar nouns by analogy.

[20] Interestingly, between the (rare) stative types that employ *essere in*, we find three of the nouns associated with *mettere*, expressing distress and anxiety (i.e., *ansia, angoscia* and *soggezione*). Apart from *essere in pena*, these are the only *essere in*-LVCs that have a causative LVC counterpart in our dataset.

As a matter of fact, in our dataset there are only 35 cases of synthetic-analytic alternations: 12 within the stative class; 2 within inchoatives; and 21 within causatives. Furthermore, in most of the cases, there seems to be a large discrepancy in the frequency of the alternants: in 24 cases out of 35 (i.e., 70% of the cases) the frequency of the SV in itWaC is at least 10 times higher than the corresponding LVC frequency. Thus, to give a faithful representation of the relationship between SVs and LVCs and to maximize the chance of unveiling meaningful factors, we selected a subset of data following two criteria: frequency of the noun and difference in frequency of the predicates. We took the top 10 most frequent nouns showing alternating constructions in (at least) one of the three event types but balancing the list to include 4 alternations (out of 10) in which the difference in frequency between the rival constructions is less marked. The selected 4 alternations include cases in which the SV frequency is 1 to 5 times the LVCs frequency, and vice-versa.

As we see in Table 3, this selection turned out to be balanced also with respect to the number of stative and causative alternations (see above). In order not to exclude inchoatives completely, we included the inchoative alternation with *paura*. Another variable kept under control is the argument-semantic role alignment of the predicates, since all the statives and the inchoative enter a Subject-Experiencer construction with an optional External Argument-Stimulus (see the *gioire* class, Belletti and Rizzi, 1988; see 13), while the causatives enter Subject-Stimulus constructions with a Direct (for the SVs, cf. 14a) or an Indirect (for the LVCs, cf. 14b) Object-Experiencer.

(13) a. *Anna gioisce (per suo fratello).*
Anna rejoice.PRS.3SG for POSS.3.M.SG brother.M.SG
'Anna rejoices (for her brother).'
 b. *Anna prova gioia (per suo fratello).*
Anna feel.PRS.3SG joy.3SG for POSS.3.M.SG brother.M.SG
'Anna feels joy (for her brother).'

(14) a. *Anna incoraggia* **gli studenti**.
Anna encourage.PRS.3SG DET.M.PL student.M.PL
'Anna encourages the students.'
 b. *Anna fa* coraggio **agli studenti**.
Anna do.PRS.3SG courage.SG to.DET.M.PL student.M.PL
'Anna gives courage to the students.'

We initially extracted 500 total occurrences of the predicates listed in Table 3, considering both written and spoken data. We employed a regular expression to match all the predicates; for LVCs we included the option of up to two words intervening between the LV and the noun, to analyze nominal modification (Section 2.1). As for spoken data, we collected all available data (191 occurrences) from three corpora:

Tab. 3: The selected alternations for the construction of the sample.

noun	SV	LVC	event type
paura 'fear'	*impaurire, spaurire*	*fare/mettere/dare paura*	causative
	impaurirsi	*prendere paura*	inchoative
dolore 'pain'	*addolorare*	*dare dolore*	causative
emozione 'excitement'	*emozionare*	*dare emozione*	causative
gioia 'joy'	*gioire*	*avere/provare/sentire gioia*	stative
coraggio 'courage'	*incoraggiare*	*fare/dare coraggio*	causative
impressione 'impression'	*impressionare*	*fare/dare impressione*	causative
timore 'fear'	*intimorire*	*dare/fare timore*	causative
fastidio 'bother'	*infastidire*	*dare fastidio*	causative
simpatia 'sympathy'	*simpatizzare*	*avere/provare simpatia*	stative
angoscia 'anguish'	*angosciarsi*	*essere in/provare angoscia*	stative

LIP (De Mauro et al., 1993), gathered in the late 80s and including several types of communicative situations (30 occurrences); KIParla (Mauri et al., 2019), gathered between 2016 and 2019 and containing semi-structured interviews, dialogic and monologic speech mainly from university settings (117 occurrences); RadioCast-It (Masini and Combei, 2024), gathered between 2017 and 2021 and containing radiophonic speech (44 occurrences). We then extracted the remaining 309 occurrences as a random sample from the written Italian corpus CORIS (Rossini Favretti et al., 2002). We excluded false positives (43 occurrences) and cases in which the predicates are employed in a non-psychological (or not-strictly psychological) sense (40 occurrences, mainly with the verb *incoraggiare* 'encourage', used in the sense of 'favor, promote' (15)), for a total of 226 occurrences. Interestingly, not only SVs turned out to be polysemous, as stated in the literature, but also LVCs, if frequent enough, such as *fare paura*, can undergo a semantic extension. For instance, in (15) *fare paura* does not mean 'frighten', but 'amaze'.

(15)   *Occorre   pertanto, adottare una   serie   di iniziative*
       is_necessary.PRS.3SG thus   adopt.INF DEF.F.SG series.SG of initiative.PL
       *per **incoraggiare** e   sviluppare il   flusso di turisti   e*
       to encourage.INF and develop.INF DET.M.SG flow.SG of tourist.PL and
       commercianti provenienti dall'   Est.
       trader.PL   coming.PL from.DET.M.SG east
       'Therefore, a number of initiatives should be taken to promote and develop the flow of tourists and traders from the East.'   (CORIS, STAMPA)

(16) [...] *dopo guardi il programma della summer school*
later look.IMP.2SG DET.M.SG program.SG of.DET.F.SG summer school
fa paura.
do.PRS.3SG fear.SG
'Later, look at the summer school programme, it's amazing.'
(KIParla, TOA3001)

Our final sample thus consists of 417 occurrences and comprises 242 LVCs (13 types) and 175 SVs (11 types). In Figure 3 we show the predicates in our sample, which interestingly do not include some of the predicates in Table 3 (mainly LVCs, such as *dare angoscia* 'give anguish', *fare simpatia* 'do sympathy', etc.).

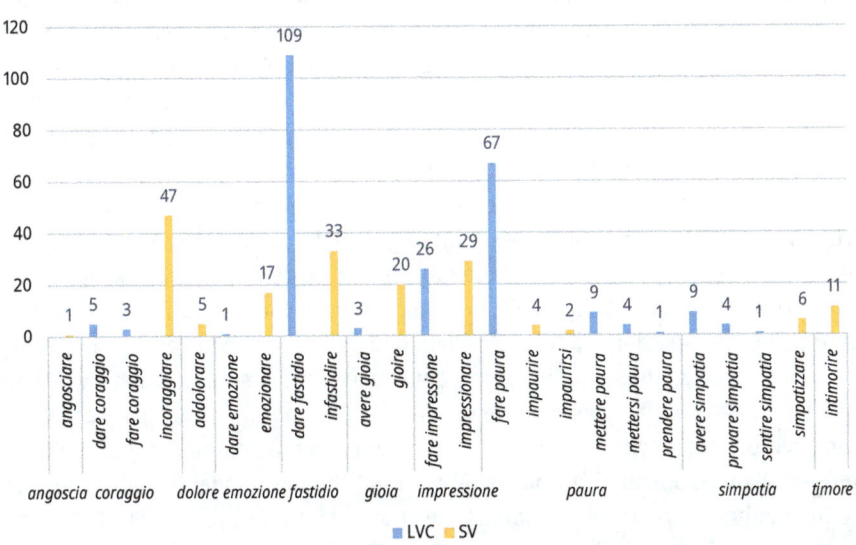

Fig. 3: Predicates in the sample, grouped by noun.

Figure 3 clearly illustrates that the SV-vs-LVC distribution varies among nouns. Thus, not only pattern selection but also the actual frequency of the specific predicates strongly depends on the nominal base. Furthermore, the predicates selected to represent statives and inchoatives turned out to occur less than we expected: causatives provide 366 of the occurrences, while we find only 44 statives and 7 inchoatives. Interestingly, no stative *essere in*-LVC and only 1 inchoative *prendere*-LVC were found. Instead, we found 4 *mettersi paura* 'get scared' (lit. put oneself fear; inchoative LVC), extracted as a false positives of *mettere paura*. We kept them in the sample, even though *mettersi*-LVC is a diatopically marked pattern (cf. De Mauro, 2011, 399). The occurrences were coded for the variables shown in Table 4.

We ran two distinct analyses. The first keeps together all event types and looks only at the 'general' variables (Corpus, Text genre, Modification, and Verb form). The second includes the semantic features of arguments. This last analysis was intended to be performed separately by event type; however, since statives and inchoatives are too few to find meaningful tendencies, the effect of semantic features was tested only on causative constructions (see the last two variables in Table 4). In both cases, we will fit a mixed-effects regression model.

Mixed-effects models are statistical models increasingly employed in linguistics (e.g., Baayen et al., 2008; Gries, 2015; Speelman et al., 2018). Like linear regression models, they allow us to predict the value of the dependent variable (or response variable, in our case binary: LVC vs. SV) based on several independent variables (or predictors), whose importance can also be ranked. Their advantage, however, is that predictors can be treated either as fixed effects or as random effects. While fixed effects are assumed to be non-random and constant across the population (the variables in Table 4), random effects represent the variability that is not captured by fixed effects and depends on the behavior of specific groups in the population. This is useful in our case, since we want to generalize as much as possible our results, avoiding the possible biases due to the specific predicates in our sample. For instance, we do not want our results to be influenced by the specific behavior of very frequent predicates derived from a certain noun, or of predicates expressing a specific event type. At the same time, we want to acknowledge the explanatory power attributable to nominal bases in the selection of SVs and LVCs. For this reason, we included the event type (only in the first model) and the nominal base as random effects. We used RBrul (Johnson, 2009) to select the best model (i.e., the one containing only the predictors that affect the choice) by running a step-up/step-down regression, and then fit the selected model in R using the *lmer4* (Bates et al., 2015) and *afex* (Henrik et al., 2023) packages to rank the effect of the predictors.

4.2.2 Modelling the SV vs LVC alternation

As we mentioned, we first modeled the alternation based on all occurrences, regardless of the aspect-causative meaning (n = 417). Thus, we included the predictors applicable to both transitive and intransitive predicates: Corpus, Text_genre, Verb_Form, and Modification as fixed effects; Noun and Event_type as random effects. The step-up/step-down procedure in RBrul selected the models containing all the predictors except Corpus (17).

Tab. 4: Variables chosen for the annotation of the occurrences.

Variable	Levels
Corpus	– Written – Spoken
Modification (adjectives or adverbs of quantity or quality)	– Modified – Non_Modified
Verb_Form	– Finite – Non Finite_Infinitive – Non Finite_Other (participles, gerunds)
Text_genre	– Dialogic_speech (face-to-face and telephone conversations) – Monologic_speech (university lessons, public speeches) – Broadcast (radio and TV speech) – Fiction_prose – Press – NonFiction_prose (academic and legal prose) – Websites (blog posts)
[causatives only] Sem_SubjStimulus (Subject-Stimulus semantics)	– Egophoric (i.e., non-3rd person stimulus, as in (*Io*) *vi do coraggio* 'I give you courage') – Animate – Inanimate – Clause & Clause_referred (i.e., *Camminare al buio fa paura* 'Walking in the dark is scary') – Unknown/Unspecified (i.e., the stimulus is not specified, as in *Ho visto un bambino impaurito* 'I saw a frightened child')
[causatives only] Sem_NonSubjExperiencer ((In)direct object-Experiencer semantics)	– Egophoric (i.e., non-3rd person experiencer *I rumori mi infastidiscono* 'Noises bother me') – Animate – Inanimate – Zero (i.e., the experiencer is not specified, as in *L'ignoto fa paura* 'The unknown is frightening' (lit. frightens))

(17)   Construction ~ Text_genre + Verb_Form + Modification + (1|Noun) + (1| Event_type)

Subsequently, we ranked the effects of the predictors with likelihood ratio tests from the *afex* package in R. Finally, we refitted the model with *lme4* package, and applied sum-to-zero contrasts with the *emmeans* package (Lenth, 2023) to evaluate the significance of the levels of the predictors. The output of the model with the predictors ranked by effect is shown in Table 5. The levels that significantly affect the choice are highlighted according to the group (pink for SVs and blue for LVCs).

Tab. 5: Output and performance of the model including all the event types.

Predictor	Levels	Estimate	Std.Error	z_ratio	p_value	
Verb_Form	Finite	0.1529	0.4962	-3.6977	0.0002	***
*** (p <.001)	NonFinite_Infinitive	1.0610	0.5227	-1.7730	0.0762	.
	NonFinite_Other	4.7493	0.9544	2.8935	0.0038	**
Text_genre	Broadcast	2.9456	0.4481	2.1377	0.0325	*
*** (p <.001)	Dialogic_speech	0.6463	0.3782	-3.5470	0.0004	***
	Fiction_prose	2.3026	0.3208	0.9814	0.3264	
	Monologic_speech	-0.3611	1.0304	-2.2796	0.0226	*
	NonFiction_prose	3.1191	0.6516	1.7363	0.0825	.
	Press	2.1809	0.3556	0.5432	0.5870	
	Websites	3.0809	0.7030	1.5548	0.1200	
Modification	Modified	1.4869	0.1975	-2.5356	0.0112	*
** (p = .009)	Non_Modified	2.4886	0.1975	2.5356	0.0112	*
Model Performance	Classification accuracy	AIC	BIC	R^2 (cond.)	R^2 (marg.)	
	0.84	351.971	401.368	0.654	0.289	

As we see in Table 5, Verb_Form and Text_genre are the most important predictors, followed by Modification. As for Verb_Form, p-values suggest that Finite is associated with LVCs, while NonFinite_Other (participles, gerunds) with SVs. For Text_genre, mainly spoken genres affect the choice significantly: Monologic_speech and, most importantly, Dialogic_speech are associated with LVCs, while Broadcast with SVs. As for written genres, we find only a weak trend associating SVs with Non-Fiction_prose. Finally, as expected, Modification is associated with LVCs.

The same procedure was applied to obtain and evaluate the model for causatives only (n = 366). We added to the formula the two predictors related to subject and non-subject semantics (Sem_NonSubjExperiecer and Sem_SubjStimulus). However, the best models included only Sem_NonSubjExperiecer:

(18) Construction ~ Text_genre + Verb_Form + Modification + Sem_NonSubjExperiecer + (1|Noun)

As we see in Table 6, the predictor concerning the semantic features of the experiencer was the highest-ranked one. In particular, Zero (i.e., the absence of the object, yielding a generic reading of the experiencer) is strongly associated with LVCs, while Animate (3rd person) experiencers with SVs. The remainder of the model displays almost the same effects as the preceding one, with the exception of some levels (Websites is associated with SVs, while Broadcast is not) and the fact that Modification is a much less important (although still significant) factor.

Tab. 6: Output and performance of the model for causative predicates.

Predictor	Levels	Estimate	Std.Error	z_ratio	p_value	
Sem_NonSubjExp *** (p <.001)	Animate	3.2237	0.3942	2.9795	0.0029	**
	Egophoric	1.6111	0.4210	-1.0405	0.2981	
	Inanimate	2.6693	0.9414	0.6589	0.5100	
	Zero	0.6922	0.4870	-2.7861	0.0053	**
Verb_Form *** (p <.001)	Finite	0.5185	0.4868	-3.1444	0.0017	**
	NonFinite_Infinitive	1.0936	0.5392	-1.7722	0.0764	.
	NonFinite_Other	4.5351	0.9225	2.6949	0.0070	**
Text_genre *** (p <.001)	Broadcast	2.8649	0.4916	1.6594	0.0970	.
	Dialogic_speech	0.8075	0.4472	-2.7760	0.0055	**
	Fiction_prose	2.0228	0.3914	-0.0671	0.9465	
	Monologic_speech	-0.2406	1.1385	-2.0111	0.0443	*
	NonFiction_prose	2.6205	0.8601	0.6643	0.5065	
	Press	2.2360	0.4320	0.4328	0.6651	
	Websites	4.0323	0.9371	2.1163	0.0343	*
Modification * (p = .035)	Modified	1.5717	0.2324	-2.0537	0.0400	*
	Non_Modified	2.5264	0.2324	2.0537	0.0400	*
Model Performance	Classification accuracy	AIC	BIC	R^2 (cond.)	R^2 (marg.)	
	0.88	270.394	325.031	0.760	0.320	

5 Discussion

5.1 A paradigm of denominal psych-predicates

As mentioned in Section 4.1, the predicates formed from psych-nouns, be they synthetic or analytic, always fall in one of three main event types. Highly frequent nouns tend to have at least one predicate per event type. Thus, we suppose that speakers' linguistic knowledge includes the fact that there are three main possible meanings expressed by denominal psych-predicates (state, inchoation, causation), and that the forms expressing these meanings may be morphologically related to each other.

Our proposal is that this situation can be fruitfully described as a derivational paradigm for psych-nouns. We can preliminarily define a derivational paradigm as a set of cells specifying the set of semantic and formal features realized by actual derivational series (cf. *paradigm*$_1$ in Hathout and Namer, 2019, 154). In our case, the paradigm is formed by three cells, corresponding to the three event types. Each cell contains the following pair of information: (i) the semantic value expressed by the denominal predicates (e.g., cause X to feel N), and (ii) the schemas (formal features) used to create these predicates (e.g., N-*are*/-*ire*, N-*izzare*, *ad*-/*in*-/*s*-N-*are*/*ire*, *fare* N, *dare* N, and *mettere* N for the causative cell).

Some arguments in favor of a derivational paradigm formed by event types come from typological research. Firstly, as we mentioned, statives, inchoatives and causatives are the most commonly lexicalized event types crosslinguistically (Croft, 1991; Talmy, 2000). Secondly, some scholars have already argued that the causative-inchoative pair forms a paradigm, with other scholars adding stative predicates too (e.g., Beavers et al., 2021). In our case, this is relevant because we assessed that anticausative morphology can form stative and not only inchoative predicates. Finally, Nichols (2019, 347) explicitly proposed that predicates denoting continuous (including states), bounded (including inchoatives) and causation events form a derivational paradigm that can be actualized in individual languages.

Our proposal can be easily translated in CxG terms (Section 3.2): psych-event types can be described as a hyperconstruction, created as an abstraction from the sets of actual morphologically related instances (e.g., *avere paura* vs *impaurirsi* vs *impaurire*). This hyperconstruction includes three cells encoding the semantic domain associated with the expression of psychological events, and paradigmatic links expressing the semantic opposition between these cells (Figure 4).

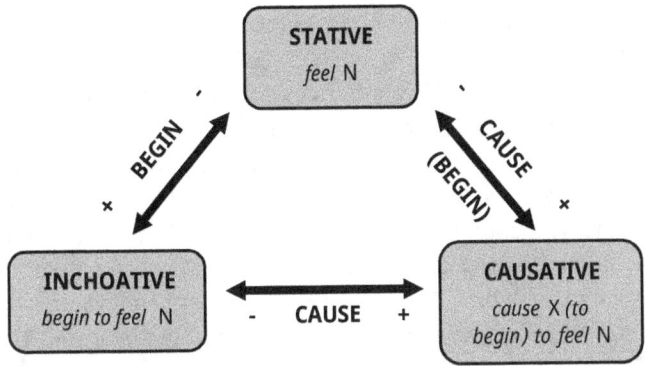

Fig. 4: The 'event types' derivational paradigm for psych-nouns.

Figure 4[21] resembles more a "content paradigm" (Stump, 2015, 5), since it only includes the abstract meanings that the predicates can express. For now, we propose this generalization, since there are several competing patterns for each cell ('differential exponence') that do not seem to form regular and predictable series: we hope future studies will shed light on this aspect. Note that differential exponence is not a problem for our proposal: the presence of multiple schemas and the lack of predictability and regularity are common in derivational paradigms and constitute a topic of debate (Bonami and Strnadová, 2019; Melloni and Dal Maso, 2022), although, as we will argue, it is possible to find a certain degree of regularity in our paradigm.

It is crucial to note that the derivational paradigm we are proposing is not a canonical one, since it includes 'periphrastic word formation'. As proposed in the literature, multiword expressions can be considered exponents in inflectional and derivational paradigms, either filling cells in complementary distribution with synthetic forms or competing with them for the same cell (Ackerman and Stump, 2004; Masini, 2019b; Cetnarowska, 2021). However, our data point precisely to broadening the notion of derivational paradigm, since LVCs do not seem to merely be 'fillers' for empty cells. Instead, the distribution of LVCs and SVs shows a quite systematic division of constructional labor, suggesting cooperation between analytic and synthetic strategies in the expression of event types:

– LVCs are the main strategy used to form stative psych predicates: LVC types (80% of which are *avere*-LVCs) are three times more numerous than the SV types. Since psych-nouns already denote states, it seems reasonable that the

---

[21] We did not split stative and dynamic causatives, since it seems a rather complex distinction, often noticeable only at the token-level, that must be further explored. However, we highlighted that the opposition in dynamicity between stative and causatives is possible, but not always present.

most natural choice is to simply add a LV to make them predicates, instead of using a denominal verb. Furthermore, as noted in the literature, stative LVCs with psych nouns are unmarked with respect to causative and inchoative ones, since in this case the LV and the noun share their actional properties and there is coreference between their arguments (Ježek, 2004; Pompei and Piunno, 2023).
– Inchoativity is generally expressed by means of anticausative SVs, formed by adding *si* to either parasynthetic (61%) or converted (39%) SVs. In fact, we found 27 SVs against 5 *prendere*-LVCs (which should be the main LVC pattern used to express anticausativity) and 1 *farsi*-LVC (*farsi coraggio*, lit 'do oneself courage'), with the LV bearing anticausative morphology, similarly to the *mettersi*-LVC (*mettersi paura*) found in the analysis. This confirms Pompei & Piunno's (2023) observation that *prendere* is not employed regularly with psych-nouns. Instead, *andare in*-LVC, though not very frequently employed (n. of types = 7), is quite regularly employed with nouns used in *essere in* stative LVC (e.g., *collera* 'wrath', *estasi* 'rapture', *panico* 'panic', etc.).
– As for causatives, there is a more complex situation since we find both SVs and LVCs and there is not a single pattern (either synthetic or analytic) that clearly predominates over the others. Hence, the causative cell shows a higher amount of 'suppletion', leading to competition at the pattern level. However, as we mentioned in Section 4.2, there seem to be some tendencies in the choice of patterns, depending on the semantics of the nominal base (e.g., *fare* shows an association with disgust and pity, *mettere* with the nouns expressing fear and anxiety, etc.) and on its sentiment polarity (positive psych-states are often expressed by converted SVs). Nonetheless, there are many cases of 'overabundance', where we find more than one strategy employed and competition between two or more available forms possibly arises.

This overview unveils some general tendencies. The link between causatives and inchoatives is weaker in the domain of LVCs (Pompei and Piunno, 2023), while it is quite strong in the domain of SVs, since it is provided more regularly by the anticausative alternation. Instead, in the domain of LVCs the counterpart of 'marked' causative LVCs are mainly statives, typically expressed through the basic *avere*-LVCs or *provare/sentire* extensions. Furthermore, the only *essere in* statives that have a causative LVC counterpart are formed from the nominal bases associated with *mettere* (see footnote 20). Finally, the only clear and regular relationship between statives and inchoatives is found between two LVCs, namely *essere in* and *andare in*.

Thus, even though further research is needed, the paradigm proposed here seems to show some degree of predictability, mainly (but not solely) provided by the division of constructional labor between analytic and synthetic strategies. However, our proposal does not downplay the differences between 'morphological' and 'periphrastic' word formation. The most evident difference pertains the entrenchment of SVs and LVCs: overall, SVs have a higher token frequency, and thus are more entrenched and more likely to influence the formation of new items. Instead, it would be difficult to claim that all the LVCs found are equally stored in the speakers' mind: for instance, the very infrequent *dare paura* 'give fear' is possibly acceptable, but it is surely not entrenched as *fare paura* 'do fear', that is frequent enough to acquire additional senses (as SVs often do, see Section 4.2.1). Moreover, there are differences in the behavior of SVs and LVCs also at the token level, which we discuss by looking at forms occupying the same cell in the paradigm.

5.2 Overabundance: the behavior of (quasi-)synonymous SVs and LVCs

Our analysis of SVs and LVCs expressing the same meaning showed that some usage differences motivate the choice between them, such as contextual distribution, formal differences but also collocational preferences at the argument structure level (at least in the case of causatives).

The first discrepancy between analytic and synthetic predicates is their different distribution across text genres, which was selected by the model over the distribution between written and spoken data. As we see in Figure 5, some genres (i.e., monologic speech, non-fiction prose, websites) comprise only few occurrences, thus it would be difficult to draw conclusions from their distribution, although it is sometimes (weakly) significant. However, more numerous groups reveal a clearer picture: in written genres, such as fiction and press, LVCs and SVs seem to be used quite evenly, whereas in dialogic speech LVCs represent the vast majority of the occurrences. This could hint at a general spoken vs. written distinction, but if we look at broadcast (i.e., radio and TV speech) we see that its distribution actually patterns with written genres, to the point that Broadcast shows a significant association with SVs in the first model (Table 5, Section 4.2.2).

These results suggest that the distribution can be explained in terms of text genres and planning, since broadcast occurrences are primarily from radio shows (from the corpus RadioCast-It), which are more planned and formal than spontaneous dialogues. This confirms the idea that the choice of LVCs "rises through registers" (Shahrokny-Prehn and Höche, 2011), and that there could be not only stylistic but also processing factors at play: LVCs allow the speaker to better monitor their linguistic production since information is dispersed over multiple highly frequent lexical units (Brugman, 2001; Amenta, 2008).

The contextual distribution of analytic and synthetic psych-predicates can help us better understand the impact of another factor, namely modification, which is

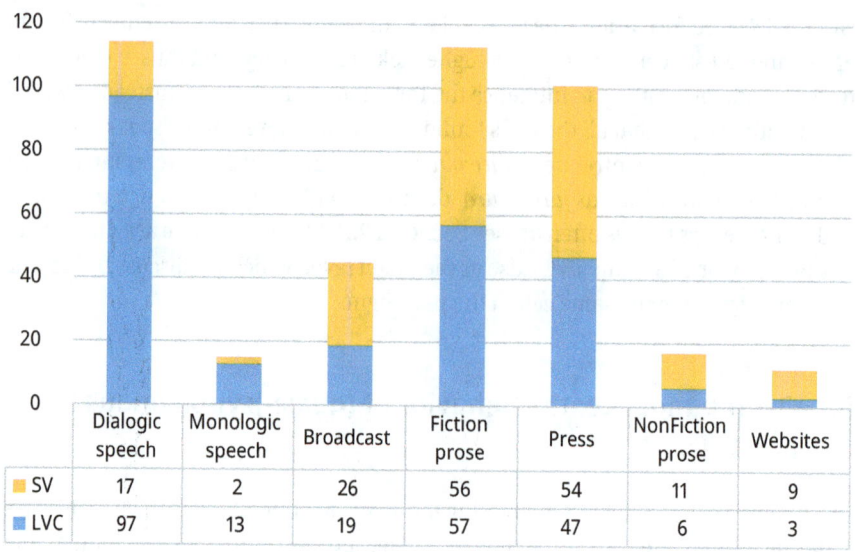

Fig. 5: Distribution of SVs and LVCs by text genre.

regarded as highly relevant in literature (Section 2.1). In our analysis, we found that, albeit significant, the putatively higher possibility of modification attributed to LVCs has a lower impact on speakers' choice than expected. Indeed, in our dataset there are many cases of adjectives (19a) and adverbs (19b) of quantity/quality interposed between the LV and the noun.

(19) a. *Mister Brontë [...] non* **aveva** *naturale simpatia per*
    Mister Brontë not have.IPFV.PST.3SG natural.F.SG sympathy.SG for
    l' infanzia
    DET.F.SG infancy.SG
    'Mr. Brontë **had no natural sympathy** for childhood' (CORIS, NARRAT)

b. *[...] faccio venire io [...] un sacco di malati, finti*
    do.PRS.1SG come.INF I DET.M.SG bag.SG of diseased.PL fake.M.PL
    naturalmente o li preferisci veri? Meglio finti,
    naturally or them prefer.PRS.1SG real.M.SG better fake.M.PL
    fanno meno impressione.
    do.PRS.3PL less impression.SG
    'I'll get a couple of journalist friends to come, and then a lot of sick people, fake of course, or do you prefer them real? It's better if they are fake, they are less shocking.' (lit. **make less impression**) (CORIS, NARRAT)

In some cases, the presence of an adjective can change the psych-state expressed by the LVC, sometimes combined with the presence of a determiner (cf. 20 with 19b). Thus, we could expect modification to crucially favor the use of LVCs, in particular adjectival modification since SVs can only be modified by adverbs (21).

(20) Ho fatto l' esame con lui la scorsa
have.PRS.3SG do.PFV.PTCP DET.M.SG exam.SG with him DET.F.SG past.f.sg
settimana, mi aveva fatto **una buona**
week.SG to-me have.IPFV.PST.3SG do.PFV.PTCP DET.F.SG good.F.SG
impressione.
impression.SG
'I took the exam with him last week; he had made **a good impression** on me.'
(CORIS, STAMPA)

(21) mi **emoziona** ancora **molto** andare al cinema [...]
me excite.PSR.3SG still a.lot go.INF to.DET.M.SG cinema.SG
'it still **excites** me **a lot** to go to the movies.' (KIParla, PTD007)

However, modification is a (significant but) minor factor in our model. Let us look at the significance of modification in different contexts. By splitting written and spoken data (for simplicity), we see that in the former LVCs appear significantly more with modifiers (chi-square yields a $p < 0.001$), and adjectives seem to play an important role (Figure 6, left graph). Instead, in spoken contexts, there is no significant association ($p = 0.08$), and visually, the contribution of adjectives is lower (Figure 6, right graph). A possible interpretation is that in contexts where there is more competition, such as written ones (where we find approximately a 50/50 distribution), modification is indeed a factor that favors the use of LVCs when the speaker wants to modify the content of the predicate, while we do not find this situation in spoken contexts, where LVCs are highly more used than SVs anyway.

Moreover, Figure 6 clearly shows that, both in written and spoken data, the presence of modification accounts for only a small part of the variation: only 20% of the occurrences are modified. Thus, modification is not frequently available as a cue for predicting the choice between LVCs and SVs.

Instead, the most relevant factor in our model turned out to be the opposition between finite and non-finite verb forms, quite unexpectedly. While LVCs tend to appear in their finite forms in 87,6% of the cases, SVs are used in a finite form only in 54,2% of the occurrences (Figure 7). This distribution does not change significantly between written (finite LVCs = 82,3%, finite SV = 51,5%) and spoken data (finite LVCs = 92,2%, finite SV = 62,2%).

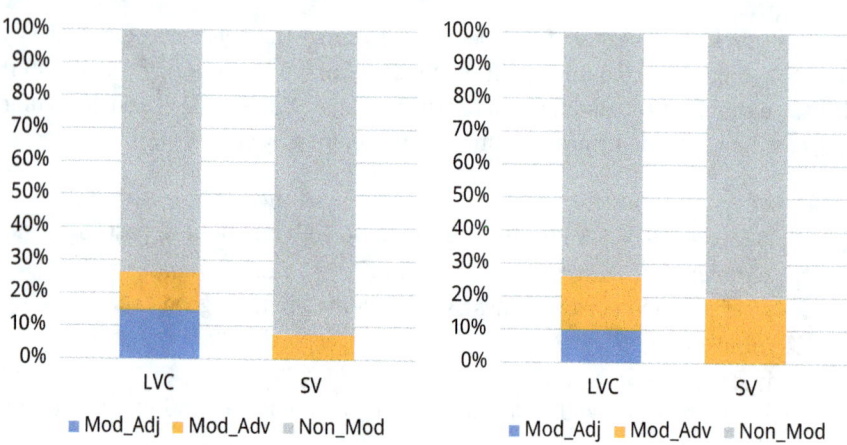

Fig. 6: Modification of LVCs and SVs in written (left) and spoken (right) data.

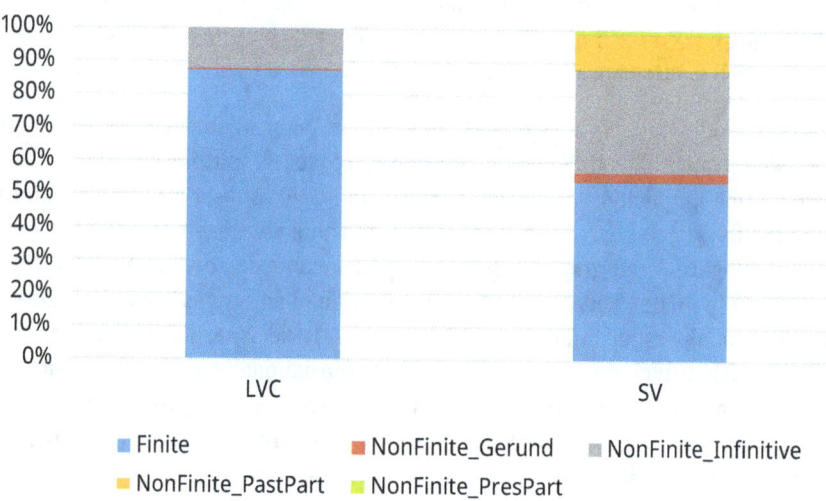

Fig. 7: Verb forms of LVCs and SVs.

This difference could partly depend on the high number of periphrases that select non-finite forms in Italian: for instance, in our dataset we find modal (22), causative (23), and aspectual (24) periphrases with infinitives.

(22) [...] *alla fine* **ha** *potuto* *gioire con*
at.DET.F.SG end.SG have.PRS.3SG be.able.PFV.PTCP rejoice.INF with
i suoi compagni per la vittoria
DET.M.PL POSS.1SG.M.PL mate.PL for DET.F.SG victory.SG
'In the end, he **was able to rejoice** with his teammates over the crucial victory'
(CORIS, STAMPA)

(23) *sono tante le cose che* **fanno** *emozionare di The*
be.PRS.3PL many.F.PL DET.F.PL thing.PL REL make.PRS.3PL excite.INF of the
Imagineering Story [...]
imagineering story
'there are so many **exciting** (lit. that **make excite**) things about The Imagineering Story.'
(RadioCast-It)

(24) *Sind Sie rasend – ha gridato il barone* [...]
have.PRSS.3SG shout.PFV.PTCP DET.M.SG baron.SG [...]
cominciando a impaurir-si *un pochino.*
begin.GER to frighten.INF-si DET.M.SG little.DIM
'Sind Sie rasend – shouted the baron, [...] **starting to get a little scared**.'
(CORIS, NARRAT)

We could argue that the use of LVCs, although surely grammatical in some of them, is generally disfavored in periphrases: their multiword nature would yield strings with a high degree of complexity, possibly more costly to process. See for instance (25), where example (22) is repeated with the SV substituted by an LVC:

(25) *Alla fine ha potuto provare gioia con*
at.DET.F.SG end.SG have.PRS.3SG be.able.PFV.PTCP feel.INF joy.SG with
i suoi compagni per la vittoria.
DET.M.PL POSS.1SG.M.PL mate.PL for DET.F.SG victory.SG
'In the end he was able to feel joy with his teammates for the crucial victory.'

However, our model also detects that infinitive forms lean more towards LVCs (even though not significantly). Clearly, we find instances of infinitive LVCs (26), but they are far less frequent than infinitive SVs.

(26) sono   stanco   // di essermi   preso   questo   ruolo
     be.PRS.1SG tired.M.SG of be.INF.for.me take.PFV.PTCP DEM.PROX.M.SG role.SG
     [...] vai   in mezzo ai   torturati   e   sei
           go.PRS.2SG in half   to.DET.M.PL tortured.PL and be.PRS.2SG
     quello   che deve   far   coraggio.
     DEM.DIST.M.SG REL must.PRS.3SG do.INF courage.SG
     'I'm tired of having this role [...] you go among the tortured and you're the
     one who has to give them courage.'   (KIParla, PTB023)

This could be due to the quasi-absence of other types of non-finite LVCs. Probably, when compared to the distribution of verb forms among SVs, infinitives are still considered as more leaning towards the LVC side overall, due to the lack of the category encompassing gerunds and participles, that are commonly used with SVs. In fact, other non-finite forms (gerunds, past and present participles) are strongly associated with SVs. This is quite expected, because, at least for past participles, LVCs, being intransitive predicates, would not assume the passive reading yielded by SVs, and thus they would be ungrammatical in the cases of adjectival-like uses of past participles (27).

(27) a. siamo   rimasti   tutti   molto ben **impressionati**
        be.PRS.1PL stay.PFV.PTCP.M.PL all.M.PL a.lot   well impress.PFV.PTCP.M.PL
        'we were all very positively **impressed**'   (LIP, NA3)
     b. *siamo   rimasti   tutti   molto ben **fatti**
        be.PRS.1PL stay.PFV.PTCP.M.PL all.M.PL a.lot   well do.PFV.PTCP.M.PL
        impressione
        impression.SG
        '*we were all very positively **made impression**'

Interestingly, whatever the full explanation may be, the byproduct of this distribution is some sort of division of constructional labor: LVCs are almost always used in prototypical predicative constructions, where they act as main clause predicates that govern directly their arguments (28), while other uses, sometimes closer to adjectives (27) or to adverbial subordinate clauses (29), are performed by SVs.

(28) non ci   vivo   quindi // i   difetti mi   danno
     not with.her live.PRS.1SG so   DET.M.PL fault.PL to.me give.PRS.3PL
     relativamente fastidio.
     relatively   annoyance.SG
     'I don't live with her so **her faults don't bother me so much**'
                                                               (KIParla, TOD2012)

(29) Io, a Bologna, ho privilegiato la produzione
I in Bologna have.PRS.1SG favor.PFV.PTCP DET.F.SG production.SG
al consumo, **incoraggiando** gli artisti.
over.DET.M.SG consumption.SG encourage.GER DET.M.PL artist.PL
'In Bologna, I favored production over consumption, **encouraging** artists.'
(CORIS, STAMPA)

As we mentioned, we also fitted a model comprising causative predicates only, in order to analyze the type and the semantics of their arguments. The first observation is a formal one: in LVCs the experiencer is aligned with the indirect object (30b) and not with the direct object (as in SVs, cf. 30a), since the object position is already filled by the psych-noun.

(30) a. *Lavoravano senza mettersi in vista, **non**
work.IPFV.PST.3PL without put.INF.themselves in sight not
infastidivano nessuno* [...].
bother.IPFV.PST.3PL anyone
'They worked without putting themselves in sight, **not bothering anyone**.'
(CORIS, NARRAT)

b. [...] *il Milan **darà fastidio** alla Lazio fino*
DET.M.SG Milan give.FUT.3SG annoyance.SG to.DET.F.SG Lazio until
all' ultimo [...].
at.DET.M.SG last.SG
'Milan **will bother** Lazio until the very end.' (CORIS, STAMPA)

While this difference in formal marking does not seem to entail a difference in meaning between the predicates in (30), it has some consequences both on the expression and the type of arguments selected. As noticed for Spanish (Cuervo, 2010; Rivas, 2016), the behavior of causative LVCs is often very similar to the one displayed by the *piacere*-class predicates (Belletti & Rizzi's 1988 third class, Section 2.2). This is particularly evident in the frequent cases (46,8% of LVC occurrences) where the experiencer coincides with the speaker and is expressed through the clitic *mi*, preposed to the predicate (31a), as in the unmarked construction for *piacere*-class verbs (31b):

(31) a. è   meglio anche per me perché **mi   dà   sempre**
        be.PRS.3SG better also for me because to.me give.PRS.3SG always
        fastidio   tenerlo   [=il microfono].
        annoyance.SG keep.INF.it
        'It's better for me too because **it always bothers me to hold** the microphone.'

        (KIParla, TOD1016)

   b. ***Mi   piacerebbe inserire***   anche idee   e   esperienze
      to-me like.COND.3SG include.INF also idea.PL and experience.PL
      altrui.
      of.others
      'I would also like (lit. **it would be pleasant to me**) to include other people's ideas and experiences.'

      (CORIS, EPHEM)

However, the model did not select this level as significant, since 62,2% of these cases are attributable to the sole *dare fastidio* 'give annoyance'. Instead, the type of experiencer-argument significantly associated with LVCs is Zero, i.e., when the experiencer is not overtly expressed, nor coreferential with any element in the context (32).

(32)   *Quel   tipo   aveva   un   modo di fare   che*
        DEM.DIST.M.SG guy.SG have.IPFV.PST.3SG DEM.M.SG way.SG of do.INF REL
        metteva   paura.
        put.IPFV.PRS.3SG fear.SG
        'The guy had a scary way about him.' (lit. had a way of behaving that **put fear**)

        (CORIS, NARRAT)

This pattern differentiates psych-LVCs from *piacere*-class verbs (Rivas, 2016), probably due to the difference in argument alignment between SVs and LVCs. We could interpret this behavior, again, as a form of complexity avoidance: if we express the experiencer as a full-PP this would make the construct more complex than the corresponding SV, given the presence of a psych-noun as the "direct object". Moreover, it seems less natural to omit the experiencer in the case of SVs, or at least some of them. For instance, the substitution of the LVC in (32) with the corresponding SV in (33) is acceptable but sounds much less natural:

(33) ?*Quel   tipo   aveva   un   modo di fare che*
      DEM.DIST.M.SG guy.SG have.IPFV.PST.3SG DET.M.SG way.SG of do.INF REL
      ***impauriva**.*
      put.IPFV.PRS.3SG
      lit. That guy had a way of behaving that **frightened**.

Examples with an unexpressed experiencer are interesting from a semantic perspective, since they convey a generic reading (34). In some cases, this may be a strategy for the speakers to background their own experience of the psych-state by attributing it potentially to the whole world, while the subject-stimulus is more foregrounded (Cuervo, 2010, 150).

(34) *I   cavalli di Agropoli, erranti   per strada*
      DET.M.PL horse.PL of Agropoli wander.IPFV.PTCP.M.PL for street.SG
      hanno   paura. Ancor di più, **fanno   paura***.*
      have.PRS.3SG fear.SG still   of more do.PRS.3PL fear.SG
      'Horses in Agropoli, wandering the streets, are scared. Even more, **they are scary**.'

(CORIS, STAMPA)

Finally, we should note that our model did not select the type of subject-stimulus as a relevant factor. LVCs do select more often clausal subjects (35), or at least subjects anaphorically or cataphorically referred to clauses (36): 30,4% of the subjects in the sample for LVCs are clausal or clause-referred, compared to 12,3% for SVs.

(35) *fa   impressione // **rileggersi il   discorso** che* [Mussolini]
      do.PRS.3SG impression.SG   reread.INF DET.M.SG speech.SG REL Mussolini
      fece
      do.PFV.PST.3SG
      'It is shocking **to reread the speech** that Mussolini gave'

(KIParla, TOD1017)

(36) *Sono   un   fuoriclasse.* **Questo**   *dà   fastidio*
      be.PRS.1SG DET.M.SG ace.SG   DEM.PROX.M.SG give.PRS.3SG annoyance.SG
      in Sicilia.
      in Sicily
      'I am an ace. **This** bothers people in Sicily.'

(CORIS, STAMPA)

The presence of clausal subjects as stimuli with LVCs is not surprising (cf., e.g., Vietri, 2017, 119-120): psych-causation is among the less prototypical forms of causation events, thus it does not necessarily entail an agentive subject (Croft, 1991, 169). However, our model factored out this predictor, since, again, it seems an effect mainly attributable to *dare fastidio*. As noted above, along with the realization of the experiencer as a clitic (see above), the lack of agentivity of the clausal stimulus, too, makes some occurrences of *dare fastidio* very close to Belletti & Rizzi's (1988) class encompassing *piacere* 'like' and similar verbs (cfr. 31).

Summing up, the factors that influence the choice between LVCs and SVs are the following:
- text genre: LVCs tend to be preferred in dialogic, unplanned speech, while in both written genres and planned speech situations (such as broadcast speech) SVs and LVCs show a more even distribution;
- verb form: LVCs are almost always used in their finite forms, while non-finite forms are mainly expressed through SVs, especially past participles with adjectival function;
- presence of modification: the possibility to modify the noun through adjectives significantly increases the number of modified LVCs in comparison with SVs, at least in written data.

Moreover, restricting our view to causative predicates, we found that LVCs are significantly more used without an overt experiencer argument, yielding an arbitrary and sometimes generic reading of the predicate. Instead, SVs tend to select animate entities as the experiencer. However, the association holds only with 3rd-person experiencers, since non-3rd-person animate experiencers (i.e., the speaker and the interlocutors) tend to be selected, even if not significantly, by LVCs.

5.3 The constructional network of psych-predicates

So far, we modeled the paradigm of event types expressed through denominal psych-predicates and assessed the competition between verbs expressing the same event type, by looking at high levels (hyperconstructions) and low levels (fully specified constructions) of abstraction. We now propose a representation of the interplay of SVs and LVCs in the constructicon, to show how the constructions at different levels are actually connected.

In CxG, relations between constructions are handled through links (Section 3.2). Thus, we need as many links as the number of different relations observed between constructions. We found at least two types of relationships between psych-predicates, namely paradigmatic opposition and semantic similarity (viz., near-synonymy). However, the full picture is more complex: for instance, we need to account for the peculiar nature of causative and anticausative predicates, and to address the problem of polysemy. For this reason, we need to discuss the links we selected (Table 7).

Tab. 7: Links employed to model the relationship between psych-LVCs and SVs.

	Link	Link direction and schematicity level of cxns	Relation between cxn_1 and cxn_2
→	instance	from cxn_1 to cxn_2 (cxn_1 more schematic than cxn_2)	cxn_1 is instantiated by cxn_2
←	S-synonymy	between cxn_1 and cxn_2 (same level of schematicity)	cxn_1 and cxn_2 are near-synonyms
↔	paradigmatic	between cxn_1 and cxn_2 (same level of schematicity)	cxn_1 and cxn_2 are in paradigmatic opposition
—•	subpart	from cxn_1 to cxn_2 (same level of schematicity)	cxn_2 is a subpart of cxn_1
┈►	metaphorical	from cxn_1 to cxn_2 (same level of schematicity)	cxn_2 is a metaphorical extension of cxn_1
——	filler-slot	from cxn_1 to $slot_2$ (cxn_1 less schematic than cxn_2)	cxn_1 fills an empty slot in cxn_2

We already presented (and employed) horizontal links: this term is used in the literature to refer both to contrast and synonymy relations between constructions. Even though there is indeed a continuum between paradigmatic contrast and semantic similarity – since we assume no (full) synonymy, or no equivalence, and thus some degree of contrast between semantically similar constructions – it's useful to distinguish the so-called horizontal links into (i) paradigmatic links (Van de Velde, 2014) and (ii) S-synonymy links (Goldberg, 1995).

The former type describes a relation between non-synonymous constructions that split a common semantic domain, and thus are suited to connect cells in a paradigm. The latter type, instead, connects constructions that are truth-semantically equivalent, but not necessarily similar from the pragmatic point of view (similarly to allostructional links, cf. Section 3.2). We chose S-synonymy over the (more commonly used) allostructional links, since allostructions are generally intended to be formal variants of a more general, formally underspecified construction (Cappelle, 2006; Perek, 2015). In our case, we are dealing with an 'alternation' that straddles the boundaries of morphology and syntax, thus making it difficult (and ad-hoc) to posit a common mother construction. Paradigmatic and S-synonymy links share some features: they connect constructions at the same level of abstraction, and are bidirectional, since constructions stand in the same relation with each other.

In Figure 8, we can see that paradigmatic links connect the constructions belonging to different cells of our paradigm. To avoid confusion in the visualization, we only connected the cells of the paradigm (the hyperconstructions), but in fact these links connect each construction in a cell with each of the constructions in another cells, as shown in Figure 9. Instead, S-synonymy links connect constructions belonging to the same cell (cf. Figure 8 and Figure 9).

In Figure 8, we also find vertical links connecting the various semi-specified schemas for LVCs with a (mother) schematic psych-LVC construction (V N_{psych}).[22] This schematic construction is generalized over the semi-specified LVCs by virtue of their common formal and functional features. We posited its existence since psych-LVCs represent a class of LVCs with their own behavior, which differentiates them from other LVCs. Furthermore, instance links connect semi-specified constructions with the corresponding fully specified ones, e.g. *fare* N_{psych} with *fare paura*.

Within this general picture, we also have to account for the peculiarity of the anticausative alternation. Causative and (mainly) inchoative SVs are not only connected by paradigmatic links, but they share most of their form, since anticausatives are formed by adding *si* to their causative counterparts. We argue that this formal similarity can be expressed by subpart links. Subpart links were proposed by Goldberg (1995) to formalize cases in which a construction is formally included in another construction, and they have been later defined as "horizontal links" since they connect constructions at the same level of abstraction (Hilpert and Diessel, 2017, 60). We posit a double link between causatives and anticausative SVs, one (paradigmatic, as between all the other constructions in paradigmatic constrast) accounting for semantic relatedness and the other (the subpart link) accounting for their formal relatedness. In this way, we motivate the stronger transparency of their relation in our paradigm with respect to the other paradigmatic contrasts.

For graphical reasons, we did not include lower-level constructions in Figure 8. Nonetheless, our proposal also accounts for fully specified constructions, which are created through filler-slot relations (Diessel, 2019). This kind of link connects a construction (often a lexical element) with empty slots in (semi-)schematic constructions, based on the slots' constraints (in our case, the filler must be a noun expressing a psych-state). In Figure 10, we show filler-slot relations at work with *fare* N and *mettere* N, with the line weight showing the strength of association between a slot and a filler.

---

[22] In order to keep the visualization of the network clear, we only included Verb + Noun light verb constructions in Figure 8. Nonetheless, in our dataset we found two Verb + Prep + Noun patterns too (*essere in* N and *andare in* N), which behave in the same way as the other constructions as far as horizontal links are concerned. The only relevant difference from other LVCs is that they are vertically linked to a schematic V Prep N construction. Since we only concentrated on two, relatively infrequent constructions motivated by this schema, we kept such schematic construction aside in the visualization of the network. Moreover, we hope that future studies will address the actual productivity (and thus the degree of entrenchment) of such schematic construction in the expression of psychological events.

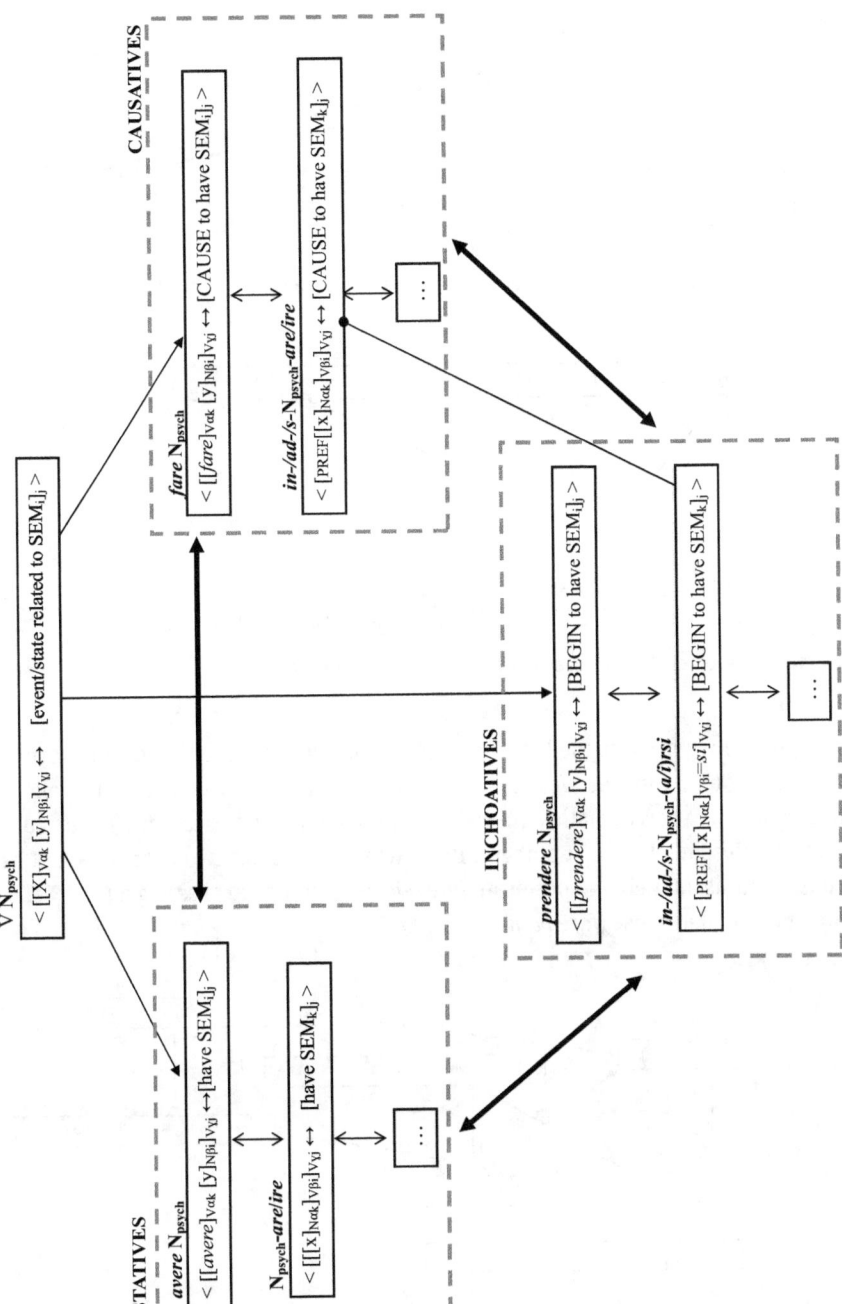

Fig. 8: The constructional network of psych-predicates.

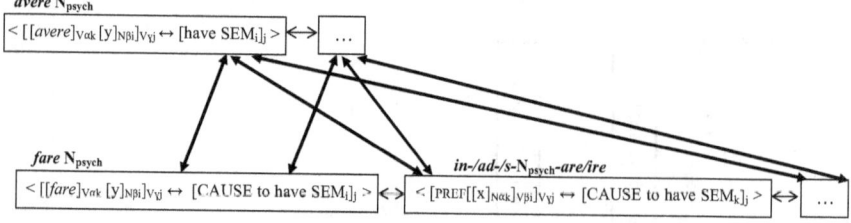

Fig. 9: Relations of similarity and paradigmatic opposition between semi-schematic stative and causative psych-predicates.

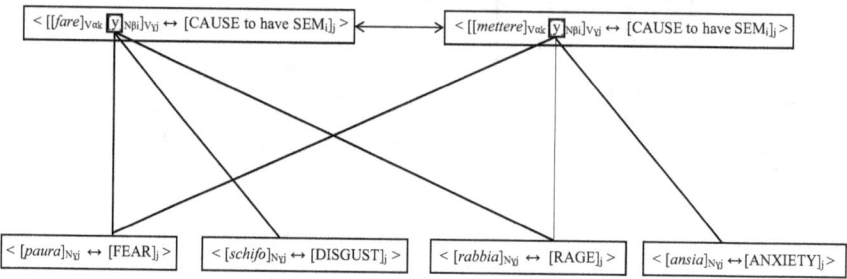

Fig. 10: Filler-slot relations between psych-nouns and *fare-* vs *mettere-*LVCs.

In Figure 11 we provide the local network for all fully specified predicates formed with the noun *paura*. As we can see, the horizontal links we posited are valid at different levels of schematicity. We also included a metaphorical link (a particular case of polysemic link, cf. Goldberg, 1995), which associates two formally identical constructions, namely the predicate *fare paura* 'frighten', expressing a basic sense, and its extended sense (*fare paura* as 'amaze').

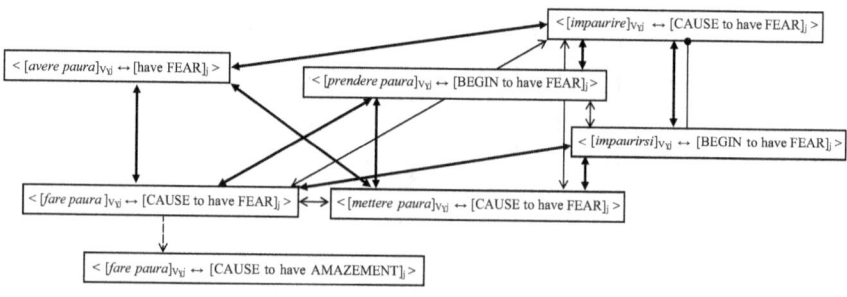

Fig. 11: Local network of fully-specified predicates formed with *paura* 'fear'.

6 Conclusion

In this paper we tried to unravel the competition between LVCs and SVs by taking noun-based psych predicates in Italian as a case study. The relationship between psych-SVs and psych-LVCs is rather complex and little investigated, since competition studies normally consider rival entities belonging to the same structural level (e.g., affix vs. affix, periphrasis vs. periphrasis, etc.). By assuming a constructionist view of language, which lacks a divide between morphology and syntax, 'analytic vs. synthetic' competition is not only possible but also an expected situation which deserves to be investigated.

We devised a methodology to tackle with this type of competition that involves quantitative analysis based on corpus data and statistical modelling. This double methodology allowed us to unveil some tendencies that contribute to regulate the distribution between psych LVCs and SVs, and therefore possibly their selection by speakers.

Overall, SVs are much more frequent, so their higher entrenchment is likely to influence the creation of new psych predicates.

At the pattern level, we found that LVCs are the preferred strategy to convey stative psych predicates, whereas inchoatives tend to be expressed by SVs (especially through -*si* verbs). Causatives are the actual battlefield, where the competition between LVCs and SVs is most active. Within causatives, the semantics of the nominal base seems to play some role, as well as its sentiment polarity.

At the level of specific lexical items, we found that the selection of LVCs vs. SVs is motivated by some usage and contextual factors: spontaneous speech definitely favors LVCs, whereas text genres with a higher level of planning, like written texts or planned speech, display a more even distribution. Modification was found to be a minor factor, playing a key role only in those texts where competition is higher, namely written texts, but not spoken texts. Quite unexpectedly, the most relevant factor turned out to be the finite vs. non-finite form of verbs. Whereas SVs are found in both forms, with a varied distribution, LVCs are strongly associated to finite forms: their occurrence appears to be disfavored within periphrases or implicit subordinate clauses, hinting at processing cost as a possible factor at play. Complexity avoidance might also be the reason why LVCs tend not to express the experiencer as a full PP, often yielding a generic reading.

Given these findings, we developed a theoretical proposal in terms of constructional network that accounts for the facts and, at the same time, might contribute to advancing our understanding of links between constructions (especially horizontal ones) and of the role of derivational paradigms within CxG.

Indeed, we regarded the triple 'stative / inchoative / causative' as a derivational paradigm where each event type corresponds to a cell, and where each cell may be filled by different strategies (SVs and LVCs). These cells are claimed to be connected by paradigmatic links, namely horizontal links between constructions at the same level of schematicity that are in some sort of paradigmatic opposition.

Paradigmatic links are, however, only part of the picture, which also includes S-synonymy links, for connecting (near-synonymous, although not fully equivalent) constructions within the same cell, as well as filler-slot relations and links of various sorts (e.g., subpart, metaphorical). Therefore, in order to provide a faithful representation of the intricate relationship between synthetic and analytic predicates, multiple links are necessary that apply at different points of the network. Our results therefore speak in favor of a highly refined network with both vertical and horizontal links of various types that encode different kinds of relationships at different levels of abstraction.

Still much remains to be done. On the one hand, the methodology proposed for this case-study could be tested for other domains, beyond psych predicates, to verify if the many factors at play are recurring and can therefore be generalized. On the other hand, further evidence could be gathered from experiments aimed at testing the tendencies we identified.

Acknowledgement

This paper is the result of a constant collaboration between the two authors, who are each 100% responsible for its contents. Flavio Pisciotta wrote Sections 1, 2, 4, 5.1 and 5.2, and Francesca Masini wrote Section 3 and 6. The two authors jointly wrote Section 5.3. We are grateful to the anonymous reviewers for useful comments, to Claudio Iacobini for his precious feedback on a previous version of the paper, and to Eliana Di Palma for help with emotive lexicons.

Data Availability Statement

The datasets analyzed in the current study are available in the OSF repository: https://doi.org/10.17605/OSF.IO/QHEJ3.

Bibliography

Ackerman, Farrell and Gregory Stump. 2004. Paradigms and periphrastic expression: A study in realization-based lexicalism. In Louisa Sadler and Andrew Spencer (eds.), *Projecting Morphology*, 111–157. Stanford: CSLI Publications.

Alba-Salas, Josep. 2002. *Light Verb Constructions in Romance: A Syntactic Analysis*. Doctoral dissertation: Cornell University, Ithaca, NY.

Alba-Salas, Josep. 2004. *Fare* light verb constructions and Italian causatives: Understanding the differences. *Rivista di Linguistica* 16(2). 283–323.

Alvarez-Morera, Georgina. 2022a. Light verb constructions in English and Spanish: state of the art. In Maria Bargalló Escrivà (ed.), *Recerca en humanitats 2021*, 9–26. Tarragona: Publicacions URV.

Alvarez-Morera, Georgina. 2022b. Modification in light verb constructions: a corpus study in Germanic and Romance languages. Presented at the 9th International Conference on Grammar and Corpora 2022, Ghent, Belgium.

Amenta, Luisa. 2008. Le polirematiche in testi parlati e scritti di italiano popolare. In Emanuela Cresti (ed.), *Prospettive nello studio del lessico italiano. Atti del IX Congresso SILFI (Proceedings e report)*, 539–546. Florence: Firenze University Press.

Aronoff, Mark. 2016. Competition and the lexicon. In Annibale Elia, Claudio Iacobini and Miriam Voghera (eds.), *Livelli di Analisi e fenomeni di interfaccia. Atti del XLVII congresso internazionale della società di linguistica Italiana*, 39–52. Rome: Bulzoni Editore.

Audring, Jenny. 2019. Mothers or sisters? The encoding of morphological knowledge. *Word Structure* 12(3). 274–296. https://doi.org/10.3366/word.2019.0150.

Baayen, R. Harald, Douglas J. Davidson and Douglas M. Bates. 2008. Mixed-effects modeling with crossed random effects for subjects and items. *Journal of Memory and Language* 59(4). 390–412. https://doi.org/10.1016/j.jml.2007.12.005.

Baroni, Marco, Silvia Bernardini, Adriano Ferraresi and Eros Zanchetta. 2009. The WaCky Wide Web: A collection of very large linguistically processed Web-crawled corpora. *Language Resources and Evaluation* 43(3). 209–226.

Bates, Douglas, Martin Maechler, Ben Bolker and Steve Walker. 2015. Fitting Linear Mixed-Effects Models Using lme4. *Journal of Statistical Software* 67(1). 1–48. https://doi.org/10.18637/jss.v067.i01.

Beavers, John, Michael Everdell, Kyle Jerro, Henri Kauhanen, Andrew Koontz-Garboden, Elise LeBovidge and Stephen Nichols. 2021. States and changes of state: A crosslinguistic study of the roots of verbal meaning. *Language* 97(3). 439–484. https://doi.org/10.1353/lan.2021.0044.

Belletti, Adriana and Luigi Rizzi. 1988. Psych-verbs and θ-theory. *Natural Language and Linguistic Theory* 6(3). 291–352. https://doi.org/10.1007/BF00133902.

Blevins, James P., Farrell Ackerman and Rob Malouf. 2019. Word and Paradigm Morphology. In Jenny Audring and Francesca Masini (eds.), *The Oxford Handbook of Morphological Theory*, 264–284. Oxford: Oxford University Press. https://doi.org/10.1093/oxfordhb/9780199668984.013.22.

Bonami, Olivier and Jana Strnadová. 2019. Paradigm structure and predictability in derivational morphology. *Morphology* 29(2). 167–197. https://doi.org/10.1007/s11525-018-9322-6.

Bonial, Claire and Kimberly A. Pollard. 2020. Choosing an event description: What a PropBank study reveals about the contrast between light verb constructions and counterpart synthetic verbs. *Journal of Linguistics* 56(3). 577–600. https://doi.org/10.1017/S0022226720000109.

Booij, Geert. 2009. Phrasal names: A constructionist analysis. *Word Structure* 2(2). 219–240.

Booij, Geert. 2010. *Construction morphology*. Oxford: Oxford University Press.

Booij, Geert and Francesca Masini. 2015. The Role of Second Order Schemas in the Construction of Complex Words. In Laurie Bauer, Lívia Körtvélyessy and Pavol Štekauer (eds.), *Semantics of Complex Words*, 47–66. Cham: Springer. https://doi.org/10.1007/978-3-319-14102-2_4.

Brugman, Claudia. 2001. Light verbs and polysemy. *Language Sciences* 23. 551–578.

Butt, Miriam. 2003. The Light Verb Jungle. *Harvard Working Papers in Linguistics, Papers from the GSAS/Dudley House Workshop on Light Verbs* 9. 1–49.

Bybee, Joan. 2013. Usage-based Theory and Exemplar Representations of Constructions. In Thomas Hoffmann and Graeme Trousdale (eds.), *The Oxford Handbook of Construction Grammar*, 49–69. Oxford: Oxford University Press.

Cappelle, Bert. 2006. Particle placement and the case for "allostructions". *Constructions* 1(7). 1–28. https://doi.org/10.24338/cons-381.

Cappelle, Bert. 2009. Can we factor out free choice? In Andreas Dufter, Jürg Fleischer and Guido Seiler (eds.), *Describing and Modeling Variation in Grammar*, 183–202. Berlin: Mouton de Gruyter. https://doi.org/10.1515/9783110216097.3.183.

Centineo, Giulia. 1995. The distribution of *si* in Italian transitive/inchoative pairs. In Mandy Simons and Theresa Galloway (eds.), *Proceedings from Semantics and Linguistic Theory V*, 54–71. Ithaca, NY: Cornell University.

Cetnarowska, Bożena. 2021. Derivational paradigms or paradigms of function? Competition between Polish affixal formations, morphological compounds and phrasal lexemes. Presented at the Second Workshop on Paradigmatic Word Formation Modelling (ParadigMo II), 3-4 June 2021, Bordeaux, France.

Cicalese, Anna. 1999. Le estensioni di verbo supporto. Uno studio introduttivo. *Studi Italiani di Linguistica Teorica e Applicata* 28(3). 447–485.

Cicalese, Anna, Emilio D'Agostino, Alberto Maria Langella and Ilaria Maria Villari. 2016. Verbi locativi in italiano come varianti di verbi supporto. *Quaderns d'Italià* 21. 153–166. https://doi.org/10.5565/rev/qdi.10.

Cifuentes Honrubia, José Luis. 2015. Causativity and psychological verbs in Spanish. In José Luis Cifuentes Honrubia Elisa Barrajón López and Susana Rodríguez Rosique (eds.), *Verb Classes and Aspect*, 110–130. Amsterdam: John Benjamin. https://doi.org/10.1075/ivitra.9.06cif.

Clark, Eve V. 1987. The Principle of Contrast: A Constraint on Language Acquisition. In Brian MacWhinney (ed.), *Mechanisms of Language Acquisition*, 1–33. Hillsdale, NJ: Erlbaum.

Crocco Galèas, Grazia and Claudio Iacobini. 1993. The Italian Parasynthetic Verbs: a Particular Kind of Circumfix. In Livia Tonelli and Wolfgang U. Dressler (eds.), *Natural Morphology. Perspectives for the Nineties*, 127–142. Padova: Unipress.

Croft, William. 1991. *Syntactic categories and grammatical relations: the cognitive organization of information*. Chicago: University of Chicago Press.

Croft, William. 1993. The role of domains in the interpretation of metaphors and metonymies. *Cognitive Linguistics* 4(4). 335–370. https://doi.org/10.1515/cogl.1993.4.4.335.

Cuervo, Maria Cristina. 2010. Two types of (apparently) ditransitive light verb constructions. In Karlos Arregi, Zsuzsanna Fagyal, Silvina A. Montrul and Annie Tremblay (eds.), *Romance Linguistics 2008: Interactions in Romance*, 139–156. Amsterdam: John Benjamins. https://doi.org/10.1075/cilt.313.14cue.

De Mauro, Tullio. 2011. *Storia linguistica dell'Italia unita*. Bari: Laterza.

De Mauro, Tullio, Federico Mancini, Massimo Vedovelli and Miriam Voghera. 1993. *Lessico di frequenza dell'italiano parlato*. Milano: Etaslibri.

de Saussure, Ferdinand. 1916. *Cours de linguistique Générale*. Lausanne: Librairie Payot & Cie.

Diessel, Holger. 2019. *The Grammar Network: How Linguistic Structure is Shaped by Language Use.* Cambridge: Cambridge University Press.

Diessel, Holger. 2023. *The Constructicon: Taxonomies and Networks.* Cambridge: Cambridge University Press. https://doi.org/10.1017/9781009327848.

Diewald, Gabriele. 2020. Paradigms lost – paradigms regained: Paradigms as hyper-constructions. In Lotte Sommerer and Elena Smirnova (eds.), *Nodes and Networks in Diachronic Construction Grammar*, 278–315. Amsterdam: John Benjamins. https://doi.org/10.1075/cal.27.08die.

Elia, Annibale, Emilio D'Agostino and Maurizio Martinelli. 1985. Tre componenti della sintassi italiana: frasi semplici, frasi a verbo supporto e frasi idiomatiche. In Annalisa Franchi De Bellis and Leonardo M. Savoia (eds.), *Sintassi e morfologia della lingua italiana d'uso. Teorie e applicazioni descrittive. Atti del XVII congresso internazionale della Società di Linguistica Italiana,* 311–325. Rome: Bulzoni.

Fernández-Domínguez, Jesús. 2019. Compounds and multi-word expressions in Spanish. In Barbara Schlücker (ed.), *Complex Lexical Units. Compounds and Multi-Word Expressions,* 189–220. Berlin: De Gruyter. https://doi.org/10.1515/9783110632446-007.

Fillmore, Charles. 1988. The Mechanisms of "Construction Grammar". *Proceedings of the Fourteenth Annual Meeting of the Berkeley Linguistics Society* 35–55.

Fillmore, Charles, Paul Kay and Mary Catherine O'Connor. 1988. Regularity and Idiomaticity in Grammatical Constructions: The Case of Let Alone. *Language* 64(3). 501–538. https://doi.org/10.2307/414531.

Fleischhauer, Jens. 2021. Simplex and Complex Predicates in Persian: An RRG Analysis. In Robert Van Valin (ed.), *Challenges at the Syntax-Semantics-Pragmatics Interface,* 31–62. Newcastle upon Tyne: Cambridge Scholars Publishing.

Fleischhauer, Jens. 2023. The 'principle of no synonymy' and light verb constructions – A case study on German stative light verbs. Presented at the 16th International Cognitive Linguistics Conference, 7–11 August 2023, Düsseldorf, Germany.

Fleischhauer, Jens and Mozhgan Neisani. 2020. Adverbial and attributive modification of Persian separable light verb constructions. *Journal of Linguistics* 56(1). 45–85. https://doi.org/10.1017/S0022226718000646.

Fleischhauer, Jens and Dila Turus. 2023. A corpus-based study on putative synonymous light verb constructions in German. Presented at the 16th International Cognitive Linguistics Conference, 7–11 August 2023, Düsseldorf, Germany.

Ganfi, Vittorio and Valentina Piunno. 2019. Costruzioni a verbo supporto con nomi di parti del corpo in italiano antico e contemporaneo. In Anna Pompei and Lunella Mereu (eds.), *Verbi supporto: fenomeni e teorie,* 187–222. Munich: LINCOM.

Giry-Schneider, Jacqueline. 1978. Interprétation Aspectuelle Des Constructions Verbales à Double Analyse. *Lingvisticae Investigationes* 2(1). 23–53. https://doi.org/10.1075/li.2.1.04gir.

Goldberg, Adele. 1995. *Constructions: A Construction Grammar Approach to Argument Structure.* Chicago: The University of Chicago Press.

Goldberg, Adele. 2003a. Constructions: A New Theoretical Approach to Language. *Trends in Cognitive Sciences* 7. 219–224. https://doi.org/10.1016/S1364-6613(03)00080-9.

Goldberg, Adele. 2003b. Words by default: The Persian complex predicate construction. In Elaine J. Francis and Laura A. Michaelis (eds.), *Mismatch: Form-Function Incongruity and the Architecture of Grammar,* 117–146. Stanford: CSLI Publication.

GRADIT. 2007. *Grande dizionario italiano dell'uso, ideated and directed by Tullio De Mauro.* Turin: UTET.

Gries, Stefan Th. 2015. The most under-used statistical method in corpus linguistics: multi-level (and mixed-effects) models. *Corpora* 10(1). 95–125. https://doi.org/10.3366/cor.2015.0068.

Gross, Maurice. 1976. Sur quelques groupes nominaux complexes. In Jean-Claude Chevalier and Maurice Gross (eds.), *Méthodes en grammaire française*, 97–119. Paris: Klincksieck.
Grossmann, Maria. 2004a. Conversione in verbi. In Maria Grossmann and Franz Rainer (eds.), *La formazione delle parole in italiano*, 534–546. Tübingen: Niemeyer.
Grossmann, Maria. 2004b. Verbi denominali. In Maria Grossmann and Franz Rainer (eds.), *La formazione delle parole in italiano*, 450–458. Tübingen: Niemeyer.
Haiman, John. 1980. The Iconicity of Grammar: Isomorphism and Motivation. *Language* 56(3). 515–540. https://doi.org/10.2307/414448.
Hathout, Nabil and Fiammetta Namer. 2019. Paradigms in word formation: what are we up to? *Morphology* 29(2). 153–165. https://doi.org/10.1007/s11525-019-09344-3.
Henrik, Singmann, Ben Bolker, Jake Westfall, Frederik Aust and Mattan S. Ben-Shachar. 2023. afex: Analysis of Factorial Experiments. R package version 1.3-0. https://CRAN.R-project.org/package=afex, last access: 25/10/2024.
Hilpert, Martin. 2019. *Construction grammar and its application to English. 2nd edition*. Edinburgh: Edinburgh University Press.
Hilpert, Martin and Holger Diessel. 2017. Entrenchment in construction grammar. In Hans-Jörg Schmid (ed.), *Entrenchment and the psychology of language learning: How we reorganize and adapt linguistic knowledge*, 57–74. Berlin: Mouton De Gruyter.
Hoffmann, Thomas and Graeme Trousdale (eds.). 2013. *The Oxford Handbook of Construction Grammar*. Oxford: Oxford University Press. https://doi.org/10.1093/oxfordhb/9780195396683.001.0001.
Hopper, Paul J. 1991. Dispersed Verbal Predicates in Vernacular Written Narrative. In Christopher Johnson Laurel A. Stutton and Ruth Shields (eds.), *Proceedings of the Seventeenth Annual Meeting of the Berkeley Linguistics Society: General Session and Parasession on The Grammar of Event Structure 17(1)*, 402–413. Berkeley: Linguistics Society of America. https://doi.org/10.3765/bls.v17i0.1609.
Huddleston, Rodney. 2002. The clause: complements. In Rodney Huddleston and Geoffrey K. Pullum (eds.), *The Cambridge Grammar of English Language*, 213–322. Cambridge: Cambridge University Press.
Iacobini, C. 2004. Parasintesi. In Maria Grossmann and Franz Rainer (eds.), *La formazione delle parole in italiano*, 165–188. Tübingen: Niemeyer.
Iacobini, Claudio and Maria Pina De Rosa. 2024. A diachronic perspective on competition in denominal verb formation in Italian. In Alexandra Bagasheva, Akiko Nagano and Vincent Renner (eds.), *Competition in word-formation*, 247–274. Amsterdam: John Benjamins. https://doi.org/10.1075/la.284.08iac.
Iacobini, Claudio and Anna Pompei. 2022. Light verbs and prefixed verbs as alternative aspectual strategies in Italian: A case study. Presented at the Societas Linguistica Europaea 55th Annual Meeting, 24-27 August 2022, Bucharest, Romania.
Jackendoff, Ray. 1990. *Semantic structures*. Cambridge, MA: MIT Press.
Jackendoff, Ray and Jenny Audring. 2020. Relational Morphology: A Cousin of Construction Grammar. *Frontiers in Psychology* 11. 1–12. https://doi.org/10.3389/fpsyg.2020.02241.
Ježek, Elisabetta. 2000. Classi verbali e composizionalità: il caso della "doppia inaccusatività" in italiano. *Studi Italiani di Linguistica Teorica e Applicata* 29(2). 289–310.
Ježek, Elisabetta. 2004. Types et degrés de verbes supports en Italien. *Lingvisticae Investigationes* 27(2). 195–201.
Ježek, Elisabetta. 2011. Verbes supports et composition sémantique. *Cahiers de lexicologie* 98(1). 29–43. 10.15122/ISBN.978-2-8124-4145-5.P.0029.

Ježek, Elisabetta. 2023. Semantic Co-composition in Light Verb Constructions. In Anna Pompei, Lunella Mereu and Valentina Piunno (eds.), *Light Verb Constructions as Complex Verbs: Features, Typology and Function*, 221–238. Berlin: De Gruyter.

Jiménez Martínez, María Isabel and Chantal Melis. 2023. A constructional approach to causative support verbs in Spanish. In Inga Hennecke and Evelyn Wiesinge (eds.), *Constructions in spanish*, 78–102. Amsterdam: John Benjamins. https://doi.org/10.1075/cal.34.04jim.

Johnson, Daniel Ezra. 2009. Getting off the GoldVarb Standard: Introducing Rbrul for Mixed-Effects Variable Rule Analysis. *Language and Linguistics Compass* 3(1). 359–383. https://doi.org/10.1111/j.1749-818X.2008.00108.x.

Lenth, Russell V. 2023. emmeans: Estimated Marginal Means, aka Least-Squares Means. R package version 1.8.9. https://CRAN.R-project.org/package=emmeans, last access: 25/10/2024.

Marini, Emanuela. 2003. Tipologia delle costruzioni a verbo supporto a det. ø in italiano antico e moderno. In Teresa Poggi Salani and Nicoletta Maraschio (eds.), *Italia linguistica anno Mille, Italia linguistica anno Duemila. Atti del XXXIV Congresso internazionale di studi della Società di linguistica italiana (SLI), Firenze, 19-21 ottobre 2000*, 259–272. Rome: Bulzoni. https://api.semanticscholar.org/CorpusID:162780242, last access: 13/01/2025.

Marín, Rafael and Louise McNally. 2011. Inchoativity, change of state, and telicity: evidence from Spanish reflexive psychological verbs. *Natural Language & Linguistic Theory* 29(2). 467–502. https://doi.org/10.1007/s11049-011-9127-3.

Masini, Francesca. 2009a. Combinazioni di parole e parole sintagmatiche. In Edoardo Lombardi Vallauri and Lunella Mereu (eds.), *Spazi linguistici: studi in onore di Raffaele Simone*, 191–210. Rome: Bulzoni.

Masini, Francesca. 2009b. Phrasal lexemes, compounds and phrases: A constructionist perspective. *Word Structure* 2(2). 254–271.

Masini, Francesca. 2019a. Competition Between Morphological Words and Multiword Expressions. In Franz Rainer, Francesco Gardani, Wolfgang U. Dressler and Hans C. Luschützky (eds.), *Competition in Inflection and Word-Formation*, 281–305. Berlin: Springer.

Masini, Francesca. 2019b. Multi-Word Expressions and Morphology. In *Oxford Research Encyclopedia of Linguistics*, Oxford: Oxford University Press. https://doi.org/10.1093/acrefore/9780199384655.013.611.

Masini, Francesca and Jenny Audring. 2019. Construction Morphology. In Jenny Audring and Francesca Masini (eds.), *The Oxford Handbook of Morphological Theory*, 264–389. Oxford: Oxford University Press. https://doi.org/10.1093/oxfordhb/9780199668984.013.25.

Masini, Francesca and Claudia Roberta Combei. 2024. RadioCast-It. Corpus di italiano della radio e dei podcast. In Silvia Ballarè, Ilaria Fiorentini and Emanuele Miola (eds.), *Le varietà dell'italiano contemporaneo*, 196–198. Rome: Carocci.

Masini, Francesca and Claudio Iacobini. 2018. Schemas and Discontinuity in Italian: The View from Construction Morphology. In Gert Booij (ed.), *The Construction of Words*, 81–109. Cham: Springer. https://doi.org/10.1007/978-3-319-74394-3_4.

Mastrofini, Roberta. 2004. Classi di costruzioni a verbo supporto in italiano: implicazioni semantico-sintattiche nel paradigma V+N. *Studi Italiani di Linguistica Teorica e Applicata* 33(3). 371–398.

Mauri, Caterina, Silvia Ballarè, Eugenio Goria, Massimo Cerruti and Francesco Suriano. 2019. KIParla corpus: a new resource for spoken Italian. In Raffaella Bernardi, Roberto Navigli and Giovanni Semeraro (eds.), *Proceedings of the Sixth Italian Conference on Computational Linguistics (CLIC-it 2019)*, 1–7.

Melloni, Chiara. 2017. Aspect-related properties in the nominal domain: The case of Italian psych nominals. In Maria Bloch-Trojnar and Anna Malicka-Kleparska (eds.), *Aspect and Valency in Nominals*, 253–284. De Gruyter. https://doi.org/10.1515/9781501505430-011.

Melloni, Chiara and Serena Dal Maso. 2022. For a topology of derivational paradigms. In Cristina Fernández-Alcaina Alba E. Ruz and Cristina Lara-Clares (eds.), *Paradigms in Word Formation: Theory and applications*, 21–56. Amsterdam: John Benjamins. https://doi.org/10.1075/slcs.225.02mel.

Mirto, Ignazio M. 2008. Analizzando analizzare: eterogeneità dei verbi in. In *Prospettive nello studio del lessico italiano: atti del IX Congresso SILFI, Firenze, 14-17 giugno 2006*, 362–365. Firenze: Firenze University Press.

Mirto, Ignazio M. and Laura Granifero. 2022. *Nomi predicativi: articoli, verbi supporto, finiture sintattiche*. Palermo: Palermo University Press.

Nesset, Tore and Laura A. Janda. 2023. A network of allostructions: quantified subject constructions in Russian. *Cognitive Linguistics* 34(1). 67–97. https://doi.org/10.1515/cog-2021-0117.

Nichols, Johanna. 2019. Suppletion or illusion?: The diachrony of suppletive derivation. In Lars Heltoft, Iván Igartua, Brian D. Joseph, Kirsten Jeppesen Kragh and Lene Schøsler (eds.), *Perspectives on Language Structure and Language Change: Studies in honor of Henning Andersen*, 345–356. Amsterdam: John Benjamins. https://doi.org/10.1075/cilt.345.16nic.

Passaro, Lucia C., Laura Pollacci and Alessandro Lenci. 2015. ItEM: A Vector Space Model to Bootstrap an Italian Emotive Lexicon. In Cristina Bosco, Sara Tonelli and Fabio Massimo Zanzotto (eds.), *Proceedings of the Second Italian Conference on Computational Linguistics CLiC-it 2015, Trento, 3-4 December 2015*, 215–220. Turin: Accademia University Press.

Perek, Florent. 2015. *Argument Structure in Usage-Based Construction Grammar*. Amsterdam: John Benjamins. https://doi.org/10.1075/cal.17.

Piera, Carlos and Soledad Varela. 1999. Relaciones entre morfología y sintaxis. In Ignacio Bosque and Violeta Demonte (eds.), *Gramática descriptiva de la lengua española. Vol. 3*, 4367––4422. Madrid: Real Academia Española.

Pijpops, Dirk and Dirk Speelman. 2017. Alternating argument constructions of Dutch psychological verbs: A theory-driven corpus investigation. *Folia Linguistica* 51(1). 207–251. https://doi.org/10.1515/flin-2017-0006.

Plutchik, Robert. 1994. *The psychology and biology of emotion*. New York: Harper Collins.

Pompei, Anna. 2017. Verbi con struttura [V+SP] e verbi supporto. Proprietà e test. *Studi e saggi linguistici* 55(2). 109–136.

Pompei, Anna, Lunella Mereu and Valentina Piunno (eds.). 2023. *Light Verb Constructions as Complex Verbs*. Berlin: De Gruyter.

Pompei, Anna and Lunella Mereu (eds.) . 2019. *Verbi supporto: fenomeni e teorie*. Munich: LINCOM.

Pompei, Anna and Valentina Piunno. 2023. Light Verb Constructions in Romance languages. An attempt to explain systematic irregularity. In Anna Pompei, Lunella Mereu and Valentina Piunno (eds.), *Light Verb Constructions as Complex Verbs*, 99–147. Berlin: Mouton de Gruyter.

Quochi, Valeria. 2016. Development and representation of Italian light-*fare* constructions. In Jiyoung Yoon and Stefan Th. Gries (eds.), *Corpus-based Approaches to Construction Grammar*, 39–64. Amsterdam: John Benjamins. https://doi.org/10.1075/cal.19.03quo.

Rivas, Javier. 2016. Verb–object compounds with Spanish *dar* 'give': an emergent *gustar* 'like'-type construction. *WORD* 62(1). 1–21. https://doi.org/10.1080/00437956.2016.1141940.

Rossini Favretti, Rema, Fabio Tamburini and Cristiana De Santis. 2002. CORIS/CODIS: A corpus of written Italian based on a defined and a dynamic model. In Andrew Wilson, Paul Rayson and Tony McEnery (eds.), *A Rainbow of Corpora: Corpus Linguistics and the Languages of the World*, 27–38. Lincom.

Salvi, Giampaolo. 1988. La frase semplice. In Lorenzo Renzi, Giampaolo Salvi and Anna Cardinaletti (eds.), *Grande grammatica italiana di consultazione*, 29–113. Bologna: Il Mulino.

Sanromán Vilas, Begoña. 2003. *Semántica, sintaxis y combinatoria léxica de los nombres de emoción en español*. Doctoral dissertation: Helsingfors Universitet.

Sanromán Vilas, Begoña. 2009. Diferencias semánticas entre construcciones con verbo de apoyo y sus correlatos verbales simples. *ELUA: Estudios Lingüísticos de la Universidad de Alicante* 23. 289–314.

Sanromán Vilas, Begoña. 2012. Aspecto léxico, sentido y colocaciones: los nombres de sentimiento. *Borealis – An International Journal of Hispanic Linguistics* 1(1). 63–100. https://doi.org/10.7557/1.1.1.2295.

Shahrokny-Prehn, Arian and Silke Höche. 2011. Rising through the registers – A corpus-based account of the stylistic constraints on Light Verb Constructions. *Corpus* 10. 239–257. https://doi.org/10.4000/corpus.2110.

Speelman, Dirk, Kris Heylen and Dirk Geeraerts. 2018. *Mixed-Effects Regression Models in Linguistics*. Cham: Springer.

Stichauer, Pavel. 2000. Su alcune costruzioni con verbo supporto in italiano. *Linguistica Pragensia* 10(1). 37–50.

Stump, Gregory. 2015. *Inflectional Paradigms: Content and Form at the Syntax-Morphology Interface*. Cambridge: Cambridge University Press. https://doi.org/10.1017/CBO9781316105290.

Stump, Gregory. 2019. Paradigm Function Morphology. In Jenny Audring and Francesca Masini (eds.), *The Oxford Handbook of Morphological Theory*, 284–304. Oxford: Oxford University Press. https://doi.org/10.1093/oxfordhb/9780199668984.013.23.

Sundquist, John D. 2022. An Exemplar-based Approach to Composite Predicates in the History of American English. *English Language and Linguistics* 26. 413–442. 10.1017/S1360674321000344.

Talmy, Leonard. 2000. *Toward a Cognitive Semantics. Typology and process in concept structuring*. Cambridge, MA: The MIT Press. https://doi.org/10.7551/mitpress/6848.001.0001.

Tomasello, Michael. 2003. *Constructing a Language: A Usage-Based Theory of Language Acquisition*. Cambridge, MA: Harvard University Press.

Ungerer, Tobias and Stefan Hartmann. 2023. *Constructionist Approaches: Past, Present, Future*. Cambridge: Cambridge University Press. https://doi.org/10.1017/9781009308717.

Van de Velde, Freek. 2014. Degeneracy: The maintenance of constructional networks. In Ronny Boogaart, Timothy Colleman and Gijsbert Rutten (eds.), *Extending the Scope of Construction Grammar*, 141–180. Berlin: De Gruyter. https://doi.org/10.1515/9783110366273.141.

Verhoeven, Elisabeth. 2010. Agentivity and stativity in experiencer verbs: Implications for a typology of verb classes. *Linguistic Typology* 14(2–3). 213–251.

Vietri, Simonetta. 2017. *Usi verbali dell'italiano: le frasi anticausative*. Rome: Carocci.

Wierzbicka, Anna. 1982. Why can you have a drink when you can't *have an eat? *Language* 58(4). 753–799. https://doi.org/10.2307/413956.

Wiskandt, Niklas. this volume. Light verb constructions with experiencer objects in Germanic and Romance – A corpus-based contrastive perspective on 'make' and 'give' patterns. In Anna Riccio and Jens Fleischhauer (eds.), *Light verbs: Synchronic and diachronic studies*, 97–122. Düsseldorf: Düsseldorf University Press.

Wiskandt, Niklas and Dila Turus. 2022. Systematic semantic differences between object-experiencer LVCs and corresponding simplex verbs in German. Presented at the 9th International Conference on Grammar and Corpora 2022, 30 June – 2 July 2022, Ghent, Belgium.

Zammuner, Vanda Lucia. 1998. Concepts of Emotion: "Emotionness"', and Dimensional Ratings of Italian Emotion Words. *Cognition and Emotion* 12(2). 243–272. https://doi.org/10.1080/026999398379745.

John Sundquist
Taking a closer look at light verb constructions in the history of American English

1 Introduction

This study examines light verb constructions (LVCs) in the history of American English, focusing primarily on *take a look* and similar expressions in texts from the Corpus of Historical American English written between 1820 and 2010. Light verbs (LVs) like *take*, along with other highly polysemous verbs in English (e.g., *give* or *make*), are semantically deficient verbs (Bowern, 2008, 163) whose generalized meaning allows them to be combined with a wide variety of NP complements that express the verbal action of the LVC as a whole. Although LVs may occur in the broader category of multi-word verbal expressions that includes various types of complex predicates, this study is focused specifically on the verbo-nominal type (LV + NP) with a transitive verb, exemplified in the following sentences:[1]

(1) Croft gazed at them and spat softly. "Go down and **take a look**," he told Red.
(Naked and the Dead, FIC, 1948)

(2) Let's **take a peak** at another adventuresome, risky arena–Wall Street.
(USA Today, MAG, 2001)

(3) However, anybody who wants to **take a gander** at the old Busch Stadium better hurry
(Washington Post, NEWS, 2005)

As seen in (1–3), there is a wide variety of NP complements that can be combined with *take* to yield an expression similar to *take a look*. The high productivity of LVCs with *take* and other light verbs is discussed in Sundquist (2020), where evidence indicates that an LVC like *take a look* may function as an exemplar for semantically similar expressions: it provides the basis for novel LVCs that occur sporadi-

---

[1] All examples come from the Corpus of Historical American English (COHA) (Davies, 2010). Examples include the relevant LVC in bold, the original source text in COHA, its genre (e.g., fiction (FIC), non-fiction (NFIC), and newspapers (NEWS)), along with its year of publication.

John Sundquist, Purdue University, USA

Open Access. © 2025 the author(s), published by De Gruyter. This work is licensed under the Creative Commons Attribution 4.0 International License.
https://doi.org/10.1515/9783111388878-007

cally while at the same time consistently increasing in token frequency itself over an extended period of time. Although it appears that most LVCs with *take* are highly productive, as Bonial (2014, 7) points out, it is perhaps more appropriate to classify them as semi-productive, since there appears to be some limitations on which NP complements may occur with particular light verbs. Moreover, as Sundquist (2022, 419) notes, novel verb-noun combinations in LVCs that share similar meanings come in and out of use at a low frequency or disappear entirely, despite the consistent rise of high frequency LVCs over time.

In the present study, I explore the LVC *take a look* and similar expressions to understand better the conditions under which the robust productivity of some LVCs increases but wanes among others. In particular, I examine the role of type and token frequency of *take* with semantically similar NP complements like (*a*) *look* over time, focusing on Goldberg's (2019) notion of coverage from a diachronic perspective. As the results of the corpus-based analysis indicate, multiple factors are at work which allow for the introduction of some new LVCs that quickly decline at the same time of a consistent increase in token frequency of exemplar LVCs over a period of several centuries.

The paper is structured as follows. Section 2 provides background on the classification of LVs and LVCs, an overview of an exemplar model in a usage-based account of LVCs, and background on the notion of coverage in the creation of new LVCs. In Section 3, the methodology of the study is presented, including an overview of the corpus and identification of LVCs with *take*. In Section 4, the results of type and token frequency analysis of LVCs similar to *take a look* are provided. In Section 5, the results are discussed, and Section 6 provides a conclusion to the paper.

2 Background

2.1 Classification of LVCs

Since the early use of the term in Jespersen (1942), there has been a lack of consensus in cross-linguistic studies on what constitutes a light verb and which NP complements should be included in the classification of LVCs.[2] Some basic assumptions allow for common ground, as pointed out in Quirk et al. (1985); Ronan (2014) and Claridge (2000). The present study is limited to an analysis of the verbo-nominal

---

[2] See studies in Brinton and Akimoto (1999) for an overview of terminology associated light verbs, light verb constructions, and types of composite predicates, particularly as it relates to early stages of English.

type of LVCs which are a type of composite predicate that consist of at least two elements: a verb with a highly generalized meaning and an NP complement that carries the semantic weight of the entire complex predicate. Consider the examples in (4):

(4) a. *Yesterday, the man and his dog took a walk.*
 b. *Yesterday, the man and his dog walked.*
 c. *Yesterday, the man took his dog on a walk.*

In (4a), *take* is a light verb that combines with an NP complement to form an LVC that expresses the same action as the verb *walked* in (4b) but does not predicate fully like *take* in (4c). Instead, the NP complement *a walk* is necessary for the phrase *take a walk* to be grammatical and meaningful as a whole.

There has been much debate on which verbs should be considered light in classifying verbo-nominal LVCs. Brinton (2008, 44) and Brinton and Traugott (2005, 130) provide helpful distinctions between categories of the broader group of composite predicates. On the one hand, the *take-a-look* group occurs with one of the following five highly frequent verbs in English: *do, give, have, make,* and *take*. They are most often combined with eventive nouns which may include a wide variety of NP types such as those with or without indefinite articles, adjectival modifiers, definite articles, or those that are zero derivations. On the other hand, *lose-sight* composite predicates, according to Brinton (2008, 45), occur with a wide variety of verbs other than the five most common, and there is less grammatical variation in the NP complements. For instance, most of these expressions include a bare NP (e.g., *lose sight*), lack any adjectival modification to the NP, and occur with a narrow range of NPs. In Allerton's (2002) comprehensive analysis or in Claridge (2000) and Ronan (2014), there is an assumption that a verb's lightness is a matter of degree, and while verbs of this second type may be polysemous, they are semantically heavier than the five highly frequent verbs which could be deemed true light verbs. In the present study, we focus the analysis mainly on *take-a-look* composite predicates, although we will offer comparison with the *lose-sight* type in discussion about the varying degrees of productivity of all LVCs.

In terms of the NP complements that should or should not be considered part of LVCs, one convincing approach to classification focuses on the semantic properties of abstract NPs rather than their various grammatical characteristics (e.g., definiteness, number, adjective modification, etc.). Bonial (2014) as well as Chen et al. (2015), for instance, use this more wide-ranging definition of LVCs based off the lexical file information of nouns in WordNet (Fellbaum, 1998) to identify eventive and stative nouns. In doing so, they allow for examples like *take a trip* or *make an effort*, in which the noun lacks a clear verbal counterpart like most LVCs (e.g., *take a drive* or *make an assumption*) but still contributes to the predicative nature of the phrase. As pointed out in Sundquist (2020, 354), this broader definition of LVCs based on semantic properties of the nouns in NP complements allows for the inclusion of a range of expressions that Fazly (2007, 9) calls multiword predicates like the LVC *take a bow* as well as 'idiomatic expressions' like *take effect*. As described in Section 3, the present study follows this more comprehensive approach in identifying LVCs similar to *take a look*.

2.2 Exemplars and a Usage-Based Approach to LVCs

Following basic assumptions within a usage-based Construction Grammar theoretical framework (Goldberg, 2003, 2006, 2009; Croft and Cruse, 2004) and diachronic extensions of this view (Hilpert, 2013, 2017; Barðdal, 2015; Perek, 2020), I suggest that expressions like *take a look* lend themselves well to an analysis in which some verb-noun pairings form a LVC that may become more and more frequent while others do not. As "stored pairings of form and function" (Goldberg, 2003, 21), these expressions fit the basic notion of a construction which, as Bybee (2006, 327) notes, becomes stored and reinforced in memory through frequent occurrence and greater repetition. In the case of verb-noun pairings in LVCs, a light verb like *take* occurs with a variety of moveable parts whose open slot for an NP complement (e.g. *a look*) may be filled with any number of different nouns (e.g., *peak, glance*). Associations that are most frequently reinforced and entrenched through speaker experience become the building blocks for retention and subsequent use in new contexts.[3]

As discussed in Sundquist (2022), LVCs also fit well into a usage-based approach like Bybee and Eddington's (2006) exemplar model that focuses on frequency, similarity, and prototype effects. Bybee (2013, 53) defines exemplars as categories formed from tokens of experience, whereby speakers map these incoming tokens onto similar existing representations. If these representations are already present and stored, they are strengthened. The mapping process involves evaluation of the degree of similarity between the existing representation and probes of new linguistic experience. In this way, exemplar clusters of relatively similar linguistic data are formed, with some members that are more central to the overall category (Bybee 2010:18). As Bonial (2014, 125) points out, an exemplar-based analysis of LVCs is convincing when we consider that there are two separate grammatical elements (i.e., the light verb and its NP complement) which form a single, meaningful unit but that similar

---

[3] For background on entrenchment, see Schmid (2020), or see Hilpert and Diessel (2017) on entrenchment in diachronic Construction Grammar. Moreover, Barðdal (2008) provides a helpful overview of type frequency effects and productivity within this approach.

elements combine with each other at times in idiosyncratic rather than systematic ways. For instance, while it is possible to combine *make* with *recommendation* along with similar nouns like *suggestion*, the combination of *make* with some nouns like *advice* is not well formed.

As discussed in previous diachronic Construction Grammar literature, both token and type frequency are essential to our understanding of the productivity of exemplars over time.[4] Sundquist (2020, 376) and Sundquist (2022, 420) argues that successful exemplars exhibit a higher token frequency than other similar representations and stand out uniquely from the group; in terms of diachrony, this success is built upon the recency of repetition as the frequency continues to rise in a 'rich get richer' type of progression, and novel structures become a single unit that is variably entrenched depending on the frequency of subsequent occurrences. In addition to token frequency, equally important to the success of exemplars is type frequency. As Bybee and Thompson (1997, 384) note, type frequency of a pattern determines its degree of productivity, as new forms are created by analogy to previously experienced utterances. Thus, in terms specific to LVCs, high-frequency verb-noun pairings may serve as exemplars for novel utterances in which a semantically similar NP complement can be paired with the same verb. By means of analogical extension based on semantic properties of the noun in the NP complements – even though the nouns may not be synonyms of each other – the number of different nouns that combine with the same verb may increase over time.

2.3 LVCs, Diachrony, and Coverage

The process whereby an exemplar's productivity increases over time resembles what Goldberg (2019) calls 'coverage'. She describes this notion as follows: "A potential productive use of an existing construction (a coinage) is acceptable to the degree that the category which would be required to include the previously attested examples and the coinage is well attested within the hyper-dimensional conceptual space in which exemplars cluster" (Goldberg, 2019, 62–62). Coverage is a function of a construction's type frequency, its semantic or phonological variability, and the similarity of a given coinage to previously attested types (Goldberg, 2019, 66). Through a series of controlled experiments related to participants' acceptability of novel verbs in ten different verb classes of a fictitious language, Suttle and Goldberg (2011) tested the effects that these three factors have on the potential acceptability of a coinage (i.e., its coverage), identifying a number of interaction effects between

---

[4] Divjak (2019) provides an overview of exemplar-based approaches in her discussion of type and token frequency and memory.

the three. They determined that greater type frequency leads to greater coverage when similarity and variability are kept the same; the degree of similarity between a coinage and previously witnessed exemplars may increase coverage if type frequency is kept the same; and an increase in type frequency inhibits greater coverage if variability is kept low Goldberg (2019, 67). In other words, an optimal case of coverage in which a coinage is accepted comes from a situation in which there is a great number of similar types that are spread out and not clustered densely in the hyper-dimensional conceptual space. This approach to coverage is synchronic in nature and is based on experimental rather than any kind of historical corpus data. However, it is interesting to consider the dynamic aspects of coverage to observe not only the point at which new LVCs come into use but also how their use plays out over time as the coverage may change.

In the case of LVCs like *take a look*, it is useful to consider these three factors in shaping the trajectories of similar verb-noun pairings. In particular, type frequency in this case can be measured by means of the number of unique verb-noun combinations that occur with *take* to form a semantically similar expression like *take a look* (e.g., *take a gander*, *take a peak*, etc.). Variability of LVCs refers to the number of different semantic types of nouns that occur with the same light verb, which in the case of *take*, is quite high on account of the high degree of polysemy of the verb (e.g., *take a trip/journey/excursion*, with nouns expressing travel, or *take a plunge/fall/dive* with nouns expressing a change of position, etc.). Lastly, similarity can be easily measured by means of the semantic relationship between nouns indicated by belonging to the same semantic frames in FrameNet (Fillmore et al., 2003) (e.g., LOOK, PEAK, GANDER, etc., as part of the 'Perception Active' semantic frame).[5] As we will see in the analysis of data in Section 4, these factors all combine to play a role in the success of an LVC like *take a look* and provide evidence of the complex relationship between them.

3 Methodology

3.1 Corpus

The quantitative portion of this analysis relies on a carefully designed sub-corpus of the larger Corpus of Historical American English (COHA, Davies, 2010), split into

---

[5] Nouns that are capitalized throughout the paper are lemmatized forms that were identified in COHA search queries. As will be shown 4.2, semantic similarity between nouns is measured here only by means of their shared listing in the same frame in FrameNet.

decades of texts written between 1820 and 2010. The sub-corpus consists of 114 million words balanced across magazines, newspapers, and fiction, with 2 million words for each genre and 6 million words per decade. This balanced design across decades and genres was necessary to avoid skewed results that come from normalizing the type and token frequencies with uneven sample sizes in longitudinal studies with texts of varying lengths, genres, or time periods (Perek, 2018).[6] This sub-corpus was used in the analysis of multiple verbs other than *take*, including *make* and *give* as well as several lexically specific verbs like *bear*, *grant*, and *lose*; results of the initial quantitative analysis are reported in Sundquist (2020) and Sundquist (2022). Using the verb *take* as a starting point in this study in the identification of LVCs like *take a look*, I ran search queries on the sub-corpus to find possible candidates of verb-noun combinations, searching by lemma for all verb-noun combinations with *take*.[7] Next, in order to compare these results across verbs, I ran the same search query on several other verbs, including *lose*, for instance, to identify verb-noun combinations that formed LVCs. For each verb lemma, I conducted an initial search that yielded all lemmatized forms of nouns that occur within five slots after the verb (e.g., *take* or *lose*). This approach is in line with synchronic analyses of English like Quirk et al. (1985) or Bonial (2014), or diachronic studies like Claridge (2000) and Ronan (2014) and Sundquist (2022), in which a variety of nouns might occur with verbs that have varying degrees of lightness and meet the basic requirements to be considered LVCs.

As a follow-up to the quantitative portion of the analysis, I examined specific verb-noun pairings with *take* similar to *take a look* in a more fine-grained post hoc analysis. Using the full COHA corpus rather than the smaller sub-corpus, this approach allowed for in-depth examination of low-frequency verb-noun pairings

---

6 Texts for the sub-corpus were selected from the larger COHA corpus according to a combinatorial optimization algorithm that takes into account each individual text's word count, genre, and decade (Sundquist and Rothwell, 2019). As a result, there is an equal number of words per decade (6 million) and number of words per genre from decade to decade (2 million), despite the varying word counts per individual text. The algorithm's code is provided here: https://github.com/corpus-based-research-lab.

7 Here is a sample query using the COHA web interface: TAKE_v + [nn*] within 5 slots; https://www.english-corpora.org/coha/?c=coha&q=99998064, last access 5.12.2024. This query retrieves all instances of the lemmas of verbal forms of *take* in which a lemma of any noun may occur within five slots after the verb. This is a collocational search that displays all instances of these combinations according to each decade between 1820 and 2010. Also, although it is possible to search slots filled by nouns before a verb in COHA, in passive constructions (e.g. *a trip was taken*) or some relative clauses (e.g. *the walk that he took yesterday*), this was not done here due to the high number of false positives that it creates. Thanks to Andrew Rothwell for help with coding, search queries, and filtering of the data using the full-text version of COHA.

and a closer evaluation of the contexts and genres in which these pairings occur. The full COHA corpus contains 475 million words split across five genres, including TV/movies, fiction, non-fiction, magazines, and newspapers written between 1820 and 2019.

3.2 Selection of Verb-Noun Pairings for Analysis

In order to get an accurate account of type and token frequencies of LVCs in each decade of the sub-corpus, several steps were followed to filter out examples of verb-noun combinations that are not LVCs. First, concreteness scores from Brysbaert et al. (2014) provided the basis for extracting only abstract nouns in NP complements to *take*, with nouns that scored 1 as being very abstract and 5 being the most concrete. I used a cutoff score of 3.5 to shorten the list to include only nouns that were independently considered more abstract than concrete.[8] For instance, the noun PIECE, as in *take a piece (of pie)*, had a high concreteness score in Brysbaert et al. (2014) of 4.14 and was filtered out as a possible LVC, while others like PLUNGE with a concreteness score of 3.04 in *take a plunge* was retained. Secondly, I used WordNet's (Fellbaum, 1998) lexical file information to check which nouns fit the categories of stative and eventive nouns, as suggested by Chen et al. (2015, 2376) and discussed in Sundquist (2022). This allowed for all pairings of lemmas with *take* and OWNERSHIP (noun.possession in WordNet), for example, or *take* and SWING (noun.action). Pairings that were omitted because they are not eventive or stative nouns according to WordNet include, for example, *take* + FACT, which does not fall into the categories of these types of nouns in Chen et al. (2015). Thirdly, I used a frequency cutoff of .05 words per million for any verb-noun pairings in the sub-corpus. This cutoff was necessary to avoid the extremely high number (i.e., several thousand isolated instances) of single verb-noun pairings that are typical of a Zipfian distribution of tokens (Zipf, 1949) and which would be difficult to filter manually. A final manual cross-check using the guidelines set up in Bonial et al. (2015) was done to check for false positives that may have been included mistakenly or for any false negatives with nouns that, for various reasons, may have been unwittingly filtered out in combinations with certain verbs like *take*.

---

8 3.5 was chosen as a conservative cutoff score that allowed for a large number of slightly more concrete nouns for consideration while staying close to the middle ranking of 3 on the 5-point scale established by raters in Brysbaert et al. (2014). As discussed below, a manual check using the context of the verb–noun pairing in COHA was performed after filtering of the data, following guidelines in Bonial et al. (2015).

After LVCs were identified, I was able to categorize nouns into families that occur as NP complements to *take*. Using the online database available via FrameNet (Fillmore et al., 2003) and its semantic categories based on human annotation of actual texts, I identified families of noun collocates that share the same semantic frame. FrameNet displays all semantic frames along with a definition and any optional frame elements or lexical units that evoke this frame.[9] In the case of nouns, for instance, while many of them are close synonyms, others are less directly related but still belong to the same semantic frame (e.g., SAFARI, PILGRIMAGE, and ODYSSEY in the 'Travel' frame). In this way, as Bonial (2014, 176) notes, it is possible to capture the semantic similarity between lexical items beyond mere synonyms, basing shared membership in categories on real-world contexts through FrameNet's annotation procedures.[10] Nouns were classified into families if there were three or more nouns that evoke the same semantic frame that were found to occur with the same verb in the sub-corpus at a rate of .05 WPM (words per million). For example, as in the case of the travel frame, a search of this frame in FrameNet reveals a number of nouns as lexical units, including TRIP, VOYAGE, EXCURSION, and JOURNEY, that co-occur with *take* in the sub-corpus at a rate above .05 WPM, but also others that are infrequent, such as JUNKET or SAFARI that occur at a low rate of only .03 words per million.[11]

---

[9] All semantic frames in the online database of FrameNet are available here: https://framenet.ics i.berkeley.edu/frameIndex. Lexical units associated with each frame are provided on that frame's listing or via the lexical unit index here: https://framenet.icsi.berkeley.edu/luIndex.

[10] Note that, as Ruppenhofer et al. (2016, 31) point out, FrameNet takes LVCs into account, referring to some of them as 'support predicates' in their Section 3.2.7.1. The noun-verb pairings that are considered LVCs in this study differ from the more narrowly-defined group of support predicates recognized in the FrameNet database; I follow Bonial (2014) and the criteria laid out in Bonial et al. (2015) in their identification of LVCs that makes use of FrameNet.

[11] The lexical units associated with the 'Travel' frame are provided here: https://framenet.icsi.be rkeley.edu/frameIndexunder the search query 'Travel'. The definition of this frame is as follows: "In this frame a Traveler goes on a journey, an activity, generally planned in advance, in which the Traveler moves from a Source location to a Goal along a Path or within an Area. The journey can be accompanied by Co-participants and Baggage. The Duration or Distance of the journey, both generally long, may also be described as may be the Mode of transportation. Words in this frame emphasize the whole process of getting from one place to another, rather than profiling merely the beginning or the end of the journey."

4 Results

4.1 Type Frequency of *take* in LVCs

After following the procedures laid out in Section 3.2, I tracked the type frequency of LVCs with *take* in each decade from 1820 to 2010, comparing this frequency to that of another verb, *lose*, in the COHA sub-corpus in Figure 1:

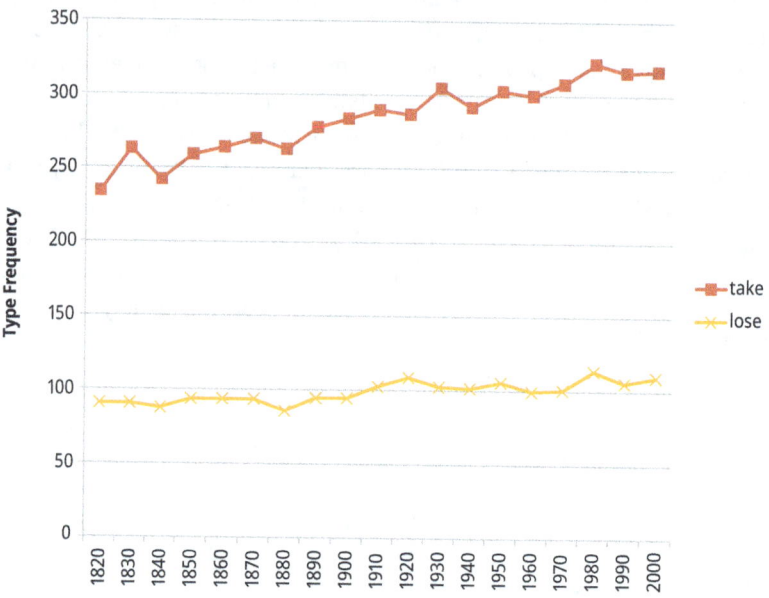

Fig. 1: Type frequency of *take* in LVCs compared to *lose* between 1820 and 2010 in the COHA sub-corpus as measured by unique verb-noun pairings.

Type frequency here relates to the number of unique verb-noun pairings associated with each verb that were selected from the sub-corpus. As Figure 1 indicates, *take* occurs with a high number of unique nouns in NP complements, while *lose* fluctuates at a low rate throughout the 19th and 20th centuries.[12] Moreover, the type frequency of *take* in LVCs tends to increase consistently over each decade, while that of *lose* is relatively flat, with only slight increases over almost 200 years. In sum: *take* has a consistently high type frequency in LVCs and occurs with an ever-growing num-

---

[12] Note that the number of unique NP-types in Figure 1 for each decade varies as some types come in and out of use.

ber of unique nouns in NP complements. A more semantically heavy verb like *lose*, on the other hand, occurs with a limited number of unique nouns in NP complements, and this type frequency remains low and flat throughout the period under investigation.

4.2 Token Frequency and Families of Nouns in LVCs with *take*

Following the procedure laid out for tracking token frequency of LVCs with *take* in Section 3.2, I examined the extent to which nouns cluster together in families by nature of their semantic similarity. Several families of varying sizes occur with *take*. Along with LOOK, for instance, there is a family which includes six other nouns that occur in LVCs with *take* in the sub-corpus that are all part of the 'Perception Active' frame of FrameNet (Fig. 2).[13]

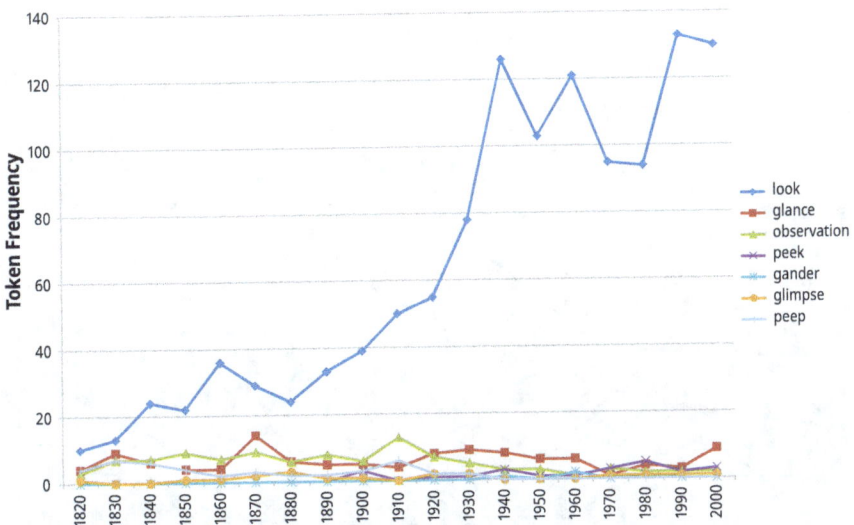

Fig. 2: Verb-Noun pairings in LVCs with *take* in the 'Perception Active' frame.

---

13 'Perception active' is provided here under the frame's name and includes a list of all associated lexical units in FrameNet: https://framenet.icsi.berkeley.edu/frameIndex. The definition of the frame is as follows: "This frame contains perception words whose perceivers intentionally direct their attention to some entity or phenomenon in order to have a perceptual experience. For this reason, we call the perceiver role in this frame 'Perceiver agentive'." Note that the 'Perception active' frame includes LOOK, GLANCE, PEEP, etc., and is marked as distinct from other similar frames

It is clear that LOOK, when paired with *take*, follows a clear trajectory in which its token frequency is higher than other nouns from the same family; this frequency continually increases over time despite some periodic decreases in some decades. Moreover, the token frequency of other nouns in this family is low and never increases substantially at any point between 1820 and 2010. As will be discussed below in Section 5, some of these nouns (e.g., GANDER) appear for the first time in combination with *take* during intermediate decades in the sub-corpus only to remain at an extremely low frequency in subsequent decades.

Upon further inspection of other nouns that occur in LVCs with *take*, we can observe clustering of semantically similar nouns into families of varying sizes. For instance, a family with slightly lower token frequency of its individual members than the 'Perception Active' family includes nouns in the 'Travel' frame (Fig. 3).

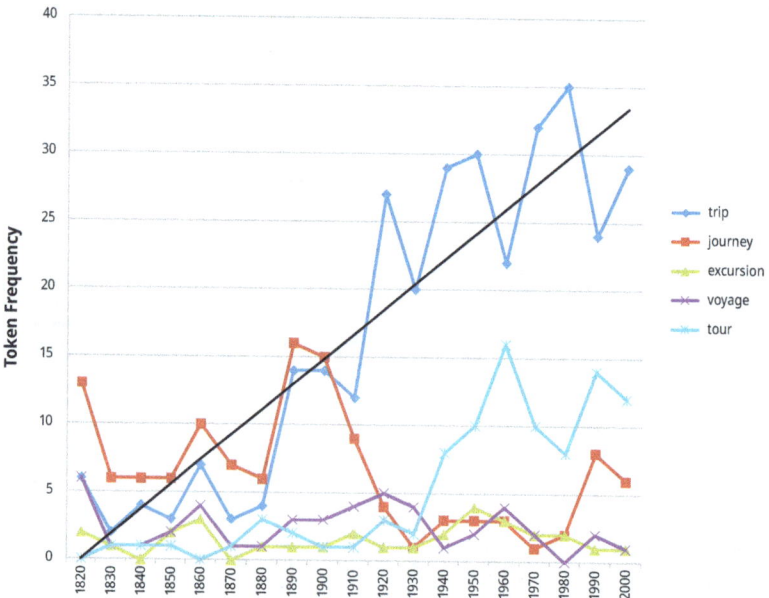

Fig. 3: Verb-Noun pairings in LVCs with *take* in the 'Travel' frame.

The token frequency of the noun TRIP with *take* clearly increases over time, while other semantically similar nouns come in and out of use as TRIP continues its rise. Many of these verb-noun combinations exhibit low, varying rates of use. The total

---

like 'Perception experience', in which the Perceiver is passive rather than active, as seen in the difference between activities like 'looking at' (active) vs. 'seeing' (passive).

membership of the family (N=5) is similar to that of the 'Perception Active' family, despite the slightly lower overall token frequency of its members in the aggregate.

Additionally, a number of nouns that all belong to the 'Change of Position' semantic frame in FrameNet form a cohesive group by nature of their shared semantic properties:

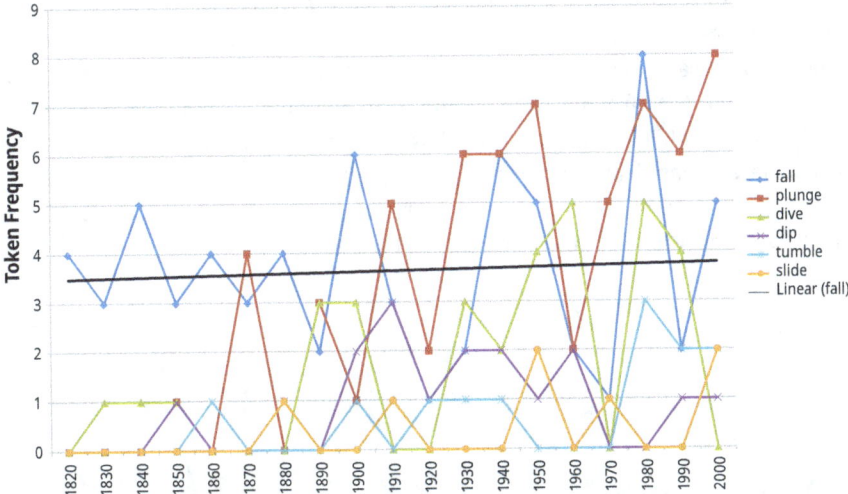

Fig. 4: Verb-Noun pairings in LVCs with *take* in the 'Change of Position' frame.

The nouns of this family all occur with relatively low token frequency, and there is no clear-cut pairing that separates itself from the others, as seen in linear trend line in Figure 4. But the number of family members of nouns in this group in the sub-corpus (N=6) is similar to that of other families in LVCs with *take*. It is clear that there are multiple family members that share the same semantic properties despite the extremely low token frequencies.

Based on the data from at least three noun families that occur as NP complements to *take*, it appears that there is variability across families. For instance, while nouns in the 'Travel' family (e.g., *trip*, *journey*, etc.) are similar in general ways to those in the 'Change of Position' family (e.g., *fall*, *tumble*, etc.) by nature of the process of movement of the agent from one position to another, they are also quite distinct from each other. In one case, the nouns are associated with an implied and intentional use of a vehicle or means of transportation; in the other case, they all involve a downward bodily movement (i.e, falling). Moreover, in the case of the 'Perception Active' frame and the nouns associated with this family (e.g., *look*, *peak*, etc.), they are quite distinct and exhibit very little semantic overlap with other families.

In other words, there is a degree of variability from one family to the other, with little clustering of the families by means of closely related semantic properties.

4.3 Comparison of *take* LVCs with *lose*

It is useful to compare type and token data from *take* and its nominal collocates with other verbs to gain an understanding of patterns that shape the formation of complex predicates over time. As noted in Section 4.1, for instance, *lose* has a much lower and flat type frequency as measured by the number of unique verb-noun combinations in LVCs. In addition, *lose* has very few families of nouns compared to *take*, where it was clear that there are multiple families of nouns of varying sizes. The only 'family' that meets the selection criteria laid out in Section 3 for *lose* is the small 'Desiring' group of nouns depicted in Figure 5:

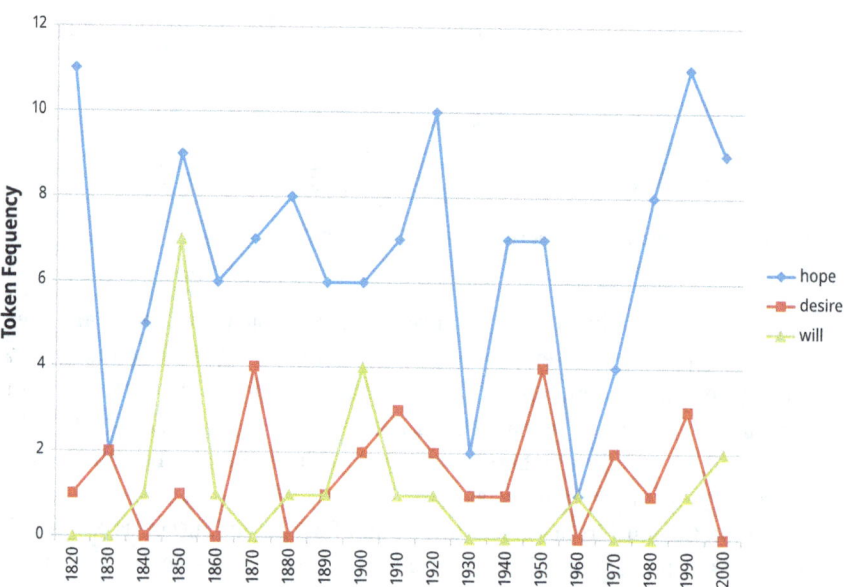

Fig. 5: Verb-Noun pairings in LVCs with *lose* in the 'Desiring' frame.

Although *lose hope* is the most frequent verb-noun combination whose noun belongs to the 'Desiring' frame, its token frequency is erratic and remains low. The other nouns, *desire* and *will*, also exhibit a consistently low token frequency with *lose*, or even fail to occur in some decades of the sub-corpus.

In terms of variability of families, the data from *lose* are sparse. In some cases, the noun does not belong to any frames that are annotated in FrameNet, and in other cases, the semantic frame with which a particular collocate noun is associated does not include enough other nouns in the sub-corpus to achieve family status. For example, *control* belongs to the same frame as *command*, as in *lose control (of)* or *lose command*; both nouns occur frequently enough with *lose* to be considered for further analysis. However, two nouns are not enough for family status, according to the data collection procedures outlined above that specify a minimum of three members. Otherwise, there are no other true families of nouns in the sub-corpus associated with *lose*, and for that reason, no variability across any potential families whatsoever.

5 Discussion

Type and token frequency data and evidence of the distribution of nouns in several families point to a high level of productivity in generating novel LVCs with *take* over time. In particular, an LVC like *take a look* exhibits five characteristics of a productive exemplar. First, the light verb *take* has, in general, a high type frequency reflected in the substantially higher number of unique nouns with which it occurs in NP complements. As noted by Sundquist (2020, 365), *take* behaves exactly like other classic light verbs such as *make* or *give* in American English, exhibiting a continuous rise in type frequency between 1800 and 2000, as the verb occurs with an ever-growing number of unique NP complements. Secondly, *take a look* displays characteristics typical of an exemplar LVC: the token frequency of the *take* + LOOK combination is high throughout the period of analysis—with only temporary decreases. This token frequency consistently rises over an extended period of time. Meanwhile, other similar verb-noun combinations like *take* + GANDER appear by analogy to *take a look* and remain in use at a low token frequency or simply disappear before other new, novel expressions first come on the scene. A third characteristic typical of a productive exemplar LVC like *take a look* relates to the semantic similarity of nouns in various families. LOOK evokes the same semantic frame as PEAK, GANDER, GLANCE, and several other nouns, according to the annotation schemes in FrameNet. In terms of the overall diachronic development, coinages or borrowings that share similar meanings are ripe for combining with *take*, even if they remain at a low token frequency. Fourthly, in addition to the general type frequency of *take* (i.e., the number of different nouns that collocate with *take* to form any kind of LVC), *take a look* also exhibits a high type frequency within the family of similar nouns. As the results in Section 4.2 indicate, there are many different nouns like LOOK that are similar in meaning and occur at a relatively high token frequency in the sub-corpus (N=7). Lastly, there is a degree of variability across families in LVCs with take that are typical of a productive LVC, as seen in how distinct the families of nouns are from each other. As a result of the high, general type frequency from such a polysemous verb as *take*, there are multiple families of nouns with a wide range of meanings that occur in NP complements to this verb. As we will see below, this type of variability allows for a greater diversity or lack of clustering of families in the sense of the hyper-conceptual space made available for coinages.

In looking at the verb-noun pairings similar to *take a look*, we see that novel expressions like *take a gander* rarely increase in token frequency, despite the consistent rise of *take a look*. In the sub-corpus in this study, GANDER first appears with *take* in the 1930s, after the steep rise of *take a look* in the late 1800s (Figure 2), as in the following passage from a 1935-mystery novel:

(5) "But those guys ain't happy unless they're workin' over some poor mug like me that ain't got any influence. **Take a gander** at this." He pointed to the strip of tape on his cheek-bone.   (Murder with Pictures, FIC, 1935)

According to the *Oxford English Dictionary*, the phrase *take a gander* first occurred as early as 1914, where the noun is listed in the Vocabulary of Criminal Slang as 'an inquisitorial glance; a searching look; an impertinent gazing or staring' with an example quote: 'Take a gander at this dump as we pass.' The example from COHA in (5) exemplifies this early, limited use in contexts of murder mysteries with gangsters and police, especially when we consider its use in early film and movies. Subsequent instances in COHA reveal some expansion to other contexts, however, including uses in other fictional writing outside crime stories like in (6), from a scene from a 1953 romantic novel:

(6) "You'll find out what happens," she [the nurse] said angrily. "Sure. You're just doing your job. So am I. **Take a gander** at the card I left and you'll see what my job is."   (Good-for-Nothing, FIC, 1953)

As an LVC, *take a gander* never completely disappears and is still attested in the COHA-sub-corpus as late as 2005, as seen in example (3) from the newspaper genre; however, it occurs only sporadically throughout the 20th century at an extremely low frequency and never increases over 8 instances in any decade of the full COHA corpus. *Take a peek* is equally infrequent and appears the most in a single decade in the 1930s when it occurs only 3 times.

Even though these novel creations appear sporadically and remain only infrequent, they provide evidence for the productivity of LVCs like *take a look* in functioning as the basis for creation of new LVCs. These novel expressions lose out in the long term due to stronger associations with the more conventional formulations (Goldberg, 2019, 61). However, the proliferation of such novel expressions contributes to the expanding type frequency necessary for creating new LVCs in the first place. As Bybee (2010, 38) points out, the most frequent exemplars (i.e., *take a look*) are the most accessible and promote faster recognition of and greater clustering with other similar forms; constructions with high type frequency will be more likely to be used simply because of the ever-increasing strength of association and the greater number of candidates on which to base analogy (Bybee, 2010, 95). In the case of LVCs like *take a look* and other similar high-frequency pairings, exemplars continue this trend by continually providing more evidence in favor of the stronger associations. Thus, *take a gander* and other similar expressions contribute to the fruitful breeding ground created by *take a look*, but remain infrequent at the expense of the growing type and token frequency of the exemplar LVC.

By contrast, a more lexically specific verb like *lose* that combines with various NP complements to form complex predicates in a similar way to *take* exhibits the opposite trend. More fine-grained analysis of individual pairings with *lose* reveals that verb-noun pairings with *lose* form complex predicates that are more idiomatic and non-compositional rather than productive, with more substitutability of component parts. For instance, a common verb-noun pairing *lose* + SIGHT (910 total tokens) exhibits high frequencies throughout the whole period between 1820 and 2010. An analysis of mutual information (MI) scores in the full COHA corpus indicates high collocational strength in each decade between 1820 and 2010. However, *lose* + SIGHT undergoes occasional decreases rather than any kind of long-term, prominent increases in token frequency. In the case of this pairing, the MI score is consistently high in each decade (mean MI score = 7.74, SD=0.36 for co-occurrence within five slots), but with a slight decrease over time (7.96 in 1820 and 7.50 in 2009). In other words, the collocational strength mirrors the high but gradually decreasing token frequency of a fixed expression in the nineteenth and twentieth centuries. The idiomatic use of this pairing is reflected in its specific meaning: of the nouns that occur with the same verb in the sub-corpus, sight does not belong to any kind of larger families of similar nouns in this frame in FrameNet. Moreover, the nouns in these kinds of complex predicates are irreplaceable (e.g. **lose vision*, **lose view* vs *lose sight*). Their token frequency remains relatively high, but they are clearly more formulaic expressions that are used only in specific contexts: *lose* + *sight* has developed a metaphorical meaning, as in 'not able to keep fresh in one's mind', alongside the more literal meaning in which one is 'no longer able to see' (Brinton, 2008, 45). In other words, complex predicates with *lose* are more often restricted to specific idiomatic usages and lack interchangeability of parts. On the other hand, LVCs with *take*, while they do occur in some more idiomatic phrases (e.g. *take the reins*), occur with a wide range of NP complements with more substitutability of component parts.

The data on *take a look* vs. *lose sight* underscore the relationship between multiple factors that contribute to coverage from a diachronic perspective. Recall that in Goldberg's (2019, 65) discussion of coverage in experimental studies, she highlighted the interaction of type frequency, similarity, and variability in predicting coverage for the acceptance of new, creative expressions. A comparison with *lose* and a complex predicate like *lose sight* reveals clear differences with respect to coverage. As the data in Section 4.1 indicate, *lose* exhibits a much lower type frequency than *take*, as seen in the low number of unique NP complements with which it occurs. As Allerton (2002, 173) describes it, there is a niche that is created by the semantic preciseness of such lexically specific verbs. The area of coverage for a verb like *lose*, therefore, is simply much smaller and inhibits the creation of new verb-noun pairings rather than promoting it, like *take* does. The high polysemy and semantic deficiency of LVs like *take* provide both variability across families and high type frequency for aiding similarity within these families. Secondly, unlike *take* or more specifically an LVC like *take a look*, in which similarity across verb-noun pairings plays a crucial role in the higher coverage, *lose* lacks noun families that are bound together by their close semantic relationship. There are plenty of high token frequency expressions with *lose*, including *lose sight* or *lose control*, but nouns in these expressions do not belong to larger families. Instead, they are idiomatic, isolated expressions whose token frequency remains high but does not increase over time or serve as an exemplar in the productive increase of similar novel expressions. Lastly, in the case of *lose* and its collocate nouns, there is little evidence of variability across any families of semantically similar nouns. Unlike *take* which has a high type frequency and many distinct nominal families associated with it, *lose* has little to no clustering of similar nouns with which it occurs. Moreover, the high token frequency of some expressions like *lose sight* fails to generate similar expressions and the productivity of *lose* in complex predicates remains low or decreases over time. In terms of Goldberg (2019), *lose sight* provides little coverage and few possibilities for any expanding coverage, due to low type frequency, and little variability and similarity across nominal families that are collocates with *lose*.

6 Conclusion

Take a look is a useful example of an LVC that reveals how several factors combine to play a role in shaping productivity under certain conditions when these factors are examined over an extended period of time. Comparison between *take a look*, on the one hand, and *take a gander* or other novel expressions, on the other hand, demonstrates that type frequency, token frequency, semantic similarity, and variability across families of nouns all contribute favorable conditions to the creation of new LVCs and the continued success of exemplar LVCs. *Take a look* exhibits consistent increases in token frequency over time which enables a consistent increase in type frequency and more variability across noun families that share semantic properties, which, in turn, perpetuates an increase in token frequency in the long run. This snowball effect of increasing token frequency of the exemplar LVC comes at the expense of the many novel expressions that are short-lived yet useful to the increase in type frequency of the similar LVCs. Thus, in a situation in which 'the rich get richer', high frequency exemplar LVCs like *take a look* promote the same conditions which allow for their growth in the first place. Other LVCs like *lose sight* demonstrate how these same conditions contribute in some way to the high token frequency of a single, idiomatic expression yet the failure to promote further productivity of new, similar expressions.

These findings have theoretical implications for our understanding of how the notion of coverage relates to language change. Goldberg's (2019) discussion of coverage relies mainly on synchronic and experimental studies, highlighting how creativity, competition between lexical and grammatical forms, and productivity affect other at a relatively limited point in time. It is useful to view coverage from a dynamic perspective, however, focusing on issues related to frequency, similarity, and variability that may undergo changes and interact in interesting, complex ways over several centuries.

Future studies may focus on a greater variety of LVCs, noun families, verbs of varying lexical specificity, and other light verbs other than *take* to understand better how coverage may change when these factors are drawn out over a longer period of time. Additional data from other families of nouns and other verbs that combine to form LVCs might shed light on how coverage plays a role in diachronic processes like grammaticalization and lexicalization.

Bibliography

Allerton, David. 2002. *Streched verb constructions in English*. London: Routledge. https://doi.org/10.4324/9780203167649.

Barðdal, Jóhanna. 2008. *Productivity: Evidence from Case and Argument Structure in Icelandic*. Amsterdam: John Benjamins.

Barðdal, Jóhanna amd Spike Gilde. 2015. Diachronic Construction Grammar: Epistemological Context, Basic Assumptions and Historical Implications. In Johanna Barðdal, Elena Smirnova, Lotte

Sommerer and Spike Gildea (eds.), *Diachronic Construction Grammar*, 1–49. Amsterdam: John Benjamins.

Bonial, Claire, Julia Bonn, Kathryn Conger, Jena Hwang, Martha Palmer and Nicholas Reese. 2015. *PropBank Annotation Guidelines*. University of Colorado at Boulder: Center for Computational Language and Education Research.

Bonial, Claire Nicole. 2014. *Take a Look at This! Form, Function and Productivity of English Light Verb Constructions*. Doctoral dissertation: University of Colorado, Boulder.

Bowern, Claire. 2008. The Diachrony of Complex Predicates. *Diachronica* 25. 161–185. https://doi.org/10.1075/dia.25.2.03bow.

Brinton, Laurel J. 2008. Where Grammar and Lexis Meet: Composite Predicates in English. In Elena Seoane, María José López-Couso and Teresa Fanego (eds.), *Theoretical and Empirical Issues in Grammaticalization*, 33–53. Amsterdam: John Benjamins.

Brinton, Laurel J. and Minoji Akimoto. 1999. *Collocational and Idiomatic Aspects of Composite Predicates in the History of English*. Amsterdam: John Benjamins.

Brinton, Laurel J. and Elizabeth Traugott. 2005. *Lexicalization and Language Change*. Cambridge: Cambridge University Press.

Brysbaert, Marc, Amy Beth Warriner and Victor Kuperman. 2014. Concreteness Ratings or 40 Thousand Generally Known English Word Lemmas. *Behavior Research Methods* 46(3). 904–911.

Bybee, Joan. 2006. From Usage to Grammar: The Mind's Response to Repetition. *Language* 82(4). 711–733. https://muse.jhu.edu/pub/24/article/208049, last access: 13701/2025.

Bybee, Joan. 2010. *Language, Usage, and Cognition*. Cambridge: Cambridge University Press.

Bybee, Joan. 2013. Usage-based Theory and Exemplar Representations of Constructions. In Thomas Hoffmann and Graeme Trousdale (eds.), *The Oxford Handbook of Construction Grammar*, 49–69. Oxford: Oxford University Press.

Bybee, Joan and Sandra A. Thompson. 1997. Three Frequency Effects in Syntax. *Berkeley Linguistics Society* 23. 65–85.

Chen, Wei-Te, Claire Bonial and Martha Palmer. 2015. English Light Verb Construction Identification Using Lexical Knowledge. In Association for the Advancement of Artificial Intelligence (ed.), *Proceedings from the Twenty-Ninth AAAI Conference on Artificial Intelligence*, 2375–2381. Palo Alto: AAAI Press. https://doi.org/10.1609/aaai.v29i1.9534.

Claridge, Claudia. 2000. *Multi-word verbs in early Modern English: A corpus-based study*. Amsterdam: Rodopi.

Croft, William and D. Alan Cruse. 2004. *Cognitive linguistics*. Cambridge: Cambridge University Press.

Davies, Mark. 2010. The Corpus of Historical American English. http://corpus.byu.edu/coha, last access: 13/01/2025.

Divjak, Dagmar. 2019. *Frequency in language: Memory, attention and learning*. Cambridge: Cambridge University Press. https://doi.org/10.1017/9781316084410.

Fazly, Afsaneh. 2007. *Automatic Acquisition of Lexical Knowledge about Multiword Predicate*. Doctoral dissertation: University of Toronto.

Fellbaum, Christiane. 1998. *An Electronic Lexical Database*. Cambridge, MA: The MIT Press.

Fillmore, Charles J., Christopher R. Johnson and Miriam R.L. Petruck. 2003. Background to FrameNet. *International Journal of Lexicography* 16(3). 235–250. https://doi.org/10.1093/ijl/16.3.235.

Goldberg, Adele. 2003. Constructions: A New Theoretical Approach to Language. *Trends in Cognitive Sciences* 7. 219–224. https://doi.org/10.1016/S1364-6613(03)00080-9.

Goldberg, Adele. 2006. *Constructions at Work: The Nature of Generalization in Language*. Oxford: Oxford University Press. https://doi.org/10.1093/acprof:oso/9780199268511.001.0001.

Goldberg, Adele. 2009. The Nature of Generalization in Language. *Cognitive Linguistics* 20(1). 93–127. DOI:10.1515/COGL.2009.005.

Goldberg, Adele. 2019. *Explain Me This*. Princeton: Princeton University Press. https://doi.org/10.1515/9780691183954.

Hilpert, Marin. 2013. *Constructional Change in English: Developments in Allomorphy, Word formation, and Syntax*. Cambridge: Cambridge University Press.

Hilpert, Martin. 2017. Frequencies in Diachronic Corpora and Knowledge of Language. In Marianne Hundt, Sandra Mollin and Simone E. Pfenninger (eds.), *The Changing English Language: Psycholinguistic Perspectives*, 49–68. Cambridge: Cambridge University Press.

Hilpert, Martin and Holger Diessel. 2017. Entrenchment in construction grammar. In Hans-Jörg Schmid (ed.), *Entrenchment and the psychology of language learning: How we reorganize and adapt linguistic knowledge*, 57–74. Berlin: Mouton De Gruyter.

Jespersen, Otto. 1942. *A Modern English Grammar on Historical Principles, Part VI, Morphology*. Copenhagen: Ejnar Munksgaard.

Perek, Florent. 2018. Recent Change in the Productivity and Schematicity of the *way*-Construction: A distributional Semantic Analysis. *Corpus Linguistics and Linguistic Theory* 14(1). 65–97. https://doi.org/10.1515/cllt-2016-0014.

Perek, Florent. 2020. Productivity and Schematicity in Constructional Change. In Lotte Sommerer and Elena Smirnova (eds.), *Nodes and networks in diachronic construction grammar*, 141–166. Amsterdam: John Benjamins. https://doi.org/10.1075/cal.27.

Quirk, Randolph, Sidney Greenbaum, Geoffrey Leech and Jan Svartvik. 1985. *A Comprehensive Grammar of the English Language*. London: Longman.

Ronan, Patricia. 2014. Light Verb Constructions in the History of English. In Kristin Davidse, Caroline Gentens, Lobke Ghesquière and Lieven Vandelanotte (eds.), *Corpus Interrogation and Grammatical Patterns*, 15–34. Amsterdam: John Benjamins.

Ruppenhofer, Josef, Michael Ellsworth, Miriam R. L. Petruck, Collin F. Baker Christopher R. Johnson and Jan Scheffczyk. 2016. *FrameNet II: Extended Theory and Practice*. Berkeley: International Computer Science Institute.

Schmid, Hans-Jörg. 2020. *The Dynamics of the Linguistic System: Usage, Conventionalization, and Entrenchment*. Oxford: Oxford University Press.

Sundquist, John D. 2020. Productivity, Richness, and Diversity of Light Verb Constructions in the History of American English. *Journal of Historical Linguistics* 103. 349–388. https://doi.org/10.1075/jhl.19009.sun.

Sundquist, John D. 2022. An Exemplar-based Approach to Composite Predicates in the History of American English. *English Language and Linguistics* 26. 413–442. 10.1017/S1360674321000344.

Sundquist, John D. and Andrew Rothwell. 2019. Combinatorial Optimization and Genetic Algorithms in Text Selection for Corpus-Based Historical Linguistics Research. www.johnsundquist.com/research, last access: 13/01/2025.

Suttle, Laura and Adele E. Goldberg. 2011. The partial productivity of constructions as induction. *Linguistics* 49. 1237–1269. https://doi.org/10.1515/ling.2011.035.

Zipf, George Kingsley. 1949. *Human Behavior and the Principle of Least Effort*. Oxford: Addison-Wesley.

David Nicoletti
Constructional semantics of Italian light verb constructions
The case of *prendere*

1 Introduction

This paper examines light verb constructions (hereinafter LVCs), which are complex predicates composed of a verbal base combined with either a noun phrase or a prepositional phrase. These constructions are widely acknowledged in numerous languages, including Italian. While in certain languages, like Farsi, LVCs are regarded as the primary means of conveying verbal meaning, Italian LVCs are comparatively less common and productive than synthetically formed verbs. Some examples of Italian LVCs are shown in (1):

(1) a. *avere paura*
       have   fear
       'to be afraid'
    b. *fare   una passeggiata*
       make a   stroll
       'to take a stroll'
    c. *dare in consegna*
       give in deliver
       'to deliver'
    d. *prendere sonno*
       take   sleep
       'to fall asleep'

The few accounts of Italian LVCs have mainly grappled with their structural features (Ježek, 2004a; Pompei, 2017), while semantic accounts have focused on the light verb's meaning contribution (Mastrofini, 2004) and its variability (Ježek, 2004b). Moreover, the LVCs under scrutiny have been the most frequent ones, namely the schema consisting of *fare* or *dare* and ATA-nominalizations, i.e. deverbal nouns derived from past participle forms (Gaeta, 2000; Samek-Lodovici, 2003; Folli and Harley, 2013; Tovena and Donazzan, 2017), which is comparable to the much discussed English schema made up of a light verb and a deverbal converted noun such as *have/take a walk* or *give a laugh* (inter alia: Wierzbicka, 1982; Dixon, 1991).

On the other hand, less productive light verbs such as *prendere* 'to take' or *mettere* 'to put' have received less attention. In particular, for *prendere* it has been suggested, albeit cursorily, that it encodes inchoative meaning (Mastrofini, 2004, 379–

David Nicoletti, University of Rome III, Italy

389, Pompei, 2023, 137–138 for an interlinguistic approach). Given the verb's peculiar distribution with other light verbs (e.g., *dare coraggio* 'to give courage' ~*prendere coraggio* 'to take courage') and the ranges of meaning it encodes (from *prendere una decisione* 'to make a decision' to *prendere fuoco* 'to take fire'), LVCs with *prendere* represent an interesting case study, especially for cognitivist and constructionist accounts of LVCs, which propose that light verbs are semantic extensions of their lexically full counterparts (Newman, 1996; Brugman, 2001).

This contribution aims to offer a quantitative and qualitative analysis of Italian LVCs with the verb *prendere*. In particular, we will consider LVCs as constructions in the sense of Construction Grammar: phrasal patterns that acquire a conventionalized meaning through frequency and routinization (Bybee and Thompson, 1997, 380).

The paper is organized as follows. Section 2 gives a general outline of the phenomenon of LVCs in Italian and in general. In particular, section 2.1 reviews earlier research on LVCs in general, while section 2.2 presents the peculiar syntactic and semantic properties of Italian LVCs. Section 3 contains the delineation of our theoretical approach as we will discuss (i) what it means to consider LVCs as constructions and (ii) how to account for the meaning of both element in a cognitivist perspective. Section 4 offers the corpus-based analysis.

2 LVcs: An overview

In this section, we will provide an overview of LVCs, both from a general perspective and with a focus on Italian. Section 2.1 will provide a concise overview of previous research on LVCs, with particular emphasis on syntactic, lexical semantics, and phraseological approaches. This discussion will lay the groundwork for section 2.2, where we show that Italian LVCs can be understood as lexical unit with respect to certain properties.

2.1 Theoretical approaches

Linguistic theories addressing LVCs have grappled with several interconnected dimensions. On one hand, LVCs exhibit "division of labor" (Nickel, 1978, 25), which involves the distribution of meaning within the analytical structure, particularly concerning the 'weight' of the light verb and the other elements involved. On the other hand, given that LVCs are (almost) formally identical to verbal phrases (sec. 2.2), the mechanisms responsible for their formation has been questioned, raising the issue of whether they belong to the lexicon or the syntax (inter alia: Goldberg, 2003; Samvelian and Faghiri, 2014).

From the point of view of meaning, LVCs are traditionally characterized by a semantically bleached verb, referred to as the *light verb* (Jespersen, 1942, 117), and a second lexical element that represents the true semantic core of the construction. This understanding was shared by the framework of *Lexique-Grammaire* theory (Gross, 1981), which introduced the notion of *verbe support*[1] 'support verb' in the French school (then embraced by the Italian tradition: Elia et al., 1985, Salvi, 1988, 79). Within this approach, the verb acts as a mere verbalizer and provides the grammatical features that the nominal element cannot express, such as tense-aspect-mood (TAM) features and person agreement (Gross, 1999, 74–75).

Syntactic-based frameworks have considered LVCs as instances of complex predicates (Jackendoff, 1974, 488), which can be understood as constructions "in which two semantically predicative elements jointly determine the structure of single syntactic clause" (Mohanan, 1994, 432). Consequently, much attention has been directed towards the argument structure of LVCs, with various proposals that elucidate how a unified argument structure is established (inter alia: Grimshaw and Mester, 1988; Mohanan, 1994; Butt, 1995, 2019). Essentially, within syntactic approaches LVCs are formed in syntax (Butt, 2019, 7).

The lexical semantic tradition represents a pivotal point in the discussion surrounding LVCs. Specifically, neostructuralist[2] approaches have sought to elucidate the combination of light verbs and nouns based on their semantic content. According to this approach, in order to explain the semantics of LVCs, two fundamental assumptions are required: i) a rich decompositional structure of lexical units, and ii) the existence of a semantic agreement mechanism (Apresjan, 2004, 4). Both Meaning Text Theory[3] and Generative Lexicon propose that the two elements in LVCs share overlapping or redundant semantic features. For instance, De Miguel (2008, 574–575), working within the Generative Lexicon approach, argues that the varying

---

[1] We consider the terms *support verb* and *light verb* to refer to the same concept (but cf. Gross, 2004, 167). Throughout this paper, we will only use the latter term.
[2] The term 'neostructuralist', as coined by Geeraerts (2010), encompasses approaches that do not neatly fit within the generative/cognitive distinction. Neostructuralist semantics share several key features, including the use of decompositional analysis, a strong demarcation between encyclopedic knowledge and lexical knowledge, and a notable interest in computational semantics (Geeraerts, 2010, 123–125). A similar categorization is offered by Sanromán Vilas (2011), who identifies authors primarily aligned with functional approaches, particularly those associated with lexicographic projects (2011, 256).
[3] Authors within Meaning Text Theory do not uniformly hold the same stance. For instance, Mel'čuk (2004, 204–205) and Alonso Ramos (2001, 99) contend that the light verb is semantically empty, whereas Sanromán Vilas (2011, 254) argues for the opposite perspective.

selection of light verbs in Spanish LVCs can be accounted in terms of co-composition, whereby the semantic features of two words interact in a dynamic fashion (Pustejovski, 1991). For Generative Lexicon, semantic features of a word include, among other things, *qualia*, i.e. single essential aspects of the word's meaning (Pustejovski, 1995, 76–81). These are instrumental in accounting for polysemy, as in the case of LVCs. See, for example, (2):

(2) a. *dar bezos* 'to give kisses'
       dar abrazos 'to give hugs'
    b. *hacer caricias* 'to make caresses'
       hacer propuestas 'to make proposals'

De Miguel (2008, 575–578) proposes that the nouns in (2) all imply some kind of recipient of the action, but in (2a), the nouns have a 'trajectory' feature ('rasgo de trayectoria': De Miguel, 2008, 576) in their *qualia* structure which aligns with the semantic structure of the verb *dar* 'to give'. In contrast, the nouns in (2b), in which the 'trajectory' feature is absent, suggest that the action involves a creation made by the subject, leading to the selection of the verb *hacer* (De Miguel, 2008, 577).

An account of LVCs based solely on a mechanism of semantic concordances does not give the full picture, as the light verbs' meaning is so general that it would be difficult to explain why another light verb is not selected instead. As Butt puts it, light verbs can be thought of as verbal "passepartouts: their lexical semantic specifications are so general that they can be used in multitude of contexts, that is, they 'fit' many constellations" (Butt, 2010, 72). A quick glance at light verbs selected by nouns signifying 'stroll' shows already significant variation:

(3) *take/have a stroll*[4]   [English]
     dar un paseo 'to give a stroll'   [Spanish]
     fazer/dar um passeio 'to make/ give a stroll'   [Portuguese]
     faire une promenade 'to make a stroll'   [French]
     einen Spaziergang machen 'to make a stroll'   [German]

Accordingly, LVCs have been considered as a type of collocation, given that the selection of the verb is conventionalized (Ježek, 2016, 204). More recently, this aspect has been reconsidered in the light of research on idioms and phraseology, leading to a new perspective that offers a way to reconcile the predictable and idiosyncratic aspects of LVCs. This line of inquiry showed that: i) idiomatic structures can still

---

[4] LVCs with *take* are common in American English and can correspond to LVCs with *have* in British and Australian varieties. It is worth noticing that not all LVCs with *have* possess an equivalent with *take* (e.g. *have a cry, have a cough* vs. **take a cry, *take a cough*).

be analyzable in their internal elements, and ii) the interpretative schema deriving from this analysis can be applied to several constructions which make a up a 'family' of constructions (Nunberg et al., 1994). Consequently, LVCs have been regarded as a type of idiomatically combining constructions (ICE), i.e. "idioms whose parts carry identifiable parts of their idiomatic meanings" (Nunberg et al., 1994, 496). This perspective has facilitated the identification of families of LVCs in specific languages, as shown in studies on Farsi (Karimi, 1997; Samvelian, 2012) and German (Fleischhauer et al., 2019). We believe that such an account is also applicable to Italian.

In the following section, we will analyze Italian LVCs as lexical units with respect to different facets of their linguistic behavior.

2.2 Italian LVCs between syntax and lexicon

Units larger than words stored in our mental lexicon in the same way as morphologically formed lexical items can be subsumed under the label multi-word expression. For phrases to be considered as part of the lexicon it means that "they form stable units with regards to various aspects" (Hüning and Schlücker, 2015, 452). The structures regarded as multi-word expressions include idiomatic expressions, proverbs, formulae and, notably, complex verbs such as verb-particle constructions and LVCs (Masini, 2005; Samvelian and Faghiri, 2013). In this section we will show that Italian LVCs also display some word-like properties using tests that will measure their syntactic fixedness, lexical specificity and semantic cohesion.[5]

Syntactic fixedness (or *figément*, Gross, 1996, 4) measures the degree to which the predicative phrase that follows the light verb is constrained or fixed. As shown by Heid, this property varies according to the referentiality of the noun (Heid, 1994, 231–232), which can be tested by surveying the range of different syntactic configurations in which the noun can occur. This is best shown by relativization (4) of the noun:

(4) a. *prendere una decisione* → *la decisione che ho preso*
  'to make a decision' → 'the decision I made'
 b. *dare una risposta* → *la riposta che mi ha dato*
  'to give an answer' → 'the answer I gave'
 c. *mettere ordine* → **l'ordine che ho messo*
  'to put order' → **'the order I put'

---

[5] The test presented in this section have been developed by multiple authors to analyze syntactic and semantic properties of LVCs, for a comprehensive survey see Langer (2004).

d. *prendere sonno* → ***il sonno che ho preso*
   'to take sleep' → *"the sleep I took"

According to this test, Italian LVCs can be categorized into two groups. When the noun is referential the typical syntactic structure is [V + ART + N] (such as (4a) and (4b)), in turn when the noun is not referential the syntactic structure is [V + N] (such as (4c) and (4d)) (Ježek, 2004a, 197–198).

Substituting the NP with a question word is very limited (Masini, 2009, 81):

(5) a. *Che cosa hai   preso?   – Una decisione.
       what   have.2SG take.PTCP a   decision
       *'What did you make? – A decision.'
    b. *Che cosa hai   dato?   – Una risposta.
       what   have.2SG give.PTCP a   answer
       *'What did you give? – An answer.'
    c. *Che cosa hai   messo?   – Ordine.
       what   have.2SG put.PTCP   order
       *'What did you bring? – Order'
    d. Che cosa hai   fatto?   – Una passeggiata.
       what   have.2SG make.PTCP a   stroll
       *'What did you make? – A stroll.'

Example (5d) only works because the verb *fare* 'to do/make' can be used as a substitute word for actions in general. The NP in LVCs is usually modifiable by adjectives:[6]

(6) a. *Mary prende una decisione importante.*
       Mary take:3SG a   decision important
       'Mary makes an important decision.'
    b. *Giulio dà   la riposta corretta.*
       Giulio give.3SG the answer correct
       'Giulio gives the correct answer.'
    c. *Il presidente ha   dato   comunicazione immediata delle*
       The president have.3SG give:PTCP communication immediate of.DET.PL
       sue   dimissioni.
       his/her resignations
       'The president immediately announced his/her resignation.'

---

[6] From a semantic point of view, (6a) and (6b) are examples of internal modification (Ernst, 1981, 51–53), whereby the modification of the NP does not target the whole idiom. According to Nunberg et al. (1994, 500), internal modification is a property of ICE and a strong argument for compositionality of such structures. On the other hand, external modification is also possible with Italian LVCs (6c). The author would like to thank the anonymous reviewer for drawing my attention to this distinction.

On the other hand, modification with negative quantifiers and possessives is not always possible:

(7) a. *Giovanni non gli ha dato alcun bacio.*
    Giovanni NEG him have.3SG give.PTCP any kiss
    'John didn't give him any kiss.'
  b. **La macchina non ha preso alcun fuoco.*
    the car NEG have.3SG take.PTCP any fire
    *'The car didn't take any fire.'
  c. **Luigi gli ha dato il suo pugno.*
    Luigi him have.3SG give.PTCP the his punch
    *'Luigi gave him his punch.'
  d. *??Gianni ha fatto la tua telefonata.*
    Gianni have.3SG make.PTCP the your phone_call
    ??'Gianni made your phone-call.'⁷

In addition, in some cases the article and the number of the NP are fixed.

(8) a. *prendere le difese*   b. **prendere una difesa*
       take the defenses   take a defense
       to stand up for

(9) a. *dare l'allarme*   b. **dare allarmi*
       give DEF=alarm   give alarms
       'to raise the alarm'

According to Voghera (2004, 59), Italian verbal multi-word expressions tend to show a low level of syntactic fixedness, particularly when compared to adverbial and adjectival multi-word expressions. However, this this does not negate the presence of lexical meaning within these expressions, as syntactic fixedness is more closely associated with pragmatic and textual functions rather than lexical meaning (Voghera, 2004, 61).

Lexical fixedness describes the extent to which the light verb in an LVC can be replaced by other elements. Typically, the light verb cannot be swapped for another light verb or a synonym without altering the meaning or grammaticality of the construction.

(10) *prendere/ *afferrare una decisione*
       take/   *grab   a decision

---

7 This could be interpreted as: 'Gianni made the phone call you were supposed to make', but its grammaticality is dubious (see note 8).

(11) a. *prendere/ *fare una decisione*
       take/   *make a   decision
    b. *fare/ *prendere una scelta*
       make /*take a   choice

(12) a. *prendere/ *mettere in considerazione*
       take/   *put   into consideration
    b. *mettere/ *prendere in conto*
       put/   *take   into account

In some cases, the light verb can be substituted by another light verb, dubbed "support verb extension" by the French school (Gross and Vivés, 1986, 18), which serves to express nuances of meaning, such as ingressive aspect (*intavolare una discussione* 'to engage in a discussion' vs. *fare una discussione* 'to have a discussion'), inchoativity (*prendere freddo* 'to get cold' vs. *avere freddo* 'to be cold') or causativity (*fare paura* 'to scare someone' vs. *avere paura* 'to be afraid') (Ježek, 2004b, 188).

Finally, semantic cohesion refers to the fact that multi-word expressions have a concept-naming function. Crucially, LVCs stand in a relation of quasi-synonymy with synthetic verbs, which are usually, but not always (cf. (13d)), morphologically related to the noun in the LVC:

(13) a. *dare un bacio ≈baciare*
       'to give a kiss' ≈'to kiss'
    b. *fare una passeggiata ≈passeggiare*
       'to take a stroll' ≈'to stroll'
    c. *prendere una decisione ≈decidere*
       'to make a choice' ≈'to choose'
    d. *prendere sonno ≈addormentarsi*
       'to fall asleep'

Moreover, Masini points out that LVCs and synthetic verbs stand in lexical competition with each other (Masini, 2019, 289). In particular, LVCs with *fare* 'to make' and nouns of psychological state may block the formation of synthetic verbs with the same nouns (14), or vice versa (15):

(14) a. *fare ribrezzo*   b. **ribrezzare*
       make disgust   'to disgust'
       'to disgust'

(15) a. *fare   preoccupazione   b. preoccupare
         make worry   'to worry'
         'to worry'

LVCs also exhibit a single argument structure:

(16) x$_{Agent}$ fa una telefonata a y$_{Recipient}$ telefonata(x, y)
      'x makes a phone call to y'

The single argument structure blocks the double realization of arguments (possible in regular verbal phrases):

(17) a. ??Luigi fa   la telefonata di Mario.
         Luigi make.3SG the phone_call of Mario
         ?? 'Luigi makes Mario's phone call.'[8]
      b. Luigi racconta la telefonata di Mario.
         Luigi tell.3SG the phone_call of Mario.
         'Luigi recounts Mario's phone call.'

To conclude this overview, we can regard Italian LVCs as lexical units that display, to varying degrees, some level of syntactic fixedness. They do not allow variability of the light verb and share with lexemes some lexical properties (concept-naming function, competition and a single argument structure). In order to address these peculiar properties, we can turn to Construction Grammar, a non-modular framework that enables a consistent treatment of both regular and idiosyncratic structures.

3 LVCs as constructions

This section deals with the implementation of LVCs within the Construction Grammar framework. We will begin by outlining the concept of construction and constructional meaning, and explain how these ideas apply to LVCs. Next, we will offer an analysis based on cognitive linguistics that illustrates the semantic shift occurring within the light verb and the related elements in the construction.

---

[8] It could be interpreted to mean: 'Luigi makes a phone call on behalf of Mario'.

3.1 Constructions and constructional meaning

In this paper, LVCs are considered syntactic structures that have been lexicalized. They are, therefore, stored in the lexicon. Usually, syntactic phrases are stored in the lexicon as idioms and are considered completely idiosyncratic, as the speakers retrieves them as a single block from their semantic memory. Contrary to the idea that the lexicon is just a list of idiosyncrasies (see inter alia: Taylor, 2012, 19–23), we adopt a vision of language that implies a continuum between syntax and lexicon. The existence of structures such as LVCs with an intermediate status with respect to syntax and lexicon is predicted by Construction Grammar (henceforth CxG), a theory of language whose development started in the '80s with the study of idiomatic expressions. According to CxG, the basic unit of language knowledge is the construction, i.e. a conventionalized form/meaning pair.[9] Any type of linguistic pattern, be it phonological, morphological or syntactic, can be described by a construction. While at first the constructionist project focused on phrasal patterns, either partially or completely filled (such as *kick the bucket* or the *let alone*-construction), it has since grappled with syntactic and morphological leaning phenomena such as argument structure, derivational morphology or multi-word expressions.

Furthermore, constructions are not organized merely as a list but rather as a network characterized by vertical links, also called inheritance links (Goldberg, 1995, 73) or taxonomic relations (Diessel, 2019, 15–17). Inheritance links denote relations between constructions at different levels of abstraction[10] and facilitate the representation of "generalizations across constructions while at the same time allowing for subregularities and exceptions" (Goldberg, 1995, 67). This type of link enables fully abstract patterns like the English Ditransitive Construction (in (18)) to possess meaning independently of the lexical semantics of the elements involved.

(18)   <FORM: Sbj V Obj Obj$_2$ ↔ FUNCTION: X CAUSES Y TO RECEIVE Z>[11]

Abstract patterns like (18) consist of open slots that can be filled by lexical items, thereby specifying the meaning of the construction. Each light verb can then corre-

---

[9] The first definition of *construction* is attributed to Fillmore (1988, 36), emphasizing the conventionalized nature of a construction's meaning. Goldberg's (1995, 4) influential definition builds on this, introducing the notion that the meaning of a construction is not "strictly predictable from [the construction's] component parts." Over time, the definition has evolved to encompass any patterns occurring with "sufficient frequency" (Goldberg, 2006, 5).
[10] Many authors suggested the existence of horizontal links, representing relations between constructions at the same level of abstraction (cf. inter alia Audring, 2019, 280; Diessel, 2015, 306. However, their epistemological status is unclear (Ungerer, 2024).
[11] The schema simplifies Goldberg (1995, 50).

spond to a syntactic frame with open slots, and LVCs, in which one of the non-verb slots is filled with specific lexical items, can be positioned at a lower level of abstraction compared to patterns like (18). This perspective is already acknowledged by Goldberg, who establishes a connection between sentences like (19), exemplifying instances of LVCs, and the ditransitive construction in (18) (Goldberg, 1995, 149):

(19) a. *She gave him a wink.*   b. *She gave him a punch.*

Similarly, Palancar's work on Spanish reflects this approach, as the author identifies groups of LVCs sharing the same semantics and links them with the 'dative construction,' denoting transfer (Palancar, 2003, 199–200). This aligns with the endeavors of other scholars aiming to identify families of LVCs (see section 2.1).

The identification of LVCs families does not always yield straightforward results. Family (2008), operating within the CxG framework on Persian LVCs with the verb *xordæn* 'to eat', introduces the concept of "notional islands". These are described as "groups of LVCs where one type of [noun] combines with a particular light verb to produce different LVCs with highly related meanings" (Family, 2008, 150), aligning closely with the notion of LVC families. However, Family notes that "not all the LVCs constructed with a specific LV are valid members of one of the islands of the LV" (Family, 2008, 150) This observation is not surprising, since it is consistent with insights from research on acquisition, revealing that constructional meaning emerges from lexical sequences sharing similar features in a bottom-up fashion (Behrens, 2009). This underscores the critical role played by lower-level constructions and detailed lexical information. As Langacker articulates, "For many constructions, the essential distributional information is supplied by lower-level schemas and specific instantiations. Higher-level schemas may either not exist or not be accessible for the sanction of novel expressions" (Langacker, 2000, 29).

The stress on low-level schemas and lexical information is also relevant for another feature of LVCs, namely the fact that they display some level of productivity (Stevenson et al., 2004, 3). An advantage of positing partially abstract patterns is that they can license the formation of novel instances of LVCs (Goldberg, 1995, 139–140; Family, 2008, 148–149). However, research has shown that there are multiple factors influencing the productivity of a construction. Specifically, the numbers of lexical elements occurring in a specific slot (type frequency, Bybee, 1985) and their semantic coherence are decisive factors in determining the level of productivity of a construction (Barðdal, 2008; Suttle and Goldberg, 2011). Accordingly, constructions with high type frequency and low internal coherence are dubbed as "open schemas" (Bybee, 1995, 430) as they can license a lot of different instances regardless of the semantic fit of its fillers, whereas low type frequency schemas usually align with a higher level of internal semantic coherence. In this last case, productivity is more motivated by item-based analogy (Boas, 2003, 260–277), where local similarities between lexical items play a crucial role in the formation and acceptability of novel instances.

The goal of this paper is to identify the constructional semantics of LVCs with the light verb *prendere* 'to take'. As we have discussed, constructional meaning emerges by clustering lexical sequences that share certain similarities. While the local nature of this generalization underscores the significance of the lexical semantics of the elements involved, it does not diminish the relevance of constructional meaning. On the contrary, it provides insight into what exactly is being generalized, even if it occurs at a local level. Specifically, in cognitive linguistics lexical meaning has access to encyclopedic knowledge, which can lead to multiple possible interpretations of lexical sequences, especially where lexemes are used in unexpected contexts which involve a shift of the conventional semantics. Constructional meaning acts as a guide in the selection of the correct interpretation (Diessel, 2019, 107–108).

Similarly to the lexical semantic perspective (see section 2.1), we consider the light verb to be polysemic. However, given the possibility of multiple readings of the same combinations of verb and noun, the existence of an entrenched constructional meaning, strengthened by frequency of occurrence, constrains the possible meanings.

In the next section we will provide a cognitivist approach to deal with (i) the meaning of the light verb with respect to its fully lexical counterpart, (ii) the conceptualization of the noun, where an eventuality is conceptualized as an entity.

3.2 Delineating a cognitive approach

The fact the light verbs can be in paradigmatic relation with their fully lexical counterparts was already envisaged by cognitive and lexical semantics approaches (see section 2.1). Specifically, cognitive approaches exploited the notion of semantic extension, whereby a lexeme extends or adapts its meaning beyond its prototypical interpretation. It is argued that meaning extends from the concrete sense, grounded in perceptual experience (Langacker, 1987, 99), to the abstract sense through processes of domain shifts, also called metaphorical extensions. For example, in sentences such as in (19), actions, namely wink and punch, are conceptualized as transferable physical entities, according to the metaphor CAUSAL EVENTS ARE TRANSFER.

This perspective on light verb's meaning was also considered by Butt and Geuder, at least for English LVCs with *give*, although the authors are doubtful about successfully connecting the light verb meaning to its fully lexical counterpart given "the referential distinctiveness of the verb *give* and the event nominalization in its object position" (Butt and Geuder, 2001, 354).

Additionally, while cases such as (19) might be considered unproblematic given the presence of a metaphorical transfer, in other instances, the semantic extension deviates significantly from the prototypical meaning. An examination of Spanish LVCs with *dar* 'give' yields interesting results, particularly when considering the semantic shift that results in a change in the number of arguments compared to *dar* as a fully lexical verb (Moncó Taracena, 2011, 131).

(20)   Transfer > Physical Implication > Motion
        dar un libro > dar un empujòn > dar un paseo > dar un silbido
        'to give a book' 'give a push' 'to take a stroll' 'to whistle'

The Physical Implication semantics involves movements or sounds produced by the body (for other kinds of sounds, the verb *hacer* 'to make' is preferred, e.g. *hacer un ruido* 'to make a noise') and is the base for the Motion semantics, which does not possess a Receiver slot, resulting in a diminished valency of the verb. The cognitive perspective is applied extensively and thoroughly by Pompei (2023, 158–166) in the analysis of Latin LVCs with the verb *dare*. The author analyzes the semantic path in (20) demonstrating how the adoption of a cognitive approach enables a uniform treatment of LVCs, since the difficulties of considering the light verb as a semantic extension, namely different semantic roles and a decrease in the number of arguments with respect to the fully lexical counterpart of the light verb, can be overcome by explaining the extension "in terms of reduction of domains within the domain matrix" (Pompei, 2023, 194) and by retaining "the terms of GIVER, THING and RECIPIENT, which constitute the profile of 'give' as a lexically full verb together with the relations holding between these entities" (Pompei, 2023, 171).

Turning to *prendere*, its the distribution in Italian LVCs is quite peculiar. Aside from *prendere una decisione* and a few others LVCs, *prendere* is mostly found in alternance with other light verbs, namely *dare* and *avere* (21). The alternance of *prendere* with *dare* and *avere* also existed in Latin, where the third element was instantiated by different verbs, *sumere* and *accipere* (García-Hernández, 2003, 140).

(21)   a.   *prendere una decisione* / — / —
          'to make a decision'
     b.   *prendere un'iniziativa* / — / —
          'to take an initiative'
     c.   *prendere controllo* / *dare controllo*   / *avere controllo*
          'to take control'   'to give control'   'to have control'
     d.   *prendere coraggio* / *dare coraggio*   / *avere coraggio*
          'to take courage'   'to give courage'   'to have courage'

e. *prendere fuoco* / *dare fuoco* / —
 'to catch fire' 'to light something on fire'

The fact that *prendere* is mainly found in alternating distribution with other light verbs is interesting also from a cognitive perspective. According to this approach, symbolic units "can be thought of as point[s] of access in a network" (Langacker, 1987, 163) that is based on the language user's experience with the world. Crucially the three verbs evoke the same domain of experience that pertains to the control and the transfer of entities.

The notion of domain is central to understanding the semantic structure of an expression and its possible extensions. Cognitive domains provide contexts "for the characterization of a semantic unit" (Langacker, 1987, 147) and can be simultaneously combined to make up a "domain matrix" (Croft, 1993, 340). For example, Newman's account of GIVE takes into consideration four domains: a) the spatio-temporal domain, b) the control domain, c) the force-dynamics domain and d) the domain of human interest (Newman, 1996, 53). On the other hand, Brugman's account of LVCs with GIVE, HAVE and TAKE subsumes under the same domain the spatio-temporal domain and the force-dynamics domain. Given the fundamental relevance of these two notions in perceptual experience, i.e. the configuration of entities in time and space and the way they interact, it makes sense to consider them together. Accordingly, the control domain and the domain of human interest represent more abstract domains, since they presuppose the other two domains (Brugman, 2001, 561–562).

In its most basic meaning, *prendere* evokes only two distinguishable entities: a TAKER and a THING. The TAKER is a person who willingly ends up being in control of an object, the THING. A relevant feature of *prendere* is its low degree of semantic specificity or granularity, which reflects "the level of precision and detail at which a situation is characterized" (Langacker, 1987, 55), e.g. *The umbrella is near the door* is less specific than *The umbrella is at the bottom left corner of the door*. A sentence such as (22), for example, can refer to different kinds of event.

(22) *La ragazza prende il libro.*
 the girl take.3SG the book
 'The girl takes the book.'

The insertion of another participant specifies the event further. A possible participant is a GIVER, namely a person that transfer the object to the girl, for example *dalla maestra* 'from the teacher'. This would make 'take' refer to a change of possession event, namely the converse of 'give'. Another possible participant is a Source, the place from which the object is being removed from, for example *dallo scaffale* 'from the shelf'. In this case, 'take' refers to a removal event (on removal events, cf.

inter alia Kopechka and Narasimhan, 2012). Moreover, even in its concrete sense *prendere* might be used in cases which presupposes some kind of choice, whereby the TAKER selects the entity among a set of equivalent possible choices (23).

(23)　　La ragazza prende il　　libro di Pasolini (anziché　　quello di Calvino).
　　　　the girl　　take.3SG the book of Pasolini instead_of that　　of Calvino
　　　　'The girl takes Pasolini's book (instead of Calvino's).'

Acknowledging these three cases, some basic consideration about the relationship between the two entities involved can be made. The spatial configuration between the two entities is describe by means of the figure-ground organization, a relationship fundamental to cognition and perception which involves an asymmetry between something, the figure, that stands out against a background, the ground (Talmy, 1972, 11).[12] A good example of a figure-ground organization is a sentence such as *The bike is near the house*, where the bike is the figure and the house is the ground. However, apart from localizing constructions the asymmetry is found in all predicates, where usually the subject is a type of figure, and the object a type of ground. In *prendere* the TAKER is not required to move in order to get in control of the THING since one might reach with their hand to grasp it (Norvig and Lakoff, 1987, 199). This means that the object is the figure, since it moves along a path to reach the subject. However, two different levels of figure-ground organization are possible (as in GIVE, cf. Newman, 1996, 41), given that one could also move with the whole body to reach an object. Substantially, what is salient from a spatial perspective about *prendere* is the motion of the THING towards the TAKER.

The interaction between the two entities is modeled in terms of force-dynamics, which describes situations between entities in terms of energy flow (Talmy, 1988; Langacker, 1991). The TAKER is framed as both the energy source and energy sink, since the energy flows from the TAKER to the THING and then reverts back to the TAKER (Newman, 1996, 58). This domain recognizes that the TAKER is both the starting point and the ending point of the action. Furthermore, even in concrete instances of 'take', the concept of force must not be considered solely in physical terms. As Brugman notices, "Marion took the book out of the library [...] could accurately describe an event in which Marion sent e-mail to the reference librarian and the librarian mailed back the book" (Brugman, 2001, 562). This can also be observed in examples like (23), where the force can be understood both as a physical force—

---

[12] The figure-ground distinction was introduced in cognitive semantics by (Talmy, 1988). Langacker uses the terms *trajector* and *landmark* as linguistic counterpart of the figure-ground organization (Langacker, 1987, 231–236). In this paper we will only use the former pair.

such as when a book is physically removed from its source location—and as a psychological force, when the book is chosen from among a set of entities.

While Newman's control domain can be subsumed under the force-dynamics domain, stating the fact that *prendere* also evokes a shift in control of an object can be advantageous. Specifically, the notion of control correlates with the semantic notion of agentivity which is quite relevant in the analysis of LVCs with *prendere* (see section 4). The term 'control' encompasses a spectrum of situations, ranging from the physical control of an object (*prendere un libro* 'to take a book') to more abstract forms of control (*prendere lo stipendio* 'to take/get a salary').

The event is illustrated in Figure 1. The force-dynamics is represented by an arrow that originates from the TAKER, extends towards the THING and flows back to the origin of the energy. The arrow also represents the motion of the THING towards the TAKER. The dashed square surrounding the THING represents the possible sphere of control of the Source, indicating that a GIVER may also play a role in the event as an additional entity.

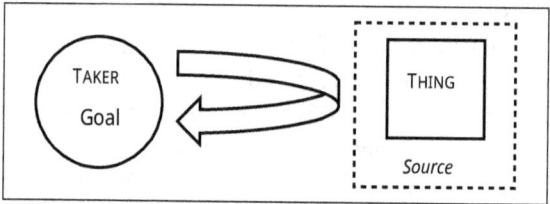

Fig. 1: Schematic representation of the event schema of *prendere* events.

The cognitive approach also posits a reconceptualization of the noun. The expressions of events (or states) as nouns, is a cognitive process Talmy dubbed as reification (Talmy, 2000, 43). If nouns are prototypically grounded in the domain of space and verbs in the domain of time, then we can identify conversion operation between the two domains. Notably, this conversion mirrors well-known correlations such as the count/mass distinction aligning with the bounded/unbounded distinction. While a lexeme might conceptualize an entity or an action as bounded or unbounded, its interaction with other linguistic structures has the potential to shift the lexical item to its opposite state by means of a cognitive operation known as bounding (Talmy, 2000, 51). For example, an unbounded entity like *water* can be reconceptualized into a bounded one through constructions such as *a body of water*. The same principle applies to actions. The (unbounded) activity *to walk* can be expressed either as an unbounded process, viz., *walking*, or as a bounded process, viz., *(a) walk*, involving a bounding operation.

Furthermore, the analogy between the two domains extends to additional categories, namely plexity and state of dividedness. Plexity refers to the "quantity's state of articulation into equivalent elements" (Talmy, 2000, 48), distinguishing between uniplex (consisting of one element) and multiplex (consisting of multiple elements). For example, while *to sigh* is uniplex, referring to a single bounded instance of sighing, *keep sighing* is multiplex. State of dividedness refers to the "quantity's internal segmentation" (Talmy, 2000, 55), viz., whether something is conceptualized as being discrete or continuous. *To breath* implies a "greater fusion across its inhalation-exhalation cycles" (Talmy, 2000, 55) than *take breaths*, the former being continuous and the latter being discrete.

Pompei argues that this characterization correlates with Aktionsart-based classification of nouns (Pompei, 2023, 169). Specifically, the author discusses Ježek's (which is based on Simone, 2003) classification of nouns based on three Vendlerian features: dynamicity, durativity and telicity (Ježek, 2016, 147–151) and argues that for this type of classification, boundedness "seems to be more relevant than telicity for nouns' Aktionsart, since the latter implies the former" (Pompei, 2023, 108). The feature of dynamicity distinguishes two noun classes: states (which are [-DYNAMIC]) and processes (which are [+DYNAMIC]). Processes can be further divided into definite, such as *walk* or *construction*, and indefinite, such as *walking* or *swimming*. The former are bounded, while the latter are not. Definite process nouns can be further divided into two subsets, whether they are telic (*construction*) or not (*walk*). Finally, punctual nouns (*start* or *jump*) are dynamic, telic and bounded but not durative.

Framing eventualities as entities makes it possible to evaluate the compatibility of the noun within the event schema. Punctual or definite process nouns are the best fit given that they are more akin to the THING as they are both bounded and of relative short extension –the former in the domain of time and the latter in the domain of space. As a result, bounded nouns such as *decisione* 'decision' or *informazione* 'information' which collocates with *prendere* merely prompt a shift of the verb's meaning from the concrete to the abstract. Additionally, the characteristics of the nouns makes them also suitable for functioning as a figure, as they are smaller and geometrically simpler compared to the other entity of the event schema, the TAKER which functions as a ground (Talmy, 2000, 315–316). A schematic representation would be quite similar to the one presented in Figure 1. In contrast, stative nouns such as *sonno* 'sleep' or *fuoco* 'fire', being unbounded, impose a bigger change on the event schema. The figure-ground asymmetry is, in this case, reversed and the unbounded nouns can serve as the ground (being larger and geometrically more complex) whereas the TAKER becomes a figure entering the state denoted by the noun.

In summary, the cognitive approach allows us to account for the semantic extension of the light verb, in terms of shift or loss of domain in the domain matrix, and the conceptualization of the noun in a comprehensive manner. In the next section, we will apply this approach to Italian LVCs with verb *prendere*.

4 The case of *prendere*

This investigation is based on data extracted from PAISÀ (Lyding et al., 2014), a large corpus of synchronic Italian consisting of approximately 250 million tokens retrieved from web. Specifically, we are interested in exploring the semantics of LVCs with the structure [*prendere* + Noun], other structures such as [*prendere* + PP] are out of the scope of this article. Through a CQL query we extracted all the instances of the construction[13] and retrieved the frequencies of co-occurrence of each noun with *prendere*. From this list we manually selected collocation of *prendere* and nouns denoting eventualities. We have discarded the cases in which the noun referred to an entity, even if the use of *prendere* was not literal, thus phrases such as *prendere un treno* 'to take a train', or *prendere una strada* 'to take a street', were discarded. Then, we performed a collostructional analysis, a family of methods developed by Stefanowitsch and Gries that identifies which lexical items are statistically biased to appear in a particular slot of a construction (Stefanowitsch and Gries, 2003, 214). Specifically, we are interested in collexeme analysis, that works by entering frequency data into a 2-by-2 contingency table. This is shown schematically in Table 1.

Tab. 1: Co-occurrence contingency table of *prendere* + N, based on (Stefanowitsch and Gries, 2003, 219).

	prendere + N	¬*prendere* + N	Total
Noun	a	b	a + b
Noun	c	d	c + d
Total	a + c	b + d	a + b + c + d

---

[13] Since the *prendere*-construction is discontinuous, relying solely on POS-based queries proved insufficient for extracting the list of concordances. Consequently, we incorporated syntactic information by retrieving all the object nouns that followed the verb *prendere*.

In Table 1, *a* is the frequency of co-occurrence of a specific noun with the *prendere* construction, *b* is the frequency of said noun occurring in every other construction – viz., the total frequency of the noun in the corpus minus *a*, *c* is the frequency of the construction in the corpus with every other noun – viz., the total frequency of the *prendere* construction minus a – and *d* is every other construction in the corpus, given that we are interested in verbal constructions this number was derived by subtracting *a*, *b* and *c* from every verb tag in the corpus. Through these four frequencies we can compute the log-likelihood ratio score, a bi-directional association measure that works well with large sets of data.[14] We selected the 50 collexemes most attracted to the construction.

Collexeme Analysis is not, strictly speaking, a hypothesis testing method, as its nature it is more exploratory. According to Stefanowitsch and Gries, the meaning of the lexical items more strongly associated with the construction reflects the meaning of the construction (Stefanowitsch and Gries, 2003, 237). However, the collexeme of a construction may vary in terms of semantic coherence (Gries and Stefanowitsch, 2004, 106). This is also true for *prendere* + Noun, as shown in Table 2 where the 14 nouns more strongly associated are listed. It is difficult to identify an underlying general semantics.

Tab. 2: The 14 collexeme most strongly attracted to *prendere* + N.

LVC	log-likelihood	LVC	log-likelihood
prendere il nome 'to take the name'	1.100361e+05	*prendere controllo* 'to take control'	1.150979e+04
prendere parte 'to take part'	2.835459e+04	*prendere il sopravvento* 'to get the upper hand'	1.014757e+04
prendere posto 'to take a seat'	2.720301e+04	*prendere forma* 'to take shape'	8.030601e+03
prendere una decisione 'to take a decision'	2.415471e+04	*prendere una posizione* 'to take a stand'	7.381638e+03
prendere il via 'to take the go'	1.818374e+04	*prendere le distanze* 'to take the distances'	6.393997e+03
prendere spunto 'to take a cue'	1.810189e+04	*prendere cura* 'to take care'	6.355200e+03
prendere possesso 'to take possession'	1.466306e+04	*prendere comando* 'to take the lead'	5.341229e+03

---

[14] The computation of association measures was conducted using the R software (R Core Team, 2021) and the Coll.Analysis 4.0 package (Gries, 2022).

In collostructional analysis, the collexemes are then usually classified into semantic classes based on qualitative or quantitative methods, each class reflecting a different subsense of the construction (Gries, 2010, 79).

There is a great deal of literature about light verbs combining with semantically coherent classes of nouns (see section 2.1 and 3). The classes at issue usually refer to generic semantic content such as communication, sounds or blows, although sometimes finer semantic classes are being distinguished, such as internally caused and externally caused emotion (Sanromán Vilas, 2011, 260). Given the semantic classification of the nouns offered in section 3.2, it is expected that the identified subtypes would be, to some degree, coherent with respect to Aktionsart properties of the noun (Duarte et al., 2010; Pompei, 2023).

In terms of semantic coherence, there is not a clear way of classifying all of *prendere*'s collexemes. The result is a rather patchy distribution of the collexemes in the semantic space, with some LVCs acting as stand-alone or only being categorized in very small groups. However, at a closer inspection some generalizations can be found. There are two relatively big groups of nouns, one denoting mental processes or activities, the other denoting states. A third one, small but quite cohesive, comprises nouns that means 'start'. These three groups make up roughly half of the LVCs retrieved. The other LVCs make up very small groups (*prendere commiato* and *prendere congedo*, both 'to take leave on absence') or are quite idiomatic (*prendere atto* 'to acknowledge', *prendere la parola* 'to begin to speak').

In the upcoming sections, we will provide an in-depth analysis of these three groups. For each group we will describe their syntactic-semantic configurations and constructional meaning in terms of semantic extensions.

4.1 Mental process nouns

The first category of nouns within the *prendere*-construction under examination comprises definite process nouns that denote mental activities. These nouns are dynamic, durative and bounded, but not telic. Morphologically, the nouns in question (Table 3) are predominantly deverbal, formed with bounding suffixes such as -*zione* and -*mento* (Gaeta, 2002, 122–124). It is noteworthy that, in some instances, the deverbal noun is lexicalized and deviates from accurately reflecting the meaning of its base. For example, *provvedimento* and *misura* denote a type of administrative decision, and there is not a direct semantic relation between *prendere un provvedimento* 'to take a measure' and *provvedere* 'to provide', or *prendere una misura* to 'take a measure' and *misurare* 'to measure'. The category also encompasses more idiomatic constructions such as *prendere partito* or *prendere le difese*, which, besides exhibiting a higher level of syntactic and lexical fixedness, share the same semantics with the other constructions and can therefore be linked to the same subtype.

Within the analysis, a nuanced categorization reveals two primary subtypes of constructions: the DECISION-type and the INFORMATION-type. The DECISION-type constitutes a semantically coherent group of nouns, sharing a common thread of representing actions or processes tied to decision-making. Examples within this subtype include *prendere una decisione* or *prendere un provvedimento* 'to take measures'. In contrast, the INFORMATION-type lacks the same internal consistency as the previous type, from both a formal and a semantic perspective. However, despite this diversity, a crucial commonality emerges – in each case, the TAKER is conceptualized as a type of COGNIZER.

Tab. 3: Mental process nouns with *prendere*.

LVC	Literal translation, translation	Frequency
prendere una decisione	'to take a decision' 'to make a decision'	2506
prendere uno spunto	'to take a cue'	1542
prendere una posizione	'to take a position/stand'	1239
prendere contatto	'to take contacts', 'to get in touch'	581
prendere un provvedimento	'to take a measure'	419
prendere una misura	'to take a measure'	361
prendere ispirazione	'to take inspiration'	329
prendere le difese	'to take the defenses', 'to stand up for'	286
prendere accordi	'to take agreements', 'to make agreements'	163
prendere un impegno	'to take a commitment'	159
prendere visione	'to take vision', 'to view'	140
prendere una precauzione	'to take precautions'	100
prendere un'informazione	'to take (in) an information'	63
prendere partito	'to take party', 'to choose'	27

The DECISION-type instantiate the schema with the article and display a higher degree of syntactic flexibility. The noun is referential and it can be, for example, modified (24), relativized and passivized:

(24) *La città prese   la controversa decisione di vendere* quel terreno
      The city take.PFV.3SG the controversial decision to sell.INF that land
      ai   Brooklyn Dodgers.
      to.the Brooklyn Dodgers
      'The city made the controversial decision to sell that land to the Brooklyn Dodgers.'

In this context, the light verb takes on a meaning closely aligned with the act of selection (see section 3.1). In these constructions, the TAKER is the entity that makes a choice from a range of possibilities, framing the action as an act of decision-making. These LVCs do not alternate with *dare* nor *avere* and the expression of a source within the event schema seems inherently implausible. Accordingly, the force and movement associated with the verb can be understood as a form of intra-psychological energy, with emphasis on the initial part of the energy flow directed towards the selected entity. Furthermore, the nouns employed in these constructions predominantly refer to administrative decisions, allowing the subject to denote administrative bodies such as a city council or an assembly (see 24). The decisions are conceptualized as bounded and discrete entities. When the noun is pluralized, the construction refers to multiple acts of decision-making:

(25)   Le forze armate indiane hanno preso numerose misure
        The forces armed indian have.3SG take.PTCP numerous measures
        anti-terrorismo.
        anti-terrorism
        'The Indian armed forces have taken numerous anti-terrorism measures.'

Conversely, the INFORMATION-type contains the indefinite article only in two cases: *prendere un'informazione* 'to take (in) an information' and *prendere uno spunto* 'to take a cue'. However, it is infrequently realized. *Prendere un'informazione* has only one instance over 63 with an article. In every other case, the noun is plural. Interestingly, *prendere uno spunto* also has only one instance over 1542 with the indefinite article. In other instances, either the bare noun or the definite article is used. These LVCs are all motivated by metaphors such as IDEAS ARE OBJECTS (Lakoff and Johnson, 1980, 10) and THE MIND IS A BODY (Sweetser, 1990, 28–35). In general, the light verb's meaning is very similar to the full verb, with the difference that the in the LVCs there is a domain shift from the concrete to the abstract. In fact, it is possible to elaborate the source (26) and to express the converse event with the light verb *dare* (27).

(26)   Il libro non riporta la fonte da cui sono state prese
        the book NEG report.3SG the source from which be.3SG be.PTCP take.3SG
        queste informazioni.
        these information
        'The book does not mention the source from which this information was taken.'

(27) La sua vicenda diede   lo spunto a romanzieri e   registi   per
     the his story   give.PFV.3SG the cue to novelists and directors for
     racconti, romanzi e   film.
     novellas novels and movies
     'His story gave inspiration to novelists and directors for short stories, novels and films.'

Additional LVCs featuring definite process nouns include *prendere accordi* 'to make agreements' and *prendere contatto* 'to get in touch'. In the former case, the noun is mostly plural, while in the latter case, the noun can be either a bare singular or plural without any changes in meaning. From a cognitive perspective, the uniplex nature of *accordo* 'agreement' or *contatto* 'contact' has been amalgamated into a multiplex continuous entity, suggesting a unique event made up of multiple blended subevents. These LVCs exemplify a reciprocal construction, as the event implies a second participant expressed with the prepositional phrase [*con* + N]:

(28) La società   ha   preso   accordi   con la Croce Rossa
     the company have.3SG take.PTCP agreements with the Red cross
     spagnola.
     Spanish
     'The company has made arrangements with the Spanish Red Cross.'

In sum, we can identify two subtypes of LVCs with Mental Process Nouns. In both cases there is a shift in terms of force-dynamics from the concrete to the abstract. However, with INFORMATION nouns the meaning of *prendere* closely resemble its full counterpart, while in the DECISION-type, given its internal semantic coherence, we can identify a constructional semantics that can be paraphrased as: 'the subject takes on the responsibility of choice N'.

4.2 Stative nouns

Prendere's collexemes also include many stative nouns (Table 4), that are durative but not dynamic nor bounded. The nouns in question do not derive from verbs but are the bases of derivates, which are usually parasynthetic verbs (on parasynthesis cf. Iacobini, 2004). From a syntactic point of view the noun is usually bare, although it can occur with indefinite articles or determiners. This entails a lower degree of referentiality, resulting in a higher degree of syntactic fixedness as passivization is not possible and relativization is very infrequent. The state nouns' semantics can be categorized in three categories: psychological or physical states (*coraggio* 'courage', *paura* 'fear', *sonno* 'sleep'), property states (*consistenza* 'consistency', *forma* 'shape', *aspetto* 'appearance') and nouns denoting the state of being in control or possessing something (*controllo* 'control', *potere* 'power', *comando* 'control, command'). The latter group has some distinctive semantic properties and will be discussed later.

Tab. 4: Stative nouns with *prendere*.

LVC	Literal translation, translation	Frequency
prendere controllo	'to take control'	1615
prendere forma	'to take shape/form'	1495
prendere possesso	'to take possession'	1491
prendere potere	'to take power', 'to seize power'	1032
prendere vita	'to take life', 'to come to life'	781
prendere comando	'to take control'	779
prendere fuoco	'to take fire'	510
prendere corpo	'to take shape'	461
prendere confidenza	'to take confidentiality', 'to familiarize with'	217
prendere aspetto	'to take appearances'	128
prendere coraggio	'to take courage'	115
prendere forza	'to take on force'	81
prendere sonno	'to take sleep', 'to fall asleep'	72
prendere consapevolezza	'to take awareness'	53
prendere colore	'to take color'	46
prendere vigore	'to take vigor'	41
prendere consistenza	'to take (on) consistency'	38
prendere paura	'to take fright'	26
prendere velocità	'to take on velocity'	24
prendere dimestichezza	'to take familiarity', 'to familiarize with'	16

Within this group the light verb *prendere* alternates with *avere* and sometimes with *dare* and *mettere*. *Avere* encodes the stative meaning, as in, for instance *avere coraggio* 'to be courageous', whereas *prendere* and *dare* or *mettere* encode, respectively, the anticausative and causative meaning, as in *prendere coraggio* and *dare/mettere coraggio* 'to encourage'. The anticausative expresses situations in which the subject undergoes a change that is presented as going on spontaneously (Haspelmath, 1987, 90). The overall semantics of this group of LVCs can thus be paraphrased as 'the subject enters the state denoted by the N'. Here the semantic shift from spatial to aspectual meaning result in a more abstract meaning of the light verb. It is quite interesting that parasynthetic verbs employ the same semantic shift, as exemplified by the *in-* prefix in *impaurirsi* 'to get scared'. The parallelism between motion and change of state events results in a particular spatial organization, whereby the entity undergoing the change of state is the figure and the property is the ground

(Talmy, 1985). In terms of force-dynamics the TAKER here is clearly the energy sink, as it shows lack volitionality and affectedness. The former can be explained by taking into account the selectional restrictions on the subject, as in this case it is not restricted to animates. As per affectedness, the *happen to* test (Cruse, 1973, 13; Beavers, 2011, 339–341 produces acceptable results:

(29) a. Ciò   che è   successo   alla   macchina è che ha
       what that be.3SG happen.PTCP to.DEF car   is that have.3SG
       preso   fuoco.
       take.PTCP fire
       'What happened to the car is that it took fire.'
    b. Ciò   che è   successo   a Eva è che ha   preso   sonno.
       what that be.3SG happen.PTCP to Eva is that have.3SG take.PTCP sleep
       'What happened to Eva is that she fell asleep.'

Furthermore, these LVCs display an interesting actional property, namely incrementality. The term incremental is usually employed to refer to mereological incremental themes (Dowty, 1991, 567) in which the action progresses by dividing the theme in incremental parts. Another type of incremental theme involves "a change in some property" (Hay et al., 1999, 129). To elucidate the difference between the two types of incremental change, compare example (30a) with (30b):

(30) a. Bill mowed half the lawn.
    b. Bill *blew the balloon up only half-way*.

In (30a) the incremental change applies to half of the parts of the lawn, while in(30b) to a scalar property of all the parts of the balloon, viz., blowing up a balloon halfway does not mean blowing up a hemisphere. This type of incremental change has been dubbed property incremental change (Croft, 2012, 72). In the LVCs, the noun denotes this property and from the aspectual point the view the event is framed as going on gradually but never really reaching its culmination (Bertinetto, 1997, 100). The unboundedness of the noun can account for this aspectual property only to a certain extent, as there seems to have taken place a cognitive operation of adoption of a proximal perspective, whereby "a perspective point is established from which the existence of any exterior bounds falls outside of view and attention" (Talmy, 2000, 62), that emerges only at a constructional level.

(31) Lo schiavo prese   via via   consapevolezza della sua forza.
     the slave take:PFV.3SG way_way awareness   of.DET his strenght
     'The slave gradually became aware of his force.'

Moreover, when the noun appears with a determiner, its degree of extension is reduced and a potential bound is expressed:

(32) *Nel corso dell' evoluzione ha preso sempre più quel*
 in.DET course of.DET evolution have.3SG take.PTCP always more that
 colore.
 colour
 'In the course of evolution, it took on more and more of that color.'

When the stative noun denotes control or possession, the overall meaning of the construction is slightly different. The subject does enter a state, but there is no affectedness as the TAKER exerts control over the process. Semantically, the light verb is more similar to the full verb as it retains more of the domain matrix.

In sum, we can identify three main subtypes with stative nouns. They can all be paraphrased as 'the subject enters into a N state', but differ with regards to control exerted by the subject.

4.3 Start nouns

Finally, we tackle nouns that denote the start of something (see Table 5). This class is very small, but it exhibits a very high degree of semantic cohesiveness. LVCs in this class represent a very cohesive syntactic unit, as the noun is not referential. The article in *prendere il via* 'take the go/start' is lexicalized.

Tab. 5: Start nouns with *prendere*.

LVC	Literal translation, translation	Frequency
prendere il via	'to take the go/start', 'to kick off'	1167
prendere avvio	'to take start/boot', 'to get started'	545
prendere inizio	'to take start', 'to get started'	112
prendere origine	'to take origin', 'to originate'	207

These constructions denote the beginning of an event:

(33) *La manifestazione ha preso inizio verso le 14.45.*
 The demonstration have.3SG take.PTCP start around the 14:45
 'The demonstration started around 2:45 pm.'

Here, although the noun's semantic is transparent, the overall meaning of the LVC is idiomatic. This group of LVCs could be considered a subtype of the LVCs with state nouns (see 4.2), as there is some degree of similarity, specifically the focus on the phasal transition into a state, which is in this case a state of existence. However, given that subjects can only be an event and that, from a syntactic point of view, they are completely fixed, they have been considered a different class.

5 Conclusion

LVCs are challenging structures for many linguistic theories. Initially, the literature focused on the semantic bleaching of the light verb, yet this characteristic has undergone reassessment over time. Recent literature reflects a shift toward more nuanced analyses, considering both the syntactic and lexical attributes of the constituents within the construction. Notably, functionalist theories of lexical semantics and cognitive linguistics have delved into elucidating the comprehensive meaning of these constructions. The lexical semantics viewpoint is based on the concordance of lexical features of light verbs and nouns, while the cognitivist perspective investigated the meaning of light verbs in terms of semantic extension from their full counterpart. Embracing this latter perspective offers a way to explain for at least some aspects of LVCs meaning. Moreover, representing LVCs as constructions enables to account for both the lexicalized and the predictable aspects of these structures. The goal of this paper was to uncover the constructional meaning of LVCs, understood as generalization emerging from similar structures.

This paper focuses on Italian LVCs with *prendere*. The findings show that it is impossible to assign a general constructional meaning to all the LVCs with *prendere*. However, the analysis reveals the presence of multiple local generalizations, leading to the identification of three distinct LVCs subtypes: i) those denoting mental activities/processes; ii) those denoting a change of state; and iii) those denoting the initiation of an event. Further subdivision of these subtypes yields narrow groups characterized by a high degree of internal semantic coherence. In terms of frequency, LVCs denoting state of change is the group with the highest type frequency (16 LVCs), but the token frequency of each member of the group is somewhat low. This is indicative of the fact that the generalization is relatively productive and entrenched. Given the aspectual distinctive traits of this type of LVCs, namely property incremental change, fairly different from the other groups of LVCs, it is quite an interesting result.

The events associated with *prendere* consistently involve self-oriented one-participant scenarios. This characteristic is rooted in the verb's force-dynamics structure, which conceptualizes the subject as the deictic center and the energy-sink. A compelling direction for future research could involve a typological comparison of the meaning ranges embraced by light verbs that share a comparable conceptual structure. Such an analysis could shed light on cross-linguistic patterns and variations in the semantic domains covered by these light verbs.

The integration of quantitative methods, such as cluster analysis (Gries, 2010) or network analysis (Dekalo and Hampe, 2017), could reveal more nuanced generalization patterns that might have gone unnoticed in this qualitative analysis of LVCs. Expanding the scope of the investigation to encompass other light verbs, particularly *dare* and *avere*, could provide a more comprehensive understanding of the network of these constructions. Additionally, the relationship between analytic and synthetic verbal strategies deserves further exploration. Clarifying whether these two means of encoding verbal meaning are in competition or serve distinct functional purposes remains an intriguing area for future research.

Acknowledgments

This contribution is a result of the research conducted within the framework of the PRIN 2020 (Progetti di Rilevante Interesse Nazionale) "VerbACxSS: on analytic verbs, complexity, synthetic verbs, and simplification. For accessibility" (Prot. 2020BJKB9M), funded by the Italian Ministero dell'Università e della Ricerca, PI: Anna Pompei.

Bibliography

Alonso Ramos, Margarita. 2001. Constructions à verbe support dans des langues SOV. *Bulletin de la Société de linguistique de Paris* 96(1). 79–106.
Apresjan, Jurij. 2004. The theory of lexical functions: An update. In *Proceedings of the Fourth International Conference on Meaning-Text Theory*, 1–14. Montréal: OLST.
Audring, Jenny. 2019. Mothers or sisters? The encoding of morphological knowledge. *Word Structure* 12(3). 274–296. https://doi.org/10.3366/word.2019.0150.
Barðdal, Jóhanna. 2008. *Productivity: Evidence from Case and Argument Structure in Icelandic*. Amsterdam: John Benjamins.
Beavers, John. 2011. On affectedness. *Natural Language and Linguistic Theory* 29. 335–370. 10.1093/jos/ffq014.
Behrens, Heike. 2009. Usage-based and emergentist approaches to language acquisition. *Linguistics* 47. 383–411. https://doi.org/10.1515/LING.2009.014.
Bertinetto, Pier Marco. 1997. *Il Dominio tempo-aspettuale. Demarcazioni, intersezioni, contrasti*. Torino: Rosenberg & Sellier.
Boas, Hans C. 2003. *A Constructional Approach to Resultatives*. Stanford, CA: CSLI Publications.
Brugman, Claudia. 2001. Light verbs and polysemy. *Language Sciences* 23. 551–578.

Butt, Miriam. 1995. *The Structure of Complex Predicates in Urdu*. Stanford: CSLI Publications.
Butt, Miriam. 2010. The light verb jungle: Still hacking away. In Mengistu Amberber, Bret Baker and Mark Harvey (eds.), *Complex Predicates in Cross-Linguistic Perspective*, 48–78. Cambridge: Cambridge University Press.
Butt, Miriam. 2019. Complex Predicates and Multidimensionality in Grammar. *Linguistic Issues in Language Technology* 17(4). 1–14. https://doi.org/10.33011/lilt.v17i.1425.
Butt, Miriam and Wilhelm Geuder. 2001. On the (semi)lexical status of Light Verbs. In Norbert Corver and Henk van Riemsdijk (eds.), *Semilexical Categories: On the Content of Function Words and the Function of Content Words*, 323–370. Berlin: Mouton de Gruyter.
Bybee, Joan. 1985. *Morphology: A Study on the Relation between Meaning and Form*. Amsterdam: John Benjamins.
Bybee, Joan. 1995. Regular morphology and the lexicon. *Language and Cognitive Processes* 10. 425–455. https://doi.org/10.1080/01690969508407111.
Bybee, Joan and Sandra A. Thompson. 1997. Three Frequency Effects in Syntax. *Berkeley Linguistics Society* 23. 65–85.
Croft, William. 1993. The role of domains in the interpretation of metaphors and metonymies. *Cognitive Linguistics* 4(4). 335–370. https://doi.org/10.1515/cogl.1993.4.4.335.
Croft, William. 2012. *Verbs: Aspect and Causal Structure*. Oxford: Oxford University Press. https://doi.org/10.1093/acprof:oso/9780199248582.001.0001.
Cruse, David A. 1973. Some thoughts on agentivity. *Journal of Linguistics* 9. 11–23. https://doi.org/10.1017/S0022226700003509.
De Miguel, Elena. 2008. Construcciones con verbos de apoyo en español. De cómo entran los nombres en la órbita de los verbos. In Inés Olza Moreno, Manuel Casado Velarde and Ramón González Ruiz (eds.), *Actas del XXXVII simposio internacional de la Sociedad Española de Lingüística*, 567–578. Pamplona: Servicio de Publicaciones de la Universidad de Navarra.
Dekalo, Volodymyr and Beate Hampe. 2017. Networks of meanings: Complementing collostructional analysis by cluster and network analyses. *Yearbook of the German Cognitive Linguistics Association* 5(1). 151–184. https://doi.org/10.1515/gcla-2017-0011.
Diessel, Holger. 2015. Usage-based construction grammar. In Ewa Dąbrowska and Dagmar Divjak (eds.), *Handbook of Cognitive Linguistics*, 296–322. Berlin: De Gruyter. https://doi.org/10.1515/9783110292022-015.
Diessel, Holger. 2019. *The Grammar Network: How Linguistic Structure is Shaped by Language Use*. Cambridge: Cambridge University Press.
Dixon, Robert M. W. 1991. *A new approach to English grammar, on semantic principles*. Oxford: Clarendon.
Dowty, David. 1991. Thematic proto-roles and argument selection. *Language* 67. 547–619. https://doi.org/10.1353/lan.1991.0021.
Duarte, Inês, Anabela Gonçalves, Matilde Miguel, Fátima Oliveria, Amália Mendes, Iris Hendrickx, Maria de Fátima Henriques da Silva Luís Filipe Cunha and Maria da Purificação Silvano. 2010. Light verbs features in European Portuguese. In Pier Luigi Bertinetto, Aanna Korhonen, Alessandro Lenci, Alissa Melinger, Sabine Schulte im Walde and Aline Villavicencio (eds.), *Proceedings of Verb 2010 Interdisciplinary Workshop on Verbs: The Identification and Representation of Verb Features*, 27–31. Pisa: Università di Pisa.
Elia, Annibale, Emilio D'Agostino and Maurizio Martinelli. 1985. Tre componenti della sintassi italiana: frasi semplici, frasi a verbo supporto e frasi idiomatiche. In Annalisa Franchi De Bellis and Leonardo M. Savoia (eds.), *Sintassi e morfologia della lingua italiana d'uso. Teorie e applicazioni*

descrittive. Atti del XVII congresso internazionale della Società di Linguistica Italiana, 311–325. Rome: Bulzoni.

Ernst, Thomas. 1981. Grist for the linguistics mill: idioms and 'extra' adjectives. *Journal of Linguistic Research* 1. 51–68.

Family, Neiloufar. 2008. Mapping semantic spaces: A constructionist account of the "light verb" xordæn "eat" in Persian. In Martine Vanhove (ed.), *From polysemy to semantic change. Towards a typology of lexical semantics associations*, 139–162. Amsterdam: John Benjamins.

Fillmore, Charles. 1988. The Mechanisms of "Construction Grammar". *Proceedings of the Fourteenth Annual Meeting of the Berkeley Linguistics Society* 35–55.

Fleischhauer, Jens, Thomas Gamerschlag, Laura Kallmeyer and Simon Petitjean. 2019. Towards a compositional analysis of German light verb constructions (LVCs) combining lexicalized tree adjoining grammar (LTAG) with frame semantics. In *Proceedings of the 13th international conference on computational semantics - long papers*, 79–90. Gothenburg: Association for Computational Linguistics. https://www.aclweb.org/anthology/W19-0407, last access: 13/01/2025.

Folli, Raffaella and Heidi Harley. 2013. The syntax of argument structure: Evidence from Italian complex predicates. *Journal of Linguistics* 49(1). 93–125. https://doi.org/10.1017/S0022226712000072.

Gaeta, Livio. 2000. On the interaction between morphology and semantics: the Italian suffix -*ata*. *Acta Linguistica Hungarica* 47(1–4). 205–229.

Gaeta, Livio. 2002. *Quando i verbi compaiono come nomi*. Milano: FrancoAngeli.

García-Hernández, Benjamín. 2003. Fraseología latina y románica. Desarrollo del sistema clasemático 'dar' – 'tener'. El testimonio de las Glosas de Reichenau. *Revista de estudios latinos* 3. 133–153.

Geeraerts, Dirk. 2010. *Theories of lexical semantics*. Oxford: Oxford University Press. https://doi.org/10.1093/acprof:oso/9780198700302.001.0001.

Goldberg, Adele. 1995. *Constructions: A Construction Grammar Approach to Argument Structure*. Chicago: The University of Chicago Press.

Goldberg, Adele. 2003. Words by default: The Persian complex predicate construction. In Elaine J. Francis and Laura A. Michaelis (eds.), *Mismatch: Form-Function Incongruity and the Architecture of Grammar*, 117–146. Stanford: CSLI Publication.

Goldberg, Adele. 2006. *Constructions at Work: The Nature of Generalization in Language*. Oxford: Oxford University Press. https://doi.org/10.1093/acprof:oso/9780199268511.001.0001.

Gries, Stefan Th. 2022. Coll.analysis 4.0. A script for R to compute perform collostructional analyses. https://www.stgries.info/teaching/groningen/index.html, last access: 13/01/2025.

Gries, Stefan Th. and Anatol Stefanowitsch. 2004. Extending collostructional analysis: a corpus-based perspective on 'alternations'. *International Journal of Corpus Linguistics* 9(1). 97–129. https://doi.org/10.1075/ijcl.9.1.06gri.

Gries, Stefan Th. amd Anatol Stefanowitsch. 2010. Cluster analysis and the identification of collexeme classes. In Sally Rice and John Newman (eds.), *Empirical and experimental methods in cognitive/functional research*, 73–90. Stanford: CSLI Publications.

Grimshaw, Jane and Armin Mester. 1988. Light verbs and θ-marking. *Linguistic Inquiry* 19. 205–232.

Gross, Gaston. 1996. *Les expression figées en français: noms composés et autres locutions*. Paris: Editions Ophrys.

Gross, Gaston. 1999. Verbes supports et conjugaison nominale. *Revue d'études francophones* 9. 70–92.

Gross, Gaston. 2004. Introduction. *Lingvisticae Investigationes* 27(2). 167–169.

Gross, Gaston and Robert Vivés. 1986. Les constructions nominales et l'élaboration d'un lexique-grammaire. *Langue Française* 69. 5–27.

Gross, Maurice. 1981. Les bases empiriques de la notion de prédicat sémantique. *Langages* 63. 7–52.

Haspelmath, Martin. 1987. *Transitivity alternations of the anticausative type*. Cologne: Institut für Sprachwissenschaft der Universität zu Köln Arbeitspapiere.

Hay, Jennifer, Christopher Kennedy and Beth Levin. 1999. Scalar structure underlies telicity in 'degree achievements'. In Tanya Matthews and Devon Strolovitch (eds.), *Proceedings of SALT 9*, 127–144. Ithaca: CLC Publications.

Heid, Ulrich. 1994. On ways words work together – topics in lexical combinatorics. In Willy Martin, Willem Meijs, Margreet Moerland, Elsemiek ten Pas, Piet van Sterkenburg and Piek Vossen (eds.), *Euralex 1994 Proceedings*, 226–257. Amsterdam: Vrije Universiteit.

Hüning, Matthias and Barbara Schlücker. 2015. Multi-word expressions. In Peter O. Müller, Ingeborg Ohnheiser, Susan Olsen and Franz Rainer (eds.), *Word Formation, An International Handbook of the Languages of Europe*, 450–467. Berlin: De Gruyter. https://doi.org/10.1515/9783110246254-026.

Iacobini, C. 2004. Parasintesi. In Maria Grossmann and Franz Rainer (eds.), *La formazione delle parole in italiano*, 165–188. Tübingen: Niemeyer.

Jackendoff, Ray. 1974. A deep structure projection rule. *Linguistic Inquiry* 5(4). 481–505.

Jespersen, Otto. 1942. *A Modern English Grammar on Historical Principles, Part VI, Morphology*. Copenhagen: Ejnar Munksgaard.

Ježek, Elisabetta. 2004a. *Lessico*. Bologna: Il Mulino.

Ježek, Elisabetta. 2004b. Types et degrés de verbes supports en Italien. *Lingvisticae Investigationes* 27(2). 195–201.

Ježek, Elisabetta. 2016. *The Lexicon. An introduction*. Oxford: Oxford University Press.

Karimi, Simin. 1997. Persian Complex Verbs: Idiomatic or Compositional? *Lexicology* 3(1). 273–318.

Kopechka, Anetta and Bhuvana Narasimhan. 2012. *Events of putting and taking*. Amsterdam: John Benjamins.

Lakoff, George and Mark Johnson. 1980. *Metaphors we live by*. Chicago: University of Chicago Press.

Langacker, Ronald. 1991. *Foundations of cognitive grammar. Vol. 2*. Stanford: Stanford University Press.

Langacker, Ronald W. 1987. *Foundations of cognitive grammar. Vol. I*. Stanford: Stanford University Press.

Langacker, Ronald W. 2000. A dynamic usage-based model. In Michael Barlow and Suzanne Kemmer (eds.), *Usage-based models of language*, 1–63. Stanford: CSLI Publications.

Langer, Stefan. 2004. A linguistic test battery for support verb constructions. *Lingvisticae Investigationes* 27(2). 171–184. https://doi.org/10.1075/li.27.2.03lan.

Lyding, Verena, Egon Stemle, Claudia Borghetti, Marco Brunello, Sara Castagnoli, Felice Dell'Orletta, Henrik Dittmann, Alessandro Lenci and Vito Pirrelli. 2014. The PAISÀ Corpus of Italian Web Texts. In *Proceedings of the 9th Web as Corpus Workshop (WaC-9)*, 36–43. Gothenburg: Association for Computational Linguistics.

Masini, Francesca. 2005. Multi-word Expressions between Syntax and the Lexicon: the Case of Italian Verb-particle Constructions. *SKY Journal of Linguistics* 18. 145–173.

Masini, Francesca. 2009. Combinazioni di parole e parole sintagmatiche. In Edoardo Lombardi Vallauri and Lunella Mereu (eds.), *Spazi linguistici: studi in onore di Raffaele Simone*, 191–210. Rome: Bulzoni.

Masini, Francesca. 2019. Competition Between Morphological Words and Multiword Expressions. In Franz Rainer, Francesco Gardani, Wolfgang U. Dressler and Hans C. Luschützky (eds.), *Competition in Inflection and Word-Formation*, 281–305. Berlin: Springer.

Mastrofini, Roberta. 2004. Classi di costruzioni a verbo supporto in italiano: implicazioni semantico-sintattiche nel paradigma V+N. *Studi Italiani di Linguistica Teorica e Applicata* 33(3). 371–398.

Mel'çuk, Igor A. 2004. Verbes supports sans peine. *Lingvisticae Investigationes* 27(2). 203–217.

Mohanan, Tara. 1994. *Argument structure in Hindi*. Stanford: CSLI Publications.

Moncó Taracena, Sofía. 2011. Étude constrastive des verbs *dar* (espagnol) et *faire* (français). In *Methodes et analyses comparatives en Sciences du langage. Actes de la 3eme edition des Journees d' Etudes Toulousaines*, 125–134. Toulouse: Universite de Toulouse.

Newman, John. 1996. *Give: A cognitive linguistic study*. Berlin: Mouton de Gruyter. https://doi.org/10.1515/9783110823714.

Nickel, Gerhard. 1978. Complex Verbal Structures in English. *International Review of Applied Linguistics* 6. 1–21. https://doi.org/10.1515/iral.1968.6.1-4.1.

Norvig, Peter and George Lakoff. 1987. Taking: a study in lexical network theory. *Proceedings of the Thirteenth Annual Meeting of the Berkeley Linguistics Society* 195–206.

Nunberg, Geoffrey, Ivan A. Sag and Thomas Wasow. 1994. Idioms. *Language* 70(3). https://doi.org/10.1353/lan.1994.0007.

Palancar, Enrique L. 2003. La polisemia dei verbi *dar, pegar* e *meter* in spagnolo. In Livio Gaeta and Silvia Luraghi (eds.), *Introduzione alla linguistica cognitiva*, 197–212. Roma: Carocci.

Pompei, Anna. 2017. Verbi con struttura [V+SP] e verbi supporto. Proprietà e test. *Studi e saggi linguistici* 55(2). 109–136.

Pompei, Anna. 2023. How light is 'give' as a Light Verb? A case study on the actionality of Latin Light Verb Constructions (with some references to Romance languages). In Anna Pompei, Lunella Mereu and Valentina Piunno (eds.), *Light Verb Constructions as Complex Verbs*, 149–200. Berlin: Mouton de Gruyter. https://doi.org/10.1515/9783110747997-006.

Pustejovski, James. 1991. The Generative Lexicon. *Computational linguistics* 17. 409–441.

Pustejovski, James. 1995. *The Generative Lexicon*. Boston: The MIT Press.

R Core Team. 2021. *R: A language and environment for statistical computing*. Vienna: R Foundation for Statistical Computing.

Salvi, Giampaolo. 1988. La frase semplice. In Lorenzo Renzi, Giampaolo Salvi and Anna Cardinaletti (eds.), *Grande grammatica italiana di consultazione*, 29–113. Bologna: Il Mulino.

Samek-Lodovici, Vieri. 2003. The internal structure of arguments and its role in complex predicate formation. *Natural Language & Linguistic Theory* 21. 835–881. https://doi.org/10.1023/A:1025588109815.

Samvelian, Pollet. 2012. *Grammaire des prédicats complexes. Les constructions nom-verbe*. Paris: Hermes Science Publications.

Samvelian, Pollet and Pegah Faghiri. 2013. Introducing PersPred, a Syntactic and Semantic Database for Persian Complex Predicates. In Valia Kordoni, Carlos Ramisch and Aline Villavicencio (eds.), *Proceedings of the 9th Workshop on Multiword Expressions (MWE 2013)*, 11–20. Atlanta: The Association for Computational Linguistics.

Samvelian, Pollet and Pegah Faghiri. 2014. Persian Complex Predicates: How Compositional Are They? *Semantics-Syntax interface* 1(1). 43–74.

Sanromán Vilas, Begoña. 2011. The unbearable lightness of light verbs. Are they semantically empty verbs? In Igor Boguslavsky and Leo Wanner (eds.), *Proceedings of the 5th International Conference on Meaning-Text Theory*, 253–262.

Simone, Raffaele. 2003. Maṣdar, 'ismu al-marrati et la frontière verbe/nom. In José Luis Giron Alconchel (ed.), *Estudios ofrecidos al profesor J. Bustos Tovar*, 901–918. Madrid: Universidad Complutense.

Stefanowitsch, Anatol and Stefan Th. Gries. 2003. Collostructions: investigating the interaction between words and constructions. *International Journal of Corpus Linguistics* 8(2). 209–243. https://doi.org/10.1075/ijcl.8.2.03ste.

Stevenson, Suzanne, Afsaneh Fazly and Ryan North. 2004. Statistical measures of the semi-productivity of light verb constructions. In Takaaki Tanaka, Aline Villavicencio, Francis Bond and

Anna Korhonen (eds.), *Proceedings of the Workshop on Multiword Expressions: Integrating Processing*, 1–8. Barcelona: Association for Computational Linguistics.

Suttle, Laura and Adele E. Goldberg. 2011. The partial productivity of constructions as induction. *Linguistics* 49. 1237–1269. https://doi.org/10.1515/ling.2011.035.

Sweetser, Eva. 1990. *From etymology to pragmatics: metaphorical and cultural aspects of semantic structure*. Cambridge: Cambridge University Press.

Talmy, Leonard. 1972. *Semantic structures in English and Atsugewi*. Doctoral dissertation: University of California, Berkeley.

Talmy, Leonard. 1985. Lexicalization patterns: Semantic structure in lexical forms. In Timothy Shopen (ed.), *Language Typology and Syntactic Description 3: Grammatical Categories and the Lexicon*, 57–149. Cambridge: Cambridge University Press.

Talmy, Leonard. 1988. Force Dynamics in Language and Cognition. *Cognitive Science* 12(1). 49–100. https://doi.org/10.1207/s15516709cog1201_2.

Talmy, Leonard. 2000. *Toward a Cognitive Semantics. Typology and process in concept structuring*. Cambridge, MA: The MIT Press. https://doi.org/10.7551/mitpress/6848.001.0001.

Taylor, John R. 2012. *The Mental Corpus: How Language is Represented in the Mind*. Oxford: Oxford University Press.

Tovena, Lucia M. and Marta Donazzan. 2017. Italian *-ata* event nouns and the *nomen vicis* interpretation. *Italian Journal of Linguistics* 29(1). 75–100. 10.26346/1120-2726-103.

Ungerer, Tobias. 2024. Vertical and horizontal links in constructional networks: two sides of the same coin? *Constructions and Frames* 16(1). 30–63. https://doi.org/10.1075/cf.22011.ung.

Voghera, Miriam. 2004. Polirematiche. In *La formazione delle parole in italiano*, 56–69. Tübingen: Niemeyer.

Wierzbicka, Anna. 1982. Why can you have a drink when you can't *have an eat? *Language* 58(4). 753–799. https://doi.org/10.2307/413956.

Hideki Kishimoto
On the light verb construction in Japanese

1 Introduction

Light verb constructions (LVCs) have predicative complexes consisting of semantically light verbs plus non-verbal elements that carry substantial predicative meanings (see e.g. Jespersen, 1942; Butt, 2010). LVCs are attested in diverse languages. Japanese is no exception. The Japanese LVC has a predicative complex formed by combining the light verb (LV) *suru* 'do' (or its potential verb *dekiru* 'can do') with a so-called 'verbal noun' (VN) marked with accusative case, as exemplified in (1).

(1) Ken-ga   benkyoo-o si-ta.
     Ken-NOM study-ACC do-PST
     'Ken studied.'

In (1), the verb *suru* expresses a general activity meaning, and the VN carries the substantive meaning of the predicative complex, i.e. 'study'. There are a number of long-standing controversies on the LVC. One of the issues figuring prominently in Japanese generative linguistics is whether or not the LV *suru* has its own argument structure with θ-roles (or thematic roles) to determine the thematic status of arguments via θ-role assignment.[1]

Grimshaw and Mester (1988) have advanced an analysis of the Japanese LVC which takes the LV *suru* to lack an argument structure of its own, i.e. the verb does not carry any θ-role of its own, while the clausal arguments receive their θ-roles from the VN via Argument Transfer. There are also some previous works (e.g. Terada, 1990; Uchida and Nakayama, 1993) claiming that *suru* appearing in the LVC can be a transitive verb, which is equivalent to saying that it can have an argument structure with θ-roles.

In this paper, I will discuss the question of how arguments are realized in the Japanese LVC from a generative perspective, and argue that the LVC is built on the transitive *suru* taking an agentive subject, i.e. *suru* is a lexical verb possessing an argument structure with its own θ-roles. It is shown that the LVC is divided into two

---

[1] Some works on Japanese LVCs done in other frameworks include Isoda (1991); Butt (1995); Matsumoto (1996); Dubinsky (1997), and Yokota (2005).

Hideki Kishimoto, Kobe University, Japan

types; one type with an agentive subject and another with a non-agentive subject. I argue that in the agentive type of LVC, *suru* has an argument structure carrying agent and theme roles, but that in the non-agentive type of LVC, *suru* has an argument structure with a theme role (lacking an agent role due to its suppression).

In this paper, the LV *suru* is argued to select a VN, which surfaces as an internal argument (i.e. the object) to the verb, whether the LVC falls into the agentive type or the non-agentive type. I suggest that in the LVC, *suru* may select nominative, dative arguments alongside the accusative VN, as (2a) illustrates, but that the VN can also supply arguments, which are rendered as clausal arguments via the raising operation referred to as 'argument ascension', as illustrated in (2b).

(2) a. [… NP-NOM NP-DAT **VN**-ACC *suru*]
    b. [… NP-NOM   NP-DAT   NP-ACC   [__ VN](-ACC)   *suru*]

The arguments raised from the VN bear various markings, including nominative, dative, and (additional) accusative case (as well as other oblique markings) depending on their thematic meanings. I will discuss cases where the raised arguments are marked with nominative, dative, and accusative case. The syntactic operation of argument ascension applies in essentially the same way across various kinds of LVCs, but certain different grammatical constraints apply according to how the arguments are case-marked.

The present paper is organized as follows. In section 2, I take a look at the general properties of the Japanese LVC. In section 3, I review two prominent approaches to the LVC, and argue that the LV *suru* is a transitive verb equipped with its own argument structure. Section 4 presents several pieces of evidence showing that the LVC involves distinct syntactic derivations depending on whether it falls into the agentive type or the non-agentive type. In section 5, I show how the argument structure of the non-agentive LVC is derived. Section 6 discusses the case marking constraints applying to the LVC. Section 7 is a conclusion.

2 Some general characteristics of the LVCs

In Japanese, the LVC is most typically formed by combining the semantically light verb *suru* 'do' with a verbal noun (VN), which belongs to a subclass of event nouns which exhibit verbal properties, i.e. they possess argument structures.[2] Note that VNs are categorically nouns, but not verbs (Martin, 1975, 869–880).

VNs combined with *suru* are construed as complex event nominals with argument structures which carry θ-roles in the sense of Grimshaw (1990). Typical VNs come from Sino-Japanese (SJ) words consisting of two Chinese characters, but there are VNs of native Japanese (NJ) and foreign (F) words.

(3) a. (SJ) *benkyoo* (勉強) 'study', *soozi* (掃除) 'cleaning', *dokusyo* (読書) 'reading', *ryoori* (料理) 'cooking', *ryokoo* (旅行) 'travel', *undoo* (運動) 'exercise'; (NJ) *aisatu* (挨拶) 'saluting', *azimi* (味見) 'tasting', *aiseki* (相席) 'seat sharing'; (F) *tesuto* 'test', *doraibu* 'driving', *kopii* 'copy'
b. *hunka* (噴火) 'eruption', *zyoohatu* (蒸発) 'evaporation', *syuuryoo* (終了) 'finish'

LVCs formed with VNs in (3a) take agentive subjects, and those formed with VNs in (3b) take non-agentive subjects, i.e. theme subjects.

LVCs built on VNs in (4) take dative arguments. The dative arguments may be supplied by *suru* or the VN depending on their thematic meaning.

(4) a. *soodan* (相談) 'consulting', *zyogen* (助言) 'advising', *zyooto* (譲渡) 'granting', *ten'i* (転移) 'shift', *toohyoo* (投票) 'vote'
b. *hunsoo* (扮装) 'dressing', *hensoo* (変装) 'disguising', *tensin* (転身) 'a job change'

In the LVCs formed with VNs in (4a), *suru* selects a goal argument. The VNs in (4b) may select result arguments, which are rendered as dative arguments if argument ascension applies, as I will discuss in section 3.

---

2 Some verbs that take VNs as their objects (e.g. *hazimeru* 'begin') show 'light verb' properties, as noted by Matsumoto (1996, 77–101). Besides, the verb *ukeru* 'receive' can express a passive meaning, when combined with a VN, as in (ib) (Kishimoto, 2010).

(i) a. *Sensei-ga   sono gakusei-o   gekirei-si-ta.*
teacher-NOM that student-ACC encouragement-do-PST
'The teacher encouraged that student.'
b. *Sono gakusei-ga sensei-kara   gekirei-o   uke-ta.*
that student-NOM teacher-from encouragement-ACC receive-PST
'That student was encouraged by the teacher.'

The complex of *gekirei-o uke-ta* in (ib) carries the meaning equivalent to the meaning of the passive *gekirei-s-are-ta* [encouragement-do-PASS-PST]. These facts might suggest that Japanese has LVs other than *suru*, but I will not go into this question.

VNs can often be decomposed into two parts, which consist of verb stems plus other elements.

(5) a. V-V: *tookai* (<*too-kai* (倒-壊) [fall-destroy]) 'collapsing'
 b. ADV-V: *sootai* (<*soo-tai* (早-退) [early-leave]) 'early leaving'
 c. V-N: *dokusyo* (<*doku-syo* (読-書) [read-book]) 'reading'

In general, the VNs can be thought to possess argument structures due to the presence of verbal elements with argument structures inside them.

The verb *suru* 'do' may be considered a Japanese counterpart of *do* in English. When *suru* is used transitively, it expresses the meaning of a volitional or non-volitional activity, but *suru* also has an intransitive use, where the verb denotes an event (see Terada, 1990; Kageyama, 1993; Miyamoto and Kishimoto, 2016). A non-exhaustive list of the uses of transitive *suru* is given in (6).[3]

(6) a. *siai-o suru*
 game-ACC do
 'play a game' [volitional action]
 b. *isya-o suru*
 doctor-ACC do
 'practice medicine' [profession]
 c. *kare-o isya-ni suru*
 him-ACC doctor-COP do
 'make him a doctor' [causative]
 d. *geri-o suru*
 diarrhea-ACC do
 'have a diarrhea' [physiological process]

The precise meaning of transitive *suru* is determined by the combination of *suru* and its complement. (7) is a non-exhaustive list of intransitive *suru*. In the case of intransitive *suru*, what the verb means can be determined by the choice of the subject.

---

3 *Suru* has the use as a dummy verb for morphological support, which is used when a bound predicative element is separated from its host, as in (i).

(i) *Kato-san-ga hon-o* {*kai-ta*/ *kaki-mo si-ta*}.
 Kato-Mr-NOM book-ACC write-ACC/ write-also do-PST
 'Mr. Kato (also) wrote a book.'

The dummy verb does not carry any lexical meaning.

(7) a. *inabikari-ga suru*
   lightning-NOM do
   'there is lightning' [natural phenomenon]
  b. *oto-ga suru*
   sound-NOM do
   'sound' [non-volitional event]
  c. *memai-ga suru*
   sound-NOM do
   'feel dizzy' [physiological sensation]
  d. *henna azi-ga suru*
   strange taste-NOM do
   'have a strange taste' [taste]
  e. *san-byaku yen suru*
   three-hundred yen do
   'cost three hundred yen' [price]

Among the uses in (6) and (7), the transitive *suru* expressing the meaning of a volitional activity in (6a) represents the most prominent use. I suggest that the LVC is built on this transitive *suru*, which has the argument structure <agent, theme> irrespective of whether it is categorized into the agentive type or the non-agentive type.

The LVC forms a transitive clause. In general, its predicative expression come in two forms. The 'VN-*o suru*' forms in (8a)/(8b) comprise two separate elements, i.e. *suru* takes the VN as its object. VN-*o suru* is an authentic form of the LVC. The 'VN-*suru*' forms in (8c–8d) are compound verbs derived by incorporating the VN into *suru* and the sentences take only one nominative argument on the surface.

(8) a. *Ken-ga benkyoo-o si-ta.*
   Ken-NOM study-ACC do-PST
   'Ken did the study.'
  b. *Kazan-ga hunka-o si-ta.*
   volcano-NOM eruption-ACC do-PST
   'The volcano erupted.'
  c. *Ken-ga benkyoo-si-ta.*
   Ken-NOM study-do-PST
   'Ken studied.'
  d. *Kazan-ga hunka-si-ta.*
   volcano-NOM eruption-do-PST
   'The volcano erupted.'

The sequence of VN-*o suru* carries the same meaning as the compound predicate VN-*suru*. Compound verbs in many cases cannot be formed if the object of *suru* is not a VN.

(9) a. *Ken-ga   tenisu-o   si-ta.*
   Ken-NOM tennis-ACC do-PST
   'Ken played tennis.'
 b. **Ken-ga   tenisu-si-ta.*
   Ken-NOM tennis-do-PST
   (lit.) 'Ken did-tennis.'

While *suru* can take a referential noun *tenisu* 'tennis' as its object, it cannot form part of a compound verb, as shown by the pair of (9a) and (9b) (see section 6).

By contrast, the compound form VN-*suru* can be formed productively in the LVC. In fact, the availability of the two forms VN-*o suru* and VN-*suru* is one notable property of the Japanese LVC. The LVC in the VN-*o suru* form refers to an event specified by the VN, showing that the VN bears the substantive meaning of the predicate complex, compared to the verb *suru*, which expresses a general activity meaning. As such, the verb *suru* can be regarded as a semantically light verb (LV).[4]

The compound form VN-*suru* is derived from the periphrastic VN counterpart VN-*o suru* via syntactic noun incorporation, i.e. by rendering a verbal noun head as part of the predicate syntactically, as in (10) (see Kageyama, 1976–1977, 1982, 1991; Kishimoto, 2019a,b).

(10)   [...   ~~VN~~   VN-*suru*]

One piece of evidence in support of this view comes from *kata*-nominalization (Kishimoto, 2006). The hallmark of *kata*-nominalization is that when a verbal predicate is nominalized with the suffix -*kata* 'way', its arguments receive genitive marking, as exemplified in (11a).

(11) a. *Ken-no   hasiri-kata*
   Ken-GEN run-way
   'Ken's way of running'

---

4 Not all complex event nominals behave like VNs in the LVC under investigation. For instance, a deverbal noun such as *tatakai* 'fighting', which is derived from the verb *tatakau* 'fight', has the use as a complex event nominal possessing an argument structure (Grimshaw, 1990), and can appear as the object of *suru*. Nevertheless, it cannot form a compound predicate with *suru*; hence the unacceptability of **tatakai-suru* 'fight-do'.

b. Ken-no {benkyoo-no si-kata/ *benkyoo-si-kata}
   Ken-GEN study-GEN do-way/ study-do-way
   'Ken's way of doing the study'
c. kazan-no {hunka-no si-kata/ *hunka-si-kata}
   volcano-GEN eruption-GEN do-way/ eruption-do-way
   'the way of volcanic eruption taking place'

Remarkably, the VN must be marked with genitive case when the LVC is nominalized, and this holds true irrespective of whether the LVC falls into the agentive type or the non-agentive type, as shown in (11b) and (11c). Note that lexical noun-verb compounds, which are registered in the lexicon, have a structure whose internal constituent is invisible to the syntax, so their noun part cannot be marked with genitive case under *kata*-nominalization.

(12) a. Mari-ga namida-si-ta.
        Mari-NOM tear-do-PST
        'Mari shed tears.'
     b. Mari-no {namida-si-kata/ *namida-no si-kata}
        Mari-GEN tear-do-PST/ tear-GEN do-PST
        'Mari's way of shedding tears.'

The referential noun *namida* 'tear' can be compound with *suru*, but cannot appear as the object of *suru* (*namida-o suru* [tear-ACC do]). Since *namida-suru* is a lexical compound verb, the noun-part cannot appear in the genitive case, as seen in (12b).

A comparison of (11b) and (12b) illustrates that *kata*-nominalization applies to the LVC at the level of syntactic representation where the VN appears separately from *suru*, and that the VN is first generated as an argument in the VN-*o suru* form. If VN-*suru* is a lexical compound, the nominalized form VN-*kata* will be available, contrary to fact. (11b) shows that the compound form VN-*suru* must be derived syntactically from the VN-*o suru* structure via noun incorporation, as illustrated in (10). If it is always the case that the VN initially appears in object position, i.e. a θ-marking position, it is fair to state that in the LVC, the VN is assigned a theme θ-role by the verb *suru*, which in turn suggests that the LV *suru* should be a verb which carries an argument structure of its own, contrary to Grimshaw & Mester's assumption.

Noun incorporation is considered to be one type of head movement cross-linguistically (Baker, 1988). Since the grammatical process of noun incorporation is subject to the Head Movement Constraint (Travis, 1984), a phrasal VN cannot form a compound predicate with *suru*.

(13) a. Ken-ga {kaisya-no/ rippana} sigoto-o si-ta.
Ken-NOM office-GEN/ excellent job-ACC do-PST
'Ken did the company's/an excellent job.'
b. *Ken-ga {kaisya-no/ rippana} sigoto-si-ta.
Ken-NOM office-GEN/ excellent job-do-PST
'Ken did the company's/an excellent job.'

Noun phrases containing a genitive phrase or an adjectival modifier cannot be compounded with *suru*, as seen in (13b), but they are allowed to occur as the object of the verb *suru*. (13a) is acceptable with no noun incorporation involved. The fact shows that the two forms of the predicative complexes in the LVC have different syntactic statuses.

3 Issues on theta-role assignment

One controversial issue pertaining to the Japanese LVC is whether or not the LV *suru* has an argument structure of its own. Two different lines of analyses have been proposed in the literature on the status of *suru* in the LVC. One analysis has been advanced by Grimshaw and Mester (1988) on the basis of an example like (14).

(14) John-wa murabito-ni ookami-ga ku-ru-to keikoku-o si-ta.
John-TOP villager-to wolf-NOM come-PRS-COMP warning-ACC do-PST
'John warned the villagers that the wolf was coming.'

According to Grimshaw and Mester, the verb *suru* does not bear any θ-role of its own to be assigned to arguments, i.e. *suru* does not select any argument, and all the θ-roles that are assigned to the clausal arguments are originated from the VN.

(15) a. keikoku (agent, goal, theme)[5]
b. suru ( ) <acc>
c. keikoku ( ) + *suru* (agent, goal, theme) <acc>

In their analysis, the θ-roles for the clausal arguments are handed from the VN to *suru* by Argument Transfer. Argument Transfer is a mechanism that allows the arguments of the VN to be assigned their θ-roles through *suru*, and thus they are realized as clausal arguments. Saito and Hoshi (2000, 267–286) propose an alternative analysis to Grimshaw and Mester's. Upholding the assumption that the LV does not have

---

[5] In Grimshaw and Mester's analysis, the quote is taken to bear a theme role in (14).

any θ-roles of its own, Saito and Hoshi argue that the θ-roles of the VN are assigned to the clausal arguments as a result of the VN incorporating into *suru* at the LF level.

Alternative analyses have been advanced by Terada (1990) and Uchida and Nakayama (1993) to the effect that the verb *suru* in the LVC of the VN-*o suru* form is a regular transitive verb. Specifically, on the basis of the observation that VN-*o suru*, but not VN-*suru*, imposes a selectional restriction on the subject, as seen in the contrast between {*John*/?**deeta*}-*ga sisa-o si-ta* [John/data-NOM suggestion-ACC do-PST] and {*John/deeta*}-*ga sisa-si-ta* [John/data-NOM suggestion-do-PST] 'John/Data made a suggestion', Terada (1990, 100–157) argues that the verb *suru* appearing in the LVC with the sequence of VN-*o suru* is a transitive verb selecting a subject and an object, whereas *suru* in VN-*suru* is an unaccusative verb. Uchida and Nakayama (1993, 624–642) claim that the availability of the VN-*o suru* form is conditioned by the aspectual properties of the VN and that *suru* is a heavy verb when it assigns accusative Case to an object.

The present paper argues, in line with the 'regular verb' analysis, that the verb *suru* appearing in the LVC has an argument structure of its own. The present paper is distinguished from the previous works advocating the regular verb analysis, in claiming that both the agentive and non-agentive types of LVC are constructed based on the most prominent use of transitive *suru*, which carries the meaning of a volitional activity. Given that *suru* in this use selects an agent, the LVC should, other things being equal, take an agent (e.g. when the VN is *sigoto* 'work') or an agentive experiencer (e.g. when the VN is *dokusyo* 'reading') as its subject. Nevertheless, the LVC is divided into two types according to whether it takes an agentive subject or a theme subject.

(16) a. *Ken-ga benkyoo-o si-ta.*
Ken-NOM study-ACC do-PST
'Ken did his study.' (Agentive Type)

b. *Kazan-ga hunka-o si-ta.*
volcano-NOM eruption-ACC do-PST
'The volcano erupted.' (Non-agentive Type)

The agentive LVC in (16a) carries the meaning of 'Ken did the act of the studying', and the non-agentive LVC in (16b) conveys the meaning of 'a volcanic eruption occurred'. I suggest that the agentive subject in (16a) is non-derived, i.e. the subject is selected by *suru*[6], but that the non-agentive subject in (16b) is derived via extraction from

---

[6] Given the vP-internal subject hypothesis, the agent subject is assigned its θ-role by *suru* in Spec-vP and is raised to the clause subject position of Spec-TP.

the VN. Under this view, the two sentences involve the distinct derivations given in (17).

(17) a. [Ken-ga benkyoo-o si$_{<\text{agent,theme(VN)}>}$-ta]

(Agentive type)

b. [Kazan-ga [~~kazan~~ hunka$_{<\text{theme}>}$]-o si$_{\text{theme(VN)}>}$-ta]

(Non-agentive type)

I suggest that the two variants of LVC can be constructed on the basis of the two types of argument structure given in (18).

(18) a. Agentive *suru* 'do': <agent, theme(VN)>
b. Non-agentive *suru* 'do': <theme(VN)>

For convenience sake, 'theme(VN)' is designated as a label for the theme role assigned to the VN. Given that *suru* in the agentive LVC in (16a) has the argument structure <agent, theme(VN)>, the agent subject and the VN *benkyoo* 'study' appear as arguments to *suru*, as (17a) illustrates. In the non-agentive LVC in (16b), *suru* possesses the argument structure <theme(VN)>, and assigns the theme role to the VN. Since *suru* does not bear an extra theme role to be assigned to the non-agentive subject, the theme subject is generated via extraction from the VN, as illustrated in (17b).

The agentive LVC in (16a) is derived on the basis of the transitive argument structure in (18a), but the non-agentive LVC in (16b) is constructed on the argument structure without an agent in (18b). Nevertheless, I propose that both agentive and non-agentive types of LVC in (16) are constructed on the transitive *suru* carrying the argument structure <agent, theme(VN)>. This claim raises the question of how the argument structure <theme(VN)> is made available, which allows the non-agentive LVC in (16b) to be derived. In answer to this question, I suggest that the argument structure <theme(VN)> in (18b) is derived by suppressing the agent role from the argument structure possessed by the transitive *suru*, as (19) illustrates.

(19) <agent, theme(VN)> → <theme(VN)>

I further suggest that both agentive and non-agentive LVCs form transitive clauses, since transitive *suru* retains a transitive case frame even if the agent role is removed from the argument structure. This means that regardless of whether the LVC is of the agentive type or of the non-agentive type, it forms a transitive clause because T assigns nominative Case to the subject and *suru* assigns accusative Case to the object (the VN) (see section 5 for empirical justifications of the argument structure derivation in (19)).

I maintain that whenever the VN has θ-roles to assign to arguments, they are assigned within the local domain of the VN, contrary to Grimshaw and Mester's (1988) claim. This is in conformity with the commonly-held view that an argument is assigned a θ-role by its θ-marking head with a local relation (see e.g. Carnie, 2013). In both agentive and non-agentive LVCs, θ-roles that are not assigned by *suru* are provided by the VN. Under the view held here, an argument receiving a θ-role from the VN can be rendered as a clausal argument only via possessor ascension, i.e. extraction from the VN.

Some VNs belong to the unaccusative type that does not allow accusative case marking on it, as discussed by Miyagawa (1989, 665-657) and Tsujimura (1990, 935-943). Unaccusative VNs like *zyoohatu* 'evaporation', *tootyaku* 'arrival', etc. take theme subjects, as with the VN *hunka* 'eruption' in (16b), so the LVC constructed on an unaccusative VN should involve the derivation in (17b), in which the subject originates from the VN (see section 6 for more discussion on unaccusative VNs). Note that the theme subject *kazan* 'volcano' in (16b) is understood to have a natural force initiating a volcanic activity by its own. Thus, *kazan* may be conceived of as an autonomous entity, which is likened to an agent performing volitional activities, and thus accusative case marking is readily tolerated on the VN *hunka* 'eruption'.[7]

Miyagawa (1989, 665) attempts to account for the case-marking facts of unaccusative VNs by appealing to Burzio's generalization (Burzio, 1986). Under his account, if the verb *suru* does not assign an external θ-role to an argument, it cannot Case-license the VN, so that the VN must be incorporated into *suru* (see also Kageyama, 1991; Miyamoto, 1999). If Burzio's generalization is viable as a grammatical constraint, the derivation of the LVC in (16b), where the VN is marked with accusative case, should not be possible, for the verb *suru* in (16b) does not assign an external θ-role (i.e. the agent role) to its subject. Importantly, however, a number of researchers such as Kageyama (2002); Sugioka (2002), and Hasegawa (2007) argue for the presence of the so-called 'unaccusative transitive' constructions. One relevant example is given in (20).

---

7 The notion of macroroles ('actor' versus 'undergoer') in Role and Reference Grammar (Van Valin and LaPolla, 1997) or the distinction of external and internal arguments utilized widely in the generative literature, does not suffice to account for the distribution of the agentive and the non-agentive LVCs at issue. These notions may be useful for accounting for the distribution of accusative case marking on the VNs, however (see section 6). Note also that speaker variation is observed on the admissibility of overt accusative case marking on VNs (see e.g. Uchida and Nakayama, 1993; Kageyama, 1991; Sode, 1995; Okutsu, 2007).

(20) *Konpyuuta-ga misu-o syoozi-ta.*
computer-NOM error-ACC occur-PST
'An error occurred on the computer.' (Kageyama, 2002, 124)

The verb *syooziru* 'occur' in (20) is a bona fide unaccusative verb, which takes a single internal argument. With this verb, it is possible to construct a transitive construction where the subject is a locative. Note that the locative cannot be an external argument. Nevertheless, the object can still be marked with accusative case. The fact suggests that Burzio's generalization does not condition accusative Case assignment, and that the LV *suru* can assign accusative Case to an object even if it does not assign an external θ-role to the subject (see section 6).

In the present perspective, the transitive *suru* in the LVC can take up to three arguments, but arguments can also be supplied by the VN. There are some asymmetries observed in the argument realization of the LVC. In the first place, the subject and the object are obligatory in the LVC. The agent subject in (16a) is selected by *suru* but the VN supplies the theme subject in (16b). In the latter case, the subject selected by the VN must be realized even if the VN takes arguments optionally, since the subject is required in the clause due to the 'Extended Projection Principle (EPP)' requirement, which demands that a finite clause has a subject (Chomsky, 1982, 17–34).[8] The VN, which appears in the object position, is also obligatory, since it forms a predicative complex with the LV *suru*.

On the other hand, *suru* can select a dative goal argument optionally if a directed motion event is conceptualized.

(21) *John-ga tomodati-ni {hentoo-o/ *benkyoo-o} si-ta.*
John-NOM friend-DAT reply-ACC/ study-ACC do-PST
'John replied/studied to his friend.'

When *suru* takes the VN *hentoo* 'reply' as its object, a transfer event is expressed, so that a dative goal argument can appear in the clause. When *suru* selects the VN *benkyoo* 'study' as its object, no directed motion is conceptualized, in which case a goal argument cannot be added to the clause. To be exact, then, the transitive *suru* conveying the sense of a volitional act has the argument structure <agent, (goal), theme>, where the goal can be included when the meaning of a directed motion is encoded.

Arguments selected by nominals with argument structures are realized optionally, as often noted (e.g. Grimshaw, 1990). For instance, a VN like *unten* 'driving' has

---

[8] To be more precise, in Japanese, the EPP requirement is imposed on a finite clause where T is active, licensing a nominative argument. See Kishimoto (2010, 2017) for the discussion on this point.

an argument structure <(agent), (theme)>, where the two θ-roles are optional. Thus, *unten* 'driving' can have four options for the argument realization given in (22).

(22) a. *unten*
          driving
          'driving'
      b. *John-no unten*
          John-GEN driving
          'John's driving'
      c. *kuruma-no unten*
          car-GEN   driving
          'the driving of a car'
      d. *John-no kuruma-no unten*
          John-GEN car-GEN driving
          'John's driving of a car'

In the LVC, arguments selected by *suru* are in most cases obligatory, but since VNs are nominals, they supply optional arguments. Note that the number of arguments realized in the clause is strictly correlated with the number of θ-roles available for *suru* and the VN in the clause, since arguments can receive one and only one θ-role, as dictated by the θ-criterion.

4 The syntactic derivations of the two kinds of LVCs

In this section, I will present empirical evidence that the agentive LVC forms a transitive clause where the transitive *suru* assigns a θ-role to the subject, but the non-agentive LVC has the theme subject derived via argument ascension from the VN since *suru* does not assign a θ-role to the theme subject. There are at least four kinds of arguments that support the present view.

One kind of evidence can be derived from the so-called 'Proper Binding Condition (PBC)' effect (cf. Saito, 1989). In the LVC, this effect is observed if an argument which has been extracted from the VN is placed in a position structurally higher than the host VN. With this in mind, observe that the VN appearing in the non-agentive LVC in (16b) cannot be moved to a position higher than the subject by the syntactic operations of relativization, pseudo-clefting, and topicalization (Kishimoto, 2019a,b; cf. Kageyama, 1991).

(23) a. *[kazan-ga   si-ta] hunka
        volcano-NOM do-PST eruption
        (lit.) 'the eruption which the volcano did' (relativization)
    b. *[Kazan-ga   si-ta] no-wa   hunka   da.
        volcano-NOM do-PST NOML-TOP eruption COP
        'What the volcano did was erupting.' (pseudo-clefting)
    c. *Hunka-wa   kazan-ga   si-ta.
        eruption-TOP volcano-NOM do-PST
        'As for eruption, the volcano did it.' (topicalization)

The facts follow given that the non-agentive subject is first generated inside the VN and then is moved into the subject position of the LVC, as (24) illustrates.

(24)   [SUBJ   [S̶U̶B̶J̶   VN]   suru]

In the relative clause in (23a) and the pseudo-cleft sentence in (23b), it can be assumed that an operator is moved to CP and is coindexed with the VN at the right end. If so, the structure in (25) can be posited for (23a) and (23b).

(25)   [[OP$_i$ SUBJ   O̶P̶   suru]   VN$_i$]

In (23c), the VN can be assumed to undergo movement to the left of the subject by topicalization, as in (26).

(26)   [VN   SUBJ   V̶N̶   suru]

In all the examples in (23), the VN ends up in a structural position higher than the subject. Since the theme subject is required to c-command its copy inside the VN, which is created by argument ascension, the syntactic operations implemented in (23) give rise to the PBC effects.

No such effects are observed in the agentive LVC in (16a) even if the VN is moved to a higher position than the subject, as illustrated in (27).

(27) a. [Ken-ga   si-ta]   benkyoo
        Ken-NOM do-PST study
        'the study which Ken did' (relativization)

b. [Ken-ga si-ta no]-wa benkyoo da.
   Ken-NOM do-PST NOML-TOP study COP
   'What Ken did was the study.' (pseudo-clefting)

c. Benkyoo-wa Ken-ga si-ta.
   study-TOP Ken-NOM do-PST
   'As for study, Ken did it.' (topicalization)

In (16a), the subject is not derived via argument ascension from the VN, since *suru* can assign an agentive role to the subject. In this case, the VN does not include a copy of the subject, so the examples in (27) are all acceptable with no PBC effect.

The difference in acceptability between (23) and (27) is determined according to whether the LV *suru* or the VN assigns a θ-role to the subject. A similar point can be made for the pair of sentences in (28) with three arguments.

(28) a. Sensei-ga Ken-ni zyogen-o si-ta.
        teacher-NOM Ken-DAT advice-ACC do-PST
        'The teacher gave advice to Ken.'

     b. Ken-ga zitugyooka-ni tensin-o si-ta.
        Ken-NOM businessman-DAT job.change-ACC do-PST
        'Ken changed his job to be a businessman.'

The two sentences in (28) take the same 'nominative-dative-accusative' case-marking pattern, but the dative arguments bear different thematic roles. In (28a) since abstract movement (i.e. transmission of messages) is conceptualized by virtue of the VN *zyogen* 'advice', *suru* has the argument structure <agent, goal, theme(VN)>, and thus the dative argument receives a θ-role from the verb *suru*, as illustrated in (29).

(29) [SUBJ-NOM Goal-DAT VN-ACC $si_{<agent,goal,theme(VN)>}$-*ta*]

On the other hand, the VN *tensin* 'job change' in (28b) describes a change of state, and the dative argument signifies the result of Ken's job change. Since the resultant state is not described by *suru*, it must be the case that the dative argument originates from the VN, which can assign a result role, as illustrated in (30).

(30) [SUBJ-NOM Result-DAT [$_{VNP}$ ~~Result~~ VN$_{<result>}$]-ACC $si_{<ag.,th.(VN)>}$-*ta*]

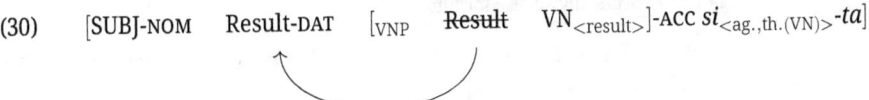

In (28b), result argument is assigned a result role within the VN, and the dative argument is derived via its extraction from the VN.[9] The result argument can remain inside the VN *tensin* if marked with genitive case, as shown in (31).

(31) *Ken-ga zitugyooka-e-no tensin-o si-ta.*
Ken-NOM businessman-to-GEN job.change-ACC do-PST
'Ken change his job to be a businessman.'

If the dative argument in (28b) is originated from the VN, we are led to the prediction that the dative argument in (28b), but not the dative argument in (28a), will display a PBC effect when the VN is moved to a position where the dative argument fails to c-command it. The anticipated PCB effect is observed if the VN *tensin* 'job change' is placed in a higher position than the dative argument in (28b).

(32) a. *[Ken-ga zitugyooka-ni si-ta] tensin*
Ken-NOM businessman-DAT do-PST job.change
'a job change, which Ken did to be a businessman.' (relativization)
b. *[Ken-ga zitugyooka-ni si-ta] no-wa tensin da.*
Ken-NOM businessman-DAT do-PST NOML-TOP job.change COP
'What Ken did to a businessman was a job change.' (pseudo-clefting)
c. *Tensin-wa Ken-ga zitugyooka-ni si-ta.*
job.change-TOP Ken-NOM businessman-DAT do-PST
'As for a job change, Ken did to be a businessman.' (topicalization)

---

9 A dative argument can also be created via extraction from a nominal in a non-LVC, as illustrated in (i).

(i) a. *Watasi-wa [kare-e-no moosiwake]-ga tata-na-i.*
I-TOP he-to-GEN excuse-NOM stand-NEG-PRS
'I cannot express any excuse for him.'
b. *Watasi-wa kare-ni moosiwake-ga tata-na-i.*
I-TOP he-DAT excuse-NOM stand-NEG-PRS
'I cannot express any excuse for him.'

Since the VN *moosiwake* 'excuse' is the host for the dative argument in (ib), the omission of the VN results in unacceptability.

(ii) *Watasi-wa Ken-ni moosiwake-ga tata-na-i-si, anata-wa Mari-ni tata-na-i.*
I-TOP Ken-DAT excuse-NOM stand-NEG-PRS-CONJ you-TOP Mari-DAT stand-NEG-PRS
'I cannot make an excuse for Ken and you cannot make for Mari.'

In (ii), the second clause does not have the VN to license the dative argument. Thus, it turns out that (ii) is unacceptable.

In contrast, no PBC effect is obtained in (28a) when the VN *zyogen* 'advice' is moved to a structural position higher than the dative argument, as shown in (33).

(33) a. [*sensei-ga gakusei-ni si-ta*] *zyogen*
  teacher-NOM student-DAT do-PST advice
  'the advice, which the teacher gave to the student' (relativization)
  b. [*Sensei-ga gakusei-ni si-ta*] *no-wa zyogen da.*
  teacher-NOM student-DAT do-PST NOML-TOP advice COP
  'What the teacher gave to the student was the advice.' (pseudo-clefting)
  c. *Zyogen-wa sensei-ga gakusei-ni si-ta.*
  advice-TOP teacher-NOM student-DAT do-PST
  'As for the advice, the teacher gave to the student.' (topicalization)

The contrast in acceptability between (32) and (33) is not expected under Grimshaw and Mester's analysis taking clausal arguments to be assigned θ-roles by the verb *suru*, which are inherited from the VN. In their analysis, all clausal arguments are realized in the same way with no extraction from within the VN, so no PBC effects are expected to obtain in (32). But this expectation is not fulfilled.

In the proposed analysis, Grimshaw and Mester's example in (14), which describes a transfer event, is expected to involve the ascension of the quote from the VN, but not the agent and the goal arguments, for *suru* carries the argument structure <agent, goal, theme(VN)>. The adequacy of this view is confirmed by (34) (cf. Isoda, 1991).

(34) a. *[*John-ga murabito-ni* [*ookami-ga ku-ru*]-*to si-ta*] *keikoku*
  John-NOM villager-to wolf-NOM come-PRS-COMP do-PST warning
  'the warning that John made to the villagers that the wolf was coming'
  b. [*John-ga murabito-ni si-ta*] *keikoku*
  John-NOM villager-to do-PST warning
  'the warning that John made to the villagers'
  c. [*John-ga si-ta*] *keikoku*
  John-NOM do-PST warning
  'the warning that John made'

(34) shows that the relative clause having the VN as its relative head is illicit when the quote is included in it. The contrast in acceptability between (34a) and (34b–34c) confirms that the quote is originated from the VN while the agent and the goal arguments are assigned their θ-roles by the verb *suru*.

In this connection, Bruening (2015, 7–8) suggests that the clausal arguments in the light verb expression *give him a kick* control into the arguments of the VN, as in (35).

(35) She₁ gave him₂ [a KICKER₁ kick KICKEE₂ in the teeth].

Given the control analysis, one might suppose that the dative argument in (28b) is related to the VN via control, as depicted in (36).

(36) [Subj-NOM Result₁-DAT [VNP PRO₁ VN<result>]-ACC si<agent,theme(VN)>-ta]

This analysis is not plausible, since a structural relation of c-command is not required between a controller and PRO in the surface strings, as exemplified in (37).

(37) a. John_i-wa [PRO_i koko-ni ku-ru]   koto-o   yakusoku-si-ta.
 John-TOP   here-to come-PRS that-ACC promise-do-PST
 'John promised to come here.'
 b. [PRO_i koko-ni ku-ru]   koto-{o/wa}_j John_i-ga t_j yakusoku-si-ta.
   here-to come-PRS that-ACC/TOP John-NOM   promise-do-PST
 'To come here, John promised.'

Note that *yakusoku-suru* 'promise' is a subject-control predicate that selects a complement with PRO. As can be seen in (37b), the control complement can be moved across the controller. Then, it should be apparent that the PBC effects in (23) cannot be accounted for under the analysis which takes clausal arguments to be related to the VN via control. The data suggest that the PBC effects arise in violation of the movement constraint on argument ascension.[10]

A second piece of evidence for the present view may be adduced from the facts of argument doubling. In the LVC, argument doubling is in principle possible when *suru* and the VN have the potential to assign the same θ-role. For instance, the agentive LVC in (16a) allows doubling of agent arguments on the 'deputy' interpretation that Ken drove on behalf of Eri yesterday (although Eri usually drives by herself), as seen in (38).

(38) Kinoo-wa   Ken-ga   kawarini [Eri-no unten]-o   si-ta.
 yesterday-TOP Ken-NOM on.behalf Eri-GEN driving-ACC do-PST
 'Ken drove on behalf of Eri.'

---

10 Needless to say, coreference is not the possibility to account for the Proper Binding Condition effects, since (i) is acceptable, where the object containing a reflexive coreferential with the subject is scrambled to the clause front.

(i) Zibun_i-no te-o   John_i-wa hura-nakat-ta.
 self-GEN hand-ACC John-TOP wave-NEG-PST
 'His hand, John did not wave.'

Genitive arguments inside the VN can often be interpreted in a number of ways if they are not accompanied by a postposition, but the crucial point here is that Eri appearing in the VN can count as an agent in (38). The acceptability of (38) under the 'deputy' interpretation is naturally expected since *suru* can assign an agent role to the subject, and the VN can assign an agent role to an argument inside the VN. Under Grimshaw and Mester's analysis which takes the view that *suru* does not carry any θ-role intrinsically, argument doubling in (38) is not expected to be possible.

Standing in contrast with the agentive LVC is the non-agentive LVC. In the non-agentive subject type of LVC in (16b), it is not possible to contain an extra theme argument, in addition to the theme subject, as shown in (39).

(39) *Huzi-san-ga [Asama-yama-no hunka]-o   si-ta.
      Fuji-Mt-NOM Asama-Mt-GEN   eruption-ACC do-PST
      'Mt. Fuji had Mt. Asama's eruption.'

The non-agentive LV *suru* does not select an agent subject, and thus carries the argument structure <theme(VN)>. The theme role which *suru* bears is assigned to the VN *hunka* 'eruption', and the LV *suru* does not have an extra theme role to be assigned to the subject.[11] Given that the non-agentive subject, i.e. the theme subject, can be assigned a theme role only by the VN, it follows that the non-agentive LVC cannot have an extra theme argument alongside the theme subject, as shown in (39).

In this connection, one might suspect that (39) is excluded for a pragmatic reason, since a mountain cannot perform a proxy act behaving like a human. On the contrary, (39) is excluded by the grammatical constraint. This fact can be confirmed by the non-agentive LVC in (40a), which allows a human subject to appear as well as an inanimate subject.

(40) a. {John-ga/ Ano suteezi setto-ga} butai-ni toozyoo-si-ta.
         John-NOM/ that stage   set-NOM   stage-on appearance-do-PST
         'John/ That stage set appeared on the stage.'
     b. *John-ga Mari-no toozyoo-o   si-ta.
         John-NOM Mari-GEN appearance-ACC do-PST
         'John made Mari's appearance on the stage.'

The theme subject *ano suteezi setto* 'that stage set' is selected by the VN in (40a), which suggests that *John* in (40a) is also a theme argument generated in the VN, and not an agent licensed by *suru* (although John might go on stage of his own will). While it is possible to imagine a situation that John went on the stage in lieu of Mari

---

11 If *Asama-yama-no* 'of Mt. Asama' is replaced with *Asama-yama-no-yoona* 'like Mt. Asama', (39) is acceptable.

by his choice, (40b) is simply not acceptable on the deputy interpretation. This gives us an indication that argument doubling is not allowed in the non-agentive LVC in (39) for the grammatical reason, but not for a pragmatic reason.[12]

The same contrast in acceptability obtained between (38) and (39)-(40b) is observed for the dative arguments in the LVC. As noted earlier, *suru* can assign a goal role to a dative argument if the VN denotes some kind of movement. The VN can have a goal argument marked with *e-no* [to-GEN] optionally (i.e. the postposition *e* indicates that the argument is identified as a goal). Accordingly, a sentence with two goal arguments can be constructed from the LVC in (28a).

(41) *Sensei-ga   Ken-ni   [Eri-e-no   zyogen]-o si-ta.*
       teacher-NOM Ken-DAT Eri-to-GEN advice-ACC do-PST
       'The teacher gave Eri's advice to Ken.'

(41) is acceptable on the 'deputy' interpretation that the teacher directed to Ken the advice that Eri should receive, that is, the intended goal (recipient) of the advice is Eri, but Ken is the person to whom the teacher actually gave advice. By contrast, when a dative argument does not receive a θ-role from *suru*, no argument doubling is possible, as exemplified in (42).

(42) **Sato-san-ga zitugyooka-ni   [kyoosi-e-no   tensin]-o   si-ta.*
       Sato-Mr-NOM businessman-DAT teacher-to-GEN job.change-ACC do-PST
       'Mr. Sato made [a job change to a teacher] to be a businessman.'

The result role can only be supplied by the VN *tensin* 'job change'. Accordingly, the result argument expressed as a clausal argument needs to be generated via argument ascension. Since the result argument can be assigned a θ-role by the VN, but not *suru*, no argument doubling is allowed for the LVC in (42).

Incidentally, when a goal argument is selected by *suru*, an extra goal argument can be licensed by the VN. Nevertheless, the latter argument cannot be rendered as a clausal argument, and (43) is not acceptable. (A 'deputy' interpretation is not possible with (43), although (41) can have this interpretation.)

(43) **Sensei-ga   Ken-ni   Eri-ni   [t_i zyogen]-o si-ta.*
       teacher-NOM Ken-DAT Eri-DAT   advice-ACC do-PST
       'The teacher gave advice to Eri to Ken.'

---

[12] If (39) is unacceptable for a pragmatic reason, the sentence should improve in a 'fairy tale' context where a mountain is construed as a willful entity like a human. But (39) is simply ungrammatical even in this context.

In (43), it must be the case that one dative argument receives a goal role from the verb *suru*, and another dative argument receives a goal role from the VN. The goal argument licensed by the VN cannot be turned into a clausal argument in this case, however, because *suru* cannot assign dative Case to more than one argument.

Thirdly, the effect of argument ascension can be assessed by looking at whether a so-called 'Specificity Condition (SC)' effect is observed.[13] In English, a SC effect is induced when an argument is extracted from a DP that has a specific reference.

(44)   a.   ?*Who$_i$ did you see [that/ Mary's portrait of t$_i$]?
            b.   Who$_i$ did you see [a portrait of t$_i$]?

As shown in (44a), *wh*-extraction is blocked from within a DP with a specific reference. If the DP is not specific, *wh*-extraction is legitimate, as in (44b).[14]

In Japanese, a difference in acceptability due to the SC emerges between the agentive and the non-agentive LVCs according to whether the VN is modified by an expression that refers to a specific point of time. Observe that the VN can be specific in the agentive LVC, but not in the non-agentive LVC, as shown in (45).

(45)   a.   *Ken-ga*   [*kinoo-no*   *sigoto*]-*o si-te*   *i-ta.*
                  Ken-NOM   yesterday-GEN work-ACC do-GER be-PST
                  'Ken was doing yesterday's work.'
           b.   ?**Kazan-ga*   [*kyonen-no*   *hunka*]-*o*   *si-te*   *i-ta.*
                  volcano-NOM   last.year-GEN eruption-ACC do-GER be-PST
                  (lit.) 'The volcano is doing last year's eruption.'

(45b) is rendered acceptable if the adnominal modifier *kyonen* 'last year' is replaced by a prenominal modifier, such as *totuzen-no* 'sudden', which does not refer to a specific point of time, as shown in (46a).

(46)   a.   *Kazan-ga*   [*totuzen-no*   *hunka*]-*o*   *si-ta.*
                  volcano-NOM   sudden-GEN eruption-ACC do-PST
                  'The volcano erupted suddenly.'
           b.   *Kazan-ga*   *kyonen*   *hunka-o*   *si-ta.*
                  volcano-NOM last.year eruption-ACC do-PST
                  'The volcano erupted last year.'

---

[13] This term is due to Fiengo and Higginbotham (1981, 402).
[14] The SC effect might be accounted for in semantic or functional terms eventually (e.g. Kuno, 1987). But the crucial point is that this effect is caused when an argument is extracted from the host noun phrase syntactically, and hence can be a yardstick to assess whether or not argument ascension is involved in the LCVs.

Further, (46b) is acceptable since *kyonen* 'last year' is used as an adverbial rather than adnominal modifier. The presence or absence of a SC effect in (45) shows that the agent subject is selected by *suru* and does not involve extraction from the VN, but that the theme subject is generated via argument ascension from the VN.

A SC effect is also induced if the clause includes a dative argument generated via extraction from the VN. In (47), the demonstrative *sono* 'that' appears with the VN, and a difference in acceptability emerges according to the type of dative argument.

(47) a. *Sensei-ga   Ken-ni   [sono zyogen]-o si-ta.*
teacher-NOM Ken-DAT that advice-ACC do-PST
'The teacher gave that advice to Ken.'

b. ?**Sato-san-ga zitugyooka-ni   [sono tensin]-o   si-ta.*
Sato-Mr-NOM businessman-DAT that job.change-ACC do-PST
'Mr. Sato made that job change to be a businessman.'

In (47a), since the dative argument *Ken* is assigned a goal role by *suru*, the sentence is acceptable. By contrast, (47b) is unacceptable in violation of the SC. If *sono* is replaced with a prenominal modifier like *kareina* 'excellent', (47b) is rendered acceptable.

(48) a. *Sato-san-ga zitugyooka-ni   [kareina tensin]-o   si-ta.*
Sato-Mr-NOM businessman-DAT excellent job.change-ACC do-PST
'Mr. Sato made an excellent change in his job to be a businessman.'

b. *Sato-san-ga [sono zitugyooka-e-no   tensin]-o   si-ta.*
Sato-Mr-NOM that businessman-to-GEN job.change-ACC do-PST
'Mr. Sato made that job change to be a businessman.'

In (48a), the VN modified by *kareina* 'excellent' does not refer to a specific event, and as such, the SC is not violated even if the dative argument appears outside the VN. (48b) shows that when *zitugyooka* 'businessman' appears inside the VN (preceded by *sono*), no SC effect is observed.[15] The data illustrate that the dative argument *zitugyooka* is originated from the VN *tensin* 'job change' in (28b).

The same kind of SC effect observed in the LVC is also obtained in the so-called 'major subject' construction. In (49a), the first nominative argument *zoo* 'elephant', which is often referred to as a major subject, is licensed by virtue of a possessive relation that holds between the two nominative nominals.[16]

---

15 The intended interpretation in (48b) is the one in which *sono* modifies the VN, but not *zitugyooka*. This interpretation is facilitated if a little pause is imposed after *sono*.
16 Major subjects are most typically licensed by holding an inalienable possession relation with the following nominal. Inalienability is expressed by constructions encoding a body-part, kinship,

(49) a. Zoo-{wa/ga}   hana-ga   naga-i.
       elephant-TOP/NOM trunk-NOM long-PRS
       'The elephant's trunk is long.'
   b. [Zoo-no   hana]-ga   naga-i.
       elephant-GEN trunk-NOM long-PRS
       'The elephant's trunk is long.'
   c. [Zoo-{wa/ga}$_i$ [t$_i$ hana]-ga naga-i]

Mainly on the basis that (49a) and (49b) express the same logical meaning, it is often claimed that (49a) is derived from (49b) via argument ascension (or 'subjectivization' in the sense of Kuno, 1973, 71). This analysis is plausible in view of the fact that (50), which has the nominal *mini* 'ear' modified by a modifier *kinoo* 'yesterday', displays a SC effect.

(50) ?*Ano zoo-wa   [kinoo-no   mimi]-ga akakat-ta.
       that elephant-TOP yesterday-GEN ear-NOM red-PST
       'That elephant's ear was red yesterday.'

No such effect is found if the second nominative nominal includes a modifier which does not have a specific reference, as shown in (51).

(51) Ano zoo-wa   [migi-no mimi]-ga akakat-ta.
     that elephant-TOP right-GEN ear-NOM red-PST
     'That elephant's right ear was red yesterday.'

(52) is also acceptable although the body-part nominal *mimi* has a temporal modifier *kinoo*.

(52) [Kinoo-no   ano zoo-no   mimi]-wa akakat-ta.
      yesterday-GEN that elephant-GEN ear-NOM red-PST
      'That elephant's ear yesterday was red.'

The acceptability of (52) is naturally expected since the argument *zoo* 'elephant' is not extracted from the body part nominal.

In Japanese, double nominative constructions can be constructed on dyadic stative predicates. Superficially, it looks as if the double nominative sentence in (53) has the same structure as (49a), since two nominative arguments appear in the clause.

---

or personal attribute relation if the possessor is animate, and it could be expressed by constructions denoting an integral part-whole or spatial relation (see Tsunoda, 1996 for the discussion on this point). In addition, the predicate of the major subject construction is most typically an individual predicate (see e.g. Kratzer, 1995).

(53) *Ano hito-wa [kinono-no (zibun-no) hurumai]-ga kiniira-nakat-ta.*
that man-TOP yesterday-GEN self-GEN behavior-NOM like-NEG-PST
'That man did not like (his own) behavior of yesterday.'

Despite the surface similarity to (49a), the first nominative argument in (53) is not derived via argument ascension from the second nominative nominal, since *kiniiru* 'like' is a dyadic predicate. Accordingly, no SC effect is observed in (53) even though the two nominative arguments are interpreted as holding a possessive relation. The major subject construction provides an independent motivation for postulating that the SC applies to argument ascension from the VN in the LVC.

Finally, the presence or absence of argument ascension out of VN in the LVC can also be detected by argument ellipsis. In the context of argument ellipsis, when an argument is sanctioned by an element other than the predicate, its licenser needs to be present in the clause. In the agentive LVC, no deterioration is detected even if the VN is omitted (Kageyama, 1980, 2009).

(54) *Kinoo-wa Ken-ga benkyoo-o si-ta-ga, kyoo-wa Eri-ga si-ta.*
yesterday-TOP Ken-NOM study-ACC do-PST-CONJ today-TOP Eri-NOM do-PST
'Ken studied yesterday, and Eri did today.'

In (54), no VN appears in the second clause, but the clause is acceptable with the intended interpretation that Eri studied. This fact suggests that the agent subject is assigned an agent role by the LV *suru*. By contrast, the non-agentive LVC is not acceptable if the VN is omitted while the theme subject is overtly expressed.

(55) **Kinoo-wa ano kazan-ga hunka-o si-ta-ga, kyoo-wa kono kazan-ga si-ta.*
yesterday-TOP that volcano-NOM eruption-ACC do-PST-CONJ today-TOP this
volcano-NOM do-PST
'That volcano erupted yesterday, and this volcano did today.'

In (55), the second clause is semantically deviant, since the subject is necessarily taken to be an agent, which is selected by *suru*. This interpretation is forced in the absence of the VN *hunka*, which assigns a theme role to the inanimate subject.

Argument ellipsis is possible with (56) as well, since the dative argument can be assigned a goal role by *suru*.

(56) *Sato-san-wa Ken-ni zyogen-o si-ta-ga, Abe-san-wa Eri-ni si-ta.*
Sato-Mr-TOP Ken-DAT advice-ACC do-PST-CONJ Abe-Mr-TOP Eri-DAT do-PST
'Mr. Sato gave advice to Ken, and Mr. Abe to Eri.'

In (56), the second clause can be taken to mean 'Mr. Abe gave advice to Eri'. By contrast, (57) is not acceptable.

(57) *Ken-wa   seizika-ni   tensin-o   si-ta-ga,   Eri-wa geizyutuka-ni
     Ken-TOP politician-DAT job.change-ACC do-PST-CONJ Eri-TOP artist-DAT
     si-ta.
     do-PST
     'Ken made a job change to be a politician, and Eri an artist.'

In the second clause in (57), the VN, which assigns a result role to the dative argument, is not present. In this case, a semantic anomaly is caused since the VN is omitted that licenses the dative argument in the second clause.

In this section, I have presented four kinds of empirical evidence showing that the agentive LVC has a non-derived subject, which is assigned a θ-role by *suru*, while the non-agentive LVC has a derived subject originated from the VN. The asymmetries observed in the two types of LVCs are not expected in Grimshaw and Mester's analysis taking the LV *suru* to assign to the clausal arguments the θ-roles inherited from the VN via Argument Transfer.

5 The source of the argument structure for the non-agentive LVC

The non-agentive LCV resorts to the syntactic operation of argument ascension to generate the subject. This derivation is invoked for the non-agentive LVC since *suru* has the argument structure <theme(VN)>. In this section, I will present evidence that the non-agentive LCV is constructed on the argument structure derived via the suppression of the agent θ-role from transitive *suru* expressing a volitional activity meaning.

To begin, the verb *suru* 'do' has an intransitive use, as well as a transitive use, as noted in section 2. In general, sentences with transitive *suru* take a nominative-accusative case-marking pattern, and sentences with intransitive *suru* have a single nominative argument, as exemplified in (58).

(58) a. *Ken-ga   yakyuu-o   si-ta.*
        Ken-NOM baseball-ACC do-PST
        'Ken played baseball.' (transitive)
     b. *Mukoo-de   inabikari-ga   si-ta.*
        over.there-in lightning-NOM do-PST
        'There was a lightning over there.' (intransitive)

The intransitive *suru* expresses the meaning of non-volitional events, including spontaneous natural phenomena, physiological sensations, and the like (see 7). The intransitive *suru* takes one nominative argument in (58b), but there are cases where it looks as if intransitive *suru* takes two arguments, as in (59).

(59) *Kono yasai-ga   henna azi-ga   si-ta.*
 this vegetable-NOM strange taste-NOM do-PST
 'This vegetable had a strange taste.'

The fact of the matter is that (59) is not a transitive clause with two arguments taken by *suru*, but an intransitive clause where the first argument is a major subject generated via argument ascension from the second argument. The status of (59) as an intransitive clause is confirmed by a PBC effect obtained when the second argument is moved over the first argument, as shown in (60).

(60) *[kono yasai-ga   si-ta] henna azi*
 this vegetable-NOM do-PST strange taste
 'the strange taste which this dish had'

Furthermore, an intransitive clause can be constructed from (59) with an appropriate choice of a modifier.

(61) *[Kono yasai-no   honrai-no   azi]-ga   si-ta.*
 this vegetable-GEN original-GEN taste-NOM do-PST
 'This vegetable had an original taste.'

The clause with the intransitive *suru* takes a 'nominative-nominative' rather than 'nominative-accusative' case-marking pattern when two verbal arguments are present in the clause. The facts of (60) and (61) show that *suru* in (59) is an intransitive verb.

The non-agentive as well as the agentive LVC takes a nominative-accusative case-marking pattern.[17] The case-marking pattern suggests that the two types of LVC

---

[17] When *suru* describes an involuntary physiological sensation, the experiencer can be expressed, in which case the clause takes a nominative-nominative case-marking pattern.

(i) *Sakki-made (kare-ga) memai-ga   si-te   i-ta.*
 moment-until he-NOM dizziness-NOM do-GER be-PST
 'He was feeling dizzy just a moment ago.'

If an overt experiencer is not present (syntactically), an intransitive clause is formed, which is interpretively understood as describing an experience of the speaker. (ii) shows that relativization is not allowed when an experiencer is expressed overtly.

are not constructed on intransitive *suru*. If the non-agentive LVC is built on the intransitive *suru*, it should be possible to construct a variant in which the VN containing the theme argument is placed in subject position marked with nominative case. This expectation is not fulfilled, however.

(62) a. *[Kazan-no   hunka]-ga   si-ta.
         volcano-GEN eruption-NOM do-PST
         (lit.) 'The volcano's eruption did.'
     b. *Kazan-ga   hunka-ga   si-ta.
         volcano-NOM eruption-NOM do-PST
         (lit.) 'The volcano, its eruption did.'

As shown in (62a), the intransitive clause where the theme argument *kazan* 'volcano' remains in the VN cannot be constructed, nor is it possible for the clause to take a double nominative case pattern, as in (62b). This is a reflection of the fact that the LV *suru* necessarily forms a transitive clause. In addition, since the subject requirement, i.e. the EPP requirement, is imposed on finite clauses, the VN appearing in the object position cannot retain its theme argument inside, as (63) shows.

(63) *[Kazan-no   hunka]-o   si-ta.
      volcano-GEN eruption-ACC do-PST
      (lit.) 'Did the volcano's eruption'

In the non-agentive LVC, *suru* does not select an agent subject, so the subject needs to be realized by way of argument ascension from the VN.

In contrast, in the LVC with *tensin-o suru* 'make a job change', the result argument *zitugyooka* 'businessman' may stay within the VN, as in (64a), or can be extracted from the VN, as in (64b).

(64) a. Ken-ga   [zitugyooka-e-no   tensin]-o   si-ta.
         Ken-NOM businessman-to-GEN job.change-ACC do-PST
         'Ken made a job change to be a businessman.'
     b. Ken-ga   zitugyooka-ni   tensin-o   si-ta.
         Ken-NOM businessman-DAT job.change-ACC do-PST
         'Ken made a job change to be a businessman.'

(ii) [Sakki-made   (*kare-ga) si-te   i-ta]   memai-wa   ima osamat-te i-ru.
     moment-until   he-NOM   do-GER be-PST dizziness-TOP now relieve-GER be-PRS
     'The dizziness which (he) was feeling a moment ago is relieved now.'

The fact suggests that the overt experiencer is supplied via argument ascension from the possessed nominal *memai* 'dizziness'.

In the case of dative arguments, argument ascension from the VN is optional since the EPP requirement is not relevant.

Note that the transitive *suru* has a non-agentive (or non-volitional) use, in which case *suru* expresses the sense of a physiological process, e.g. *miburui-o suru* [trembling-ACC do] 'tremble' (cf. 6d). Nevertheless, the non-agentive LVC is not built on *suru* in this use, since the non-agentive LVC is derived via argument ascension from the VN.

The generalization on the impossibility of forming an intransitive clause applies to the agentive LVC as well, as shown in (65).

(65) a. *[*Ken-no benkyoo*]-ga si-ta.*
      Ken-GEN study-NOM do-PST
      (lit.) 'Ken's study did.'
   b. **Ke-ga   benkyoo-ga si-ta.*
      Ken-NOM study-NOM do-PST
      (lit.) 'Ken, his study did.'

Both agentive and non-agentive LVC need to have one argument marked with nominative case and another argument, i.e. the VN, with accusative case (although the VN can be incorporated into *suru* optionally). The data suggest that the two types of LVC are built on the transitive *suru*.

The present analysis gains further support from *hazimeru* 'begin' (Matsumoto, 1996; Yokota, 2005).[18] Observe that the transitive verb *hazimeru* can take either an agentive or a non-agentive subject, as with the LV *suru*.

(66) a. *Ken-ga   benkyoo-o hazime-ta.*
        Ken-NOM study-ACC begin-PST
        'Ken began to study.'
   b. *Kazan-ga   hunka-o   hazime-ta.*
      volcano-NOM eruption-ACC begin-PST
      'The volcano began to erupt.'

In (66b), the theme subject is derived via extraction from the VN. This is confirmed by the examples in (67).

---

18 Matsumoto (1996, 77-83) observes that a number of verbs such as *hazimeru* 'begin', *kokoromiru* 'attempt', etc. possess light verb properties, in that they can take VNs as their objects, and behave in a similar way to the LVC with *suru* (see also Yokota, 2005). Nevertheless, they do not form compound predicates with the VNs (e.g. *benkyoo-o hazimeru* [study-ACC begin] versus **benkyoo-hazimeru* [study-begin] 'begin to study').

(67) a. *[kazan-ga   hazime-ta] hunka
        volcano-NOM begin-PST   eruption
        'the eruption which the volcano began' (relativization)
    b. *[Kazan-ga   hazime-ta no]-wa   hunka da.
        volcano-NOM begin-PST NOML-TOP eruption COP
        'What the volcano began was erupting.' (pseudo-clefting)
    c. *Hunka-wa   kazan-ga   hazime-ta.
        eruption-TOP volcano-NOM begin-PST
        'As for eruption, the volcano began.' (topicalization)

The verb *hazimeru* 'begin (trans.)' has an intransitive form *hazimaru* 'begin (intr.)'. Notably, an intransitive construction can be constructed with intransitive *hazimaru* (but not transitive *hazimeru*), as shown in (68).

(68) a. [Ken-no   benkyoo]-ga {hazimat-ta/ *hazime-ta}.
        Ken-GEN study-NOM   begin-PST   begin-PST
        'Ken's study began.'
    b. [Kazan-no   hunka]-ga   {hazimat-ta/ *hazime-ta}.
        volcano-GEN eruption-NOM begin-PST   begin-PST
        'The volcanic eruption began.'

The constructions in (68), where the VNs include the arguments corresponding to the subjects in (62), are possible with the intransitive verb *hazimaru*, since these arguments can be supplied by the VNs.

The verb *suru* differs from the transitive *hazimeru*, which has an intransitive counterpart *hazimaru*, in that it can be used only transitively in the LVC. If *suru* appearing in the LVC can have an intransitive use, the variants in which the theme argument remains inside the VN should be available when the VN appears in the subject position marked with nominative case. But the ungrammaticality of the examples in (62) indicates that this type of clause cannot be formed, thereby showing that *suru* in the LVC is a transitive predicate.

The data discussed thus far suggest that the LV *suru* is a transitive verb. In the agentive LVC describing a change of state, *suru* has the argument structure <agent, theme(VN)>, so that the clause has a non-derived agent subject alongside an accusative VN. In the non-agentive LVC, *suru* has the argument structure <theme(VN)>, where the agent role is suppressed, and as a consequence, the non-agentive subject must be supplied by the VN. Even in this case, the LV *suru* is transitive, and thus forms a transitive clause which has the subject and the object (although a VN in the object position may later be incorporated into *suru*).

It is worth noting at this point that in Japanese, an inanimate argument can often be placed as the subject of a transitive verb in lieu of an agent subject with the verbal morphology remaining intact although this grammatical process is generally not available in a language like English (Kishimoto and Kageyama, 2011, 292–297). (69) represents a case in point.

(69)   *Nattoo-ga (*wazato)   nagai ito-o   hii-te   i-ru.*
natto-NOM   intentionally long   string-ACC pull-GER be-PRS
'The natto is stringy and has long strings (on purpose).'

The hallmark of (69) is that the subject *nattoo* 'fermented soybeans' bears a possessive relation with the accusative argument. Thus, the sequence of the subject and the object is understood to have the same meaning as the nominal structure in (70).

(70)   *Nattoo-no nagai ito*
natto-GEN long   string
'the natto's long strings'

Note, however, that the verb *hiku* 'pull' normally takes an agentive subject, as in (71).

(71)   *Kodomo-ga (wazato)   himo-o   hii-te   i-ru.*
child-NOM   intentionally rope-ACC pull-GER be-PRS
'The child is pulling the rope (on purpose).'

(71) is an ordinary transitive construction where the subject is selected by the verb *hiku*. (69), unlike (71), has a non-agentive subject. Accordingly, an intentional adverb such as *wazato* 'intentionally' is compatible with (71), but not (69).

The verb *hiku* 'pull' is intrinsically transitive, and does not have an intransitive use. The absence of an intransitive use for the verb *hiku* is confirmed by (72).

(72)   **Nattoo-no nagai ito-ga   hii-ta.*
natto-GEN long   string-NOM pull-PST
(lit.) 'The natto's long strings pulled.'

If the verb *hiku* 'pull' has an intransitive use, it should be possible for the clause to include only one nominative argument, which comprises the theme argument *nattoo* marked with genitive case Nevertheless, the intransitive clause in (72) is not legitimate.

The data illustrate that *hiku* 'pull' is a transitive verb that possesses the argument structure <agent, theme>, but (69) has an inanimate subject, which bears a possessor-possessed relation with the object. The fact suggests that the argument structure <theme> of *hiku* 'pull' can be derived by way of suppressing the agent role. With this change in the verb's argument structure, the derivation in (73) can be invoked for (69).

(73) [SUBJ [S̶U̶B̶J̶ N]-ACC V]

In (73), the non-agent subject is derived via its extraction from the accusative argument. The same kind of derivation is involved in the formation of the non-agentive LVC, since its derivation is motivated by the suppression of the agent role in the argument structure of the transitive *suru*.

There are several pieces of evidence that the inanimate subject is assigned a θ-role inside the accusative nominal in (69). In the first place, the examples in (74) confirm that the inanimate subject *nattoo* is derived via extraction from the accusative DP.

(74) a. *[nattoo-ga hii-te i-ta] ito
    natto-NOM pull-GER be-PST string
    'the strings which the natto was pulling' (relativization)
  b. *[Nattoo-ga hii-te i-ta no]-wa ito da.
    natto-NOM pull-GER be-PST NOML-TOP string COP
    'What the natto was pulling was the strings.' (pseudo-clefting)
  c. *Ito-wa nattoo-ga hii-te i-ta.
    string-TOP natto-NOM pull-GER be-PST
    'As for the strings, the natto was pulling.' (topicalization)

The examples in (74) are deviant since the accusative object is moved to a higher position than the non-agentive subject. The PBC effects observed in (74) suggest that the non-agentive subject is derived by way of its extraction from within the object.

Secondly, the fact that argument doubling is not allowed in (75a) suggests that the theme subject has been extracted from the accusative argument.

(75) a. *Nattoo-ga [okura-no ito]-o hii-te i-ru.
    natto-NOM okura-GEN string-ACC pull-GER be-PRS
    'The natto is pulling the okura's string.'
  b. Eri-ga [Ken-no himo]-o hii-te i-ru.
    Eri-NOM Ken-GEN rope-ACC pull-GER be-PRS
    'Eri is pulling Ken's rope.'

In (75b), since both *suru* and VN have the potential to assign the agent θ-role, argument doubling is possible on the 'deputy' interpretation that Eri pulled the rope in lieu of Ken. The unacceptability of (75a) suggests that the theme subject in (69) is derived by argument ascension from the DP in object position, unlike the agentive subject counterpart in (71).

Moreover, a contrast in acceptability emerges between (69) and (71) if *ito* 'string' is preceded by *kinoo-no* instead of *nagai*, as shown in (76).

(76)   a.   ?*Nattoo-ga [kinoo-no   ito]-o   hii-te   i-ru.*
                 natto-NOM   yesterday-GEN string-ACC pull-GER be-PRS
                 'The natto is pulling yesterday's strings.'
       b.   *Kodomo-ga [kinoo-no   himo]-o   hii-te   i-ru.*
                 child-NOM   yesterday-GEN rope-ACC pull-GER be-PRS
                 'The child is pulling yesterday's rope.'

(76a) is deviant since the nominal *ito* 'string' with *kinoo-no* refers to an entity at a specific point of time. Note that when *ito* is modified by an adjective like *nagai* 'long', no deterioration of the sentence is observed, as in (69). Then the presence of a SC effect in (76a) shows that the theme subject is generated by argument ascension from the DP *nagai ito*. This effect is absent in (76b) since the agent subject is selected by *hiku*.

Expressing a non-agentive event by a transitive verb with a possessor-possessed relation between the subject and the object seems to be fairly unique to Japanese, but it is not difficult in the language to find the same type of construction formed on transitive verbs, as in (77).

(77)   a.   *Nikuman-ga   yuge-o   tate-te   i-ru.*
                 meat.bun-NOM steam-ACC put.up-GER be-PRS
                 'The meat bun put up steams (=The steam is coming out of the meat bun).'
       b.   *Konpyuutaa-ga netu-o   mot-ta.*
                 computer-NOM heat-ACC hold-PST
                 'The computer had a heat (=The computer heated up).'
       c.   *Kaoku-ga   hono'o-o age-ta.*
                 house-NOM fire-ACC   raise-PST
                 'The houses raised fires (=The houses were on fire).'

The inanimate subjects in (77) bear a possessive relation with the objects, and the sentences pattern with (69) with regard to the diagnostics for argument ascension, although the relevant examples are not provided here for reasons of space.

The non-agentive LVC shares the above-noted properties with the inanimate subject clause with the transitive verb *hiku* in (69), in that the subject is derived via argument ascension. Crucially, in the non-agentive LVC, the LV *suru* has the argument structure <theme(VN)> derived from <agent, theme(VN)> by suppressing the agent role, and the argument to which a theme role is assigned by the VN is turned into a clausal subject via argument ascension. Even so, the LVC with *suru* forms a transitive clause, which takes the VN as an object (although it can be incorporated into *suru* optionally).[19]

6 The surface case-marking constraints in the LVC

In this section, I will look at some (surface) case-marking constraints imposed on the LVC in Japanese. First, observe that two variants of the LVC can be constructed on the VN is *soozi* 'cleaning', as in (78) (Tanomura, 1989).

(78) a. *Ken-ga [sono heya-no soozi]-o si-ta.*
Ken-NOM that room-GEN cleaning-ACC do-PST
'Ken did the cleaning of that room.'
b. *Ken-ga sono heya-o soozi-si-ta.*
Ken-NOM that room-ACC cleaning-do-PST
'Ken cleaned that room.'

(78a) is a periphrastic variant of the LVC where the theme argument *heya* 'room' stays inside the VN. The predicate in (78b) has a compound form. The compound variant in (78b) is derived by extracting the theme argument *sono heya* 'that room' from the VN *soozi* 'cleaning', which is later incorporated into the verb to form a complex predicate.

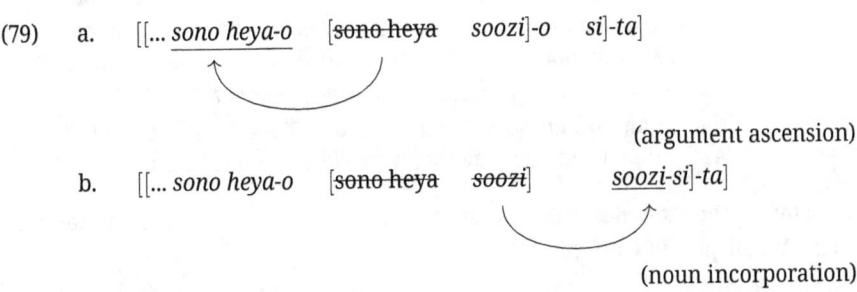

(79) a. [[... *sono heya-o* [~~sono heya~~ *soozi*]-*o* *si*]-*ta*]

(argument ascension)

b. [[... *sono heya-o* [~~sono heya~~ ~~soozi~~] *soozi-si*]-*ta*]

(noun incorporation)

The derivation of (78b) involves the two syntactic operations of argument ascension and noun incorporation, as illustrated in (79). The LVC in (80), which corresponds to (79a), has the form before noun incorporation applies, but is not well-formed due to the double-*o* constraint.

---

[19] The fact that the LVC always forms a transitive clause suggests that the VN can be incorporated into *suru* even if it is assigned accusative Case.

(80) *Ken-ga   sono heya-o$_i$ [t$_i$ soozi]-o   si-ta.
     Ken-NOM that room-ACC   cleaning-ACC do-PST
     'Ken did the cleaning of that room.'

The double-*o* constraint applying to the LVC is a surface case-marking constraint (see Harada, 1986; Poser, 2002; Saito and Hoshi, 2000). Thus (80) is rendered acceptable if the accusative case marking on the VN or the theme argument is eliminated with the addition of an adverbial particle.

(81) a. *Ken-ga   sono heya-o$_i$ [t$_i$ soozi]-mo   si-nakat-ta.*
        Ken-NOM that room-ACC   cleaning-also do-NEG-PST
        'Ken did not even do the cleaning of that room.'
     b. *Ken-ga   sono heya-mo$_i$ [t$_i$ soozi]-o   si-nakat-ta.*
        Ken-NOM that room-also   cleaning-ACC do-NEG-PST
        'Ken did not do the cleaning of even that room.'

There is evidence that the theme argument *sono heya* in (78b) is created via argument ascension from the VN *soozi*. To make this point, first observe that the theme argument can be moved by relativization, pseudo-clefting, and topicalization.

(82) a. *[Ken-ga   soozi-{o/   mo} si-nakat-ta] sono heya*
        Ken-NOM cleaning-ACC also do-NEG-PST that room
        'that room, which Ken did not (even) clean' (relativization)
     b. *[Ken-ga   soozi-{o/   mo} si-nakat-ta no]-wa   sono heya da.*
        Ken-NOM cleaning-ACC also do-NEG-PST NOML-TOP that room COP
        'What Ken did not (even) clean was that room.' (pseudo-clefting)
     c. *Sono heya-wa Ken-ga   soozi-{o/   mo} si-nakat-ta.*
        that room-to Ken-NOM cleaning-ACC also do-NEG-PST
        'As for that room, Ken did not (even) clean.' (topicalization)

By contrast, the examples in (83), where the same syntactic operations have applied to the VN, display PBC effects.

(83) a. *[Ken-ga   sono heya-o   si-nakat-ta] soozi
        Ken-NOM that room-NOM do-NEG-PST cleaning
        'that room, of which Ken did not do the cleaning' (relativization)
     b. *[Ken-ga   sono heya-o   si-nakat-ta no]-wa   soozi   da.
        Ken-NOM that room-ACC do-NEG-PST NOML-TOP cleaning COP
        'What Ken did not do to that room was cleaning.' (pseudo-clefting)
     c. *Soozi-wa   Ken-ga   sono heya-o   si-nakat-ta.
        cleaning-TOP Ken-NOM that room-ACC do-NEG-PST
        'As for cleaning, Ken did not do to that room.' (topicalization)

In addition, a SC effect is observed in (84), which has the premodifier *kinoo-no* in the VN.

(84) ?*Ken-wa sono heya-o   [kinoo-no   soozi]-sae   si-nakat-ta.
     Ken-TOP that room-ACC yesterday-GEN cleaning-even do-NEG-PST
     'Ken did not even do the yesterday's cleaning of that room.'

The data in (83) and (84) illustrate that the theme argument *sono heya* is originated from the VN *soozi*.

Furthermore, the two objects in (78) show an asymmetry with regard to direct passivization. The theme argument *kono heya* 'this room' can be turned into a passive subject, as in (85).

(85) Kono heya-ga   {soozi-o   s-are-te/   soozi-s-are-te}
     this room-NOM cleaning-ACC do-PASS-GER cleaning-do-PASS-GER
     i-nakat-ta.
     be-NEG-PST
     'This room has not been cleaned.'

By contrast, the VN cannot be turned into a passive subject, as in (86).

(86) a. *Soozi-ga   kono heya-o   s-are-te   i-nakat-ta.
        cleaning-NOM this room-ACC do-PASS-GER be-NEG-PST
        'Cleaning has not been done for this room.'
     b. *Kono heya-o soozi-ga   s-are-te   i-nakat-ta.
        this room-ACC cleaning-NOM do-PASS-GER be-NEG-PST
        'For this room, cleaning has not been done.'

The VN *soozi* contains a copy of the theme argument *kono heya* created by argument ascension. In (86a) the VN is raised across the theme argument in the object position under direct passivization. In this configuration, the theme argument fails to c-command its copy inside the VN *soozi*. Consequently, a PBC violation is incurred in (86a). In (86b), the theme argument appears to the left of the VN by scrambling, but the sentence is not acceptable since, in this case, the VN fails to c-command the copy of the theme argument in the pre-scrambling object position, which contains a copy of the VN.

The well-formedness of (87a) illustrates that the VN *soozi* can be turned into passive subject by direct passivization when it includes the theme argument in it.

(87) a. [Kono heya-no   soozi]-ga   s-are-te   i-nakat-ta.
        this room-GEN cleaning-NOM do-PASS-GER be-NEG-PST
        'Cleaning has not been done for this room.'

b. *Kono heya-wa soozi-ga s-are-te i-nakat-ta.*
　　this　room-TOP cleaning-NOM do-PASS-GER be-NEG-PST
　　'For this room, cleaning has not been done.'

(87b) is well-formed in spite of the fact that the word order is the same as (86b). *Kono heya* in (87b) can be a major subject generated via argument ascension from the passive subject. In this case, *kono heya* can c-command the copy inside the passive subject. This derivation is not available for *kono heya* in (86b), which is marked with accusative case. Given that the VN *seisoo* cannot be moved across *kono heya*, which has been exttracted from the VN, it is easy to see that the examples in (86) are excluded in violation of the PBC.

In this connection, observe that unaccusative VNs such as *zyoohatu* 'evaporation' resist overt accusative case marking.

(88)　*Mizu-ga　{?*zyoohatu-o　si-ta/ zyoohatu-si-ta}.*
　　　water-NOM　evaporation-ACC do-PST evaporation-do-PST
　　　'The water evaporated.'

The LVC with the VN *zyoohatu* 'evaporation' has a non-agentive subject. In the present perspective, the VN is expected to provide the subject, i.e. the subject is generated via extraction from the VN, as illustrated in (89).

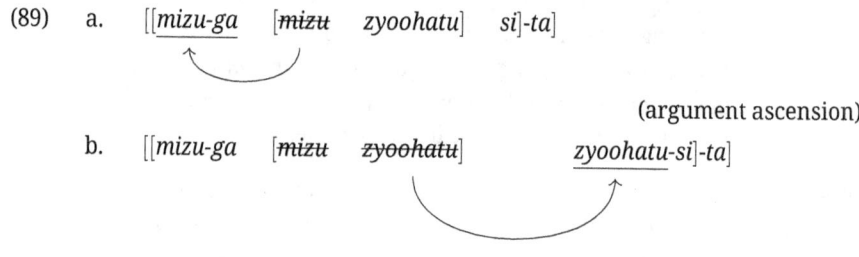

Miyagawa (1989) assumes that the compound form of the unaccusative VN-*suru* is formed in the lexicon, but I claim that the VN is generated as an argument separate from the LV *suru*, and then undergoes incorporation into *suru*, as (89b) illustrates. The adequacy of the present view is confirmed by *kata*-nominalization.

(90)　*mizu-no　{zyoohatu-no　si-kata/ *zyoohatu-si-kata}*
　　　water-GEN　evaporation-GEN do-way　evaporation-do-way
　　　'the way of water's evaporating'

(90) shows that the VN appears separately from *suru*, marked with genitive case under *kata*-nominalization. The unacceptability of the nominalized form **zoohatu-si-*

kata illustrates that unaccusative VNs are initially generated in a structural position separate from the verb *suru* (pace Miyagawa, 1989).

The VN *zyoohatu* cannot appear in the accusative case, but it can remain in the argument (object) position when the overt accusative case is suppressed by an adverbial particle (Kishimoto, 2019a,b).

(91) *Mizu-ga   zyoohatu-wa   (mattaku) si-nakat-ta.*
      water-NOM evaporation-TOP at.all   do-NEG-PST
      'The water did not evaporate (at all).'

The VN occurring with a particle is not incorporated into *suru*, so that an adverb like *mattaku* 'at all' can intervene between them. Even if the VN with an adverbial particle is separable from *suru*, it is not possible to move the VN across the subject.

(92) a. **Zyoohatu-wa   mizu-ga   si-nakat-ta.*
          evaporation-TOP water-NOM do-NEG-PST
          'The water did not evaporate.'

      b. * [[~~mizu zyoohatu~~]-wa   mizu-ga   [~~mizu zyoohatu~~]   si-nakat-ta]

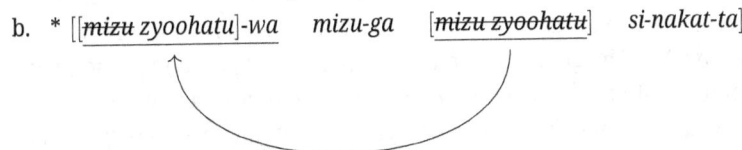

The subject in (92a), generated via extraction from the VN, fails to c-command its copy inside the VN created by movement, as illustrated in (92b), and hence a PCB violation is incurred in (92a). In a similar vein, VN ellipsis is not possible in the LVC with an unaccusative VN.

(93) **Kono mizu-wa zyoohatu-mo   si-nakat-ta-ga,   ano mizu-wa si-ta.*
      this water-TOP evaporation-also do-NEG-PST-CONJ that water-TOP do-PST
      'This water did not even evaporate, but that water did.'

The unacceptability of VN ellipsis further corroborates the adequacy of the view that the theme subject is originated from the unaccusative VN.

As suggested in section 3, Burzio's generalization is not a viable grammatical constraint to account for the facts of the LVC with an unaccusative VN. There is in fact good reason to believe that the formation of the LVC with an unaccusative VN is not dictated by Burzio's generalization, despite Miyagawa's (1989, 665) claim to the contrary. Under Miyagawa's analysis which draws on Burzio's generalization, accusative Case is not assigned to the unaccusative VN since the subject is not assigned an external θ-role. This account leads to the prediction that the LVC with an accusative VN will be well-formed if the VN appears in the subject position while containing a theme argument.

(94) *Mizu-no   zyoohatu-ga   si-ta.
     water-GEN evaporation-NOM do-PST
     (lit.) 'The water's evaporation did.'

(94) is an ordinary intransitive construction, which does not violate Burizo's generalization. Nevertheless, (94) is not grammatical. Miyagawa's analysis is also called into question, given the well-formedness of (91). If, as Miyagawa assumes, an unaccusative VN cannot appear in the object position of *suru*, the LVC with *zyoohatu* in (91) should not be available. But this expectation is not met.

The case-marking facts of unaccusative VNs can be best characterized as a condition on the surface (or morphological) case marking rather than a grammatical constraint on the assignment of structural Case. Recall that overt accusative marking is allowed on the VN if an inanimate subject is taken to be an autonomous entity, as discussed in section 3. This kind of case-marking phenomenon is naturally expected if a surface case-marking constraint is applicable to the LVC with an unaccusative VN. The generalization is that noun incorporation is chosen over overt morphological accusative case marking for the unaccusative VN when the VN is conceived of as selecting a theme argument referring to a non-autonomous entity (Pustejovski, 1995, 206–207; Levin and Rappaport Hovav, 1995, 90–101) (and hence the unacceptability of ?*zyoohatu-o suru).[20]

Noun incorporation can be implemented productively in the LVC, but it is worth mentioning that this grammatical process can sometimes be applied to non-VNs, as shown in (95), although it is not fully productive.

---

[20] Hosokawa (1993, 396–397) notes that accusative case marking is allowed when unaccusative VNs are phrasal. This generalization applies to the VN *zyoohatu* 'evaporation', as shown in (i).

(i)   Mizu-ga   [kyuugeki-na zyoohatu]-o   si-ta.
      water-NOM rapid   evaporation-ACC do-PST
      'The water made a rapid evaporation.'

This fact also suggests that Burzio's generalization is not relevant for the formation of the LVC with an unaccusative VN. Given the well-formedenss of (i) and (91), it is plausible to postulate that the verb *suru* assigns accusative Case to an unaccusative VN in object position irrespective of whether it is later incorporated into *suru*, hence, the well-formedness of *zyoohatu-mo suru* [evaporation-also do] and [*kyuugeki-na zyoohatu*]-*o suru* [rapid evaporation-ACC do]. See Kishimoto (2001, 2019a) for the discussion that simple, but not phrasal, VNs can be incorporated into *suru* at LF.

(95) {koi-o   su-ru/ koi-su-ru} hito
       love-ACC do-PRS love-do-PRS man
       'a man who falls in love'

The noun *koi* 'love, romance' refers to a mental state but not an event, and thus is not a VN. Nevertheless, *koi* can appear with *suru* in the two forms. The *kata*-nominalization fact in (96) shows that the compound form is derived via syntactic noun incorporation.

(96) Ano hito-no   {koi-no   si-kata/ *koi-si-kata}
      that man-NOM   love-ACC do-way   love-do-way
      'the man's way of falling in love'

In contrast, a noun *ai* 'love, affection', which has a similar meaning to *koi*, can only appear in a compound form if combined with *suru*, and hence the contrast in grammaticality between *ai-suru* [love-do] and *ai-o suru* [love-ACC do]. *Kata*-nominalization confirms that *ai* cannot occur separately from *suru*.

(97) Ken-no {*ai-no   si-kata/ ai-si-kata}
      Ken-NOM love-ACC do-way love-do-way
      'Ken's way of loving'

The data illustrate that non-VNs can sometimes be incorporated into *suru*, but it has a limited applicability in the case of non-VNs.[21]

In a nutshell, noun incorporation is implemented quite productively in the LVC, but this is not unique to the LVC. Furthermore, the suppression of an agent role in argument structure at first sight looks unique to the LVCs, but this process is also found elsewhere in Japanese, as discussed in section 5. Notably, the compound form 'NV-*suru*' is derived by first generating the VN in a θ-marking object position of *suru*. This fact suggests that the VN is assigned a θ-role by *suru*. Such being the case, the LV *suru* cannot be a thematically empty verb. Rather, the LV *suru* is a regular transitive verb.

One perennial issue regarding the LVC is whether the verb appearing with a non-verbal element that supplies a substantial predicative meaning is a light verb or a regular lexical verb (see e.g. Cattell, 1984; Butt, 2010; Bruening, 2015). The VN-*o suru* construction can be thought of as falling into a species of the LVC since the VN carries the substantive meaning of the predicative sequence 'NV-*o suru*'. But this is largely

---

[21] Just as compound verbs can be created by combining verbal nouns with *suru* 'do' via noun incorporation (Kageyama, 1982, 245–248), so complex adjectives can be formed by combining nouns with the adjective *nai* 'null' via noun incorporation (Kishimoto and Booij, 2014).

due to the fact that *suru* used in the LVC expresses a general activity meaning. The LV *suru* appearing in the LVC has the same essential properties as the transitive *suru*, and thus it is reasonable to identify the LV *suru* as a regular transitive verb. As far as Japanese is concerned, there is no a priori reason for sustaining the assumption on the light verb *suru* as a thematically empty verb (entertained by some works such as Grimshaw and Mester, 1988 and Saito and Hoshi, 2000).

7 Conclusion

In Japanese, the LVC is constructed if a predicative complex is formed by combining *suru* with a VN. I have shown that the LVCs are divided into the agentive type formed on the argument structure <agent, (goal), theme(VN)> and the non-agentive type formed on the argument structure <theme(VN)>. In the agentive LVC, the subject is selected by *suru*, but in the non-agentive LVC, the subject is derived via argument ascension from the VN. The LV *suru* can take up to three arguments, but additional clausal arguments can be supplied by the VN. Such arguments receive their θ-roles from the VN and are turned into clausal arguments by argument ascension. In both agentive and non-agentive LVCs, the LV *suru* selects a VN as its complement, which entails that the LV *suru* is equipped with its own argument structure, although some arguments of the LVC may be furnished by the VN.

Acknowledgments

Earlier versions of the present paper were presented in my lectures delivered at Institut National des Langues et Civilisations Orientales, Paris (October, 2023), at the Faculty of Asian and Middle Eastern Studies, University of Oxford, United Kingdom (March, 2024), and at the Research Faculty of Media and Communication, Hokkaido University, Japan (March, 2024). I am grateful to Yayoi Nakamura-Delloye, Akiko Takaemura, Jean Bazantay, Bjarke Frellesvig, Satoshi Oku, Shiori Ikawa, Masanobu Ueda, and the audience at these meetings for comments and suggestions. I am also thankful to the two anonymous reviewers for their comments suggesting that some basic issues concerning the light verb construction should be discussed. This work is supported by Grant-in-Aid for Scientific Research (C) (grant no. 20K00605).

Bibliography

Baker, Mark. 1988. *Incorporation: A Theory of Grammatical Function Changing*. Chicago: University of Chicago Press.
Bruening, Benjamin. 2015. Light verbs are just regular verbs. *U. Penn Working Papers in Linguistics* 21(1). 1–10.
Burzio, Luigi. 1986. *Italian Syntax: A Government-Binding Approach*. Dordrecht: Reidel.
Butt, Miriam. 1995. *The Structure of Complex Predicates in Urdu*. Stanford: CSLI Publications.
Butt, Miriam. 2010. The light verb jungle: Still hacking away. In Mengistu Amberber, Bret Baker and Mark Harvey (eds.), *Complex Predicates in Cross-Linguistic Perspective*, 48–78. Cambridge: Cambridge University Press.
Carnie, Andrew. 2013. *Syntax: A Generative Introduction*. Oxford: Wiley-Blackwell 2nd edn.
Cattell, Ray. 1984. *Composite Predicates in English*. Sydney: Academic Press.
Chomsky, Noam. 1982. *Some Concepts and Consequences of the Theory of Government and Binding*. Cambridge, MA: The MIT Press.
Dubinsky, Stanley. 1997. Syntactic underspecification and the light-verb phenomena in Japanese. *Linguistics* 35. 627–672. https://doi.org/10.1515/ling.1997.35.4.627.
Fiengo, Robert and James Higginbotham. 1981. Opacity in NP. *Linguistic Analysis* 7. 347–373.
Grimshaw, Jane. 1990. *Argument Structure*. Cambridge, MA: The MIT Press.
Grimshaw, Jane and Armin Mester. 1988. Light verbs and θ-marking. *Linguistic Inquiry* 19. 205–232.
Harada, Shin-Ichi. 1986. Counter equi-NP deletion. *Journal of Japanese Linguistics* 11(1-2). 157–202. https://doi.org/10.1515/jjl-1986-1-205.
Hasegawa, Nobuko. 2007. The possessor raising construction and the interpretation of the subject. In Simin Karimi, Vida Samiian and Wendy K. Wilkins (eds.), *Phrasal and Clausal Architecture: Syntactic Derivation and Interpretation*, 62–99. Amsterdam: John Benjamins.
Hosokawa, Hirofumi. 1993. Remarks on light verb structures in Japanese. In *Gengogaku-kara-no Chooboo [perspectives from linguistics]*, 391–404. Fukoka: Kyushuu Daigaku Shuppankai.
Isoda, Michio. 1991. The light verb construction in Japanese. In *CLS 27: Papers from the 27th Regional Meeting of the Chicago Linguistic Society 1991 Part One, The General Session*, vol. 27 1, 261–275.
Jespersen, Otto. 1942. *A Modern English Grammar on Historical Principles, Part VI, Morphology*. Copenhagen: Ejnar Munksgaard.
Kageyama, Taro. 1976–1977. Incorporation and Sino-Japanese verbs. *Papers in Japanese Linguistics* 5. 117–156.
Kageyama, Taro. 1980. *Nichi-ei Hikaku Goi-no Koozoo [Lexical Structures: A Comparative Study of Japanese and English]*. Tokyo: Shohakusha.
Kageyama, Taro. 1982. Word formation in Japanese. *Lingua* 57. 215–258.
Kageyama, Taro. 1991. Light verb constructions and the syntax-morphology interface. In Heizo Nakajima (ed.), *Current English Linguistics in Japan*, 169–203. Berlin: Mouton de Gruyter.
Kageyama, Taro. 1993. *Bunpoo to Gokeisei [Grammar and Word Formation]*. Tokyo: Hituzi Syobo.
Kageyama, Taro. 2002. Hitaikaku-koozoo-no tadooshi: Imi-to toogo-no intaafeisu [Transitive verbs with unaccusative structures: The interface between semantics and syntax]. In Takane Ito (ed.), *Bunpoo Riron: Rekishikon-to Toogo [Grammatical Theory: Lexicon and Syntax]*, 119–145. Tokyo Daigaku Shuppan Kai.
Kageyama, Taro. 2009. Isolate: Japanese. In Rochelle Lieber and Pavol Stekauer (eds.), *The Oxford Handbook of Compounding*, 512–526. Oxford University Press. https://doi.org/10.1093/oxfordhb/9780199695720.013.0028.

Kishimoto, Hideki. 2001. Binding of indeterminate pronouns and clause structure in Japanese. *Linguistic Inquiry* 32. 597–633. https://doi.org/10.1162/002438901753373014.
Kishimoto, Hideki. 2006. Japanese syntactic nominalization and VP-internal syntax. *Lingua* 116(6). 771–810. https://doi.org/10.1016/j.lingua.2005.03.005.
Kishimoto, Hideki. 2010. Ukemi-no imi-o arawasu 'ukeru'-no goi-gainen-koozoo [The lexical conceptual structure for 'ukeru' that expresses a passive meaning]. In Taro Kageyama (ed.), *Lexicon Forum No. 5*, 201–218. Tokyo: Hituzi Syobo.
Kishimoto, Hideki. 2017. Negative polarity, A-Movement, and clause architecture in Japanese. *Journal of East Asian Linguistics* 17. 109–161. https://doi.org/10.1007/s10831-016-9153-6.
Kishimoto, Hideki. 2019a. Keidooshi-koobun-niokeru imiyakuwari-fuyo-no mekanizumu [The mechanism of thematic role assignment in the light verb construction]. In Hideki Kishimoto (ed.), *Rekishikon-no Gendai Riron-to Sono Ooyoo [Modern Theories of Lexicon and Their Applications]*, 99–126. Tokyo: Kurosio Publishers.
Kishimoto, Hideki. 2019b. Keidooshi-koobun-no idoo-genshoo: Koo-jooshoo-to meishi hennyuu [Movement phenomena in light verb constructions: Argument ascension and noun incorporation]. In Testuo Nishihara, Haruko Miyakoda, Koichiro Nakamura, Yoko Yonekura and Shinichi Tanaka (eds.), *Gengo-niokeru Intaafeisu [Interfaces in Language]*, 11–24. Tokyo: Kaitakusha.
Kishimoto, Hideki and Geert Booij. 2014. Complex negative adjectives in Japanese: The relation between syntactic and morphological constructions. *Word Structure* 7(1). 55–87.
Kishimoto, Hideki and Taro Kageyama. 2011. Koobun kootai-to koo-no gugenka [Alternations and argument realizations]. In Taro Kageyama (ed.), *Nichi-ei-taishoo Meishi-no Imi-to Koobun [Japanese and English Contrasted: The Meanings and Constructions of Nouns]*, 270–304. Tokyo: Taishukan.
Kratzer, Angelika. 1995. Stage-level and individual-level predicates. In Greg Carlson and Francis J. Pelletier (eds.), *The Generic Book*, 125–175. Chicago: University of Chicago Press.
Kuno, Susumu. 1973. *The Structure of the Japanese Language*. Cambridge, MA: The MIT Press.
Kuno, Susumu. 1987. *Functional Syntax: Anaphora, Discourse and Empathy*. Chicago: University of Chicago Press.
Levin, Beth and Malka Rappaport Hovav. 1995. *Unaccusativity: At the Syntax-Lexical Semantics Interface*. Cambridge, MA: The MIT Press.
Martin, Samuel E. 1975. *A Reference Grammar of Japanese*. New Haven: Yale University Press.
Matsumoto, Yo. 1996. *Complex Predicates in Japanese: A Syntactic and Semantic Study of the Notion 'Word'*. Tokyo: Kurosio Publishers/ CSLI Publications.
Miyagawa, Shigeru. 1989. Light verbs and the ergative hypothesis. *Linguistic Inquiry* 20. 659–668.
Miyamoto, Tadao. 1999. *The Light Verb Construction in Japanese: The Role of the Verbal Noun*. Amsterdam: John Benjamins.
Miyamoto, Tadao and Hideki Kishimoto. 2016. Light verb constructions with verbal nouns. In Taro Kageyama and Hideki Kishimoto (eds.), *The Mouton Handbook of Japanese Lexicon and Word Formation*, 425–458. Berlin: Mouton de Gruyter. https://doi.org/10.1515/9781614512097-016.
Okutsu, Keiichiro. 2007. *Rentai Soku Renkyoo? [Attributive Equals Adverbial?]*. Tokyo: Hituzi Syobo.
Poser, William. 2002. The double-*o* constraint in Japanese. Manuscript.
Pustejovski, James. 1995. *The Generative Lexicon*. Boston: The MIT Press.
Saito, Mamoru. 1989. Scrambling as semantically vacuous A'-movement. In Baltin Mark and Anthony Kroch (eds.), *Alternative Conceptions of Phrase Structure*, 182–200. Chicago: University of Chicago Press.
Saito, Mamoru and Hiroto Hoshi. 2000. The Japanese light verb construction and the minimalist programs. In Roger Martin, David Michael and Juan Uriagereka (eds.), *Step by Step: Essays on Minimalist Syntax in Honor of Howard Lasnik*, 261–295. Cambridge, MA: The MIT Press.

Sode, Rumiko. 1995. Intentionality and VN-*suru* constructions in Japanese. *Journal of the Association of the Teachers of Japanese* 29(2). 22–54. https://www.jstor.org/stable/i221299, last access: 13/01/2025.

Sugioka, Yoko. 2002. Keiyooshi-kara hasei-suru dooshi-no jita-kootai-o megutte [On the transitivity alternation of deadjectival verbs]. In Takane Ito (ed.), *Bunpoo Riron: Rekishikon-to Toogo [Grammatical Theory: Lexicon and Syntax]*, 91–116. Tokyo: University of Tokyo Press.

Tanomura, Tadahura. 1989. 'Heya-o soozi-suru' to 'heya-no soozi-o suru' ['Do the cleaning of the room' versus 'do the room cleaning']. *Nihongogaku* 7(11). 70–80.

Terada, Michiko. 1990. *Incorporation and Argument Structure in Japanese*. Doctoral dissertation: University of Massachusetts Amherst.

Travis, Lisa. 1984. *Parameters and Effects of Word Order Variation*. Doctoral dissertation: MIT.

Tsujimura, Natsuko. 1990. Ergativity of nouns and case assignment. *Linguistic Inquiry* 21. 277–287.

Tsunoda, Tasaku. 1996. The possession cline in Japanese and other languages. In Hillary Chapel and William McGregor (eds.), *The Grammar of Inalienability: A Typological Perspective on Body Part Terms and the Part-Whole Relation*, 565–630. Berlin: Mouton de Gruyter.

Uchida, Yoshiko and Mineharu Nakayama. 1993. Japanese verbal noun constructions. *Linguistics* 31. 623–666. https://doi.org/10.1515/ling.1993.31.4.623.

Van Valin, Robert and Randy LaPolla. 1997. *Syntax*. Cambridge: Cambridge University Press. https://doi.org/10.1017/CBO9781139166799.

Yokota, Kenji. 2005. The structure and meaning of Japanese light verbs. *Language Sciences* 27. 247–280. https://doi.org/10.1016/j.langsci.2004.02.002.

Index

Affectedness 33, 223
Aktionsart, 5, 215
Allostruction 134
Anticausative 129
Applicative 91
Argument
– causer 99
– correlate 99
– experiencer 99
– external 243
– internal 243
– non-experiencer 99
– stimulus 99
– theme 99
Argument ascension 234, 253, 255, 264
Argument structure 207, 233, 240
Argument transfer 233, 240

Bare nouns 86
Bleaching 18

Causativity 103
Cohesion 56
Collemxe analysis 216, 217
Collocation 18, 202
Collostructional analysis 218
Compositionality 6, 204
Concreteness 184
Constructicon 131, 133
Construction 131, 180, 208
– daughter 133
– hyper- 134, 150, 163
– mother 133
Construction Grammar 131, 180, 208
Construction Morphology 131
Coordination 61
Coverage 181
Cue availability 127
Cue reliability 127

Desemanticization 18
Determination 72
Dividedness 215

Event structure 128

Event type 129, 130
Eventuality 3

Family
– construction 134, 203
– light verb construction 18, 209
– light verb constructions 16
– noun 185
Figure-Ground 213
Fixedness
– lexical 205
– syntactic 203
Force dynamics 19, 213
Frequency
– token 181, 187
– type 181, 186

Generative Lexicon 202
Grammaticalization 59, 62
– cline 59

Head Movement Constraint 239
Horizontal relation 134

Idiom 4, 18
Idiomatically combining expression 6, 203
Incorporation 56, 90, 91, 237–239, 241, 270, 271
Inheritance link 133

Light verb construction 3, 15, 17, 43, 100, 179, 199, 233
– object-experiencer 99
– psych 101, 124, 130
– subject-experiencer 99

Macrorole 243
Modification 55, 72, 73, 127, 204
– adjectival 69, 73, 127
– adverbial 69, 127
– internal 204
Multi-word expression 1, 203

Neostructuralist approaches 201
Nominal
– event 235

Noun
– deverbal 18
– eventive 17
– psych 130, 150
– state 124
– verbal 48, 233–236
Number 72

Paradigm
– derivational 150
Phraseological continuum 18
Phraseological unit 18
Plexity 215
Polysemy 126
Possessor ascension 243
Predicate
– complex 1, 56, 201
– composite 179
Principle of No Synonymy 123, 126, 134
Proper Binding Condition 245

Referentiality 203

Schema, 132
– second-order, 134

Support verb construction 1
Synonymy 133

Telicity 26, 27, 30, 37, 68, 126
Theta-role assignment 233, 240, 243
Topicalization 56

Verb
– analytic 126
– auxiliary 59, 60, 62
– compound 237
– dummy 236
– experiencer 97, 99
– formation 130
– heavy 3, 15, 19, 43, 48
– light 1, 2, 15, 19, 43, 48, 66, 177, 201, 202
– object-experiencer 97, 99, 100
– parasynthetic 132
– psych 99, 128–130
– support 1, 5, 201
– synthetic 126

Word formation, 130
Word-and-Paradigm, 131

www.ingramcontent.com/pod-product-compliance
Lightning Source LLC
Chambersburg PA
CBHW061708300426
44115CB00014B/2600